Microsoft®

Word 2010 FOR DUMMIES®

eLEARNING KIT

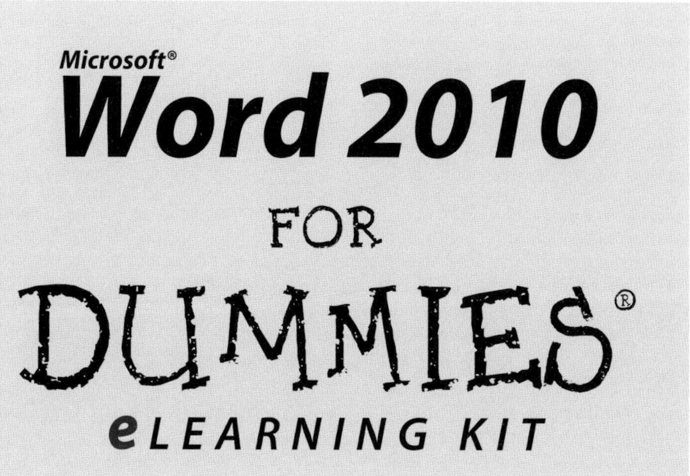

by Lois Lowe

John Wiley & Sons, Inc.

Microsoft® Word 2010 eLearning Kit For Dummies®

Published by
John Wiley & Sons, Inc.
111 River Street
Hoboken, NJ 07030-5774
www.wiley.com

Published by John Wiley & Sons, Inc., Hoboken, New Jersey

Published simultaneously in Canada

For general information on our other products and services, please contact our Customer Care Department within the U.S. at 877-762-2974, outside the U.S. at 317-572-3993, or fax 317-572-4002.

For technical support, please visit www.wiley.com/techsupport.

Wiley publishes in a variety of print and electronic formats and by print-on-demand. Some material included with standard print versions of this book may not be included in e-books or in print-on-demand. If this book refers to media such as a CD or DVD that is not included in the version you purchased, you may download this material at http://booksupport.wiley.com. For more information about Wiley products, visit www.wiley.com.

Library of Congress Control Number: 2012937922

ISBN 978-1-118-33699-1 (pbk); ISBN 978-1-118-38164-9 (ebk); ISBN 978-1-118-38167-0 (ebk); ISBN 978-1-118-39002-3 (ebk)

Manufactured in the United States of America

10 9 8 7 6 5 4 3 2 1

About the Author

Lois Lowe is the author of several books on Microsoft Office applications and Windows, and a Microsoft Office Master Instructor and A+ certified PC technician. She has also taught Office applications in both academic and corporate settings, as well as developed online courseware and web content.

Dedication

To the first Lois Lowe, whose name I carry on. A one-of-a-kind original.

Author's Acknowledgments

I'd like to thank my wonderful editorial team at Wiley, headed up by Katie Mohr and Pat O'Brien, for their professionalism and good cheer throughout this project.

Publisher's Acknowledgments

We're proud of this book; please send us your comments at http://dummies.custhelp.com. For other comments, please contact our Customer Care Department within the U.S. at 877-762-2974, outside the U.S. at 317-572-3993, or fax 317-572-4002.

Some of the people who helped bring this book to market include the following:

Acquisitions, Editorial, and Vertical Websites

Project Editor: Pat O'Brien

Acquisitions Editor: Katie Mohr

Copy Editor: Jen Riggs

Technical Editor: Sharon Mealka

Editorial Manager: Kevin Kirschner

Vertical Websites: Jenny Swisher, Producer

Editorial Assistant: Amanda Graham

Sr. Editorial Assistant: Cherie Case

Cover Photos: ©iStockphoto.com / imagedepotpro; ©iStockphoto.com / Neustockimages; ©iStockphoto.com / Johnny Greig

Cartoons: Rich Tennant (www.the5thwave.com)

Composition Services

Project Coordinator: Sheree Montgomery

Layout and Graphics: Jennifer Henry

Proofreaders: Debbye Butler, Melissa Cossell

Indexer: BIM Indexing & Proofreading Services

Special Help: Tracy Barr

Publishing and Editorial for Technology Dummies

Richard Swadley, Vice President and Executive Group Publisher

Andy Cummings, Vice President and Publisher

Mary Bednarek, Executive Acquisitions Director

Mary C. Corder, Editorial Director

Publishing for Consumer Dummies

Kathleen Nebenhaus, Vice President and Executive Publisher

Composition Services

Debbie Stailey, Director of Composition Services

Contents at a Glance

Table of Contents

Introduction

If you've been thinking about taking a class on the Internet (it is all the rage these days), but you're concerned about getting lost in the electronic fray, worry no longer. *Microsoft Word 2010 eLearning Kit For Dummies* is here to help you, providing you with an integrated learning experience that includes not only the book and CD you hold in your hands but also an online version of the course at `www.dummieselearning.com`. Consider this Introduction your primer.

About This Kit

Each piece of this eLearning kit works in conjunction with the others, although you don't need them all to gain valuable understanding of the key concepts covered here. Whether you pop the CD into your computer to start the lessons electronically, follow along with the book (or not), or go online for the courses, *Microsoft Word 2010 eLearning Kit For Dummies* teaches you how to

- Create basic documents and navigate the Word interface — no previous experience required!
- Format and print attractive documents that use various fonts, colors, borders, and page layouts.
- Simplify and standardize formatting across entire documents with headers, footers, styles, and templates.
- Present complex data clearly with tables.
- Use many types of graphics, including scanned photos, clip art, and line drawings.
- Automate business tasks, such as envelope printing and mail merge.

- Bring order to long documents with footnotes, Table of Contents, and indexes.
- Protect a document from changes and share documents with others.

This book is split into 11 lessons:

1: Getting to Know Word 2010

2: Creating a Word Document

3: Formatting Text

4: Formatting Paragraphs

5: Working with Styles and Templates

6: Working with Pages and Sections

7: Creating and Formatting Tables

8: Inserting and Formatting Graphics

9: Managing Correspondence

10: Preparing Professional Reports

11: Protecting and Sharing a Document

The appendix briefly outlines what the CD in the front of this book contains and what you'll find in the online courses (available at `www.dummieselearning.com`). The appendix also contains a few technical details about using the CD and troubleshooting tips, should you need them.

How This Book Works with the Electronic Lessons

Microsoft Word 2010 eLearning Kit For Dummies merges a tutorial-based *For Dummies* book with eLearning instruction contained on the CD and in online courses. Each of the easy-to-access components features foundational instruction, self-assessment questions, skill-building exercises, plentiful illustrations, resources, and examples. The CD contains interactive electronic lessons. You also find the practice files for the lessons in the book online at `www.dummies.com/go/word2010elearningkit`. Used in conjunction with the tutorial text, the electronic components give learners the tools needed for a productive and self-guided eLearning experience.

- **Lesson-opener questions:** To get you warmed up and ready for class, the questions quiz you on particular points of interest. If you don't know the answer, a page number heads you in the right direction to find the answer.
- **Summing Up:** This section appears at the end of the lesson; it briefly reiterates the content you just learned.
- **Try-it-yourself lab:** Test your knowledge of the content just covered by performing an activity *from scratch* — that is, using general steps only and no sample files.
- **Know this tech talk:** Each lesson contains a brief glossary of related terms.

Conventions Used in This Book

A few style conventions help you navigate the book piece of this kit efficiently:

- Names of the files needed to follow along with the step lists are *italicized.*
- Website addresses, or URLs, are shown in a special monofont typeface, `like this.`
- Numbered steps that you need to follow and characters you need to type are set in **bold.**

Foolish Assumptions

For starters, I assume you know what eLearning is, need to find out how to use Office (and fast!), and want to get a piece of this academic action the fun and easy way with *Microsoft Word 2010 eLearning Kit For Dummies.* I assume you have basic Windows and computer skills, such as starting the computer and using the mouse.

Icons Used in This Kit

The familiar and helpful *For Dummies* icons point you in the direction of really great information that's sure to help you as you work your way through assignments. Look for these icons throughout the *Microsoft Word 2010 eLearning Kit For Dummies,* in the book and in the electronic lessons, too:

The Tip icon points out helpful information that's likely to make your job easier.

This icon marks a general interesting and useful fact — something that you might want to remember for later use.

The Warning icon highlights lurking danger. When you see this icon, you know to pay attention and proceed with caution.

Sometimes I might change things up by directing you to repeat a set of steps but with different parameters. If you're up for the challenge, look for the Practice icon.

Sometimes I point you to resources on the Internet. Look for the Go Online icon.

In addition to the icons, you also find two friendly study aids that bring your attention to certain pieces of information:

- **Lingo:** When you see the Lingo box, look for a definition of a key term or concept.
- **Extra Info:** This box highlights something to pay close attention to in a figure or points out other useful information that's related to the discussion at hand.

Class Is In

Occasionally, we have updates to our technology books. If this book has any technical updates, they will be posted at `www.dummies.com/go/word2010elearningupdates`. Now that you're primed and ready, time to begin.

Lesson 1

Getting to Know Word 2010

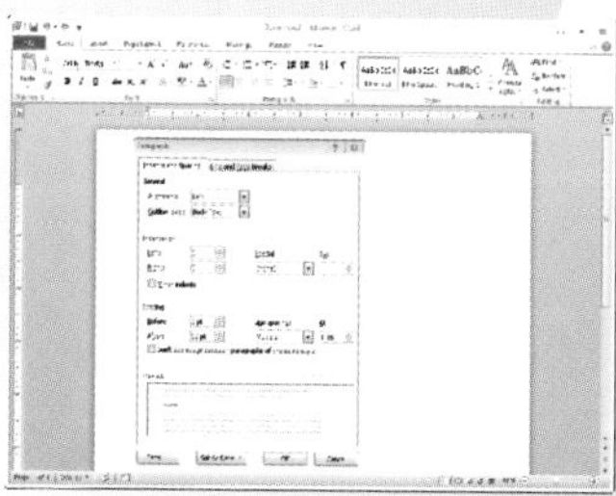

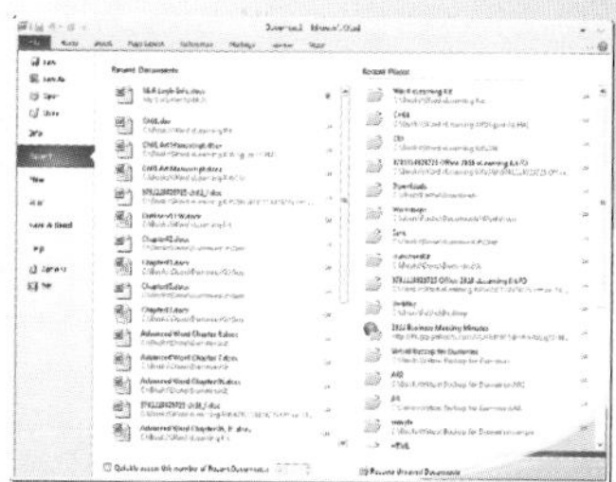

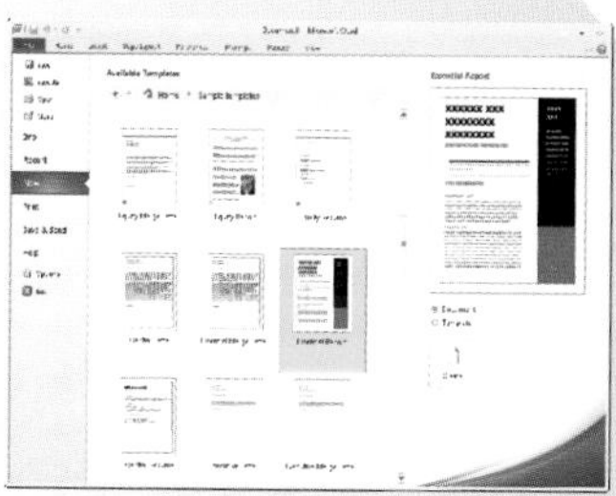

- Moving around in a document enables you to view different parts of the document that may not be onscreen at the moment. You can use scroll bars, arrow keys, and keyboard shortcuts in any combination.
- Changing the onscreen view helps you focus on the important parts of the document for the task you want to perform. Each application has its own unique set of views, as well as a Zoom control.
- Saving and opening documents lets you store your work for later use and then recall it to the screen when you're ready to continue. The Save As and Open dialog boxes share a common look and feel in all applications.

1. How do you start Word?

Open to page 7

2. How can you find out what a certain button on the Ribbon is for?

Buttons take a bow on page 12

3. What is Backstage view?

Peek through the curtain to page 16

4. After you save a file, how can you reopen the Save As dialog box so you can save it with a different name?

Boxes bounce back on page 26

5. How can you quickly reopen a recently opened document?

Race over to page 33

Microsoft Word is a word-processing application that can help you create many kinds of written documents, including reports, letters, newsletters, and labels. Word excels at any kind of text-based task.

Word is part of the Microsoft Office suite. A *suite* is a group of applications that are designed to work together and to have similar user interfaces that cut down on the learning curve for each one.

The time you spend now learning the Word interface will benefit you later if you decide to tackle any of the other Office applications.

Starting Word

The most straightforward way to start Word is to choose it from the Start menu in Windows. You can navigate through the folders by choosing Start➪All Programs, or you can start typing the application's name and then click its name at the top of the Start menu when it appears.

Depending on how your PC is set up, you may also have shortcuts to one or more of the Office apps on your desktop and/or on the taskbar.

You can double-click a data file that's associated with one of the apps, but if you haven't created any documents, you can't do that now.

LINGO

Technically, a **program** can be any type of software, including Windows itself, whereas an **application** is a specific type of program that performs a useful user task, such as word processing. Most nongeeky computer users don't recognize that distinction, though, and they use the terms interchangeably. So do I in this book.

When you're finished with an application, you can either click its Close (X) button in its upper-right corner, or you can choose File⇨Exit. If you have any unsaved work, you're prompted to save it.

In the following exercise, you practice opening and closing Microsoft Word.

Files needed: None

1. **In Windows, click the Start button.**

   The Start menu opens. See Figure 1-1.

> **EXTRA INFO**
>
> On the left side of the Start menu, shortcuts to recently or frequently used applications appear. If the application you want happens to appear there after Step 1, you can click it to open the application. If not, continue to Step 2.

Figure 1-1

2. **Choose All Programs.**

   A list of all installed applications appears. Some of the applications are organized into folders.

3. **Click the Microsoft Office folder.**

   A list of the Microsoft Office 2010 applications appears. See Figure 1-2.

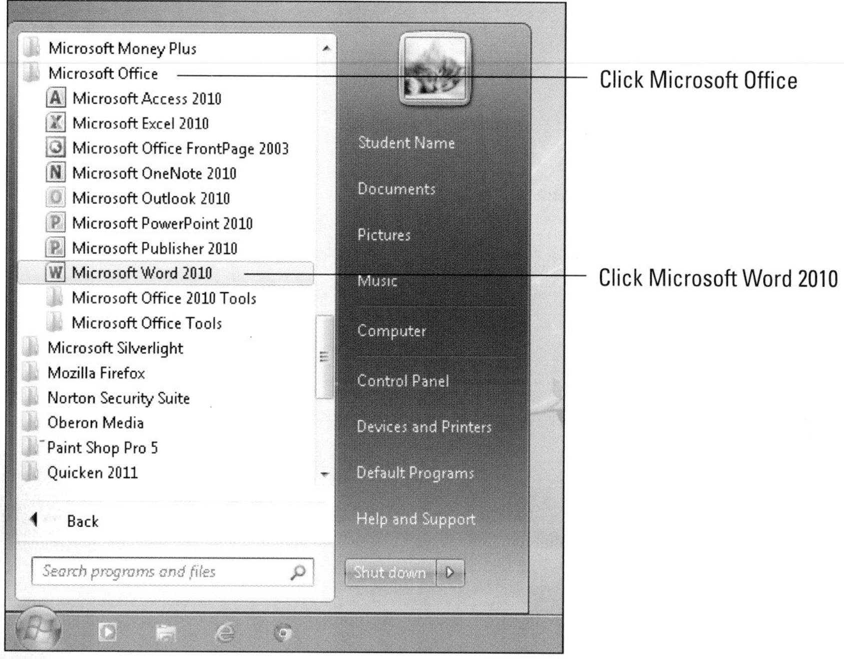

Figure 1-2

4. **Click Microsoft Word 2010.**

   The Word application opens.

5. **Click the Close (X) button in the upper-right corner of the Word window. (See Figure 1-3.)**

   The Word application window closes.

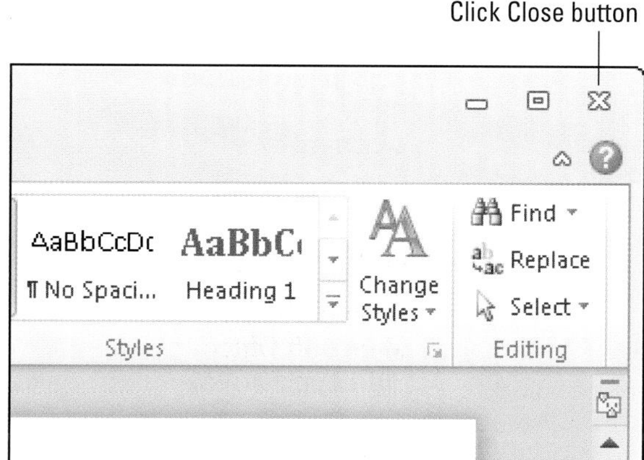

Figure 1-3

6. **Click the Start button and then type** Word **in the search box.**

   The Start menu filters applications that contain those letters in their names. See Figure 1-4.

7. **From the list of applications that appears, click Microsoft Word 2010.**

   The Word application opens.

8. **Click the File tab in the upper-left corner, and from the menu that opens (see Figure 1-5), choose Exit.**

   The Word application closes.

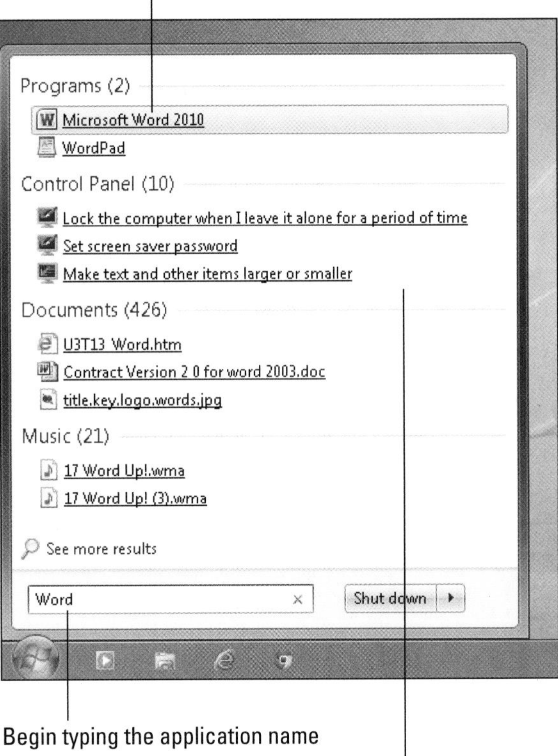

Figure 1-4

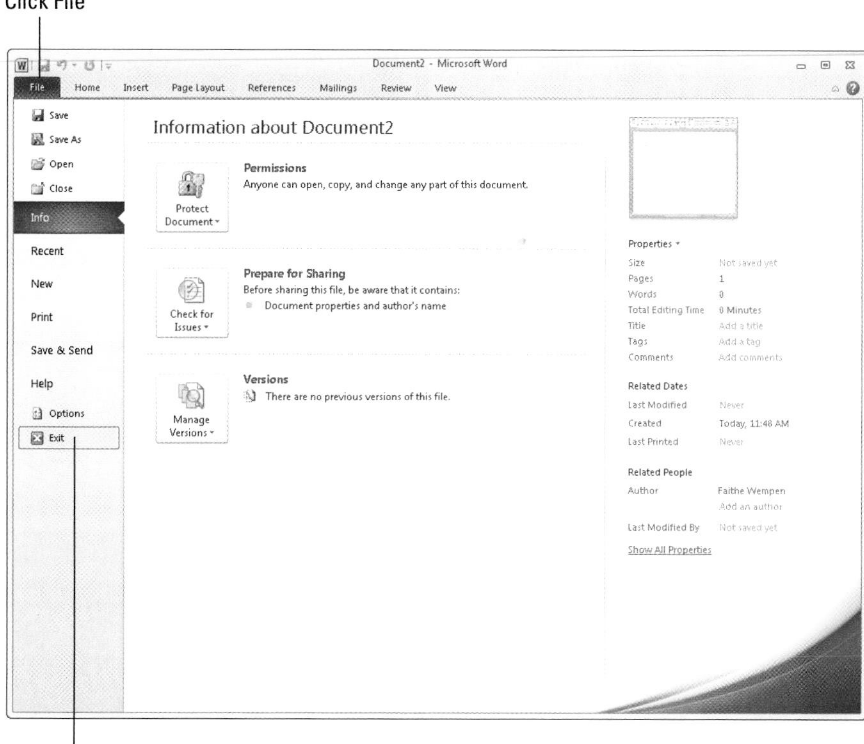

Figure 1-5

9. **Click Start.**

   A shortcut for Word appears in the left side of the Start menu because the application was used recently. See Figure 1-6.

EXTRA INFO

This menu system is also called Backstage view, which you explore in greater detail in an upcoming exercise.

10. Click Microsoft Word 2010.

The Word application opens.

Leave Word open for the next exercise.

Click Word on the top level of the Start menu

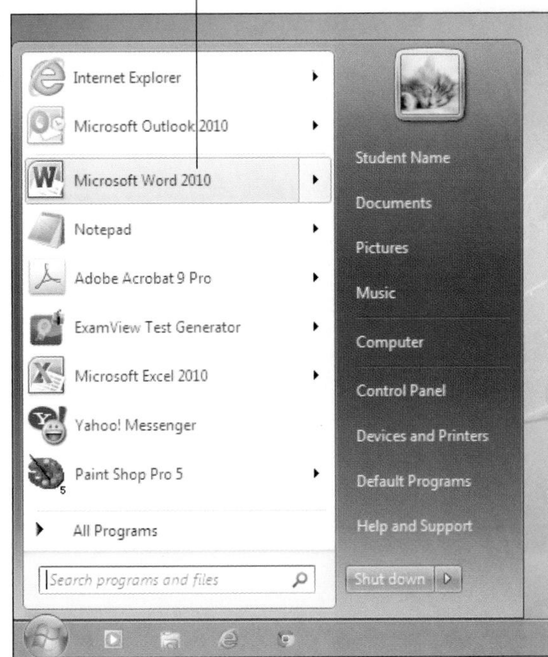

Figure 1-6

Exploring the Word Interface

The Word 2010 interface consists of a tabbed Ribbon, a File menu, a status bar, window controls, and other common features. In the following sections, you become familiar with these common elements.

Exploring the Ribbon and tabs

All Office 2010 applications have a common system of navigation called the *Ribbon,* which is a tabbed bar across the top of the application window. Each tab is like a page of buttons. You click different tabs to access different sets of buttons and features.

In the following exercise, you practice using the commands on the Ribbon in Microsoft Word.

Files needed: None

1. **If Word isn't already open from the preceding exercise, open it.**
2. **On the Ribbon, click the Insert tab.**

   Buttons for inserting various types of content appear.

The buttons are organized into *groups;* the group names appear at the bottom. For example, the Pages group is the leftmost group.

3. **In the Links group, hover the mouse pointer over the Hyperlink button.**

   A ScreenTip appears, telling you the button's name and purpose and showing a keyboard shortcut (Ctrl+K) that you can optionally use to select that command. See Figure 1-7.

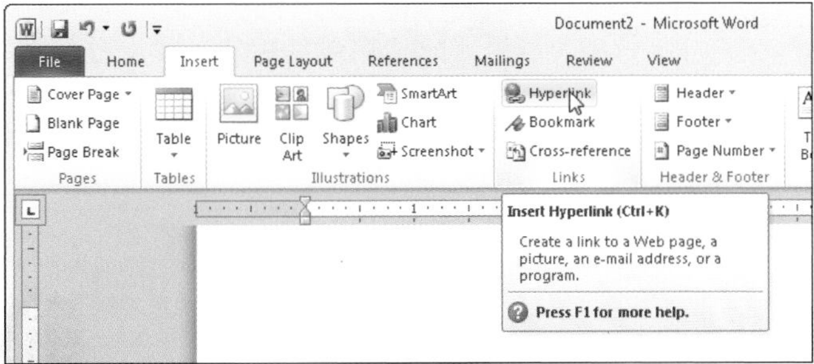

Figure 1-7

4. **In the Links group, click the Hyperlink button.**

   An Insert Hyperlink dialog box opens. See Figure 1-8.

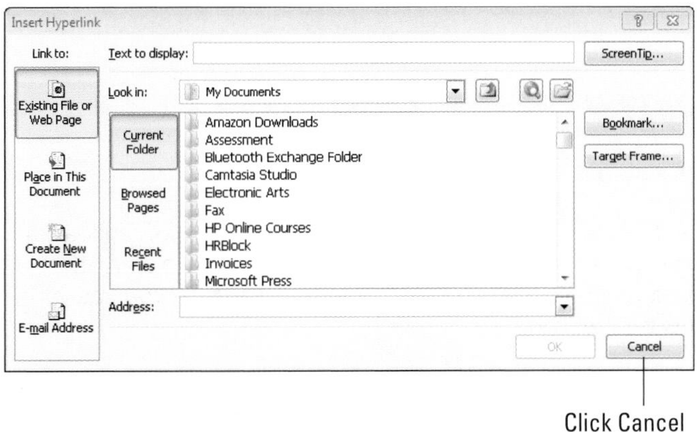

Figure 1-8

5. **Click Cancel in the dialog box to close it.**

6. **In the Header & Footer group, click the Header button.**

   A menu opens. See Figure 1-9.

You can tell the Header button opens a menu because the button has a down-pointing arrow on it.

The Gold button is an on/off toggle

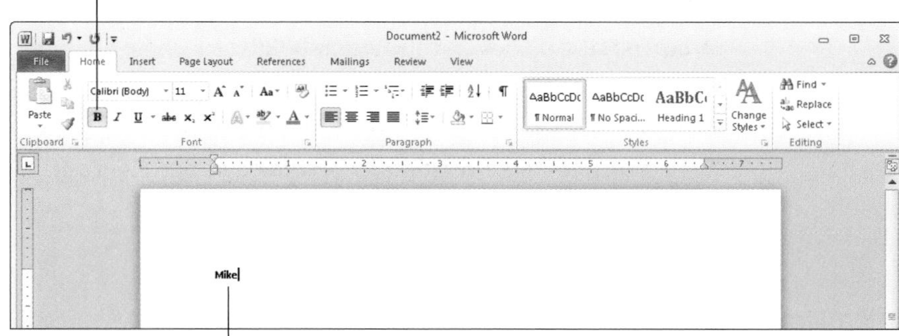

Text typed after clicking the Bold button appears bold

Figure 1-9

7. **Drag the scroll bar on the right side of the menu to view its content, and then click away from the menu without making a selection to close it.**
8. **Click the Home tab.**

   The buttons change to the ones on that tab.
9. **In the Font group, click the Bold button to toggle on the Bold attribute; then type your first name.**

   Your first name appears in bold. See Figure 1-10.

The Bold button is an on/off toggle

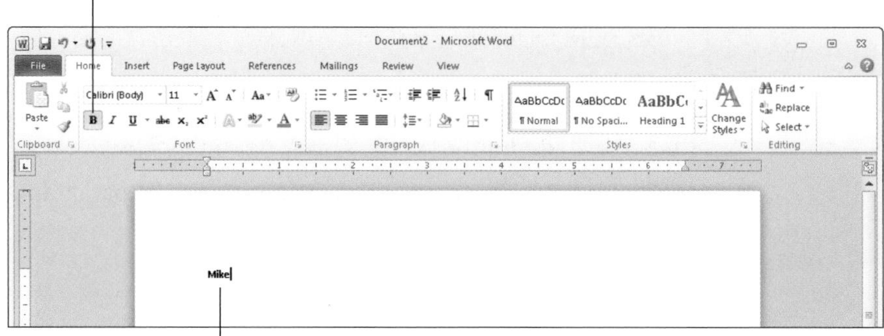

Text typed after clicking the Bold button appears bold

Figure 1-10

10. **Click the Bold button again to toggle off the Bold attribute; then type your last name.**

    Your last name does not appear in bold.

11. **In the Paragraph group, notice that the Align Text Left button is selected; click the Center button in the Paragraph group.**

    Your name centers horizontally on the page. See Figure 1-11.

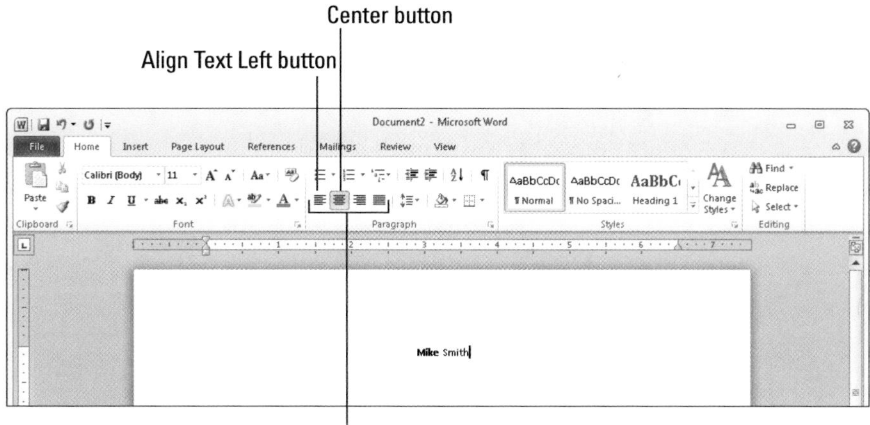

Figure 1-11

The paragraph alignment buttons are a set; when you select one, the previously selected button is deselected.

12. **Click the Undo button on the Quick Access toolbar.**

    See Figure 1-12. The last action is undone, and the paragraph alignment goes back to left alignment.

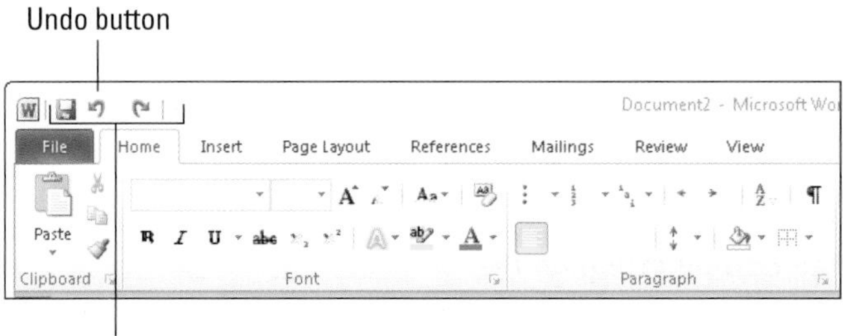

Figure 1-12

13. **Click the dialog box launcher in the bottom-right corner of the Paragraph group.**

    A Paragraph dialog box opens. See Figure 1-13.

14. **Click Cancel to close the Paragraph dialog box.**

Dialog box launcher

Figure 1-13

15. **If the Word window is maximized, click the Restore button in the upper-right corner so that the window is resizable (see Figure 1-14).**

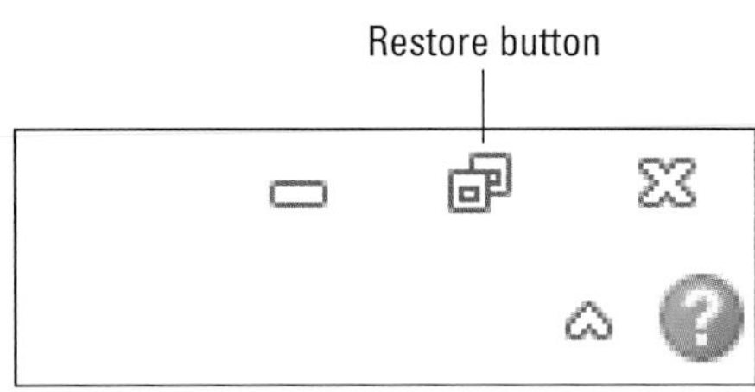

Figure 1-14

16. **Note the buttons available in the Editing group on the Home tab.**

    These buttons enable you to find, replace, and select text in a document.

17. **Drag the right border of the Word window toward the left, decreasing the size of the Word window until the Editing group collapses into one button (see Figure 1-15), and then click the Editing button.**

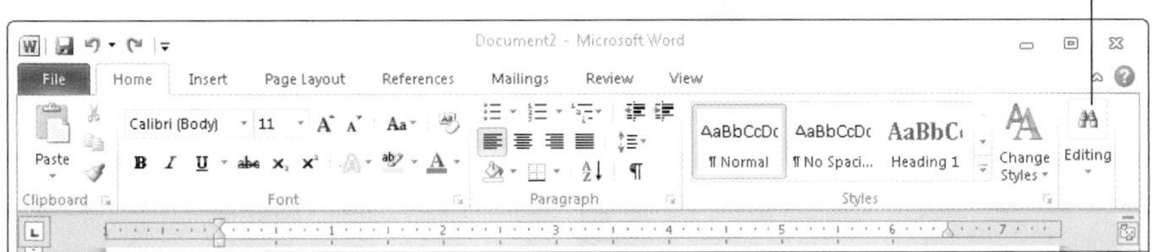

Figure 1-15

The menu that opens contains the buttons that were previously available from the Editing group. See Figure 1-16.

18. **Drag the right border of the Word window toward the right until the Editing group is expanded again.**

19. **Exit the Word application. When you're prompted to save changes, click No.**

Leave Word open for the next exercise.

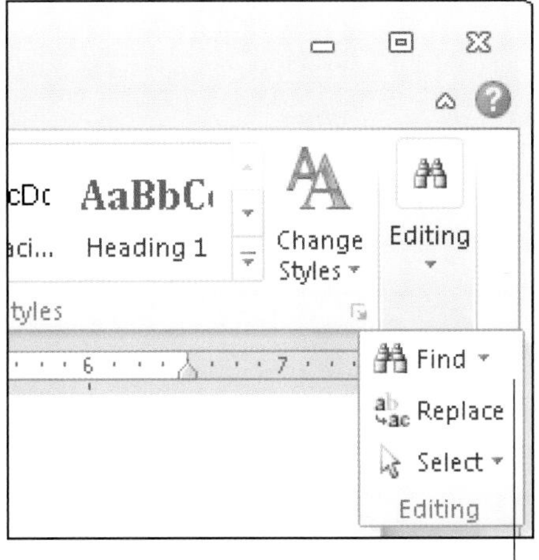

Figure 1-16

Understanding the File menu

Clicking the File tab opens the File menu, also known as *Backstage view.* Backstage view provides access to commands that have to do with the document you're working with — things like saving, opening, printing, mailing, and checking its properties.

To leave Backstage view, click some other tab or press the Esc key.

In the following exercise, you practice using the File menu.

Files needed: None

1. **If Word isn't already open from the preceding exercise, open it.**
2. **Click the File tab on the Ribbon.**

   The File menu opens. Categories of commands are listed at the left.

The category that appears by default depends on whether any changes have been made to the blank document that opens by default when the application starts.

3. **Choose Recent if that category doesn't already appear by default.**

   This category provides shortcuts for reopening recently used files. See Figure 1-17.
4. **Choose File⇨Info and examine the commands available.**

   This category provides commands for permissions, sharing, and versions, as well as basic information about the file itself.

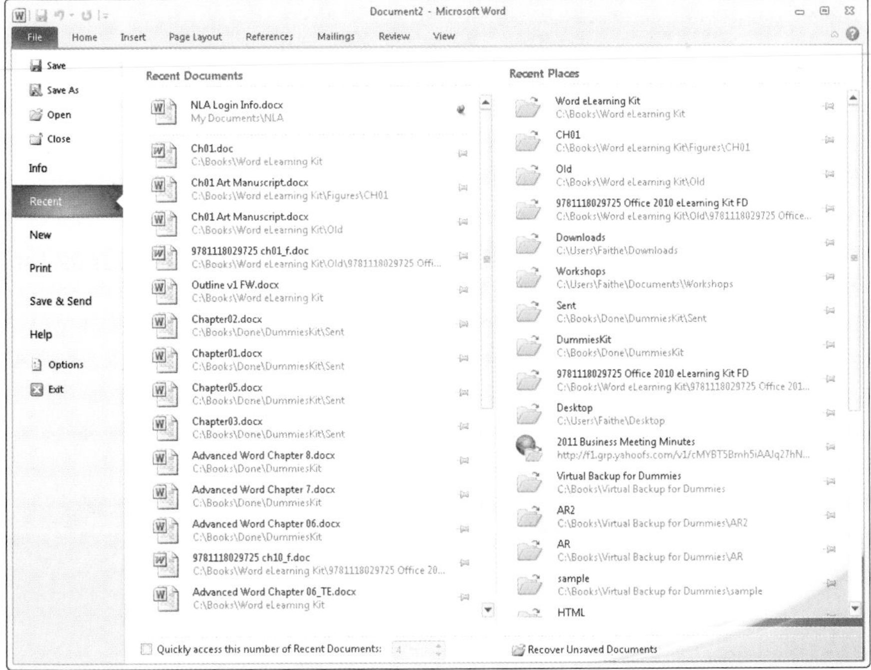

Figure 1-17

5. **Click the Manage Versions button.**

   This button opens a menu of additional commands. See Figure 1-18.

6. **Click away from the menu without choosing a command from it.**

   The menu closes.

7. **Choose File➪New.**

   Buttons appear for creating a new document based on a variety of templates.

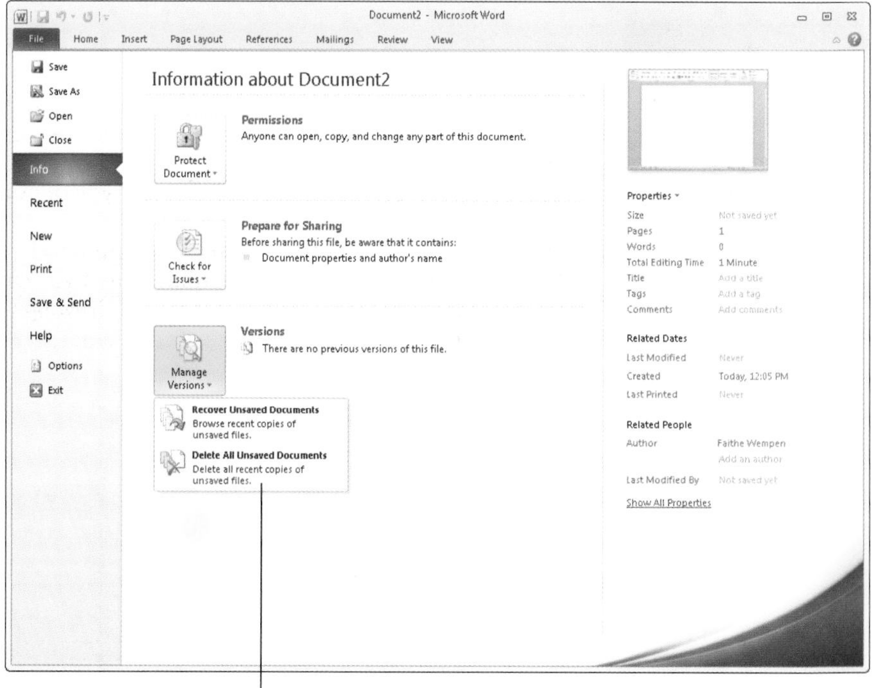

Figure 1-18

8. **Choose File➪Print.**

   Buttons appear for printing the active document.

9. **Choose File➪Save & Send.**

   Buttons appear for saving and distributing the active document in different formats.

10. **Choose File➪Help.**

    Options appear for getting help with the application.

11. **Choose File➪Close.**

    The active document and Backstage view close. Word remains open.

12. **Choose File➪Exit.**

    The Word application window closes.

Creating Your First Document

When you start Word, a new, blank document appears automatically, as you saw in the section "Starting Word." You can begin creating new content in this document and then save your work when you're finished. Alternatively, you can open an existing document or start a different type of document.

After starting a new document, you type or insert content into it. Documents can contain text, graphic objects, or a combination of the two. You can use many types of graphic objects, such as photos, clip art, drawings, diagrams, and charts. You learn about these object types in Lesson 8.

Starting a new, blank document

In the following exercise, you start several new Word documents using various methods.

Files needed: None

1. **Start Microsoft Word 2010 using any method you like.**

   A new, blank document opens automatically.

2. **Choose File⇨New.**

   Icons for various template types appear.

3. **Click the Sample Templates icon, choose Essential Report (see Figure 1-19), and then click the Create button.**

   A document appears with several types of placeholder content.

4. **Press the down-arrow key on the keyboard several times.**

   The various types of placeholders come into view.

5. **Choose File⇨Close to close the new document.**

   No documents are open. The new, blank one that was created by default when Word started closed automatically because you didn't use it.

6. **Press Ctrl+N to start a new, blank presentation.**

7. **Choose File⇨New, click the Blank Presentation icon, and then click the Create button.**

   A blank document opens.

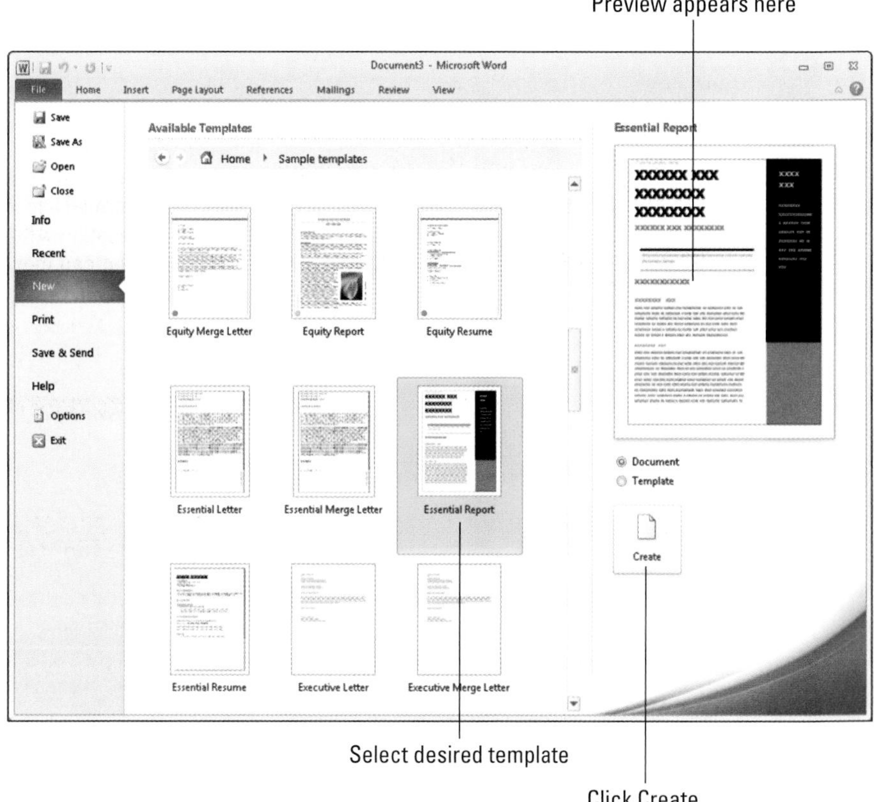

Figure 1-19

8. **Choose File⇨Exit to close Word.**

   A prompt appears asking whether you want to save changes to the document you created using the template. You aren't prompted to save the blank document you created in Step 7 because it contains no content (either placeholder or user-entered).

9. **Click Don't Save.**

   Word exits.

Typing text

You can type any text you like into a Word document, creating various document types from posters to dissertations. Just click in the large blank area in the center of the Word window and begin typing.

In the following exercise, you place text into a Word document.

Files needed: None

> **LINGO**
>
> Text that you type appears at the **insertion point,** which is a blinking vertical line that marks the active location. After you type some text, you can move the insertion point around within the text by clicking or by pressing the arrow keys on the keyboard.

1. **Start Microsoft Word 2010 by using any method you like.**

   A new, blank document opens.

2. **Type** ACME Engineering**, press Enter to start a new paragraph, and then type** Making smart engineering decisions since 1962 **(see Figure 1-20).**

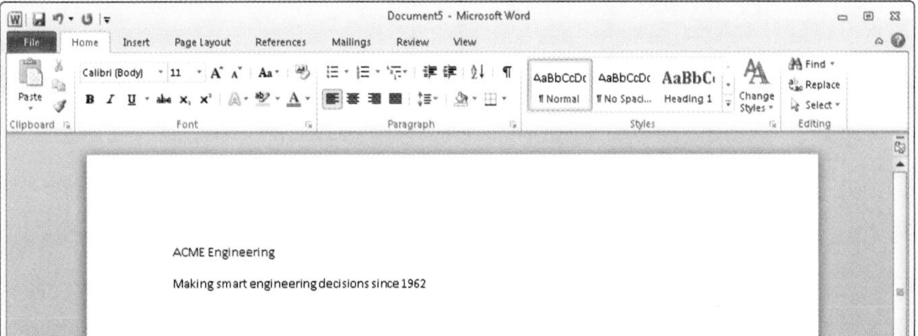

Figure 1-20

3. **Press Enter to move the insertion point to the next line, and then press the up-arrow key once to move the insertion point back into the text you typed.**

   The insertion point appears at the beginning of the word *Making.*

4. **Press the right-arrow key until the insertion point appears between 6 and 2 (see Figure 1-21), and then press the Backspace key to delete the 6.**

Insertion point

ACME Engineering

Making smart engineering decisions since 1962

Figure 1-21

If no text is selected, pressing Backspace removes the character to the *left* of the insertion point.

5. **Type** 7 **and then press the left-arrow key once.**

   The insertion point moves to the left of the 7.

6. **Press the Delete key to delete the 7.**

If no text is selected, pressing Delete removes the character to the *right* of the insertion point.

7. **Type** 6.

   The date once again appears as 1962.

Leave the document open for the next exercise.

Inserting a picture

One of the most common graphic types is a *picture from file* (a picture that's saved as a separate file outside of Word already). You can get pictures from the Internet, from friends, or from your own scanner or digital camera.

In the following exercise, you place a graphic into a Word document.

Files needed: `01Graphic01.jpg`

LINGO

Word supports a wide variety of picture formats. Some of the most common formats include JPEG, TIF, GIF, BMP, and PNG. Those are **file extensions.** Most filenames include a period (.) followed by an extension, a code that indicates the file's type. Extensions are customarily three characters long, but do not have to be.

1. **Start with the Word document open from the preceding exercise.**

If you didn't do the preceding exercise, go back and perform Steps 1–4 there.

2. **Click below the second paragraph to move the insertion point there; then click the Insert tab on the Ribbon and click the Picture button.**

   The Insert Picture dialog box opens.

3. **Navigate to the folder containing the data files for this lesson, select `01Graphic01.jpg` (see Figure 1-22), and click the Insert button.**

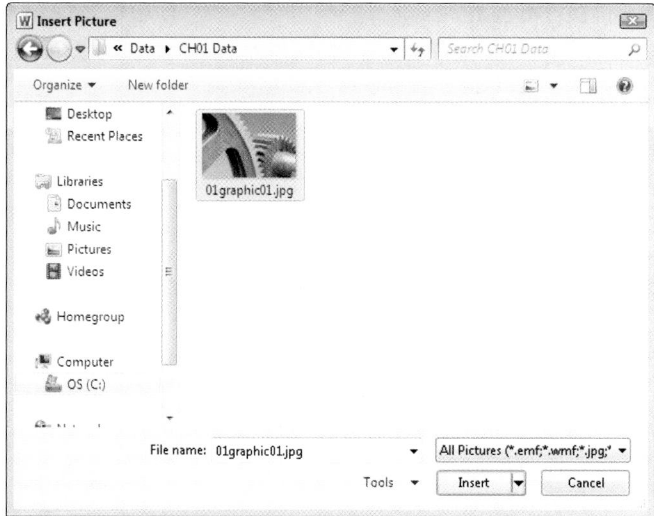

Figure 1-22

The picture is inserted in the document at the insertion point position.

The picture appears very large — larger than you might want it to be. Lesson 8 covers resizing a picture.

Leave the document open for the next exercise.

Saving and Opening Documents

Word can create, open, and save documents that contain the text, graphics, and other content you have entered into Word. If you don't save your work, whatever you've entered disappears when you close the application or turn off your computer.

Throughout the rest of this book, many of the exercises begin with an instruction to open a particular data file and end with an instruction to save it; when instructed to do those things, you can refer back to this section for help as needed.

Saving a document for the first time

As you work in Word, the content you create is stored in the computer's memory. This memory is only temporary storage. When you exit the application or shut down the computer, whatever is stored in memory is flushed away forever — unless you save it.

The first time you save a file, Word prompts you to enter a name for it in the Save As dialog box. You can also choose a different save location and/or file type.

When you resave an already saved file, the Save As dialog box doesn't reappear; the file saves with the most recent settings.

If you want to change the settings (such as the location or file type) or save under a different name, choose File➪Save As to make the Save As dialog box appear.

Word saves its documents in a Word Document (`.docx`) format, by default, but it can also save in other formats for compatibility with other applications or for special uses. Two of the most common alternative file formats are

- **Macro-enabled files:** If you need to store macros in a Word document, you can save it in Word Macro-Enabled Document (`.docm`) format.

> **LINGO**
>
> **Macros** are recorded bits of code that can automate certain activities in a program. For example, a macro can record keystrokes for performing a task that needs to be repeated over and over, saving the user time. However, macros can also carry viruses. The default Word format doesn't support macros for that reason.

- **Word 97–2003:** Word includes a file format for backward compatibility with earlier versions of the application (versions 97 through 2003; the file format for Word 2007 is identical to that of Word 2010, so you don't need a special format for backward compatibility with Word 2007). Some minor functionality may be lost when saving in this format. The file extension for it is `.doc`, and it does not have macro-enabled and non-macro-enabled variants; all are macro-enabled.

In this exercise, you save a document in Word several times with different names and file types.

Files needed: None

1. **In Word, with the document still open from the preceding exercise, choose File➪Save.**

   The Save As dialog box opens. A default name, ACME Engineering, is already filled in the File Name text box. Word took this from the first line of the document.

2. **In the File Name text box, type** Engineering, **replacing the default name (see Figure 1-23), and then click Save.**

> **EXTRA INFO**
>
> The save location is whatever is set as the default for your user account (probably the Documents library). For now, you can leave the location as-is.

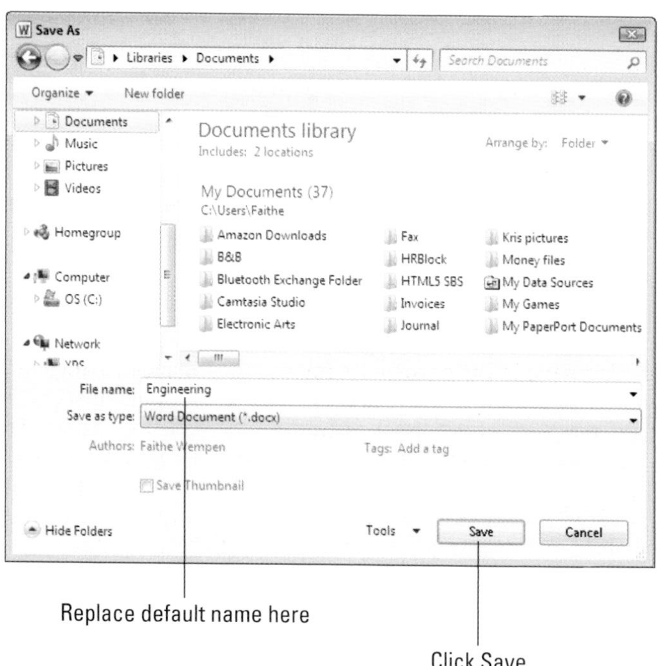

Figure 1-23

The file is saved. Engineering appears in the title bar of the Word application window.

3. **In the document, double-click the word** Engineering **to select it, type the word** Consulting **to replace it, and on the Quick Access toolbar, click the Save button.**

   See Figure 1-24. The changes to the document are saved.

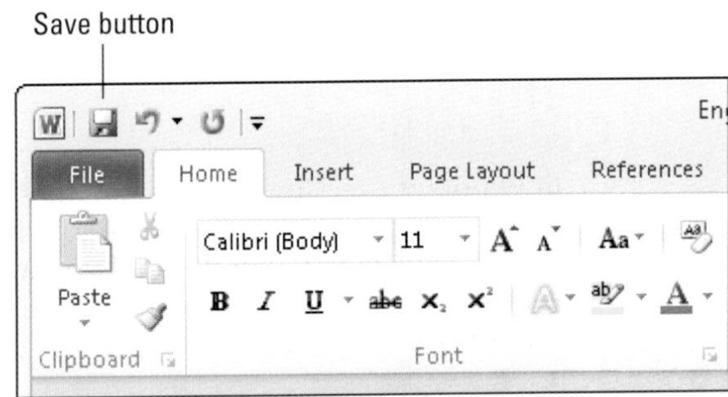

Figure 1-24

4. **Press Ctrl+S.**

   The changes are saved again.

5. **Choose File⇨Save As.**

   The Save As dialog box opens.

6. **In the File Name text box, change the filename to** Consulting; **from the Save as Type drop-down list, choose Word 97–2003 Document (see Figure 1-25); and click Save.**

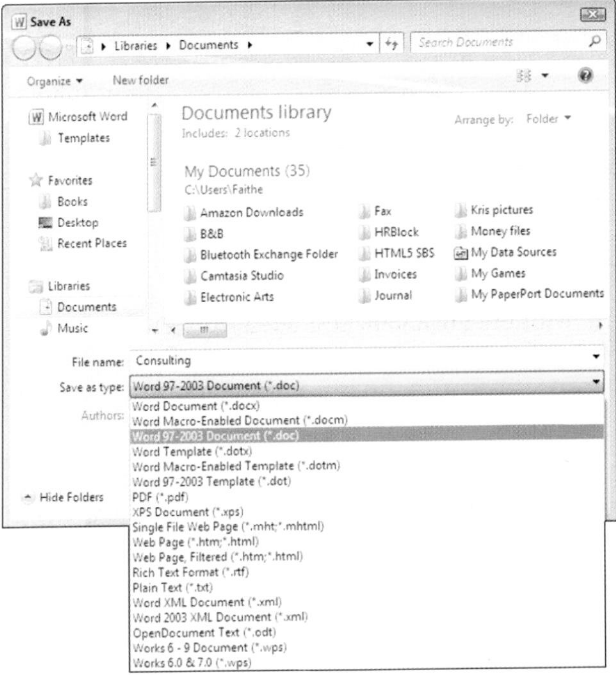

Figure 1-25

The document is resaved with a different name and a different file type.

Leave the document open in Word for the next exercise.

Navigating in the Save and Open dialog boxes

In Windows (versions Vista and later), each user has his own Documents folder based on who is logged in to Windows at the moment. That's the default save location in Word. If you want to save somewhere else, you must use the controls in the Save As dialog box to change to a different location before you save.

To understand how to change save locations, you should first understand the concept of a file path. Files are organized into folders, and you can have folders *inside* folders. For example, you might have

- A Work folder
- Within that folder, a Job Search folder
- Within that folder, a Word Resume.docx file

The path for such a file would be

```
C:\Work\Job Search\Resume.docx
```

When you change the save location, you're changing to a different path for the file. You do that by navigating through the file system via the Save As dialog box. The Save As dialog box provides several ways of navigating, so you can pick the one you like best.

In this exercise, you experiment with several ways of changing the save location in the Save As dialog box.

Files needed: None

1. **In Word, with the document still open from the preceding exercise, choose File⇨Save As.**

   The Save As dialog box opens. See Figure 1-26.

This exercise assumes you're using Windows 7. In Windows Vista, the Save As dialog box may not show any folders or locations by default. If it doesn't, click the Browse Folders button at the bottom left of the dialog box.

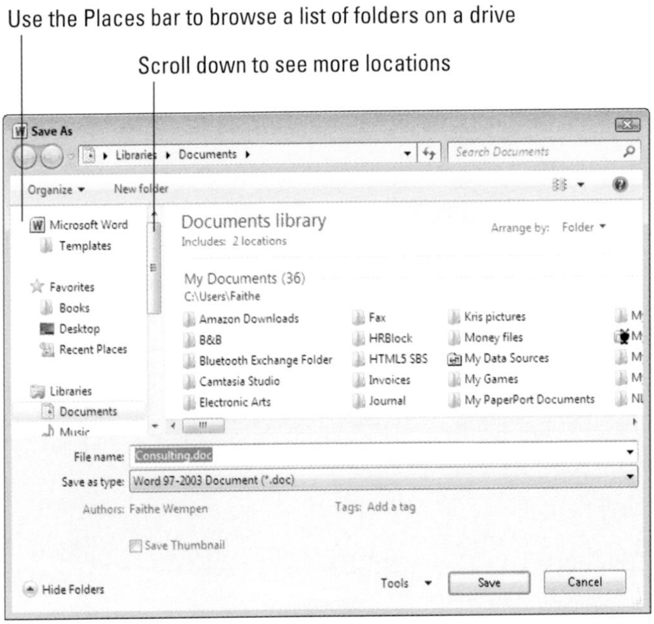

Use the Places bar to browse a list of folders on a drive

Scroll down to see more locations

Figure 1-26

2. **Scroll through the Places bar to see the available locations for saving files, and then double-click Computer.**

   A list of drives appears.

3. **Double-click the `C:` drive.**

   A list of folders on the `C:` drive appears. See Figure 1-27.

> **EXTRA INFO**
>
> The bar at the left side of the dialog box is the Places bar. It provides shortcuts for various places you can save files. The bar across the top is the Address bar. It shows the current location.

4. **Scroll up in the Places bar to locate the Documents shortcut and double-click it.**

   The Documents folder's content appears.

5. **Right-click an empty spot in right pane of the dialog box and click New Folder.**

   A new folder appears, with the name highlighted, ready for you to name it.

6. **Type** Dummies Kit **and press Enter to name the folder.**

   You've just created a folder that you can use to store all the work that you do for this class.

7. **Drag the Dummies Kit folder and drop it into the Favorites list at the left (see Figure 1-28).**

Folders on the C: drive appear here

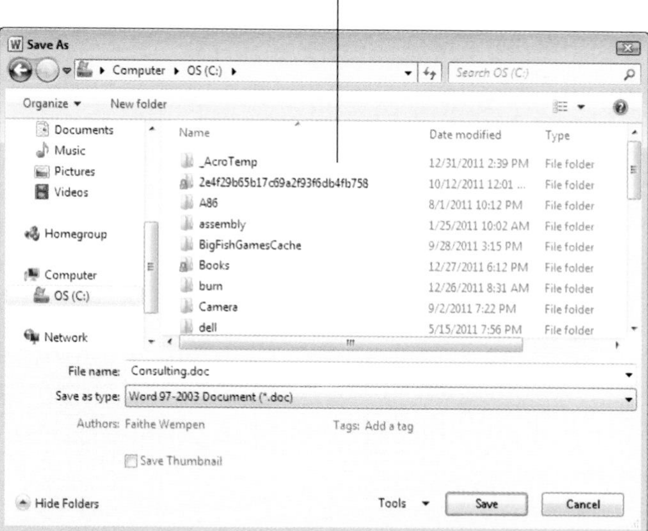

Figure 1-27

Drag new folder and drop it under Favorites heading

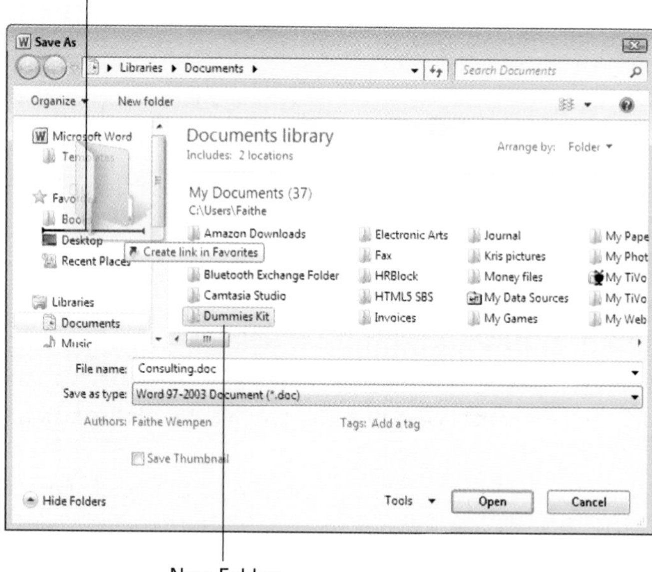

New Folder

Figure 1-28

8. **Double-click the Dummies Kit folder to open it, and in the Address bar, click the right-pointing arrow to the left of Dummies Kit.**

   A list of all the other folders in the Documents folder appears.

In the Address bar, the parts of a path are separated by right-pointing triangles rather than by slashes. You can click any of the triangles to open a drop-down list containing all the *subfolders* (that is, the folders within that folder).

9. **Click any of the folders on that list to switch to that folder, and then in the Favorites list, click Documents.**

   The Documents folder reappears.

10. **In the Address bar, click Libraries.**

    A list of the libraries for Windows 7 appears: Documents, Pictures, Music, and Videos.

11. **Scroll up near the top of the Places bar and click Desktop.**

    You can save directly to your desktop by saving to this location.

12. **On the Favorites list, click Dummies Kit.**

    The Dummies Kit folder reappears.

13. **In the File Name text box, type** Lesson 1 Practice**; from the Save as Type drop-down list, choose Word Document (see Figure 1-29); and click Save.**

    The file is saved.

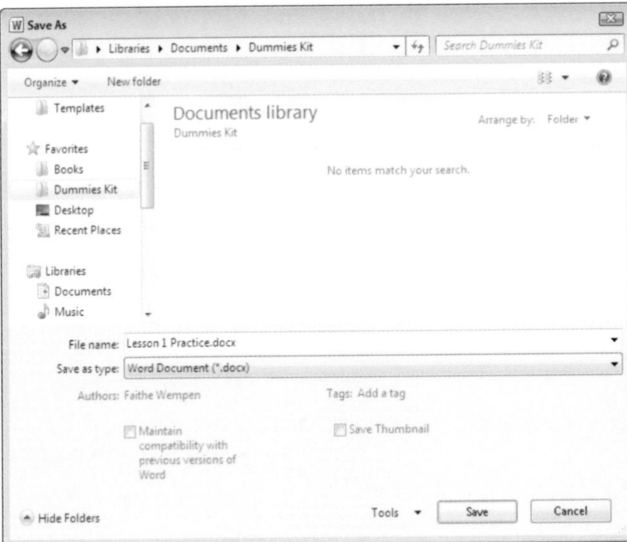

Figure 1-29

14. Choose File➪Close to close the document without exiting Word.

Leave Word open for the next exercise.

Opening a document

When you open a file, you copy it from your hard drive (or other storage location) into the computer's memory, where Word can access it for viewing and modifying it.

The Open dialog box's navigation controls are almost exactly the same as those in the Save As dialog box, so you can browse to a different storage location if needed.

If you want to reopen a recently used file, there's an even quicker way than using the Open dialog box. Choose File➪Recent, and then click the file's name on the Recent Files list.

In this exercise, you open a saved file.

Files needed: Any saved Word document, such as the Lesson 1 Practice file you saved in the preceding exercise

1. **In Word, choose File➪Open.**

   The Open dialog box appears.

2. **On the Favorites list in the Places bar, click Dummies Kit.**
3. **Click Lesson 1 Practice (see Figure 1-30), and then click Open.**

   The file opens in Word.

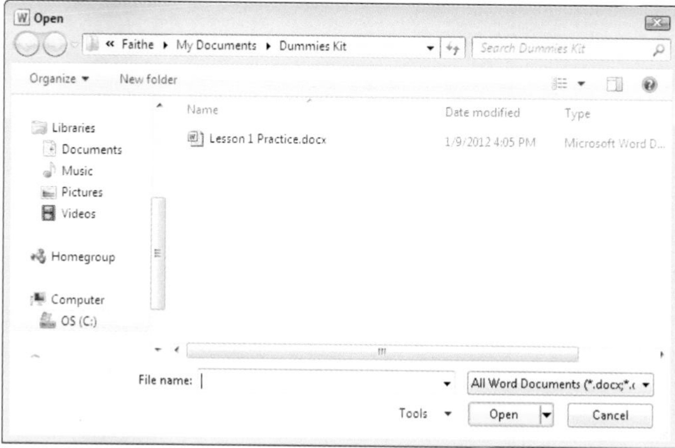

Figure 1-30

4. **Choose File⇨Close to close the document without exiting Word, and then choose File⇨Recent.**

   A list of recently opened files appears.

5. **Click Lesson 1 Practice to reopen the file, and then choose File⇨Close to close the document again.**

Leave Word open for the next exercise.

Recovering lost work

Computers lock up occasionally, and applications crash in the middle of important projects. When that happens, any work that you haven't saved is gone.

To minimize the pain of those situations, Word has an AutoRecover feature that silently saves your drafts as you work, once every ten minutes or at some other interval you specify. These drafts are saved in temporary hidden files that are deleted when you close the application successfully (that is, not abruptly because of a lockup, crash, or power outage). If the application crashes, those temporary saved files appear for your perusal when the program starts back up. You can choose to do either of the following:

- Save them if their versions are newer than the ones you have on your hard drive.
- Discard them if they contain nothing you need.

In this exercise, you change the interval at which Word saves backup drafts for AutoRecover.

Files needed: None

1. **In Word, choose File⇨Options.**

   The Word Options dialog box opens.

2. **Click the Save category on the left.**
3. **Make sure that the Save AutoRecover Information Every xx Minutes check box is selected.**
4. **If desired, change the value in the Minutes box to another number.**

   For example, to save every five minutes, type **5** there. See Figure 1-31.

5. **Click OK.**

Leave Word open for the next exercise.

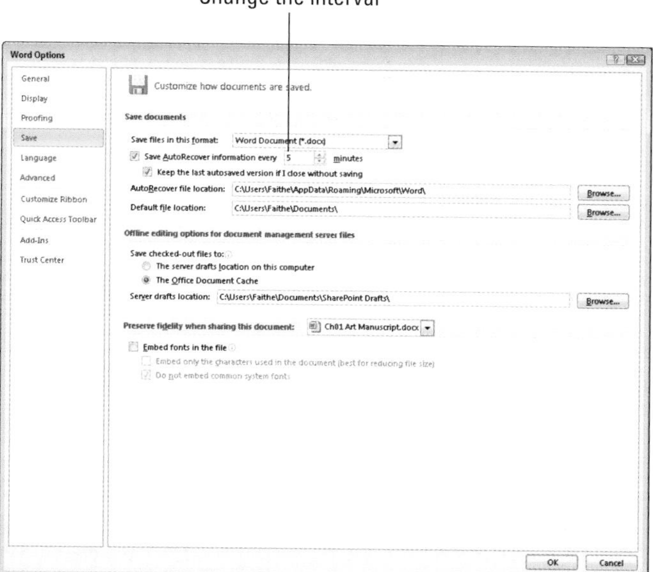

Figure 1-31

Moving Around

As you work in Word, you may add so much content that you can't see it all onscreen at once. You might need to scroll through the document to view different parts of it. The simplest way to scroll through a document is by using the *scroll bars* with your mouse.

Scrolling through a document with the scroll bars doesn't move the insertion point, so what you type or insert doesn't necessarily appear in the location that shows onscreen.

You can also get around by moving the insertion point. When you do so, the document view scrolls automatically so you can see the newly selected location. You can move the insertion point either by clicking where you want it or by using keyboard shortcuts.

Moving with the mouse

Here's a summary of the available mouse movements:

- Click a scroll arrow to scroll a small amount in that direction.
- Click above or below the scroll box to scroll one full screen in that direction if the document is tall/wide enough that there's undisplayed content in that direction.
- Drag the scroll box to scroll quickly in the direction you're dragging.

Now practice those skills in the following exercise.

In the following exercise, you move around in a Word document via the mouse.

Files needed: Lesson 1 Syllabus.docx

1. **In Word, open Lesson 1 Syllabus and save it as Lesson 1 Syllabus Practice.**
2. **Click the bottom scroll arrow on the vertical scroll bar three times.**

   Each time you click, the display scrolls down a small amount. See Figure 1-32.
3. **Click once below the scroll box.**

   The display scrolls down one screenful.
4. **Drag the scroll box up as high as it will go.**

   The top of the document comes back into view.
5. **Click and hold down the mouse button on the top scroll arrow.**

   The bottom of the document comes into view.

Leave the document open for the next exercise.

EXTRA INFO

The size of the scroll box is an indicator of how much of the document is undisplayed at the moment. In Figure 1-32, the scroll boxes take up about ⅓ of the vertical scroll bar, indicating that the portion displayed onscreen is approximately ⅓ of the total document.

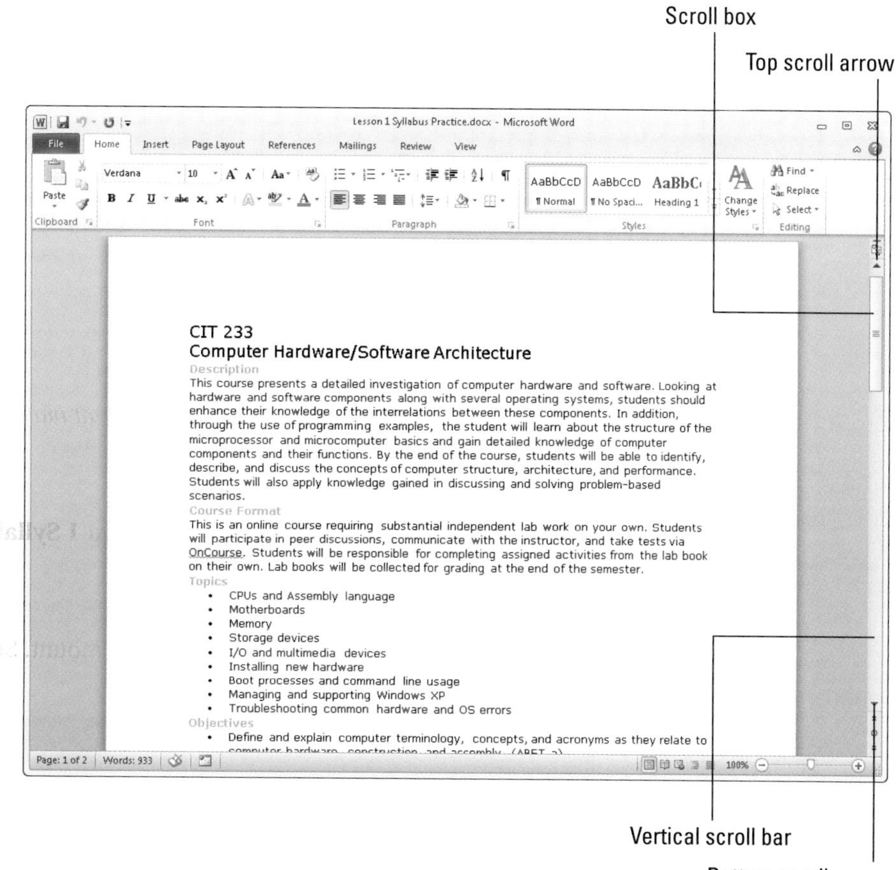

Figure 1-32

Moving with the keyboard

Here's a summary of the ways you can move around in a document via the keyboard:

- Press an arrow key to move the insertion point in the direction of the arrow. The up- and down-arrow keys move one line, and the right- and left-arrow keys move one character.
- Press the Page Up or Page Down key to scroll one full screen in that direction.

- Press the Home key to move to the left side of the current line.
- Press the End key to move to the right side of the current line.
- Press Ctrl+Home to move to the beginning of the document.
- Press Ctrl+End to move to the end of the document.

Now practice those skills in the following exercise.

In the following exercise, you move around in a Word document via the keyboard.

Files needed: Lesson 1 Syllabus Practice.docx, open from the preceding exercise

1. **In Lesson 1 Syllabus Practice, press Ctrl+Home.**

   The insertion point moves to the beginning of the document.

2. **Press the right-arrow key on the keyboard twice.**

   The insertion point moves two spaces to the right.

3. **Press the down-arrow key twice.**

   The insertion point moves two lines down so that it is in the Description paragraph. See Figure 1-33.

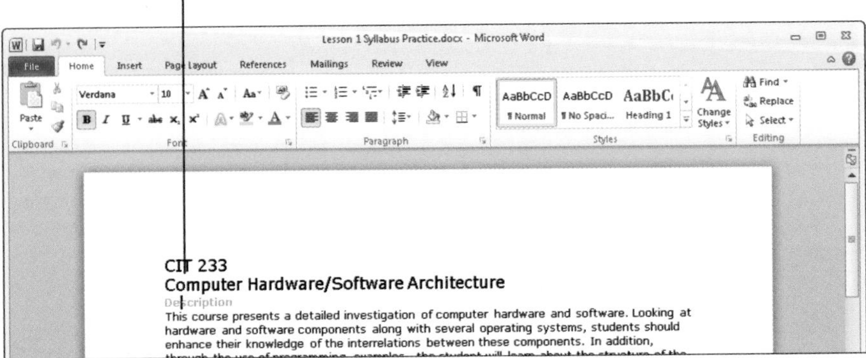

Figure 1-33

4. **Hold down the Ctrl key and press the down-arrow key.**

   The insertion point moves to the beginning of the next paragraph.

5. **Hold down the Ctrl key and press the right-arrow key.**

   The insertion point moves to the next word in the paragraph.

6. **Press the Home key.**

   The cell cursor moves back to the beginning of the paragraph.

7. **Press the Page Down key.**

   The page scrolls down one full screenful. (The exact amount depends on your screen size.)

8. **Press Ctrl+Home.**

   The cell cursor moves back to the top of the document.

Leave the document open for the next exercise.

Changing the Onscreen View

Word has multiple viewing modes you can switch among to make it easier to do different kinds of writing and editing. For example, Word's Outline view is optimal for creating outlines, and Full Screen Reading view works well for reading long documents on a computer monitor.

In addition, Word has Zoom commands that can make the text and graphics appear larger or smaller onscreen while you work.

Zooming has no relationship to the size of the text or graphics when they print; it affects only the onscreen view.

Changing views

The default view in Word is Print Layout; it displays a document very similarly to the way it will print, including all graphics, multi-column layouts, and page breaks.

The alternatives to Print Layout view are

- **Full Screen Reading:** A view designed to optimize readability onscreen, including a two-column display like in a printed book.
- **Web Layout:** A view designed to mimic web content; use this view to see how your document might look if saved in web format.
- **Outline:** A hierarchical view in which each heading level is a level in an outline, and body text can optionally be hidden.
- **Draft:** A simple text-only view that hides most graphics and ignores multi-column layouts and page headers and footers.

In this exercise, you explore the available views in Word.

Files needed: Lesson 1 Syllabus Practice.docx, open from the preceding exercise

1. **In Lesson 1 Syllabus Practice, click the View tab.**

   Buttons for each of the available views appear on the Ribbon. See Figure 1-34.

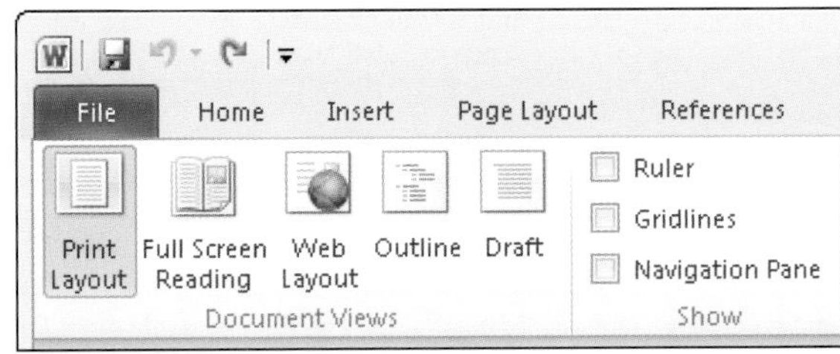

Figure 1-34

2. **Choose View➪Full Screen Reading.**

   The display changes to show the document in a two-column, full-screen view. See Figure 1-35.

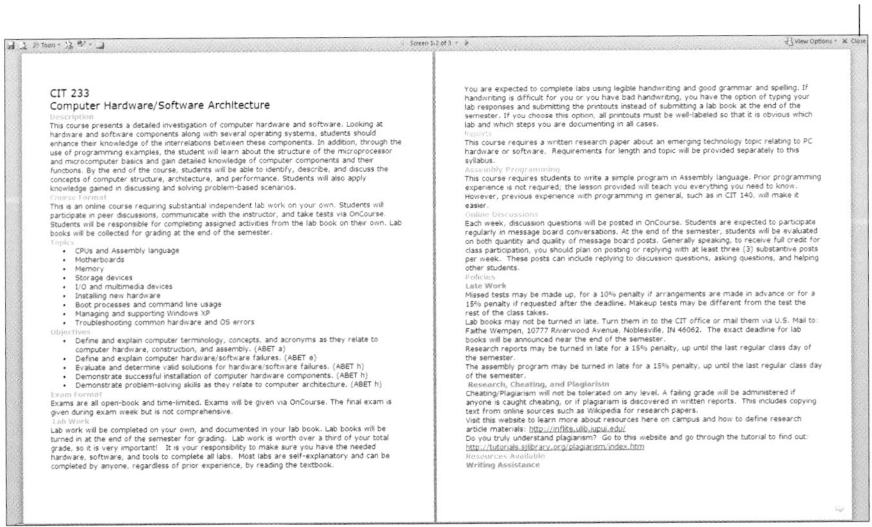

Figure 1-35

3. **Click the Close button in the upper-right corner to exit Full Screen Reading view, and then choose View➪Web Layout.**

   The display changes to show the document in a margin-less layout that resembles a web page.

4. **Choose View➪Draft.**

   The display changes to show the document in Draft view.

5. **Scroll through the document in Draft view.**

EXTRA INFO

Draft view shows the text in a very basic format, without multiple columns, headers/footers, or other layout elements.

Page breaks are indicated by dotted lines. See Figure 1-36.

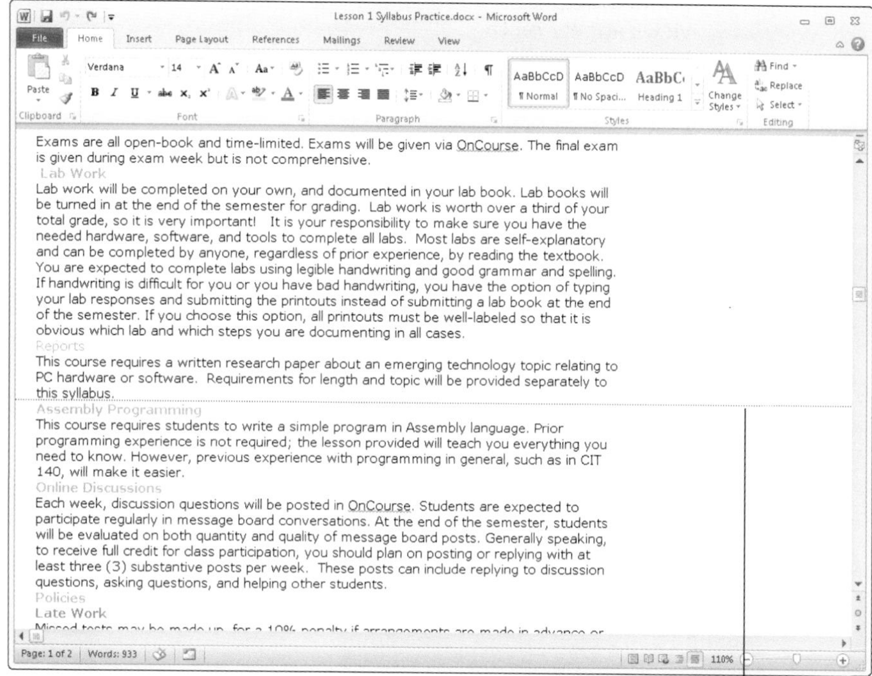

Figure 1-36

6. **Choose View⇨Outline.**

   The display changes to show the document in Outline view. An Outlining tab appears on the Ribbon. This document doesn't outline very well because no headings have been set up in this document yet.

7. **Choose Outlining⇨Close Outline View.**

   The display returns to Print Layout view.

8. **Hover the mouse over the Draft button on the status bar.**

   A ScreenTip appears indicating it is the Draft button. See Figure 1-37.

View buttons in a status bar

Figure 1-37

9. **Hover the mouse over each of the other view buttons on the status bar to see their names.**

Leave Word open for the next exercise.

> **EXTRA INFO**
>
> Each of the views has an equivalent button on the status bar for quick view changes, so you don't have to open the View tab each time you want to change the view.

Zooming in and out

Zooming changes the magnification of the data shown onscreen. Zooming doesn't change the magnification of the application window itself (for example, the Ribbon), and it doesn't change the size of the data on printouts.

Zooming in increases the magnification, and zooming out decreases it.

In this exercise, you explore the Zoom feature in Word.

Files needed: Lesson 1 Syllabus Practice.docx, open from the preceding exercise

1. **In Lesson 1 Syllabus Practice, drag the Zoom slider all the way to the right.**

   The Zoom slider is located in the bottom-right corner of the Word window. The zoom level increases to 500 percent.

2. **Drag the Zoom slider to the left to the 50% setting.**

   The zoom magnification decreases to 50%. Two pages of the document display side by side.

3. **Click the plus sign at the right end of the Zoom slider.**

   The zoom increases slightly.

4. **Click the minus sign at the left end of the Zoom slider.**

   The zoom decreases slightly.

5. **Click the current zoom percentage (the number to the left of the Zoom slider).**

   The Zoom dialog box opens.

You can also open the Zoom dialog box by clicking the View tab on the Ribbon and clicking the Zoom button.

6. **In the Zoom dialog box, select 100% and then click OK.**

   The zoom changes back to 100 percent (the default).

7. **Close the document. Do not save changes if prompted.**

Exit Word.

Summing Up

In this lesson, you explored the Word interface. You learned how to start and exit Word, move around in a document, create and save your work, and adjust the view.

- The Ribbon and Start menu provide a consistent interface for managing files and issuing commands in each application.
- Word starts a new, blank document when it opens. You can use this document, or you can open an existing one.
- To enter text in a document, click where you want to place it; that moves the insertion point there. Then type.
- To insert a picture, click the Insert tab on the Ribbon and then click the Picture button.
- Scroll bars enable you to scroll to different parts of a document. You can also move around by clicking where you want to go or by using the arrow keys to move the insertion point.
- To save your work, choose File⇨Save, press Ctrl+S, or click the Save button on the Quick Access toolbar.

- To open a file, choose File⇨Open. You can also select a recently used file from the Recent section of the File menu.
- You can switch among views on the View tab.
- The Zoom feature increases or decreases the magnification of the data displayed onscreen. Use the Zoom slider and controls in the lower-right corner of the application window.

Try-it-yourself lab

For more practice with the features covered in this lesson, try the following exercise on your own."

1. **Start Word and, in the new document that appears, type** Grocery List.
2. **Press Enter to start a new paragraph, and then type a grocery shopping list of at least six items, pressing Enter after each one.**
3. **Save the file as** Lesson 1 Grocery List **in the Dummies Kit folder you created earlier and close Word.**

Know this tech talk

application: A program that performs a useful user task, such as creating a word-processing document or calculating a number.

Backstage view: The section of Word that appears when the File menu is open. It contains commands for working with files, setting program options, importing, exporting, and printing.

document: A data file in a word-processing program. Can also refer generically to any data file.

file extension: The code following the period at the end of a filename, indicating the file's type.

folder: An organizing container on a hard drive in which to store files.

insertion point: A flashing vertical line indicating where text will be inserted when typed.

scroll bar: A bar along the right and/or bottom side of a window that can be used to change the viewing area.

scroll box: The movable box inside the scroll bar.

Lesson 2

Creating a Word Document

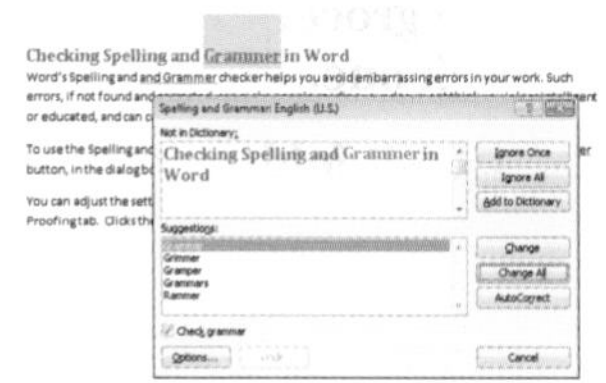

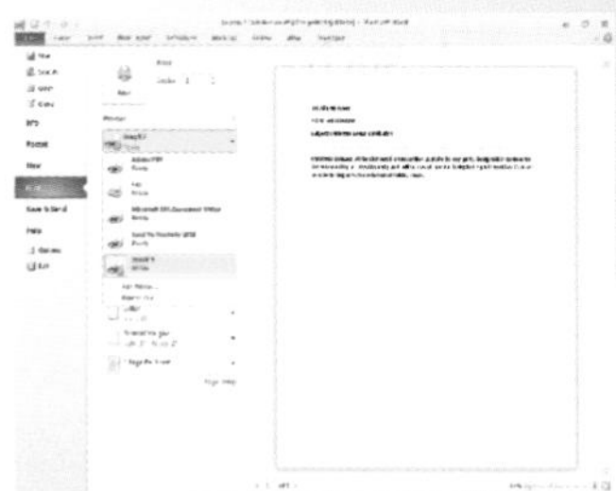

- Starting new documents based on templates can save time and provide guidance as to what content to insert and where to place it. Many templates are available for free via Office.com.
- Selecting text before issuing a command enables you to act on large blocks of text at a time. You can select text either with the keyboard or the mouse.
- Finding and replacing text makes editing easier. You can identify all instances of a particular word or phrase and replace them with a different word or phrase.
- Check your spelling and grammar to avoid embarrassing errors in documents you distribute to others. Word can help you check individual words and the entire document easily.
- You can share your documents with other people via e-mail or by printing them. You can begin sending a document via e-mail from within Word, and your default e-mail program opens to send the message.

1. How do you start a document based on an online template?

Guide yourself to page 48

2. How can you change a document's margins?

There's space on page.. 52

3. How do you set the paper size and page orientation?

Find your bearings on page 54

4. How do you locate all instances of a word in a document?

Search for that information on page 62

5. How do you alphabetize a list?

Sort that out on page.. 65

6. What does it mean when text has a wavy red underline?

There are all kinds of squiggles on page.. 66

7. How do you send Word documents via e-mail?

For electronic greetings, seek page 69

Microsoft Word is the most popular Office application because nearly everyone needs to create text documents of one type or another. With Word, you can create everything from fax cover sheets to school research papers to family holiday letters.

In this lesson, I explain how to create, edit, proofread, and share simple documents. By the end of this lesson, you have a good grasp of the entire process of document creation, from start to finish, including how to share your work with others via print or e-mail. Later lessons then build on this knowledge, adding in the fancier aspects, such as using formatting, styles, graphics, and multiple sections.

Starting a New Word Document

As you learn in Lesson 1, you can create a blank new document or you can base a new document on a template. Word has some templates that are stored locally on your hard drive and many more that are available via the Internet. After starting a new document, you can adjust the paper size and orientation if needed.

Even when you start a blank document, you still (technically) use a template. The blank document uses a Normal template, and it specifies certain default settings for a new blank document, such as the default fonts (Calibri for body text and Cambria for headings), default font sizes (11 point for body text), and margins (1 inch on all sides).

LINGO

A **template** is a special type of document that's designed to be a model for new documents. Templates have a different file extension than regular documents (either `.dotx` or `.dotm`). When you start a new document based on a template, the template file itself is unaffected, so the template is always the same each time you use it.

Creating a new document using a template

You can easily create a new document based on a template. This new document has all the characteristics of the template, including margins, paper size, default fonts, and any sample content that the template contains.

In the following exercise, you start two new Word documents. One uses a local template, and one uses a template from Office.com.

Files needed: None

1. **In Word, choose File⇨New.**

   Icons for creating new documents appear, as shown in Figure 2-1.

2. **In the Office.com Templates section, click Brochures and Booklets.**

   A set of three folders appears: Brochures, Catalogs, and Programs.

3. **Double-click the Brochures folder.**

   Word uses your Internet connection to retrieve a list of available brochure templates.

EXTRA INFO

When you create a new document by clicking the Blank Document icon or by pressing Ctrl+N, the resulting document is based on the Normal template. If you stick with the default values for the Normal template's definition, the Normal template doesn't exist as a separate file; it's built into Word itself. You won't find the template if you search your hard drive for it. However, if you make a change to one or more of the Normal template's settings, Word saves them to a `Normal.dotm` file. If Word at any point can't find `Normal.dotm`, it reverts to its internally stored copy and goes back to the default values.

That's important to know because if you ever accidentally redefine the Normal template so that it produces documents with unwanted settings or if it ever gets corrupted, all you have to do is find and delete `Normal.dotm` from your hard drive, and you go back to a fresh-from-the-factory version of the default settings for new, blank documents. The template is stored in `C:\Users\`*`user`*`\AppData\Roaming\Microsoft\Templates`, in which *user* is the logged-in username.

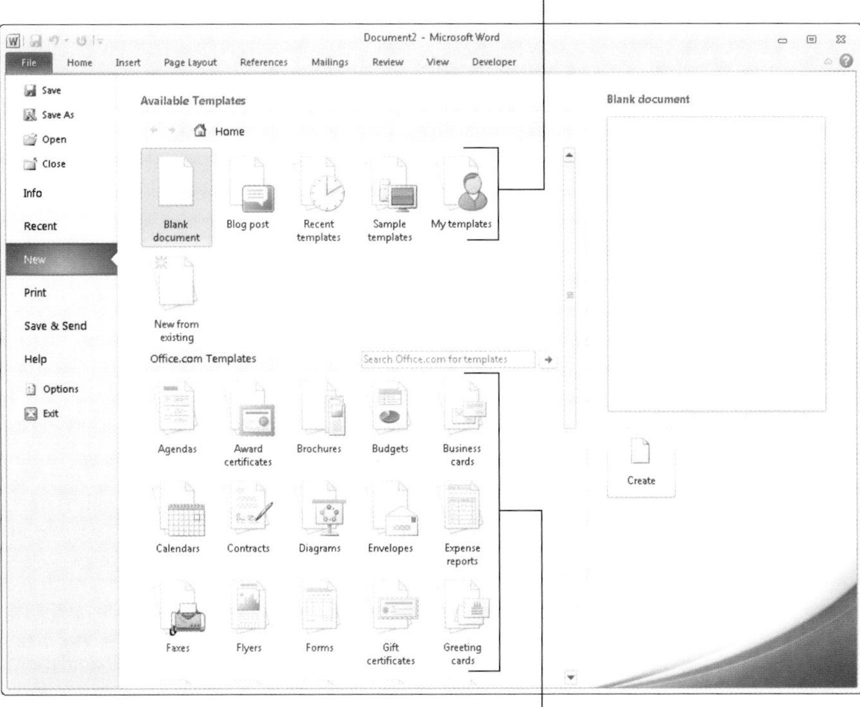

Figure 2-1

4. **Scroll down and click the Hawaii Brochure template.**

   A preview of it appears. See Figure 2-2.

5. **Click the Download button below the preview.**

   A license agreement appears.

6. **Click I Accept.**

   The template is downloaded, and a new document appears based on it. See Figure 2-3.

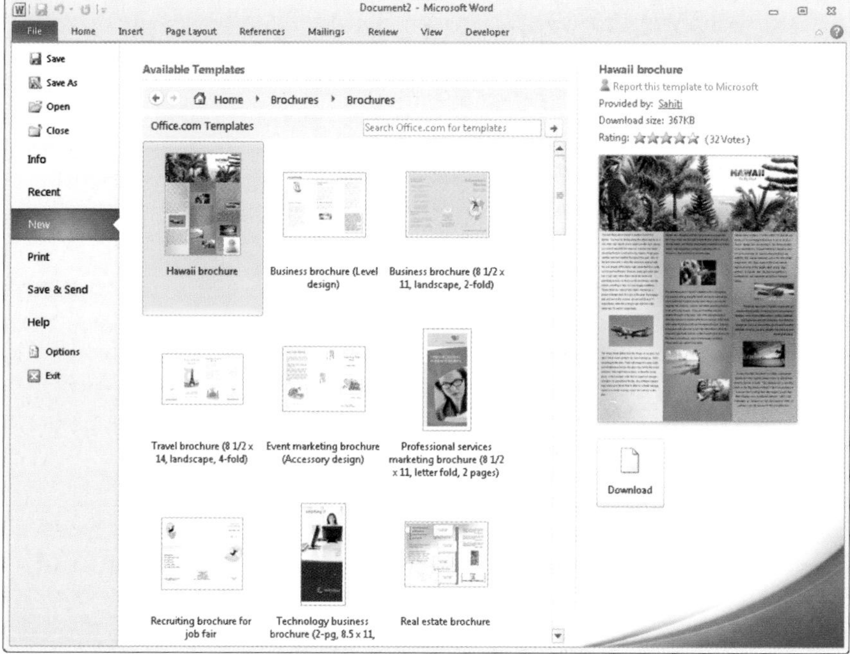

Figure 2-2

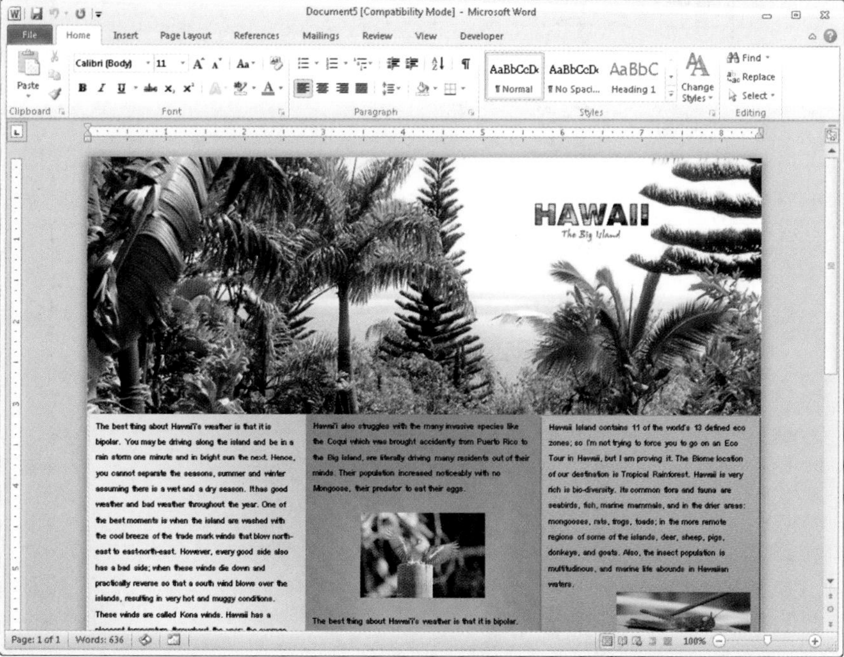

Figure 2-3

7. **Examine the document to see what types of content the template provides, choose File⇨Close to close the document, and if prompted to save your changes, click Don't Save.**

8. **Choose File⇨New.**

   The icons reappear for new document types.

9. **Click Sample Templates.**

   A list of the templates stored on your local hard drive appears.

10. **Scroll down to the bottom of the listing and click Urban Report.**

    A sample of the template appears. See Figure 2-4.

11. **Click the Create button.**

    A new document opens based on the selected template.

EXTRA INFO

Notice that the title bar contains the words Compatibility Mode. That's because this template is backward-compatible with Word 97–2003.

EXTRA INFO

This template's layout is atypical because it uses colored text boxes to hold the text; in most Word documents, you type directly onto the page.

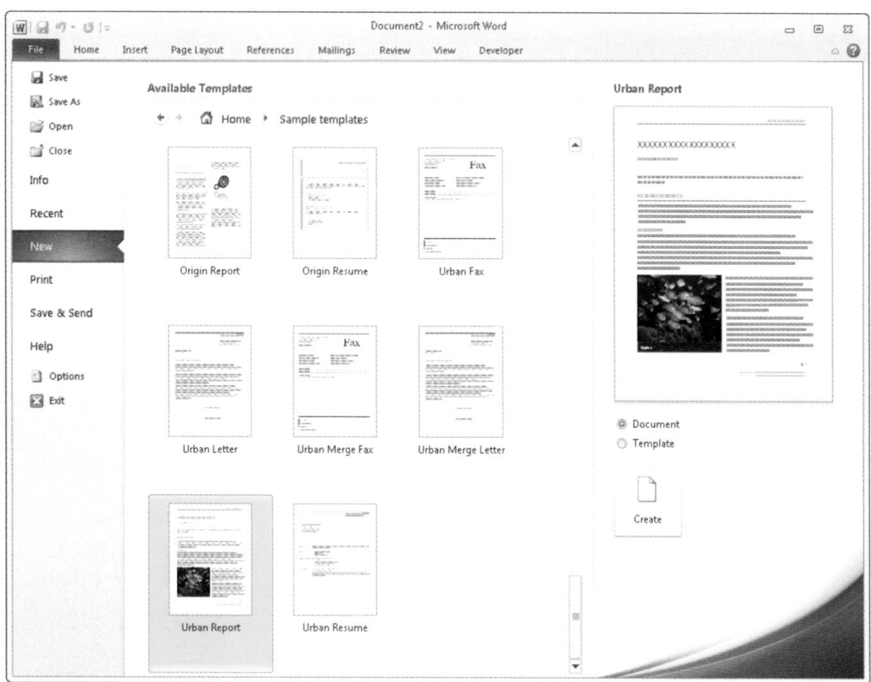

Figure 2-4

12. **Scroll through the new document and notice the placeholders ready for you to fill in to create your own version of the report.**
13. **Save the document as *Lesson 2 Practice.***

Leave the document open for the next exercise.

For more practice, create several more new documents by using different templates. Don't save any of them.

Setting page margins

Word provides several easy-to-use presets. You can also individually specify the margins for each side of the page if you prefer.

In the following exercise, you change the page margins in two ways: using a preset and using an exact value.

Files needed: Lesson 2 Practice, open from the preceding exercise

1. **In the Lesson 2 Practice document, choose Page Layout⇨Margins⇨Narrow (see Figure 2-5).**

   Presets for narrow margins are applied to the top, bottom, right, and left margins for the document.
2. **Click the Margins button again, and then choose Custom Margins.**

   The Page Setup dialog box opens.

LINGO

Margins are the amounts of blank space that Word reserves on each side of the paper. In most cases, you want them to be roughly the same on all sides, or at least the same at both the right/left, so the document looks symmetrical. In special cases, though, such as when you're going to bind the document on the left or at the top, you may want to leave more blank space on one particular side.

EXTRA INFO

The Mirrored margin option enables you to specify different margins for right and left, depending on whether the page number is odd or even. This option allows you to print pages for a two-sided booklet with the extra space on whichever side of the page will be binded.

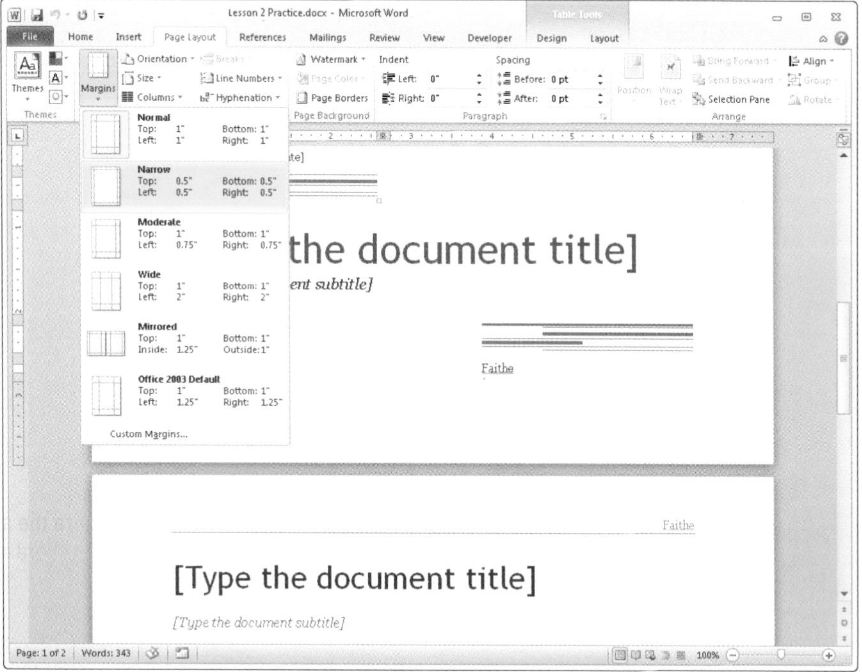

Figure 2-5

3. **In the Top, Bottom, Right, and Left boxes, type** 1.3, **as shown in Figure 2-6, and then click OK.**

   The margins change.

You can tell because the sample text is positioned differently on the pages.

4. **Save your work.**

Leave the document open for the next exercise.

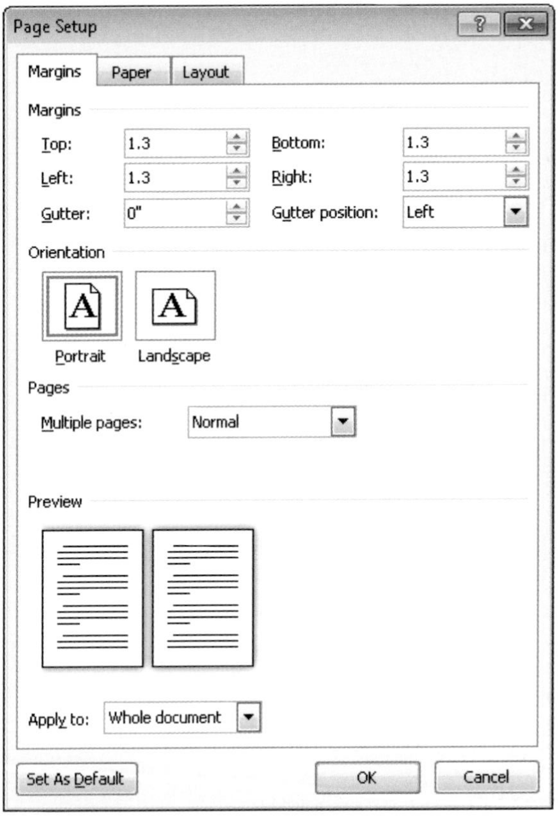

Figure 2-6

Setting page size and orientation

A template might not always use the right paper size or page orientation for the work you want to create. In some cases, either or both may require adjustment.

The standard paper size in the U.S. is 8.5 x 11 inches, also known as Letter. Most of the templates available through Word use this paper size, although some exceptions exist. For example, an Envelopes template might use a page size that matches a standard business envelope, or a legal brief template might use legal-size paper (8.5 x 14 inches).

LINGO

A document's **orientation** can be in either Portrait or Landscape mode. **Portrait** is a standard page in which the long side of the paper runs along the left and right. **Landscape** is a rotated page in which the long side of the paper runs along the top and bottom.

In the following exercise, you set the page orientation of a document to Landscape and change its paper size.

Files needed: Lesson 2 Practice, open from the preceding exercise

1. **In the Lesson 2 Practice document, choose Page Layout➪Orientation➪ Landscape (see Figure 2-7).**

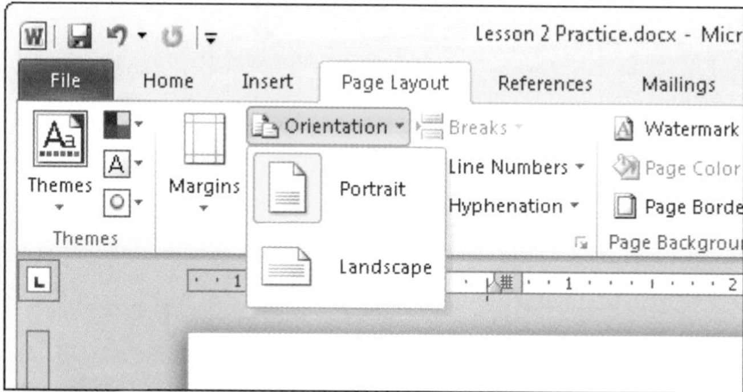

Figure 2-7

   The page changes to Landscape mode.

2. **Click the Orientation button and choose Portrait to change the orientation back to Portrait mode.**
3. **Click the Size button, and in the drop-down list that appears (see Figure 2-8), choose A4 210x297mm.**

   You may need to scroll down to find this option.

   The paper size changes.

EXTRA INFO

A4 is a commonly used paper size in Europe.

Look online for websites that explain the paper sizes common in various countries. Here's one such site: `www.cl.cam.ac.uk/~mgk25/iso-paper.html`.

Changing the paper size in Word doesn't change the paper size in your printer, of course, so if you print on a different sized paper than you tell Word you're using, the printing may not be centered on the paper.

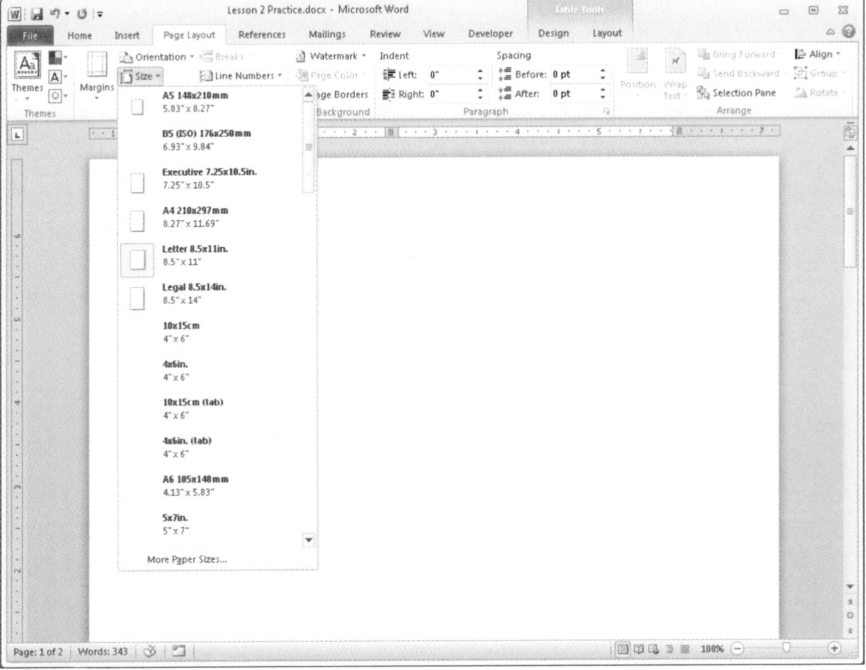

Figure 2-8

For more practice, click the Size button, choose More Paper Sizes, and set up a custom paper size by entering a width and height on the Paper tab of the Page Setup dialog box.

4. **Save your work.**

Leave the document open for the next exercise.

Editing Text

After creating a document and settings its basic properties, such as margins, orientation, and page size, you're ready to edit its content. Editing can include adding text, deleting text, modifying text, and moving and copying blocks of text from one location to another.

If you used a template to get started, you may already have some sample content in the document (text and/or graphics). You can edit this content, or you can delete it and start from scratch.

Filling text placeholders

Some templates include placeholders to guide you in creating content in a specific format. You aren't required to use the placeholders; you can delete them if you like. However, if you aren't sure how to get started with a particular type of document, the template's placeholders can be helpful guides.

In the following exercise, you edit a document's text by filling in placeholders.

Files needed: Lesson 2 Practice, open from the preceding exercise

1. **In the Lesson 2 Practice document, click in the *[Type the document title]* placeholder on the first page.**

   The placeholder becomes highlighted. See Figure 2-9.
2. **Type** Mountain Vista Vacations**.**

   The text appears in the placeholder box.

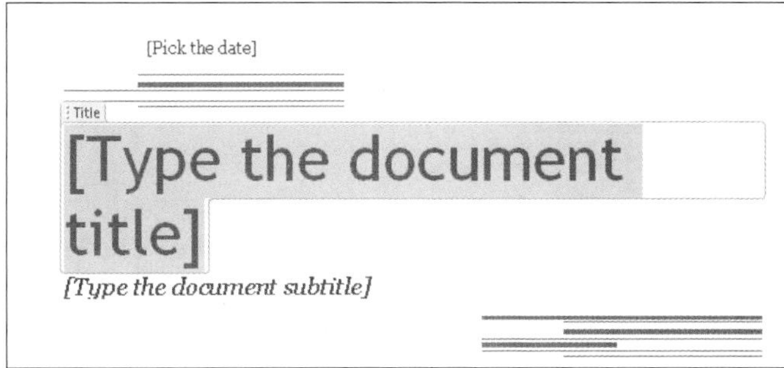

Figure 2-9

3. **Click in the *[Type the document subtitle]* placeholder and type** Affordable Family Fun**.**
4. **Click in the *[Pick the date]* placeholder.**

   The text becomes highlighted, and a drop-down arrow appears to its right.
5. **Click the arrow to open a date picker (see Figure 2-10), click the Today button to select today's date, and click the name that appears in the document.**

   By default, the name that appears is the name of the registered user of this copy of Word.
6. **If it's not your name that appears already, type your own name.**

   The cover page information is now complete, as shown in Figure 2-11.

Figure 2-10

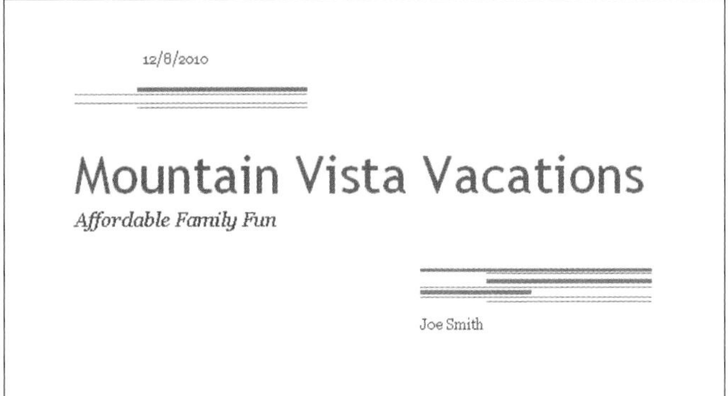

Figure 2-11

7. **Save your work and close the document.**

Leave Word open for the next exercise.

Typing and editing text

Most documents don't contain text placeholders, so you're on your own in deciding what to type. Fortunately, you can easily type and edit text in Word.

When you type in Word, the insertion point automatically moves to the next line when you run out of room at the right margin. You don't have to press Enter to break each line manually. The only time you need to press Enter is when you want to start a new paragraph.

You can press the Delete key to delete text to the right of the insertion point, or press the Backspace key to delete text to the left of the insertion point. To delete more than one character at once, select the block of text to delete, and then press either Delete or Backspace.

You can also select some text and then type over it. When you type after selecting text, the selected text is replaced by what you type.

In the following exercise, you type some text in a new document and then edit it using several editing techniques.

Files needed: None

1. **In Word, press Ctrl+N to start a new blank document.**
2. **Type the following text in the document:**

   Dear Karen:

   Florida is certainly a long way from home, and although we are enjoying our trip, we're looking forward to being home again with our good friends.

   We're having a wonderful time on our vacation. The weather has been perfect. Elroy and George have been collecting shells, and Judy and I have been enjoying the pool.
3. **Triple-click the last paragraph to select it.**
4. **Click and drag the paragraph up, and then drop it between the other two paragraphs (between the salutation and the first body paragraph). See Figure 2-12.**

Dear Karen:

We are having a wonderful time on our vacation. The weather has been perfect. Elroy and George have been collecting shells, and Judy and I have been enjoying the pool.

(Ctrl)

Florida is certainly a long way from home, and although we are enjoying our trip, we are looking forward to being home again with our good friends.

Figure 2-12

5. **Double-click the name *Karen* in the first paragraph and type** Rosie.
6. **Click to move the insertion point after the word *Florida* in the last paragraph. Press the Backspace key until the entire word is deleted, and then type** California.
7. **Use the arrow keys to move the insertion point before *shells* in the second paragraph, and then type** sea.

   The document resembles Figure 2-13.

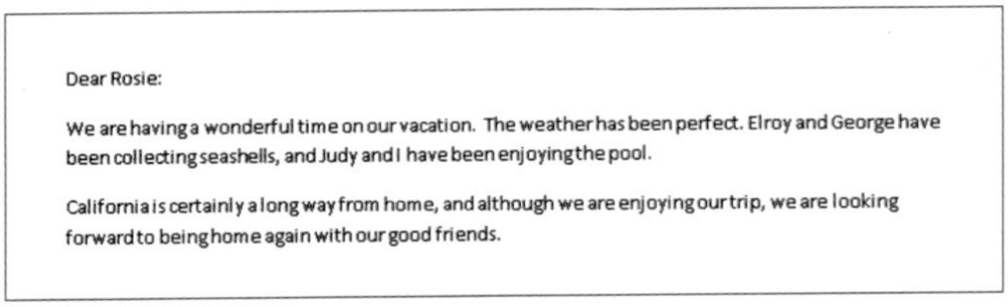

Dear Rosie:

We are having a wonderful time on our vacation. The weather has been perfect. Elroy and George have been collecting seashells, and Judy and I have been enjoying the pool.

California is certainly a long way from home, and although we are enjoying our trip, we are looking forward to being home again with our good friends.

Figure 2-13

8. **Save the document as *Lesson 2 Vacation*.**

Leave the document open for the next exercise.

Selecting Text

Selecting blocks of text before you issue an editing or formatting command allows you to act on the entire block at once. For example, you can select multiple paragraphs before applying new line spacing or indentation settings, and those settings apply to every paragraph in the selection.

You have many ways to select text:

- Click and drag across the text with the left mouse button pressed to select any amount of text.
- Move the insertion point to the beginning of the text, and then hold down the Shift key while you press the arrow keys to extend the selection.
- Press the F8 key to turn on Extend mode, and then you can use the arrow keys to extend the selection.
- Double-click a word to select it or triple-click a paragraph to select it.
- Press Ctrl+A to select the entire document.
- Click to the left of a line to select that line.

In the following exercise, you practice selecting parts of a document.

Files needed: Lesson 2 Vacation, open from the preceding exercise

1. **In the Lesson 2 Vacation file, triple-click the middle paragraph to select it.**
2. **Hold down the Shift key and press the down-arrow key twice to extend the selection to the next paragraph (see Figure 2-14).**

Triple-click this paragraph to select it ...

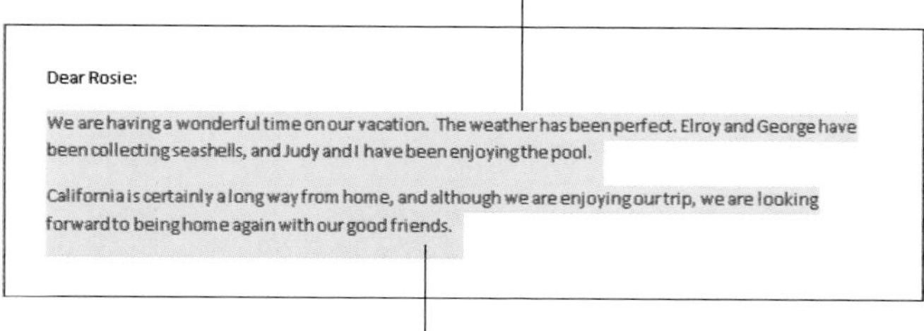
Dear Rosie:

We are having a wonderful time on our vacation. The weather has been perfect. Elroy and George have been collecting seashells, and Judy and I have been enjoying the pool.

California is certainly a long way from home, and although we are enjoying our trip, we are looking forward to being home again with our good friends.

... then hold down Shift and press the down-arrow key twice to extend the selection to this paragraph

Figure 2-14

For more practice, click away from the selected paragraphs to deselect them, and then double-click several words to select them. Then double-click one word and hold down the Shift key while you double-click a different word. Try it again with the Ctrl key instead of Shift.

3. **Press Ctrl+A to select the entire document, and then click away from the selected text to deselect it.**
4. **Drag the mouse across the word *wonderful* to select it, and then position the mouse pointer to the left of the first line in the second paragraph.**

   The mouse pointer turns into a white arrow that points diagonally up and to the right.

If you don't see the arrow, make sure you are in Print Layout view. On the View tab, click Print Layout.

5. **Click to select the line (see Figure 2-15).**
6. **Close the document without saving your changes because you didn't make any in this exercise.**

Leave Word open for the next exercise.

Mouse pointer

Dear Rosie:

We are having a wonderful time on our vacation. The weather has been perfect. Elroy and George have been collecting seashells, and Judy and I have been enjoying the pool.

California is certainly a long way from home, and although we are enjoying our trip, we are looking forward to being home again with our good friends.

Figure 2-15

Manipulating Text

You can manually move around in a document making edits and rearranging text, but it is often more efficient to use the tools in Word that are especially designed for helping you find, replace, and sort text.

In the following sections, you learn about the Find pane in Word and how to use it to quickly find all instances of a text string. You also learn how to replace one text string with another and how to sort a list of items alphabetically without manually rearranging them.

Finding text

The Navigation pane in Word serves several purposes. One of these is to display the results of a search for a text string you enter. You can open the Navigation pane by pressing Ctrl+F or by selecting the Navigation Pane check box on the View tab. In the Navigation pane, you can enter the text string you want to find in the Search Document box at the top. A list of all the instances of that text string appears in the Navigation pane. You can jump to any instance by clicking it in the pane.

> **EXTRA INFO**
>
> In earlier Word versions, a Find dialog box opened when you pressed Ctrl+F, enabling you to search through the document via a dialog box interface. That interface is still available, but you have to work a little harder to get to it now. From the Navigation pane, click the down arrow to the right of the Search Document box and choose Advanced Find from the menu that appears. The Find and Replace dialog box appears. This is the same dialog box, by the way, that you use when you replace text (which I cover in the next section). The keyboard shortcut for replace is Ctrl+H, so one quick way to get to the Find feature in the Find and Replace dialog box is to press Ctrl+H and then click the Find tab.

In the following exercise, you use the Find feature to find instances of some text.

Files needed: Lesson 2 Letter.docx

1. **In Word, open the Lesson 2 Letter file and save it as Lesson 2 Letter Practice.**
2. **Choose Home⇨Find.**

   The Navigation pane opens with the Find tab displayed.

Ctrl+F is the keyboard shortcut for Find.

3. **In the Search Document box at the top of the Navigation pane, type** King **and press Enter.**

   Both instances of King are highlighted in the letter. The first instance is selected in the document. See Figure 2-16.

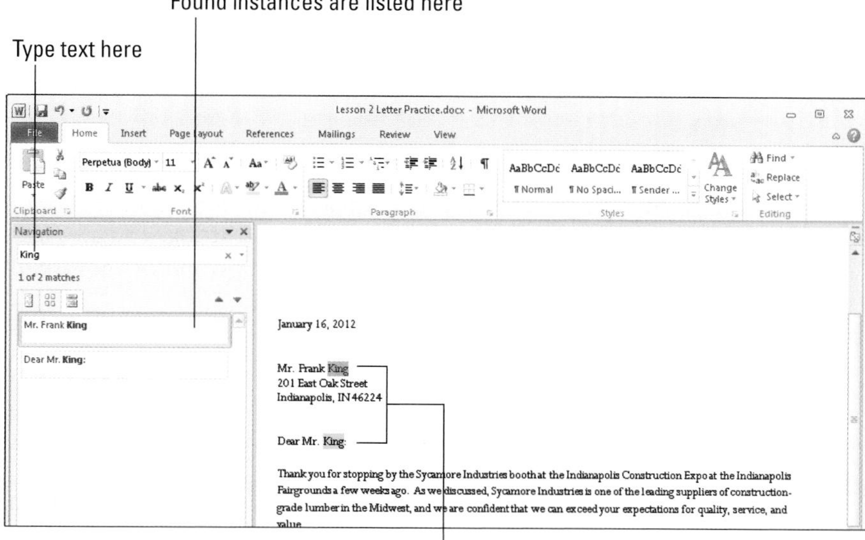

Figure 2-16

4. **In the Navigation pane, click the second instance.**

   The second instance is selected in the document.

5. **In the Search Document box of the Navigation pane, select King, type** Sycamore Industries **to replace it, and press Enter.**

   Four instances of Sycamore Industries are highlighted in the document.

6. **In the Navigation pane, click each of the instances to jump to it in the document.**

7. **Click the Close (X) button in the upper-right corner of the Navigation pane to close it.**

Leave the document open for the next exercise.

Replacing text

Not only can you find specific text in a document, but you can also replace it with other text. This can be helpful, for example, if a company or person changes its name and you need to make a report or letter reflect that.

You can change individual instances one-by-one, or you can use the Replace All feature to replace all instances at once.

Replace All is very convenient, but be careful that you don't make unintended changes with it; sometimes a text string you replace is part of another word or phrase that shouldn't be changed.

In the following exercise, you use the Replace feature to change the name of a company in a letter.

Files needed: Lesson 2 Letter Practice.docx, open from the preceding exercise

1. **In Lesson 2 Letter Practice, press Ctrl+Home to move the insertion point to the top of the document.**
2. **Choose Home⇨Replace.**

   The Find and Replace dialog box opens with the Replace tab displayed.

Ctrl+H is the keyboard shortcut for Replace.

3. **In the Find What box, type** Sycamore Industries **and in the Replace With box, type** Dumont Fabrication **(see Figure 2-17).**

Figure 2-17

4. **Click the Find Next button.**

   The first instance of Sycamore Industries appears highlighted in the document.

You can drag the title bar of the Find and Replace dialog box to move the dialog box out of the way if it obscures the found text.

5. **Click the Replace button to replace the first instance, click the More button to reveal additional options, and then select the Match Case check box.**

   The operation is restricted to instances that match the Find What text string's capitalization. See Figure 2-18.

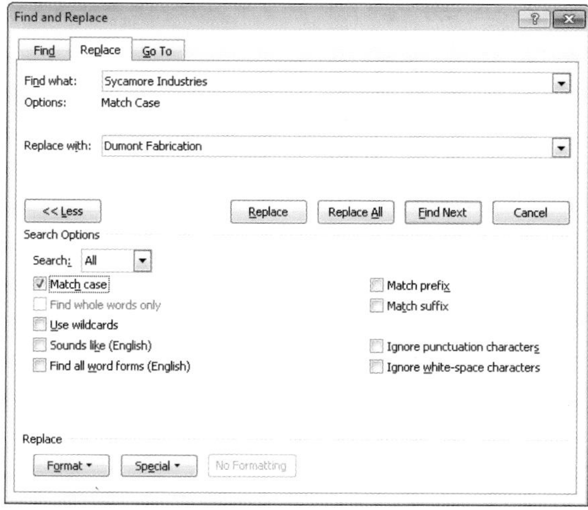

Figure 2-18

6. **Click the Replace All button.**

   All remaining instances that match in capitalization are replaced. A dialog box appears stating that Word has reached the end of the document and three replacements were made.

7. **Click the Close button to close the Find and Replace dialog box, and then save the document by pressing Ctrl+S.**

Leave the document open for the next exercise.

Sorting a list

As you type a list of items, it might not occur to you that you want them sorted into alphabetical order. Never fear, though — it's easy to sort a list alphabetically in Word. Word sorts by the first letter of each paragraph, so each item in the list must be a separate paragraph.

LINGO

Sorts can be **ascending,** which means A to Z, or **descending,** which means Z to A. In an ascending sort, numbers and symbols come before letters; in a descending sort, they come after letters.

In the following exercise, you use the Sort feature to reorder a list.

Files needed: Lesson 2 Letter Practice.docx, open from the preceding exercise

1. **In Lesson 2 Letter Practice, select the bulleted list.**

   To do so, click and drag the mouse pointer across the entire bulleted list.

2. **Choose Home⇨Sort and in the Sort Text dialog box that opens (see Figure 2-19), click OK.**

   The list is sorted in ascending order. See Figure 2-20.

3. **Save and close the document.**

Leave Word open for the next exercise.

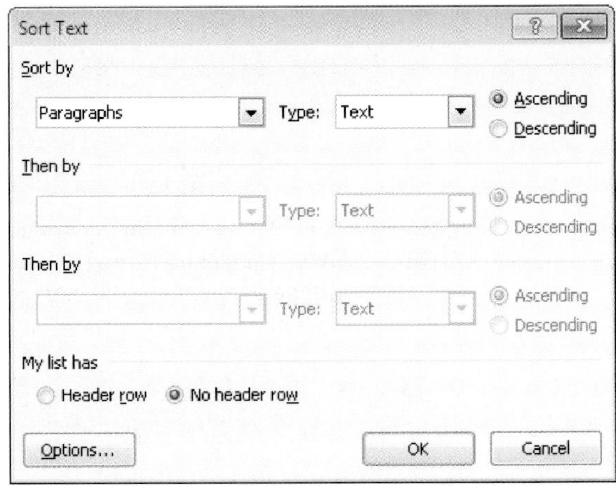

Figure 2-19

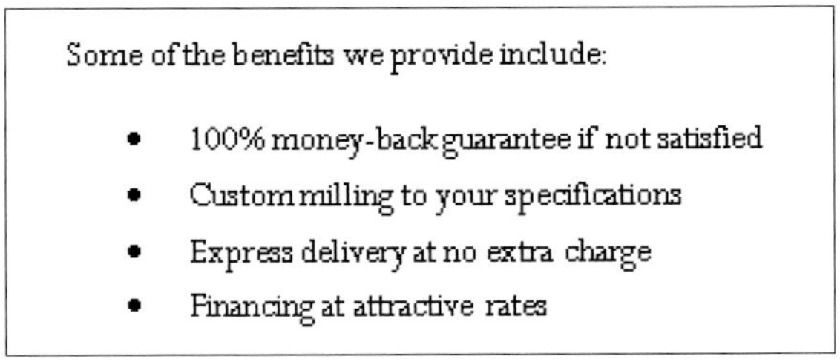

Some of the benefits we provide include:

- 100% money-back guarantee if not satisfied
- Custom milling to your specifications
- Express delivery at no extra charge
- Financing at attractive rates

Figure 2-20

Checking Spelling and Grammar

Spelling and grammar errors in your documents can leave a bad impression with your audience and cause lost customers, jobs, and opportunities. Fortunately, Word can help save you from the consequences of such errors, whether they're errors because of carelessness or because of a lack of spelling and grammar knowledge.

Word automatically checks your spelling and grammar as you type. Wavy red underlines indicate possible spelling errors, and wavy blue underlines indicate possible grammar errors. To correct one of these errors on the fly, right-click the underlined text and choose a quick correction from the shortcut menu.

You can also run the full-blown Spelling and Grammar feature within Word to check the entire document at once. One by one, each potential error appears in a dialog box, and you click buttons to decide how to deal with each one.

One of the choices when dealing with a potentially misspelled word is to add the word to the dictionary so that it isn't flagged as misspelled in any future spell check in any document. The Dictionary file is common to all Office applications, so any word you add to the dictionary in Word is no longer flagged as misspelled in Excel, PowerPoint, or Outlook.

Word has a more robust and powerful Spelling and Grammar feature than the other Office applications, but they all have similar functionality. Therefore, after you learn how to check spelling and grammar in Word, you can also do so in the other Office apps.

In the following exercise, you correct spelling and grammar errors in a document.

Files needed: Lesson 2 Spelling.docx

1. **In Word, open the Lesson 2 Spelling file and save it as Lesson 2 Spelling Corrected.**
2. **Right-click the misspelled word *eerors* and on the shortcut menu that appears, choose the correct spelling, *errors* (see Figure 2-21).**
3. **Click at the beginning of the document to move the insertion point there, and then choose Review➪Spelling & Grammar.**

   The Spelling and Grammar dialog box opens, with the first mistake (Grammer) highlighted. See Figure 2-22.

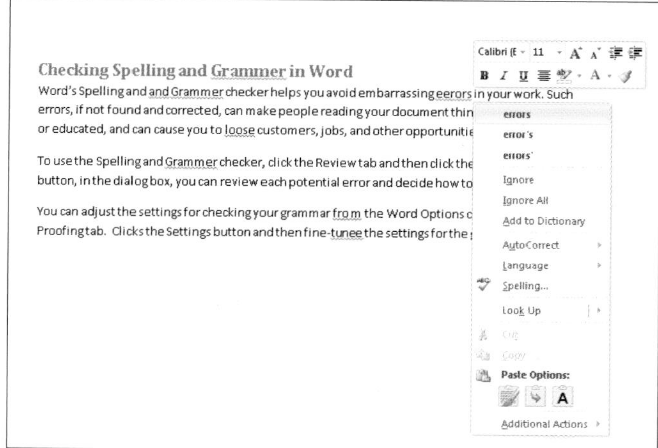

Figure 2-21

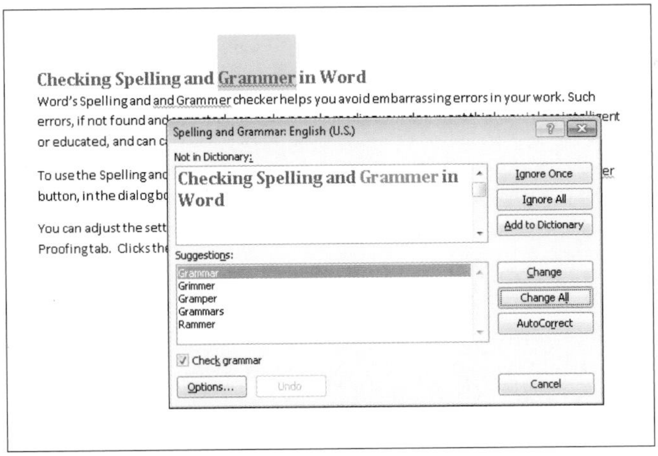

Figure 2-22

4. **Click the Change All button to change all instances of *grammer* to *grammar.***

   The next mistake found is the duplicate word: *and and.*

5. **Click Delete to delete one of the instances of *and.***

   The next mistake found is a possible grammar area: the capitalization of *Spelling.* In this case, the capitalization is correct.

6. **Click the Ignore Once button to skip the correctly capitalized word.**

   The next mistake found is the misuse *lose* as *loose.*

7. **Click the Change button to change to the correct word.**

   The next mistake found is an extra space in the word *from.*

8. **Click the Change button to remove the extra space.**

   The next mistake is the misspelling of *tune* as *tunee.*

9. **Click the Change button to correct the spelling.**

   A dialog box appears to tell you that the spell check is complete.

10. **Click OK and then save your work.**

Leave the document open for the next exercise.

Sharing Your Document with Others

If the people with whom you want to share your work are also Office 2010 users, sharing with them is easy. Just give them your data file. You can transfer a data file to someone else via a USB drive, a portable disc such as a writable CD or DVD, or e-mail. Users of Office 2007 can also work freely with your Office 2010 data files because the file formats are identical.

To share with people who don't have Office 2007 or 2010, you can save in other formats. Word (and the other Office apps) supports a variety of saving formats, so you're sure to find a format that bridges the distance between Office and the program that your recipient has to work with.

E-mailing your document to others

Some versions of Office include *Microsoft Outlook,* an e-mail, calendar, and contact management program. If you don't have Outlook, you might have some other e-mail program, such as Windows Live Mail, which comes with Windows Vista and is available for free download for other Windows versions; Outlook Express, which comes with Windows XP; or some non-Microsoft program, such as Eudora. When you send a document via e-mail from within Word, Word calls up your default e-mail application, whatever that may be. The steps in this book assume Outlook 2010 is your default e-mail application; your steps might be different if you have something else.

LINGO

One way to distribute your work to others is to send it to them via e-mail. Your document piggybacks on an e-mail as an attachment. An **attachment** is a file that's separate from the body of the e-mail, travelling along with the e-mail to its destination.

If you use a web-based e-mail application, such as Hotmail, Gmail, or Yahoo! Mail, you can't follow along with the steps in this section. You can still send Word files as e-mail attachments, but you can't initiate the process from within Word. You start a new e-mail message from within the web interface, and then attach the file from there.

In the following exercise, you send a document to yourself as an e-mail attachment. These steps assume that Outlook is your default e-mail program and that your e-mail account is already set up in it.

Files needed: Lesson 2 Spelling.docx, open from the preceding exercise

1. **In Lesson 2 Spelling, choose File⇨Save & Send, and then click Send as Attachment.**

   A new message opens in Outlook (or your default e-mail application) with the Lesson 2 Spelling file already attached. The filename also appears in the Subject line. See Figure 2-23.

2. **Click in the To box and type your own e-mail address there, and then click the Send button.**

   The file is sent to you.

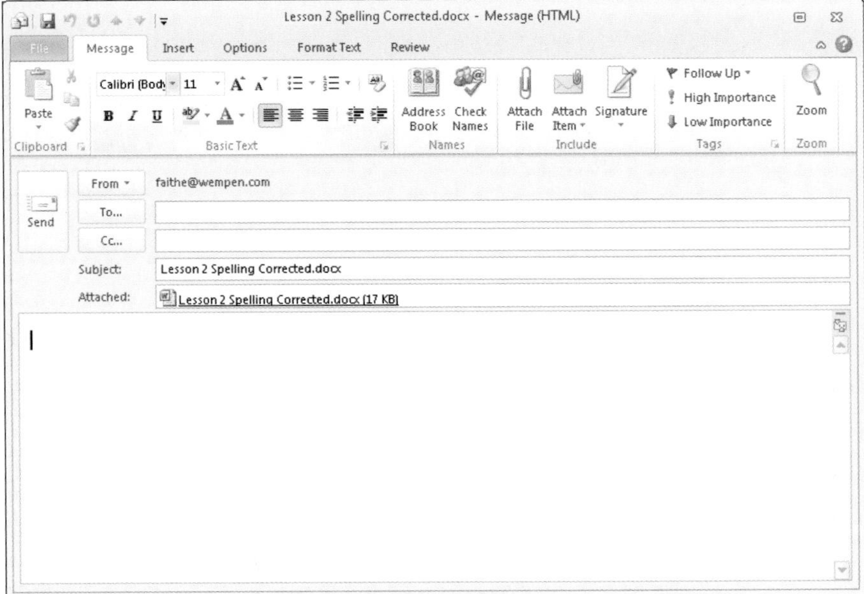

Figure 2-23

3. **In Outlook, choose Home➪Send/Receive All Folders.**

   You receive the sent file as a new message in your inbox.

If the message doesn't appear right away, click Send/Receive All Folders again.

4. **Close Outlook and return to Word.**
5. **Close the document (but not Word), saving your changes if prompted.**

Leave Word open for the next exercise.

Sharing your document in other formats

If your intended recipients use earlier versions of Office or don't have Office at all, you must save your work in another format before transferring the file to them. All the Office programs allow you to export your work in other formats, so you can transfer just about any data to just about any other application.

The further away you get from the original version of the file, the more formatting features you lose. For example, saving in the Word 2010 format preserves the most features, and saving in Word 97–2003 format loses some features. RTF loses even more, and plain text loses all formatting.

In the following exercise, you save a file in two formats.

Files needed: Lesson 2 Distribution.docx

1. **In Word, open the Lesson 2 Distribution file and choose File⇨Save As.**

   The Save As dialog box opens.

2. **From the Save as Type drop-down list, choose Word 97–2003 Document (see Figure 2-24) and then click Save.**

   Your document is saved in a format that's compatible with earlier Word versions (Word 97 through Word 2003); it's also usable in Word 2007 and Word 2010.

3. **Choose File⇨Save As, and from the Save as Type drop-down list, choose Rich Text Format.**

4. **Click the Save button.**

   Your document is saved in Rich Text Format. This format is useful for exchanging data with someone who has a different brand of word processor, such as WordPerfect.

Leave the document open for the next exercise.

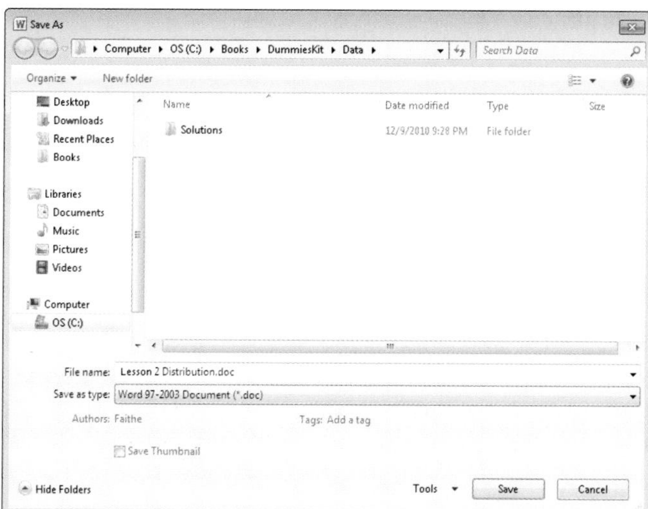

Figure 2-24

Printing Your Work

Another way to distribute your work is by printing it, provided you have access to a printer. You can do a quick print with the default settings, or you can specify a certain printer, number of copies, page range, and other settings.

EXTRA INFO

Some of the items on the list of printers are not actually printers, such as Microsoft XPS Document Writer or Send to OneNote 2010. Word outputs to some external formats by treating the converter utilities as printers. You "print" to the driver, which generates a file of the document in a different format.

In the following exercise, you print a document.

Files needed: Lesson 2 Distribution.docx, open from the preceding exercise

1. **In Lesson 2 Distribution, choose File⇨Print.**
2. **In the Copies box, click the up arrow once to change the number to 2. Then click the down arrow to change it back to 1.**
3. **Open the Printer drop-down list and choose the printer you want to use (see Figure 2-25).**

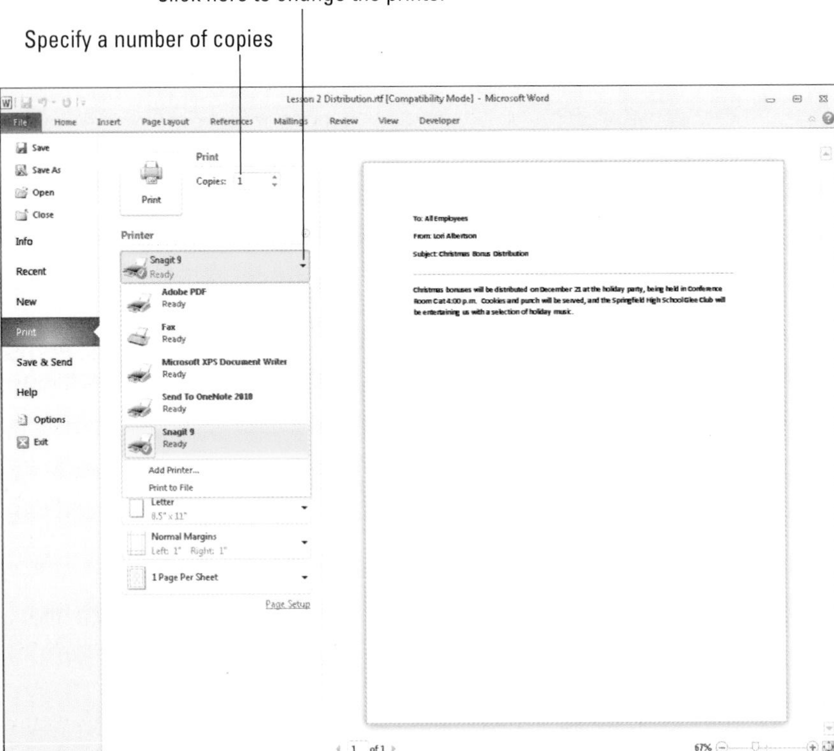

Figure 2-25

For more practice, check out the additional print options. For example, you can change the page range, orientation, paper size, margins, and duplex setting (that is, print one-sided or two-sided). The settings for duplex and collation, as well as for printing only specific pages, don't apply to the document used in this exercise because it has only one page.

4. **Click the Print button.**

   The document prints.

Exit Word.

Want more help learning the basics of Word document creation and editing? You can find Word tutorials here: `http://office.microsoft.com/en-us/word-help/CH010369478.aspx`.

Summing Up

Word makes it easy to create a basic document. You can either start typing in the blank document that opens automatically at startup, or choose one of the templates provided. Here are the key points this lesson covered:

- To start a new blank document, press Ctrl+N, or choose File⇨New and then click Blank Document.
- To start a document based on a template, choose File⇨New, pick the template you want, and then click Create.
- To set page margins, choose Page Layout⇨Margins.
- To change the paper size, choose Page Layout⇨Size.
- Portrait and Landscape are the two page orientations. Portrait is the default. To switch, choose Page Layout⇨Orientation⇨Landscape.
- To find text, use the Navigation pane; press Ctrl+F to open it, or choose Home⇨Find.
- To replace text, use the Find and Replace dialog box; Ctrl+H opens it, or choose Home⇨Replace.
- To sort a list, select the list and choose Home⇨Sort.
- Word checks spelling and grammar automatically, and underlines errors with a red wavy underline (for spelling) or a blue wavy underline (for grammar).
- You can also launch a full spelling and grammar check by choosing Review⇨Spelling & Grammar.

- To e-mail your document to others, choose File⇨Save & Send and then click Send as Attachment.
- To print your document, choose File⇨Print.

Try-it-yourself lab

For more practice with the features covered in this lesson, try the following exercise on your own:

1. **Start Word and write a description of a funny or embarrassing incident that happened recently to you or someone you know.**
2. **Add a new paragraph at the beginning of the document and type a title there, such as** My Most Embarrassing Day Ever.
3. **Check your spelling and grammar, and then make any corrections needed.**
4. **E-mail the document to yourself or to a friend you want to share it with.**
5. **Print one copy of the document and then close Word.**

Know this tech talk

ascending: A to Z order. Numbers and symbols precede letters.

attachment: A file attached to an e-mail so that the file is sent along with the message.

descending: Z to A order. Numbers and symbols follow letters.

landscape: A page orientation in which the wide part of the paper forms the top and bottom.

margins: The space between the edge of the paper and the text.

orientation: The direction the text runs on a piece of paper where one dimension is greater than the other. See also *portrait* and *landscape.*

portrait: A page orientation in which the narrow part of the paper forms the top and bottom.

Lesson 3
Formatting Text

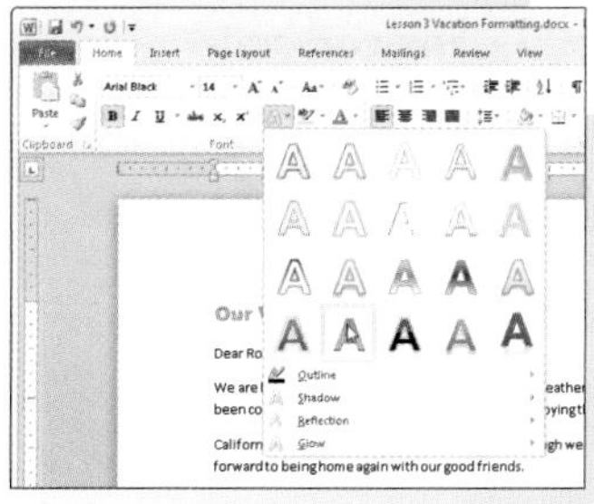

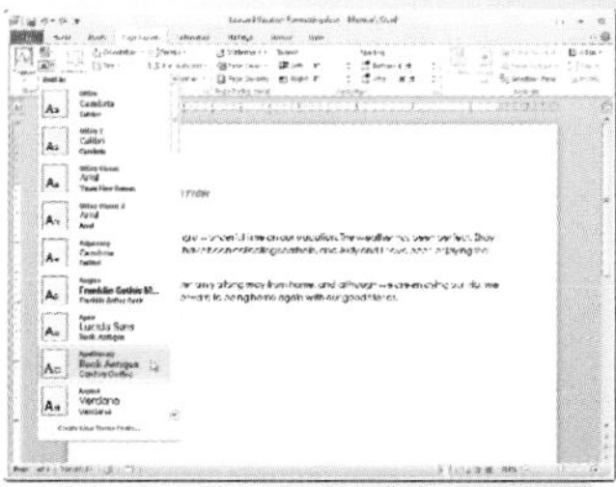

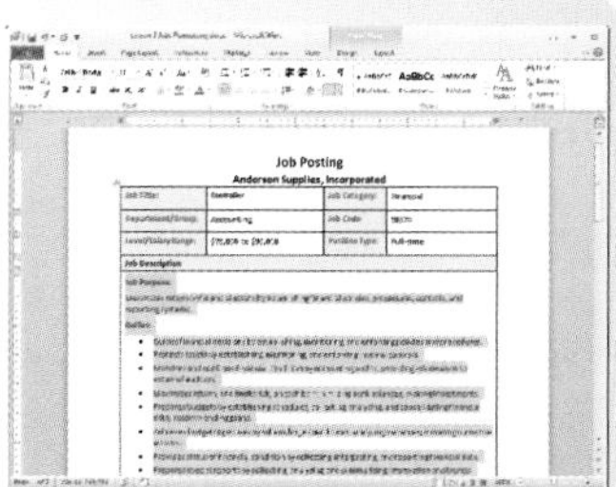

- Formatting text makes your documents more attractive and readable. You can apply different fonts, sizes, and colors, as well as use style sets and themes to automate the process of formatting an entire document.
- Themes make it easier to apply consistent formatting within a document and between documents.
- WordArt enables you to easily format text with fancy special effects that blur the line between text formatting and artwork.
- Custom character spacing and scale settings provide precise control for professional-quality typesetting.

Without formatting, text can be dull and dreary. You'll probably want to pep up your prose by applying various fonts, attributes, colors, and themes to capture your readers' interest.

In this lesson, I explain how to format text in a Word document. By the end of this lesson, you'll be able to choose fonts, sizes, and colors that are appropriate for the job at hand, and how to copy and clear formatting from text. You also find out how to use WordArt to make text extra-special, and how to adjust typographical settings that can make text look like it was professionally typeset.

Formatting Text

Text formatting can make a big difference in the readability of a document. By making certain text larger, boldface, or a different font, you can call attention to it and add interest for your readers.

You can apply each type of character formatting individually, or you can use style sets or themes to apply multiple types of formatting at once.

LINGO

The type of formatting covered in this lesson is commonly known as **character formatting** (formatting that can be applied to individual characters). Character formatting includes fonts, font sizes, text attributes (such as italics), character spacing (spacing between letters), and text color.

Choosing text font, size, and color

The text in the document appears using a certain style of lettering, dubbed a *font* or *typeface.* Word comes with dozens of fonts, so you're sure to find one that meets the needs of whatever project you create.

Each font is available in a wide variety of sizes measured in *points,* with each point being 1⁄72 of an inch on a printout. (The size it appears onscreen depends on the display zoom. You learn about zoom in Lesson 1.) Text sizes vary

LINGO

The style of lettering is a **font,** or **typeface.** Fonts are measured in **points.** Fonts can be in **standard colors,** which doesn't change when you change a document theme, or in **theme colors,** which change with the theme.

from very small (6 points) to very large (100 points or more). An average document uses body text that's between 10 and 12 points, and headings between 12 and 18 points.

You can also color each font by using either a *standard color,* which doesn't change when you change document themes, or a *theme color,* which does change. Later in the lesson, you learn how to change themes and you see what happens to the text colors you've applied when the theme colors change.

You can apply fonts, sizes, and colors either from the Home tab of the Ribbon or from the Mini Toolbar.

In the following exercise, you format some text by applying different fonts, sizes, and colors to it.

Files needed: Lesson 3 Vacation.docx

1. **In Word, open Lesson 3 Vacation and save it as Lesson 3 Vacation Formatting.**
2. **Place the insertion point at the beginning of the document, press Enter to create a new line, press the up-arrow key once to move the insertion point into the new line, and then type** Our Vacation.
3. **Triple-click Our Vacation to select the entire paragraph.**
4. **Point the mouse pointer at the selected paragraph so that the Mini Toolbar appears. At first it appears dim, so move the mouse over the Mini Toolbar to make it brighter (see Figure 3-1).**
5. **From the Font drop-down list on the Mini Toolbar, choose Arial Black; from the Font Size drop-down list, choose 14.**

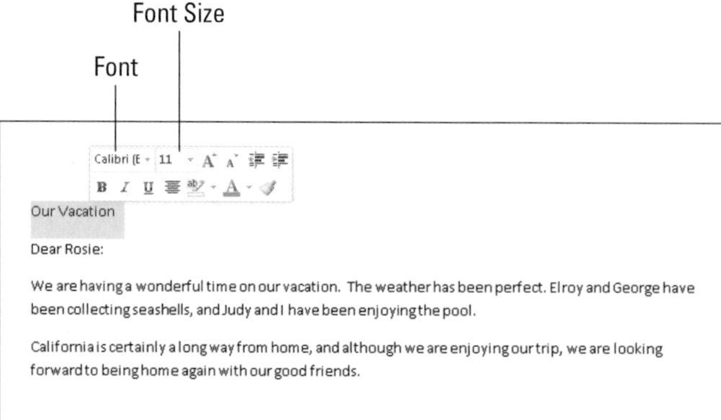

Figure 3-1

If the Mini Toolbar is no longer visible, right-click the text to make the Mini Toolbar reappear.

For more practice, change the font and font size by using the controls on the Home tab in the Font group on the Ribbon.

6. **On the Ribbon, choose Home➪Grow Font to increase the font size of the selected text to 16 points (see Figure 3-2) and then click the Font Color button.**

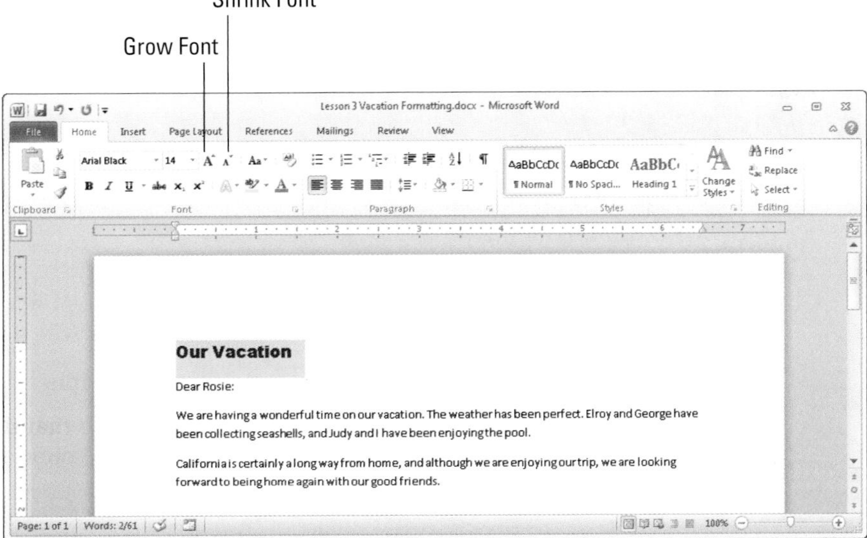

Figure 3-2

Whatever color was already displayed on the button is applied to the text. (The color that appears depends on the most recently used font color.)

7. **Click the down arrow to the right of the Font Color button, and in the palette of colors that appears (see Figure 3-3), click the red square under Standard Colors.**

   The text becomes red.

8. **Click the down arrow on the Font Color button again to reopen the color palette and then click the Red, Accent 2 square on the top row of the Theme Colors section.**

Pointing at a square makes its name appear in a ScreenTip.

Font Color button

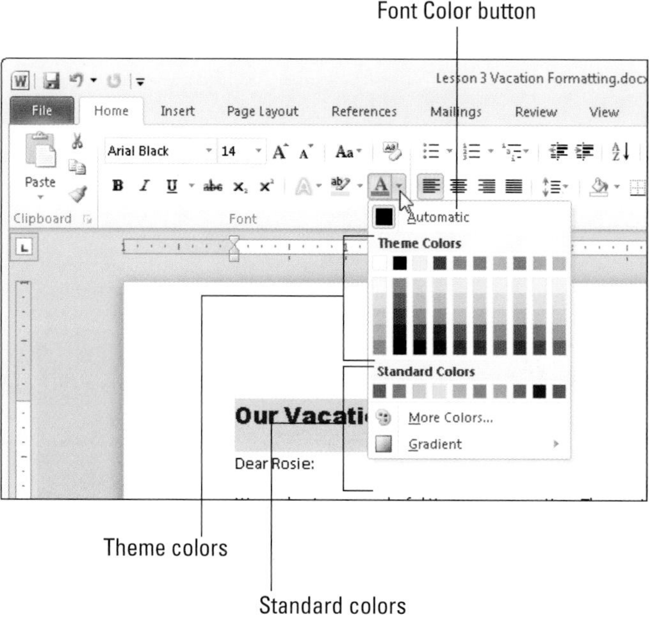

Theme colors

Standard colors

Figure 3-3

For more practice, try some of the tints and shades below the theme colors.

Leave the document open for the next exercise.

> **LINGO**
>
> A **tint** is a lighter version of a color, and a **shade** is a darker version of it.

Applying text attributes and WordArt effects

You can modify text with a variety of *attributes,* such as bold, italic, underlining, and so on. Some of these can be applied from the Mini Toolbar and/or the Font group on the Home tab. Others are available in the Font dialog box. Some of them also have keyboard shortcuts.

Figure 3-4 displays some of these attributes. Table 3-1 summarizes the keyboard shortcuts for them.

> **LINGO**
>
> **Attributes** are typographical styles such as bold, italic, and underline. **Text effects,** or **WordArt effects,** are special types of effects, such as reflection or glow, that are unique to Office applications.

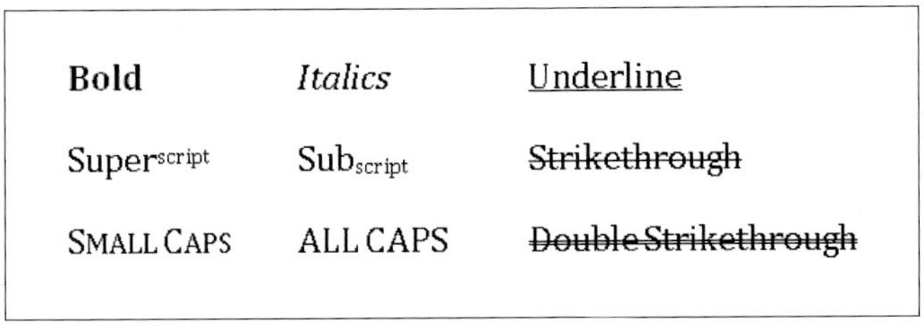

Bold	*Italics*	Underline
Super^{script}	Sub$_{script}$	~~Strikethrough~~
SMALL CAPS	ALL CAPS	~~Double Strikethrough~~

Figure 3-4

Table 3-1 Keyboard Shortcuts for Applying Text Attributes

Attribute	*Keyboard Shortcut*
Bold	Ctrl+B
Italic	Ctrl+I
Underline	Ctrl+U
Subscript	Ctrl+=
Superscript	Ctrl+Shift++ (plus sign)
Underline words but not space	Ctrl+Shift+W
Double underline text	Ctrl+Shift+D
Small caps	Ctrl+Shift+K
All caps	Ctrl+Shift+A

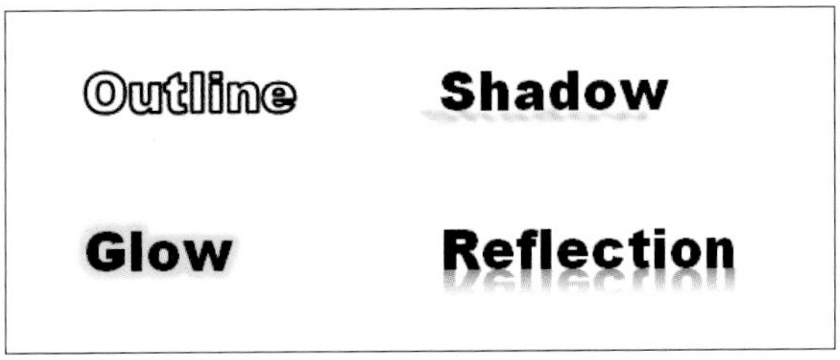

Outline	Shadow
Glow	Reflection

Figure 3-5

You can apply *text effects,* or *WordArt effects,* such as outline, shadow, reflection, and glow. Figure 3-5 shows some examples of these effects, accessed from the Text Effects button's menu on the Home tab. The Text Effects button's menu also includes a number of presets that combine color fills, outlines, and other effects in one operation.

In the following exercise, you format some text by applying some attributes and effects to it.

Files needed: Lesson 3 Vacation Practice.docx, open from the preceding exercise

1. **In Lesson 3 Vacation Practice, triple-click the Our Vacation title to select it if it's not already selected.**
2. **Choose Home⇨Text Effects (see Figure 3-6) and then click the second sample in the bottom row.**

   The text is formatted with an orange gradient fill and an inner shadow.

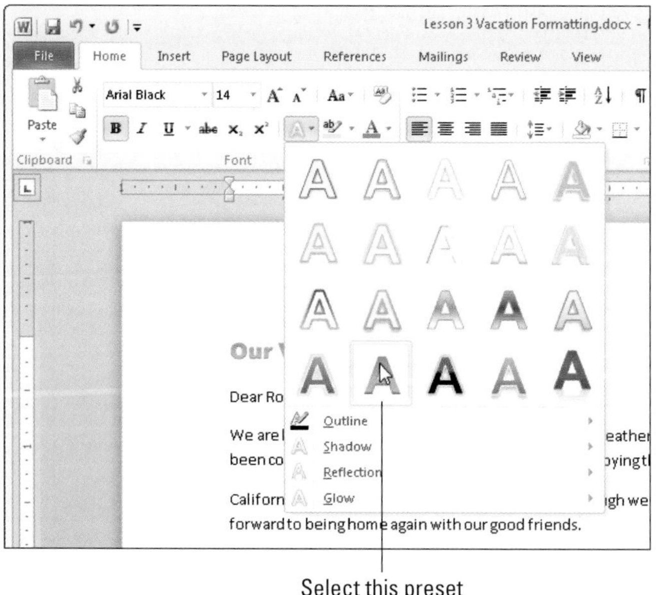

Figure 3-6

3. **Click the Text Effects button again, point to Reflection, and click the first effect in the Reflection Variations section (see Figure 3-7).**
4. **Choose Home⇨Italic to italicize the text, and then click the dialog box launcher in the lower-right corner of the Font group on the Home tab (see Figure 3-8).**

   The Font dialog box opens.

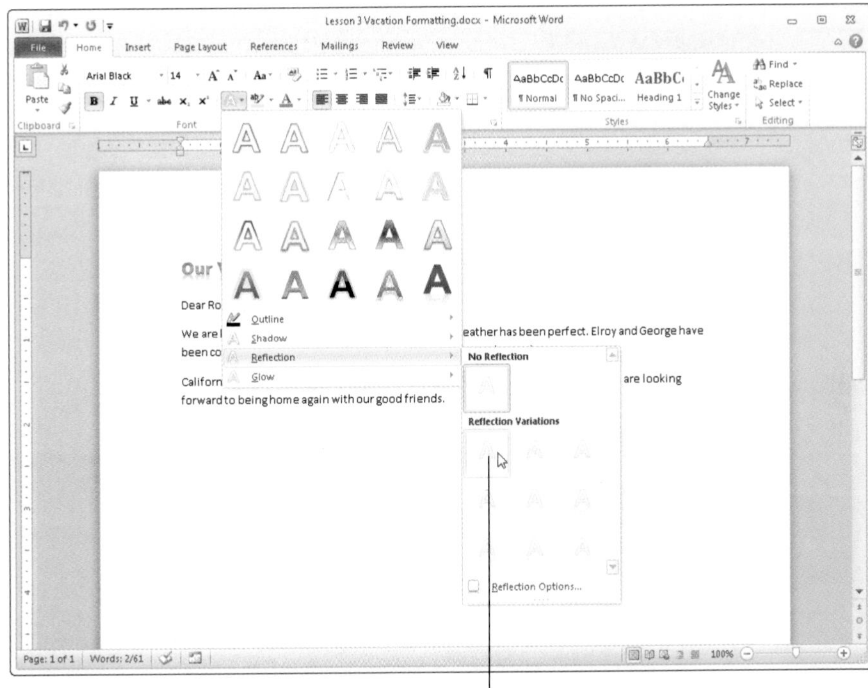

Select this reflection effect

Figure 3-7

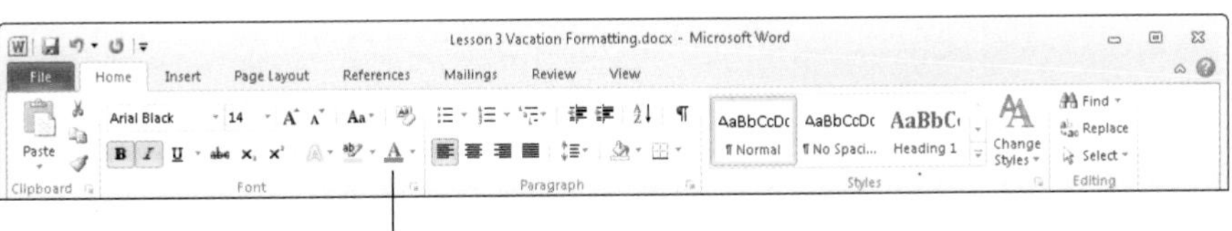

Dialog box launcher

Figure 3-8

5. **Select the Small Caps check box, as shown in Figure 3-9, and then click OK.**
6. **Save your work.**

Leave the document open for the next exercise.

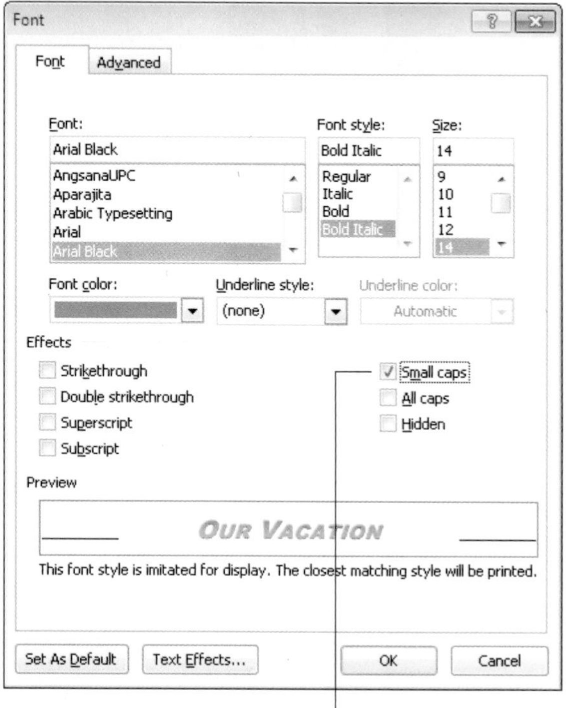

Mark the Small Caps check box

Figure 3-9

Working with Themes

Themes enable you to dramatically change the look of a document quickly. They apply several types of preset formatting to text, including font, color, and object formatting. In a Word document that contains only text, you won't notice the effect changes when you switch to a different theme, but the font and color changes will be apparent.

All the Office applications use the same set of themes, so themes can help you standardize the look of your work across multiple applications. For example, you could make the fonts and colors on a brochure you create in Word similar to a presentation you create in PowerPoint.

You can also apply color themes, font themes, and/or effect themes separately. This ability is useful when none of the available themes exactly match what you want. After you make the selections you want to create the right combination of colors, fonts, and effects, you can save your choices as a new theme to use in other documents (including in Excel, PowerPoint, and Word).

LINGO

A **theme** is a file that contains settings for fonts (heading and body), colors, and object formatting effects.

Themes affect only text that hasn't had manual formatting applied that overrides the defaults. For example, if you've specified a certain font or font color for some text, that text doesn't change when you change the theme. You can strip off manual formatting with the Clear Formatting button on the Home tab or by pressing Ctrl+spacebar.

In the following exercise, you format some text by applying some attributes and effects to it.

Files needed: Lesson 3 Vacation Practice.docx, open from the preceding exercise

1. **In the Lesson 3 Vacation Practice file, choose Page Layout➪Themes, and in the list of themes that appears (see Figure 3-10), choose Apex.**

   The colors and fonts in the document change to match the theme. The text that was previously orange is now purple, and the font for body text is now Book Antiqua. The font for the first paragraph did not change because it was manually set earlier; themes do not override manual formatting.

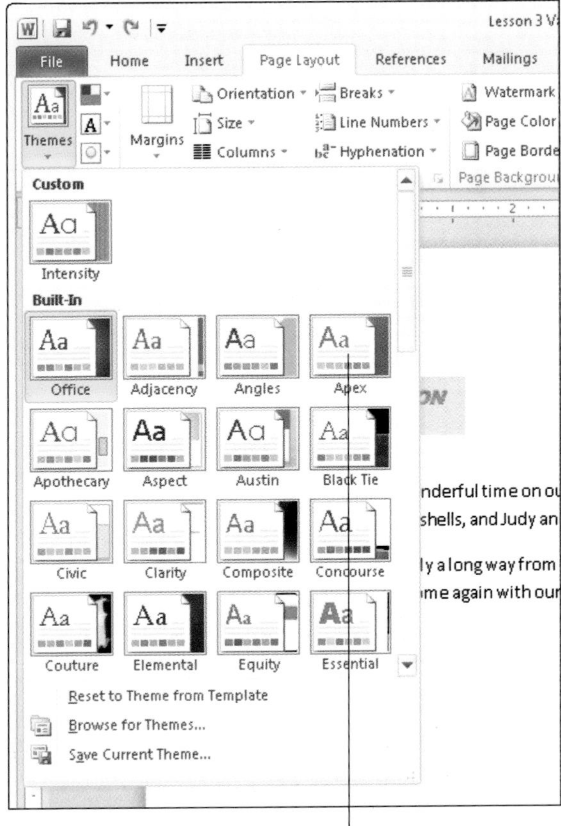

Figure 3-10

Point the mouse at several other themes and see their effects in the text behind the open menu.

2. **Click the Theme Fonts button, and in the list of available theme font sets that appears (see Figure 3-11), choose Apothecary.**

   The fonts in the document change to Century Gothic.

Point the mouse at several other font themes and see their effects in the text behind the open menu.

> **EXTRA INFO**
>
> To use a theme that someone else has given you, choose Page Layout⇨Themes⇨Browse for Themes. You can then specify the location where the theme file is stored.

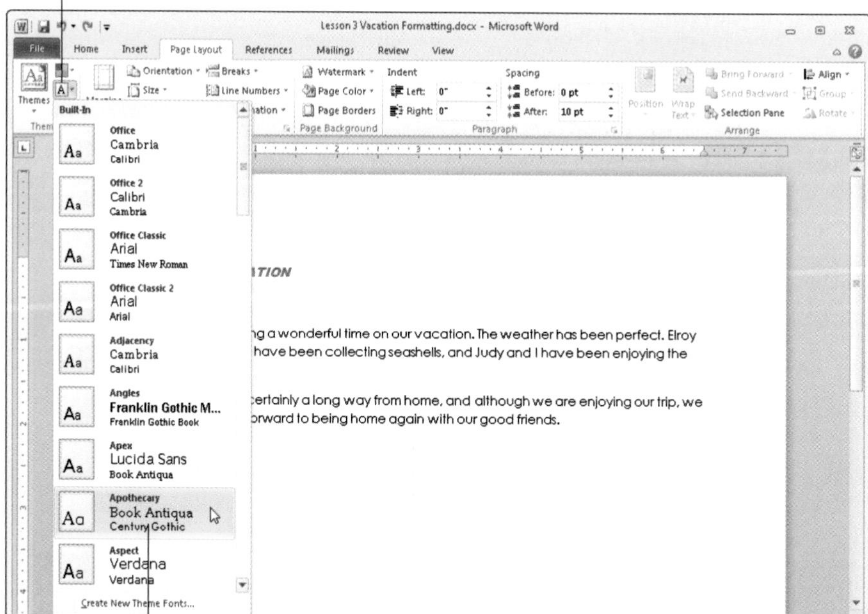

Figure 3-11

3. **Click the Theme Colors button, and in the list of available theme color sets that appears (see Figure 3-12), choose Module.**

   The color of the heading changes from purple to red.

Theme Colors button

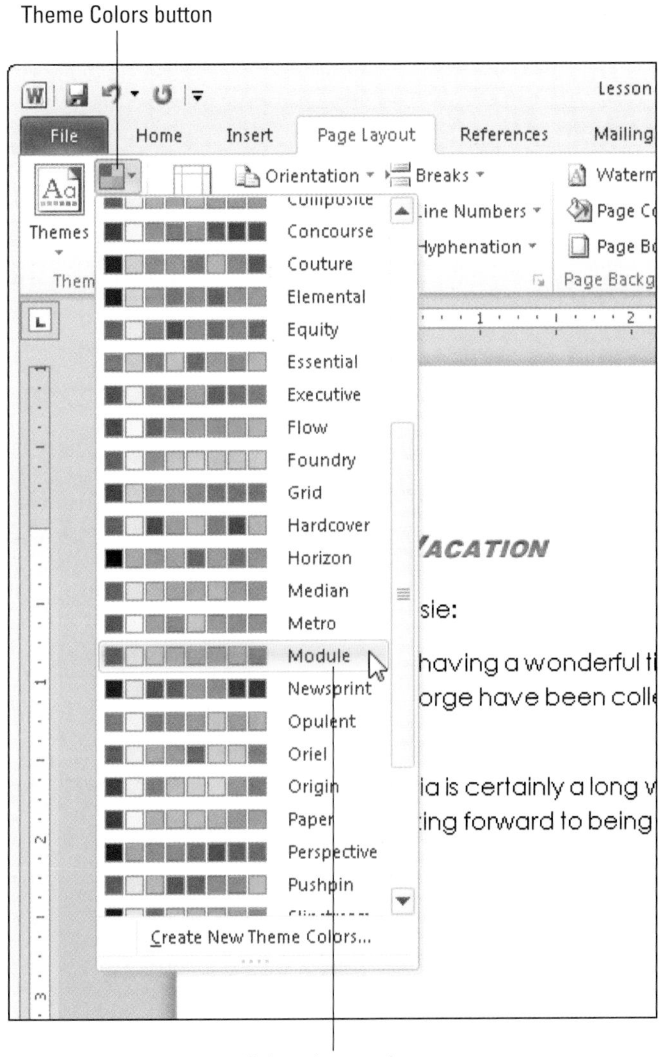

Select these colors

Figure 3-12

4. **Save your work.**

Leave the document open for the next exercise.

Applying Style Sets

At the top of the Font drop-down list on the Home tab are two entries: one designated for headings and one for body. If you use these settings rather than specifying individual fonts, you can reformat the document by choosing a different style set.

LINGO

A **style set** is a preset combination of fonts, paragraph line spacing, character spacing, and indentation. Style sets enable you to quickly change the look of the document without manually reformatting each paragraph.

If you've manually applied specific fonts, you won't see a change when you apply a different style set. If you don't get the results you expect with a style set, select the entire document (press Ctrl+A) and then clear the formatting by clicking the Clear Formatting button on the Home tab or by pressing Ctrl+spacebar.

In the following exercise, you format some text by applying different fonts, sizes, and colors to it.

Files needed: Lesson 3 Vacation Practice.docx, open from the preceding exercise

1. **In the Lesson 3 Vacation Practice file, triple-click the Our Vacation title to select it, if it's not already selected.**
2. **Choose Home⇨Clear Formatting to remove all the formatting you've applied to the selected text.**

   See Figure 3-13. Notice that the manual formatting is cleared, but the font choice applied by the theme applied in the preceding exercise remains.

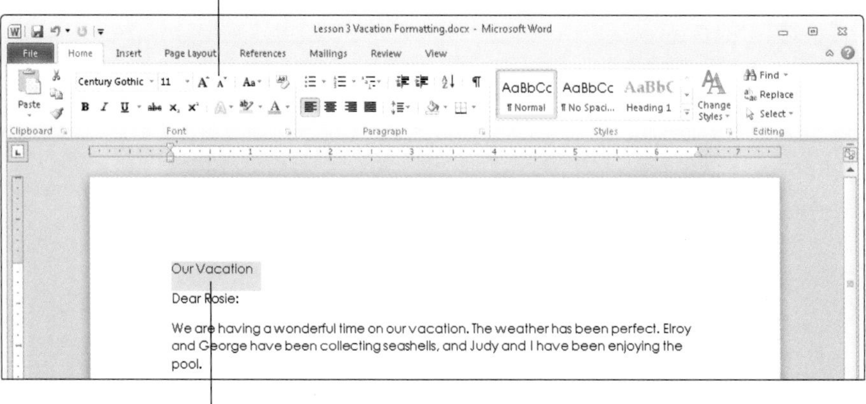

Figure 3-13

3. **From the Font drop-down list, click Book Antiqua (Headings) at the top of the list.**

   The Our Vacation text changes to the Book Antiqua font.

If you did not complete the preceding exercise, some other font may appear at the top of the list, with (Headings) next to it. If so, choose that font. The important part is that you choose the font with (Headings) next to it.

The rest of the text in the document is already formatted using the font marked as (Body) at the top of the Font drop-down list: Century Gothic. That's because unless you manually make a change, all text in the document is automatically shown in whatever font is specified as the body text font.

4. **Click the Change Styles button and point to Style Set.**

   A list of available style sets appears. See Figure 3-14.

Pointing to an item previews it. Point to each of the styles sets on the Style Set menu, one by one, and watch the document's formatting change.

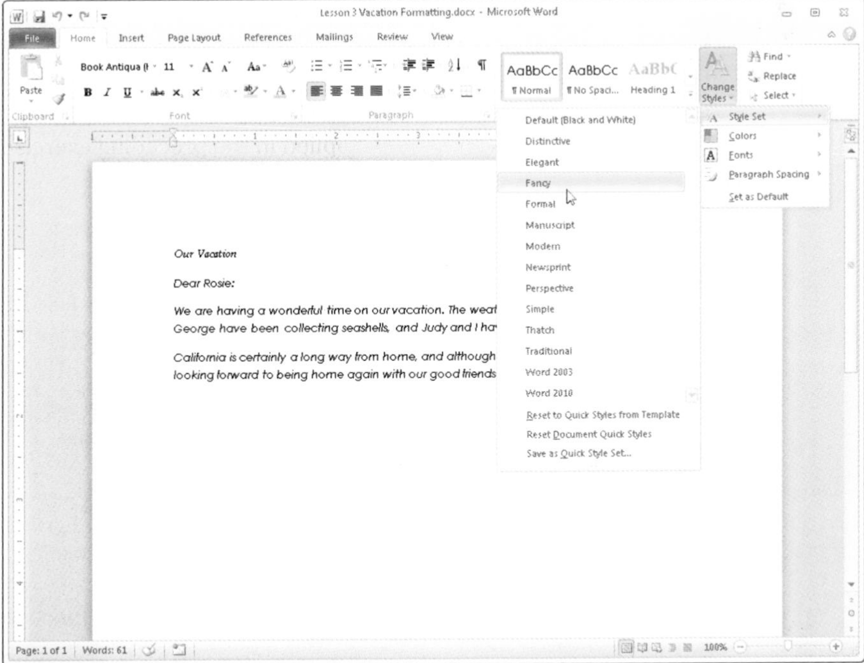

Figure 3-14

5. **Choose Fancy.**

   The Fancy style set is applied. The paragraph formatted as a heading changes to the new font designated for headings, and the paragraphs formatted as body change to the new font designated for body text.

6. **Triple-click the Our Vacation heading and change the font size to 18 point. Then click away from the text to deselect it.**

   The document looks like Figure 3-15.

7. **Save your work and close the document.**

Leave Word open for the next exercise.

Our Vacation

Dear Rosie:

We are having a wonderful time on our vacation. The weather has been perfect. Elroy and George have been collecting seashells, and Judy and I have been enjoying the pool.

California is certainly a long way from home, and although we are enjoying our trip, we are looking forward to being home again with our good friends.

Figure 3-15

Copying Formats with Format Painter

When many blocks of text need to be formatted the same way, it can be tedious to select and format each block. As a shortcut, Word offers the Format Painter feature. Format Painter picks up the formatting from one block of text and applies it to another.

If you select the destination text, Format Painter copies only *character-based formatting* (that is, the type of formatting created by the commands in the Font group of the Home tab). If you click in a paragraph as the destination, rather than selecting, Word copies both character and paragraph settings. Paragraph settings include things like left and right indents, tab stops, and spacing between lines.

In the following exercise, you copy the formatting from one block of text to another.

Files needed: Lesson 3 Jobs.docx

1. **Open Lesson 3 Jobs and save it as Lesson 3 Jobs Formatting.**
2. **Click and drag the mouse across the text *Job Title* to select it and then choose Home⇨Format Painter (see Figure 3-16).**

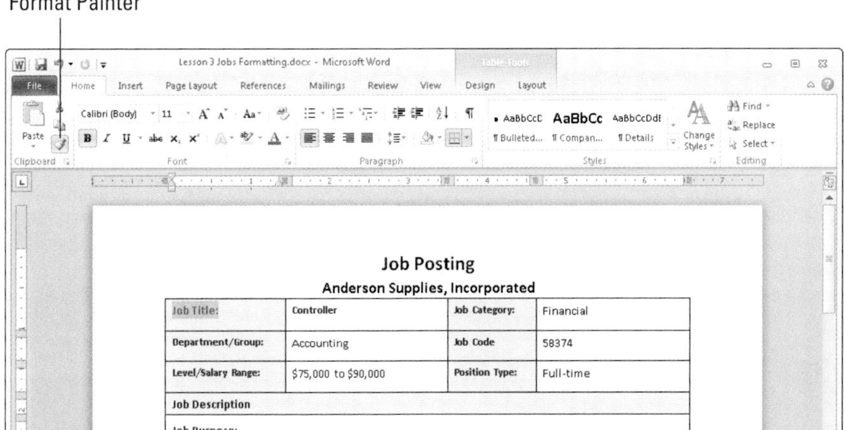

Figure 3-16

3. **Click and drag across the text *Department/Group:* to paint the formatting onto that text.**

   The Format Painter feature turns itself off automatically.

4. **With the *Department/Group:* text still selected, double-click the Format Painter button.**

   Double-clicking Format Painter rather than clicking it turns it on so that it remains on until you turn it off.

5. **Drag across each of the other headings in the blue-background boxes, one after the other.**

   The formatting is copied to each of those blocks of text. When you're finished, the formatting looks like Figure 3-17.

6. **Click the Format Painter button to turn off the feature and then save your work.**

Leave the document open for the next exercise.

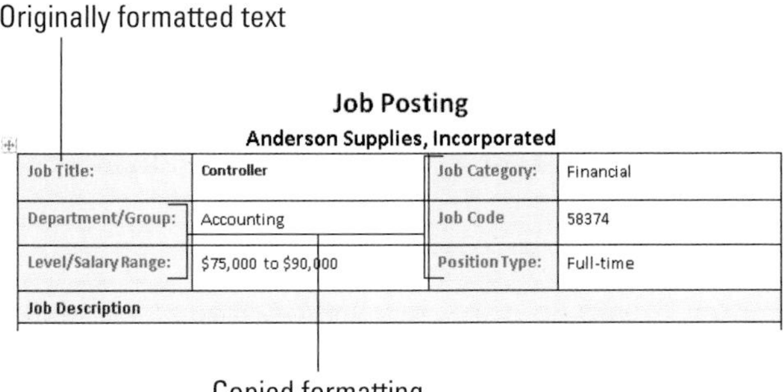

Figure 3-17

Adjusting Character Spacing

As you type in Word, Word automatically handles the character spacing for you, so you normally don't have to think about it. In some cases, though, you may want to adjust those automatic settings to create special effects.

LINGO

Character spacing refers to the spacing between individual characters, and also secondarily to a character's individual vertical positioning, such as with superscript and subscript.

Text scale and spacing changes can help you fit your text into an available space by subtly changing the spacing between each letter. It may not be obvious to your reader that you've made such a change, but the overall effect will be to increase or decrease the amount of space that text occupies on the page.

On Sale Now 80%

On Sale Now 100%

On Sale Now 150%

Figure 3-18

The Scale setting controls the width of each character. Changing the scale makes the characters wider or narrower in relation to their height. For example, Figure 3-18 shows the same text at 75-, 100-, and 150-percent scaling. The 150-percent version looks like it is taller than the others, but that's an optical illusion; they're all the same height. Only the width changes.

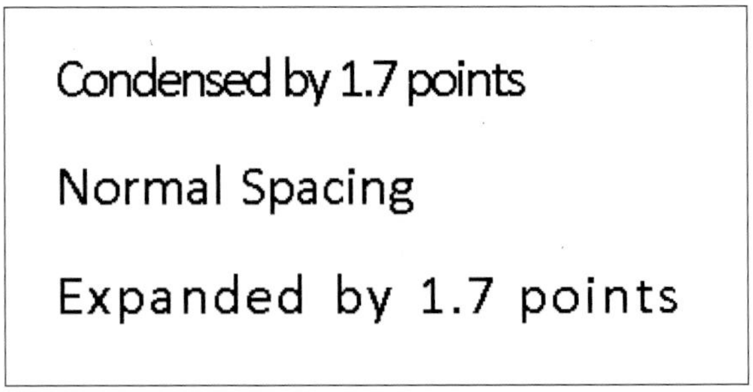

Condensed by 1.7 points

Normal Spacing

Expanded by 1.7 points

Figure 3-19

The Spacing setting controls the blank space between letters. For example, Figure 3-19 shows the same text with different amounts of spacing. Condensed spacing jams the letters together; expanded spacing spreads them out. These examples are dramatic to show the differences more clearly, but in most documents, an adjustment of one point or less may be sufficient.

In this exercise, you adjust the text scale and text spacing.

Files needed: Lesson 3 Jobs Formatting.docx, open from the preceding exercise

1. **In Lesson 3 Jobs Formatting, scroll down to the bottom of the document.**

   Notice that the text doesn't quite fit on one page.

2. **Select all the text in the bottommost table cell, beginning with the Job Purpose heading.**

3. **On the Home tab, click the dialog box launcher in the Font group (see Figure 3-20).**

   The Font dialog box opens.

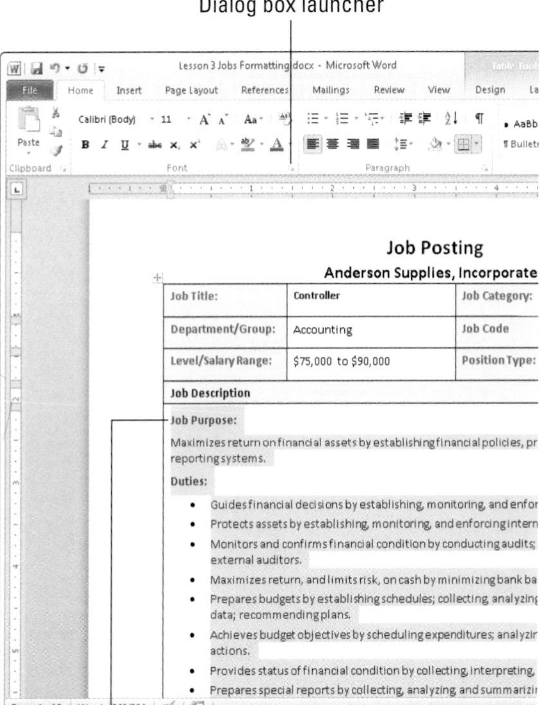

Figure 3-20

4. **In the Font dialog box, click the Advanced tab; from the Scale drop-down list, choose 90% (see Figure 3-21); and then click OK.**

5. **Scroll to the bottom of the page to see whether the text all fits on one page now and then click the dialog box launcher for the Font group to reopen the Font dialog box.**
6. **From the Scale drop-down list, choose 100% to restore the text's original spacing; from the Spacing drop-down list, choose Condensed; in the By box next to Spacing, click the up arrow to set the amount of condensing to 0.4 point (see Figure 3-22), and then click OK.**

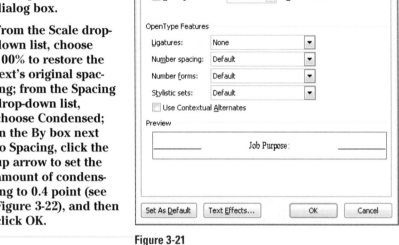

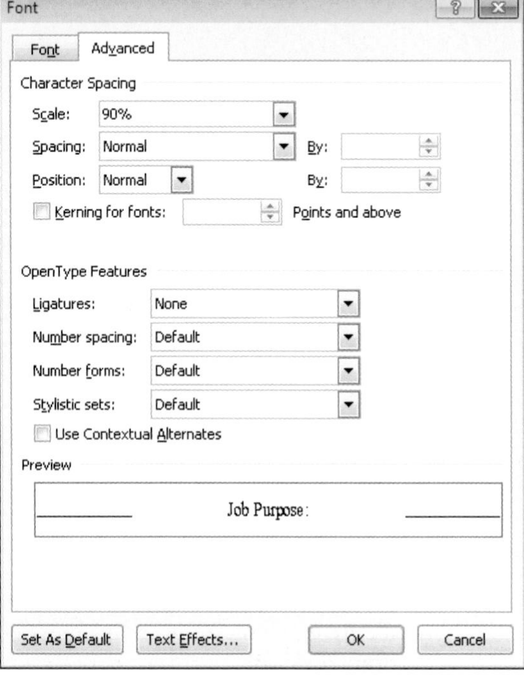

Figure 3-21

You'd think that clicking the up arrow would increase the amount of the setting, but because it's dealing with condensing the text, a smaller number makes it *less* condensed, so the up arrow is used.

7. **Scroll again to the bottom of the document and notice that the text fits on one page.**
8. **Save the document.**

Leave the document open for the next exercise.

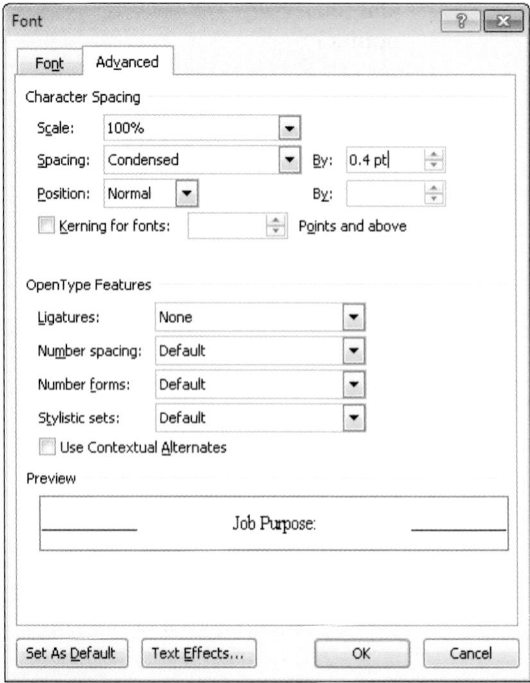

Figure 3-22

Making Advanced Typesetting Adjustments

Word processing and page layout have certainly come a long way since the days of the typewriter. Nowadays you can fine-tune the typesetting in your document as precisely as the most high-end typesetting equipment of 20 years ago could do. Even though Word isn't considered a high-end desktop publishing program like QuarkXPress or Adobe InDesign, it still has several features for adjusting the typesetting in your document.

Enabling kerning

Kerning decreases the space between certain pairs of letters based on their shapes. Kerning can make a visual difference when two large letters are adjacent to each other and their shapes happen to fit together, such as a V and an A. Kerning places them closer together than they normally would be, so it doesn't look like there is too much space between them. Kerning is typically done only when the text is over a certain point size because at smaller sizes, it's not noticeable. Figure 3-23 shows examples of kerned and unkerned text in Times New Roman at 100 points in size.

> **LINGO**
>
> **Kerning** is a spacing adjustment made between two letters based on their shapes.

In this exercise, you enable kerning for text 18 points and larger.

Files needed: Lesson 3 Jobs Formatting.docx, open from the preceding exercise

1. **In Lesson 3 Jobs Formatting, triple-click the Job Posting heading at the top of the page to select it.**
2. **On the Home tab, click the dialog box launcher in the Font group.**

   The Font dialog box opens.

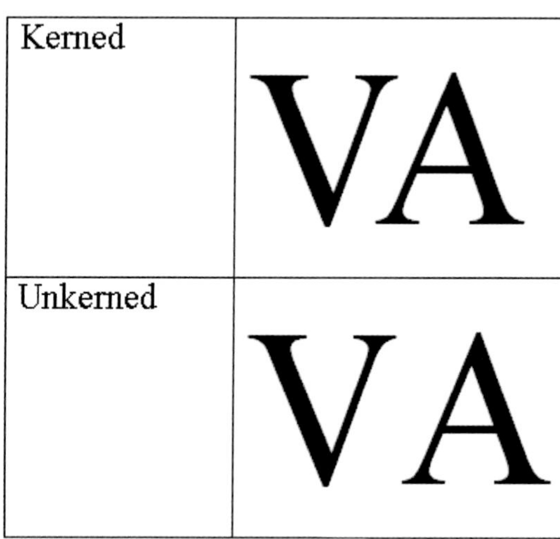

Figure 3-23

3. **On the Advanced tab, click the Kerning for Fonts xx Points and Above check box but leave the default setting of 18 points as-is (see Figure 3-24). Click OK.**

   The selected text is kerned. The difference is subtle, so you might not notice the change.

4. **Save the document.**

Leave the document open for the next exercise.

Figure 3-24

Creating custom superscript and subscript

You can change the vertical position of a character, moving it up or down in relation to the other characters around it. This is useful, for example, when you want to adjust the position of a superscript or subscript character. By adjusting the character position, you can increase or decrease the amount of raising or lowering.

LINGO

Superscript characters are raised a certain amount above the baseline, and **subscript** characters are lowered a certain amount.

In this exercise, you adjust the position of a superscript numeral.

Files needed: Lesson 3 Jobs Formatting.docx, open from the preceding exercise

1. **In Lesson 3 Jobs Formatting, click to move the insertion point after $90,000 on the third row of the table and then type** 1.

2. **Select the 1 you just typed, and choose Home➪Superscript to make the character smaller and raise it above the baseline (see Figure 3-25).**

   Note the position of the 1 in relation to the adjacent 0.

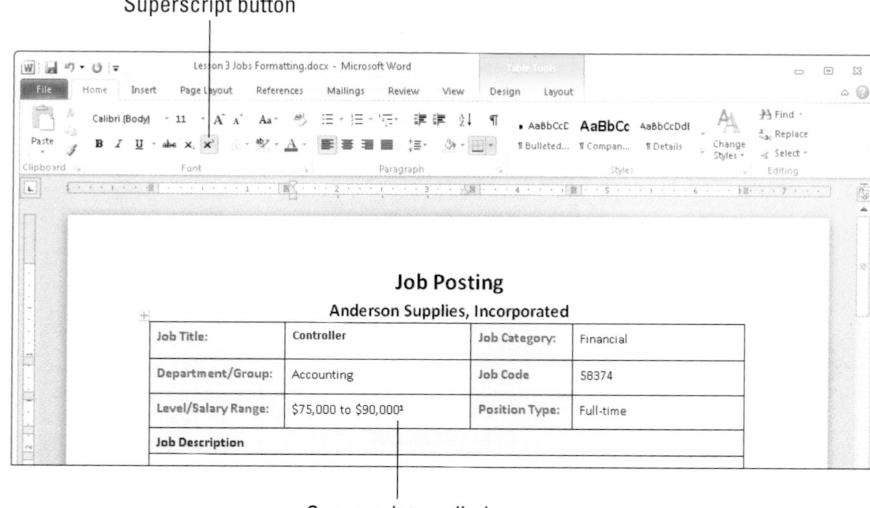

Figure 3-25

3. **With the 1 still selected, click the dialog box launcher for the Font group, opening the Font dialog box.**

4. **On the Advanced tab, from the Position drop-down list, choose Raised but in the By box, leave the default setting of 3 pt as-is (see Figure 3-26), and then click OK.**

   Notice that the 1 is now significantly higher than the 0 adjacent to it. See Figure 3-27.

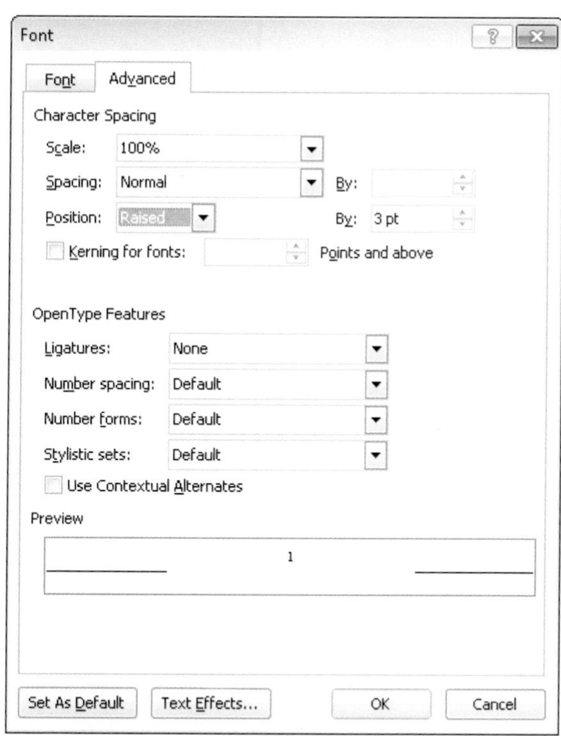

Figure 3-26

5. **Save the document.**

Leave the document open for the next exercise.

$75,000 to $90,000[1]

Figure 3-27

Controlling OpenType font options

OpenType is a kind of font file that Windows and Macintosh computers use. Like the older TrueType fonts, OpenType fonts are fully scalable to any size, but they also offer special capabilities as well for fine-tuning typeface settings, such as

- **Ligatures:** A ligature is a combination of characters that is written as a *glyph*, that is, as though they together were a single character. Most often ligatures are made up of pairs of letters, such as when the letter f is combined with others. Look at the two *f's* in *different* in Figure 3-28; the first word one does not use a ligature, and the second one does. In the ligature version, the horizontal lines on the f's are fused.

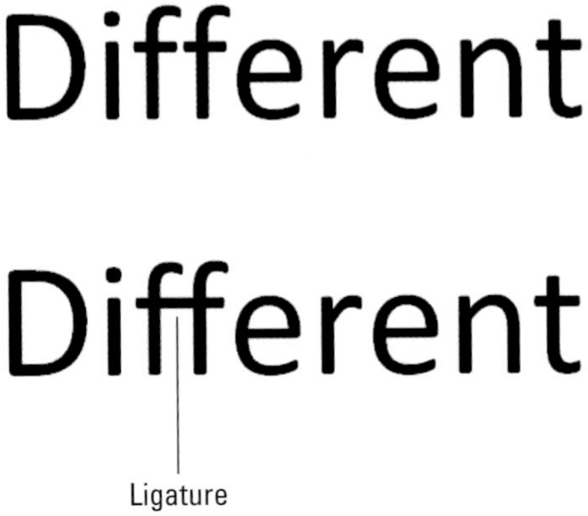

Different

Different

Ligature

Figure 3-28

- **Number spacing:** Number character spacing can be either *proportional* (where numbers are spaced like letters, with varying widths) or *tabular* (where each number has the same width). Each font has a default setting, but you can override it.
- **Number forms:** Numbers can be either *lining* (not extending below the baseline of the text, and all the same height) or *old-style* (extending below the baseline or centered higher on the line). Each font has a default setting, but you can override it.
- **Stylistic sets:** Some fonts contain multiple *stylistic sets* (up to 20), which contain alternately formed versions of some characters. You can choose among the stylistic sets that a font provides (if any).

- **Contextual alternates:** This feature, when enabled, changes the shapes of letters or combinations of letters based on surrounding characters. This can be used to make script fonts look more natural and flowing, or to use alternate letter forms at the start or end of words or next to punctuation.

For more information about OpenType features in Word, see `http://office.microsoft.com/en-us/word-help/opentype-options-in-the-font-dialog-box-HA101809106.aspx`.

Not all OpenType fonts include all these features. The Calibri, Cambria, Candara, Consolas, Contantia, and Corbel fonts all contain various OpenType features, as does Gabriola, a font that comes with Windows 7. If you have Gabriola available, it's the best one to experiment with because it contains the most OpenType features.

In this exercise, you modify OpenType options.

Files needed: Lesson 3 Jobs Formatting.docx, open from the preceding exercise

1. **In Lesson 3 Jobs Formatting, select the two paragraphs of text above the table.**
2. **On the Home tab, click the dialog box launcher to open the Font dialog box.**
3. **In the Font dialog box that appears, on the Advanced tab, open the Ligatures drop-down list, choose All, and click OK.**

   Notice that now the *t* and the *i* in *Posting* run together.
4. **Press Ctrl+Z to undo the action to see how it used to look before applying the ligature; then press Ctrl+Y to redo the action to reapply the ligature.**
5. **Select the salary range ($75,000 to $90,000[1]) and then click the dialog box launcher in the Font group to reopen the Font dialog box.**
6. **In the Font dialog box, on the Advanced tab, from the Number Spacing drop-down list, choose Proportional, review the sample in the bottom of the dialog box to see how the text will change, and then click OK to apply the change.**
7. **Select the job code (58374), and then click the dialog box launcher in the Font group to reopen the Font dialog box.**

8. **In the Font dialog box, on the Advanced tab, from the Number Forms drop-down list, choose Old-Style, review the sample in the bottom of the dialog box to see how the text will change, and click OK.**

9. **Save the document and close it.**

Exit Word.

Summing Up

Word makes it easy to create a basic document. You can either start typing in the blank document that opens automatically at startup or choose one of the templates provided. Here are the key points this lesson covered:

- Fonts, or typefaces, are lettering styles. Choose a font from the Home tab or from the Mini Toolbar.
- Font sizes are measured in points. A point is 1⁄72 of an inch. Choose font sizes from the Home tab or from the Mini Toolbar.
- A style set applies a different appearance to a document, including fonts, paragraph spacing, character spacing, and indentation. To change the style set, choose Home⇨Change Styles⇨Style Set.
- Some text attributes and effects can be applied from the Mini Toolbar or the Font group on the Home tab. Others must be applied from the Font dialog box. To open the Font dialog box, click the dialog box launcher in the Font group.
- A theme is a file that contains settings for fonts, colors, and object formatting effects. Apply a theme by choosing Page Layout⇨Themes.
- Scale is the width of each character; spacing is the blank space between characters.
- You can control scale and spacing on the Advanced tab of the Font dialog box. Click the dialog box launcher for the Font group to access it.
- Kerning adjusts spacing between two characters based on their shapes.
- Some OpenType fonts offer special typesetting options. For example, a ligature is a combination of characters that is written as though they were a single character.

Try-it-yourself lab

For more practice with the features covered in this lesson, try the following exercise on your own:

1. **Open the file Lesson 3 Summary.docx and save the file as Lesson 3 Try It.docx.**
2. **Change the style set to Modern and then change the theme to Apex.**
3. **Select the entire document and clear all manual formatting from it.**
4. **Apply the Cambria font to the body text of the article and then condense the body text by 0.5 point.**
5. **Enable ligatures of all types and then set the scale on the title (Wuthering Heights) to 150 percent.**
6. **Close Word, saving all changes if prompted.**

Know this tech talk

attributes: Formatting options such as bold, italics, and underline.

character formatting: Formatting that affects individual characters, such as font choices. Contrast this to paragraph formatting, such as indentation and line spacing, that affects only entire paragraphs.

character spacing: The spacing between the individual characters in a paragraph.

effects: Special WordArt-style effects, such as glow, reflection, and shadow, applied to text.

font: Also called a *typeface.* A style of lettering, such as Arial, Times New Roman, or Calibri.

ligature: The combination of two letters together, forming a glyph (or graphic).

lining number form: Numbers that begin at the baseline and are of the same height.

old-style number form: Numbers that may be above or below the baseline and may be different heights.

OpenType: An advanced type of scalable font that includes special typesetting features.

point: A unit of measure that's $\frac{1}{72}$ of an inch. Font size is measured in points.

proportional spacing: Spacing that's dependent on the width of the character.

scale: The setting that modifies the width of each character from its default of 100 percent.

spacing: A setting that controls the blank space between letters.

standard color: A fixed color that doesn't change when you change to a different theme.

style set: A set of font, indentation, and line spacing options.

stylistic set: An alternate set of characters stored in an OpenType font file, dictating different looks for certain characters.

tabular spacing: Spacing that's the same for every character.

template: An example file on which new documents may be based.

theme: A set of font, color, and graphic effect settings stored in a separate file, accessible to all Office applications.

theme color: A set of color choices that are applied to color placeholders in a document.

typeface: See *font*.

Lesson 4

Formatting Paragraphs

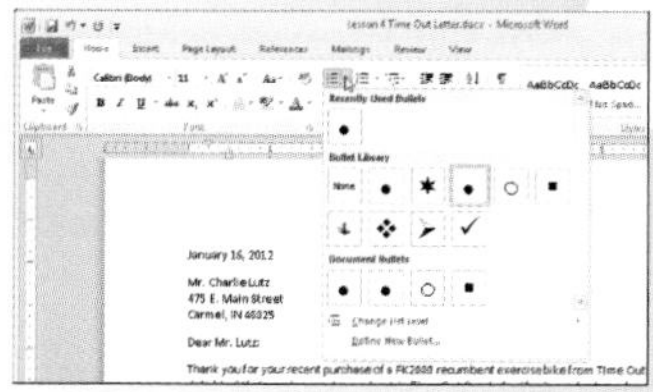

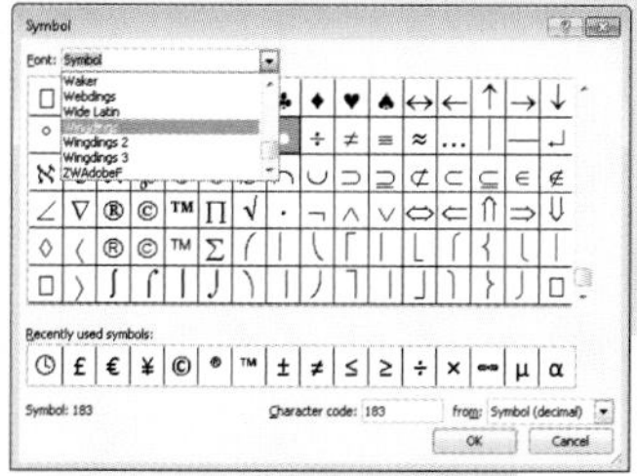

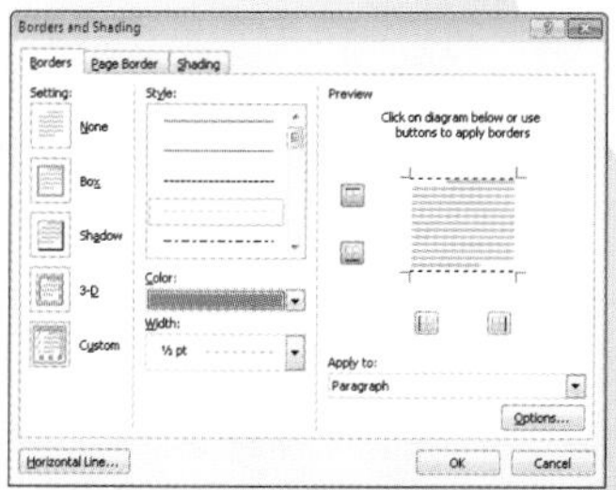

- Paragraph formatting enables you to control the indentation, line spacing, and horizontal alignment of a paragraph.
- Indenting a paragraph can set it off visually from the rest of the document for greater emphasis.
- To make a text-heavy document easier to read, increase its line spacing so that more space appears between each line.
- Create a numbered list to organize a list in which the order of the items is significant; use a bulleted list when the order is not significant.
- Custom tab stops enable you to control the position the insertion point moves into when you press the Tab key.
- Adding a border or shading to a paragraph makes it stand out from the rest of the document.

1. What is justified alignment?

   Justify your answer on page 106
2. How do you double-space a document?

   The answer is taking up space on page 108
3. How do you indent a paragraph?

   Check out page 112
4. How do you create a hanging indent?

   The answer is hanging out on page 113
5. What is a tab leader?

   Here's the page that leads the way 118
6. How do you create a numbered list that uses Roman numerals?

   Roam on over to page 126
7. How can you create a shaded box around a paragraph?

   It's made in the shade on page 129

Paragraphs are essential building blocks in a Word document. Each time you press Enter, you start a new paragraph. If you've ever seen a document where the author didn't use paragraph breaks, you know how important paragraphs can be. They break up the content into more easily understandable chunks, which help the reader both visually and logically.

In this lesson, you learn how to apply various types of formatting to paragraphs. For example, you learn how to adjust the spacing and alignment of a paragraph, how to create bulleted and numbered lists, and how to manage tab stops and indents. You also find out how to spotlight a paragraph by adding a border and shading to it.

Formatting Paragraphs

Paragraph formatting is formatting that affects whole paragraphs and cannot be applied to individual characters. For example, line spacing is a type of paragraph formatting, along with indentation and alignment.

If you apply paragraph formatting when no text is selected, the formatting applies to the paragraph in which the insertion point is currently located.

> **LINGO**
>
> **Paragraph formatting** applies to entire paragraphs, not individual characters.

If you apply paragraph formatting when text is selected, the formatting applies to whatever paragraphs are included in that selection, even if only one character of the paragraph is included. Being able to format paragraphs this way is useful because you can select multiple paragraphs at once and then format them as a group.

To set the paragraph formatting for the entire document at once, press Ctrl+A to select the entire document and then issue the paragraph formatting commands.

Applying horizontal alignment

Horizontal alignment determines where the paragraph will align in relation to the right and left margins. The horizontal alignment choices in Word are Align Text Left, Align Text Right, Center, and Justify. Figure 4-1 shows an example of each of the alignment types.

> **LINGO**
>
> **Horizontal alignment** refers to the positioning of the paragraph between the right and left margins.

Each of those is pretty self-evident except the last one. *Justify* aligns both the left and right sides of the paragraph with the margins, stretching out or compressing the text in each line as needed to make it fit. The final line in the paragraph is exempt and appears left-aligned.

Left alignment aligns with the left margin.

Center alignment centers the paragraph between the right and left margins.

Right alignment aligns with the right margin.

Justify alignment with a single-line paragraph looks just like left alignment.

Justify alignment with a multi-line paragraph spreads out each of the lines to touch both the right and left margins, except for the last line. The last line is left-aligned. Justify alignment with a multi-line paragraph spreads out each of the lines to touch both the right and left margins, except for the last line. The last line is left-aligned.

Figure 4-1

If you apply Justify alignment to a paragraph that contains only one line, it looks like it's left-aligned. However, if you then type more text into the paragraph so it wraps to additional lines, the Justify alignment becomes apparent.

In the following exercise, you apply horizontal alignment changes to a business letter.

Files needed: Lesson 4 Time Out.docx

1. **In Word, open Lesson 4 Time Out from the data files for this lesson and save it as Lesson 4 Time Out Letter.**
2. **Select the first three lines (the facility's name and address) and then choose Home⇨Center or press Ctrl+E (see Figure 4-2).**

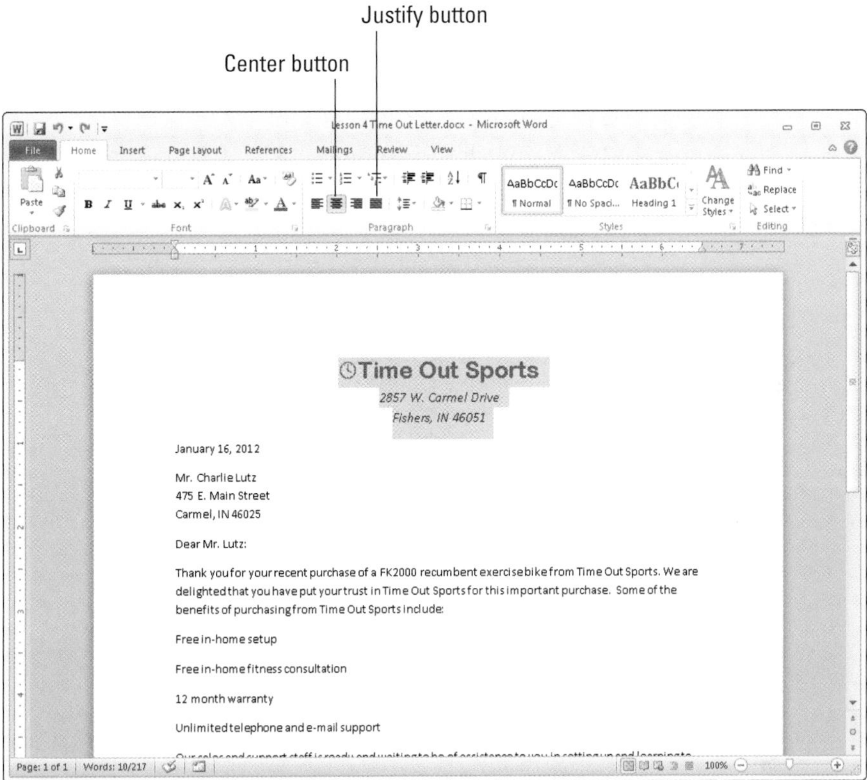

Figure 4-2

3. **Click in the first body paragraph (the paragraph that starts with *"Thank you . . ."*) and then choose Home⇨Justify or press Ctrl+J.**

   The paragraph changes to Justify alignment.

4. **Select the last four body paragraphs of the document (starting with *"Our sales and support staff . . ."*) and click the Justify button again.**

   Those paragraphs change to Justify alignment. Figure 4-3 shows the results.

5. **Save the changes to the document.**

Leave the document open for the next exercise.

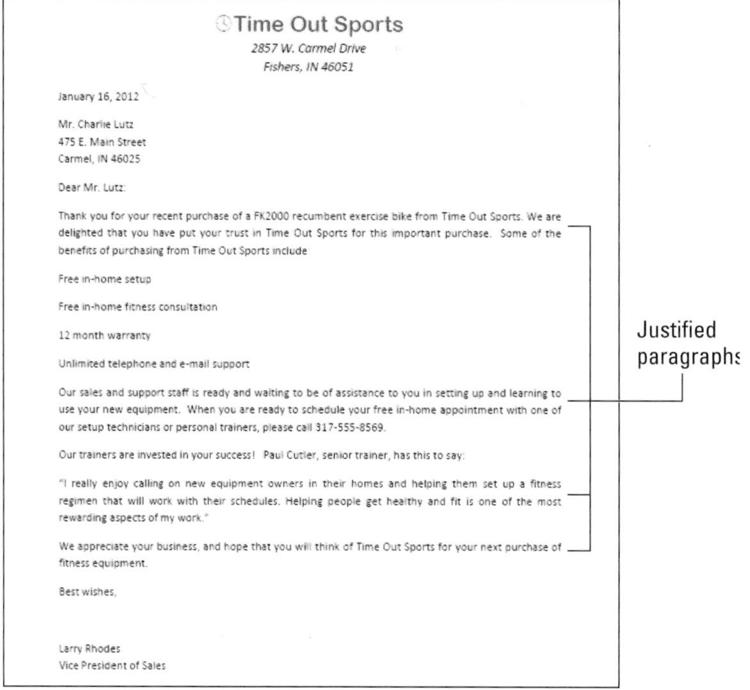
Time Out Sports
2857 W. Carmel Drive
Fishers, IN 46051

January 16, 2012

Mr. Charlie Lutz
475 E. Main Street
Carmel, IN 46025

Dear Mr. Lutz:

Thank you for your recent purchase of a FK2000 recumbent exercise bike from Time Out Sports. We are delighted that you have put your trust in Time Out Sports for this important purchase. Some of the benefits of purchasing from Time Out Sports include:

Free in-home setup

Free in-home fitness consultation

12 month warranty

Unlimited telephone and e-mail support

Our sales and support staff is ready and waiting to be of assistance to you in setting up and learning to use your new equipment. When you are ready to schedule your free in-home appointment with one of our setup technicians or personal trainers, please call 317-555-8569.

Our trainers are invested in your success! Paul Cutler, senior trainer, has this to say:

"I really enjoy calling on new equipment owners in their homes and helping them set up a fitness regimen that will work with their schedules. Helping people get healthy and fit is one of the most rewarding aspects of my work."

We appreciate your business, and hope that you will think of Time Out Sports for your next purchase of fitness equipment.

Best wishes,

Larry Rhodes
Vice President of Sales

Figure 4-3

Changing vertical spacing

You can set line spacing (that is, the vertical spacing between the lines of a paragraph) to any of several presets, such as Single, Double, and 1.5 Lines, or to an exact value, measured in points. You may remember from Lesson 3 that a *point* is 1/72 of an inch. Space before and after a paragraph is specified in points, too.

LINGO

Vertical spacing refers to the amount of space (also known as the **leading**) between each line. A paragraph has three values you can set for its spacing: *Line spacing,* which is the space between the lines within a multi-line paragraph; *Before,* which is extra spacing added above the first line of the paragraph; and *After,* which is extra spacing added below the last line of the paragraph.

If you specify an exact amount of space per line and you change the font size, the text may not look right anymore. For example, if you change the font size to a larger size than the exact spacing is set for, the lines might overlap vertically. If you aren't sure what font sizes you need, don't use exact spacing.

In the following exercise, you change the vertical spacing for paragraphs in a letter.

Files needed: Lesson 4 Time Out Letter.docx, open from the preceding exercise

1. **In the Lesson 4 Time Out Letter document, press Ctrl+A to select the entire document.**
2. **Choose Home⇨Line Spacing⇨1.0 (see Figure 4-4).**

   The line spacing in every paragraph changes to single spacing.
3. **Select the paragraph beginning with *"Free in-home setup . . ."* and the next two paragraphs following it.**

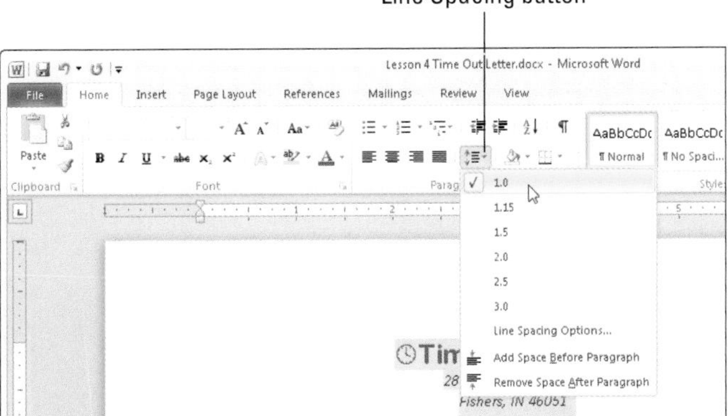

Figure 4-4

4. **Click the Line Spacing button again and then choose Remove Space After Paragraph (see Figure 4-5).**
5. **Select the Time Out Sports heading at the top of the document.**
6. **Click the Line Spacing button again and then choose Line Spacing Options.**

   The Paragraph dialog box opens.

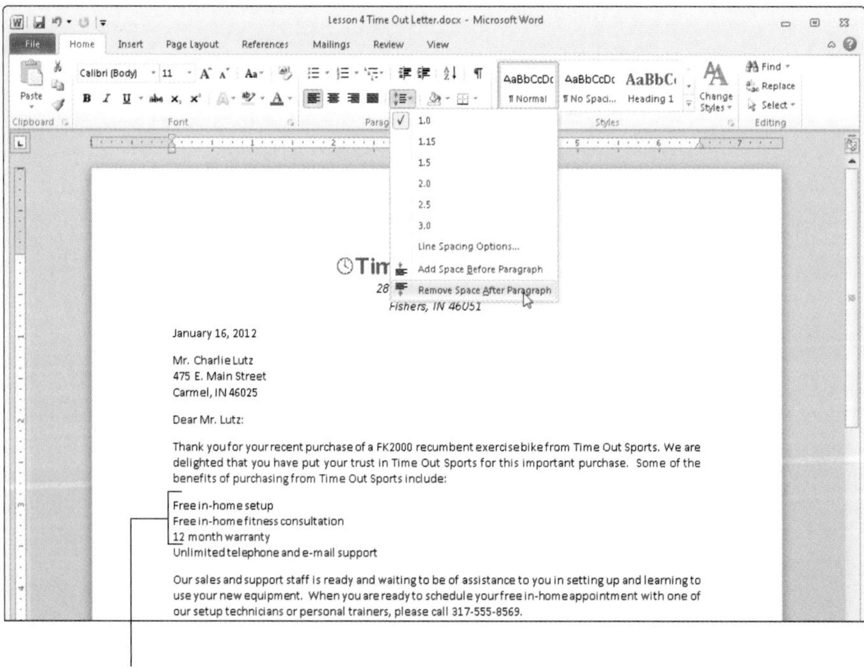

Figure 4-5

You can also click the dialog box launcher for the Paragraph group to open the Paragraph dialog box if you prefer that method.

7. **Decrease the value in the After text box to 6 pt (see Figure 4-6) and then click OK to accept the new setting.**
8. **Triple-click the quotation paragraph to select it, and then click the Line Spacing button again and choose Line Spacing Options.**

   The Paragraph dialog box opens again.

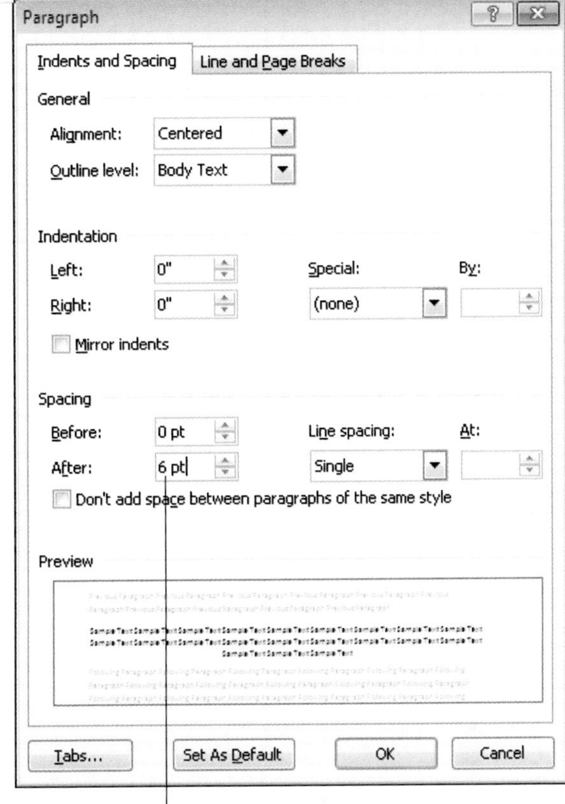

Figure 4-6

9. **From the Line Spacing drop-down list, choose Exactly; then type** 15 **into the text box to its right (see Figure 4-7) and click OK.**

For more practice, set the font size for the paragraph you just formatted to 24 points and watch what happens to the line spacing; it stays at 15 points, and the lines overlap. Press Ctrl+Z to undo when you're finished experimenting.

10. **Save the changes to the document.**

Leave the document open for the next exercise.

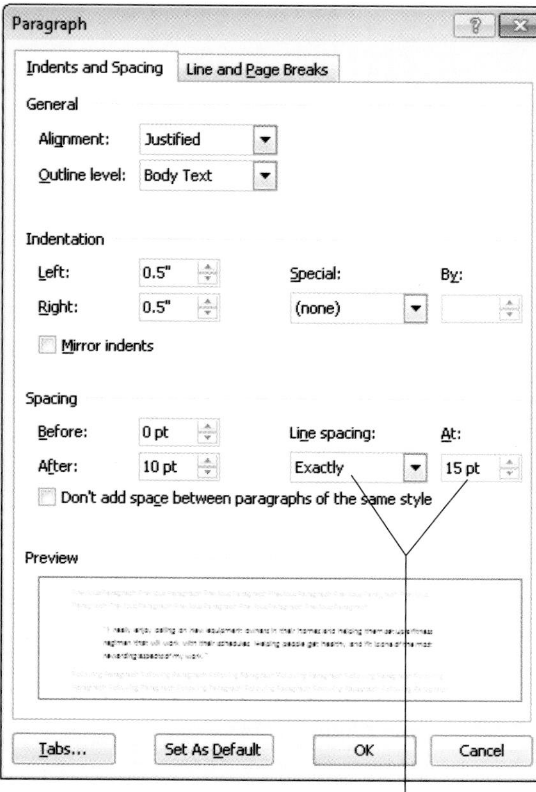

Figure 4-7

Indenting a paragraph

When a paragraph has no indentation, it's allowed to take up the full range of space between the left and right margins. When you set indentation for a paragraph, its left and/or right sides are inset by the amount you specify. Many people like to indent quotations to set them apart from the rest of the text for emphasis, for example, as shown in Figure 4-8.

LINGO

Indentation is the amount that a paragraph is inset in relation to the left and right margins. A **first-line indent** is present when the first line's indentation is more than that of the subsequent lines. A **hanging indent** is the reverse — the first line is indented less than the other lines.

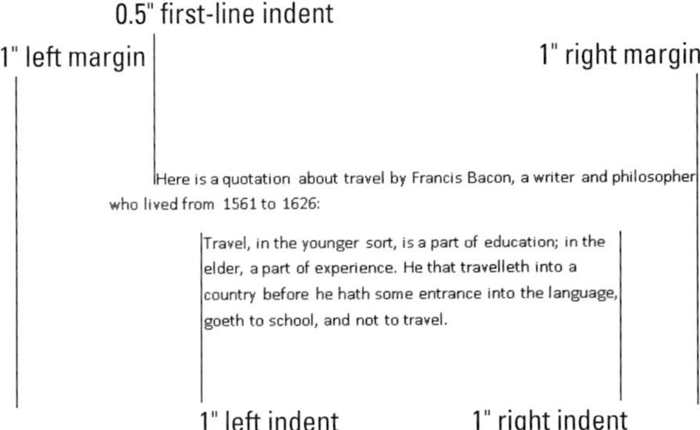

Figure 4-8

In addition to a left and right indent value, each paragraph can optionally have a special indent for the first line:

- **A first-line indent (clever name) occurs when the first line is indented more than the rest of the paragraph.** First-line indents are sometimes used in reports and books to help the reader's eye catch the beginning of a paragraph. In layouts where vertical space is between paragraphs, first-line indents are less useful because it's easy to see where a new paragraph begins without help.
- **A hanging indent occurs when the first line is indented less than the rest of the paragraph.** Hanging indents are typically used to create listings. In a bulleted or numbered list, the bullet or number hangs off the left edge of the paragraph in a hanging indent. However, in Word, when you create bulleted or numbered lists (covered later in this lesson), Word adjusts the paragraph's hanging indent automatically, so you don't have to think about it.

In the following exercise, you apply indents to paragraphs in a letter.

Files needed: Lesson 4 Time Out Letter.docx, open from the preceding exercise

1. **In the Lesson 4 Time Out Letter document, triple-click the paragraph containing the quotation to select it (the paragraph that begins with *"I really enjoy . . ."*).**

2. **Choose Home⇨Increase Indent.**

   The left indent increases by 0.5 inch. See Figure 4-9.

3. **Click the dialog box launcher in the Paragraph group to open the Paragraph dialog box.**

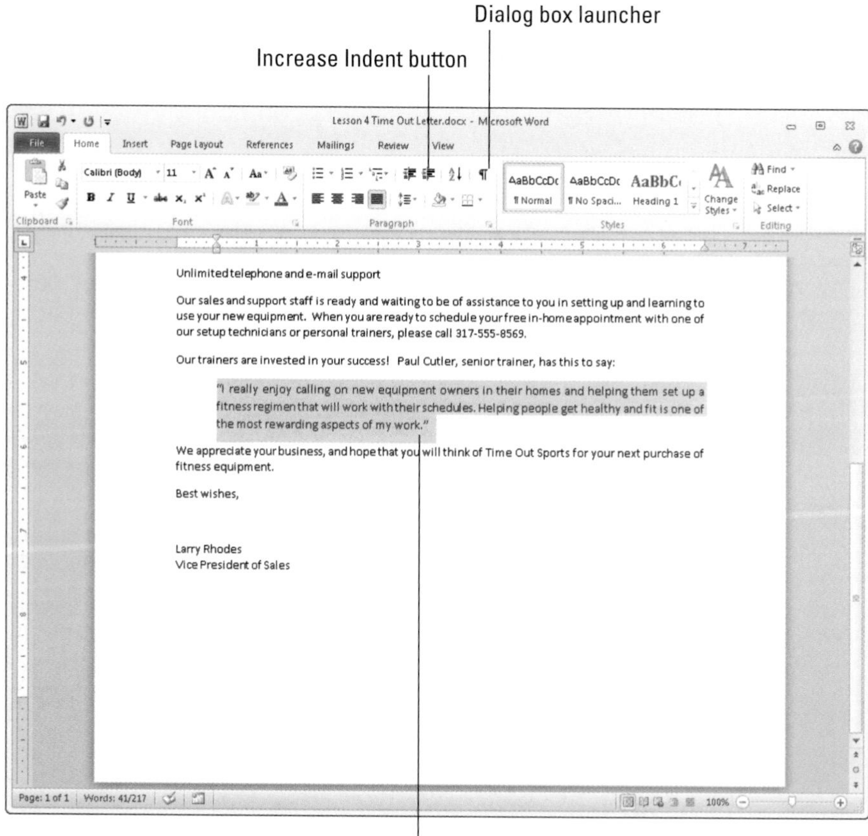

Figure 4-9

4. **Click the up arrow on the Right text box to increase the right indent to 0.5 inch (see Figure 4-10) and then click OK.**

   The paragraph is indented 0.5 inch on each side.

5. **Click in the paragraph that begins *"Our sales . . ."* and then click the dialog box launcher again to reopen the Paragraph dialog box.**

6. **From the Special drop-down list, choose First Line.**

   A first-line indent default value of 0.5 inch appears. See Figure 4-11.

7. **Click OK.**

   That paragraph is now first-line indented by 0.5 inch.

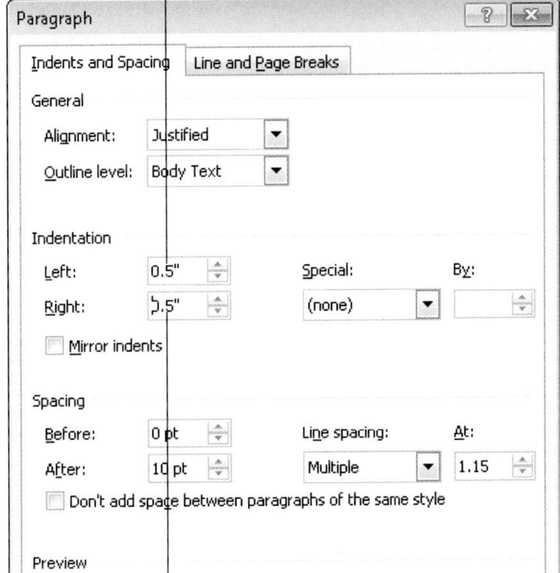

Figure 4-10

For more practice, try setting a hanging indent for one of the remaining paragraphs. Choose Hanging from the Special drop-down list in the Paragraph dialog box. When you're finished, press Ctrl+Z to undo.

EXTRA INFO

You can also create a first-line indent by positioning the insertion point at the beginning of a paragraph and pressing the Tab key. Normally this would place a 0.5-inch tab at the beginning of the paragraph, but Word's AutoCorrect feature immediately converts it to a real first-line indent for you.

8. **Save the changes to the document and close it.**

Leave Word open for the next exercise.

Adjusting indents with the Ruler

If the Ruler is displayed in Word, you can see indent markers on it showing where the current paragraph is indented. If no indents are applied, the indent markers coincide with the margins.

The margins are represented on the Ruler by the areas where the Ruler's color changes from dark gray to light gray. (Choose View⇨Ruler to toggle the Ruler on or off.)

The indent markers are as follows:

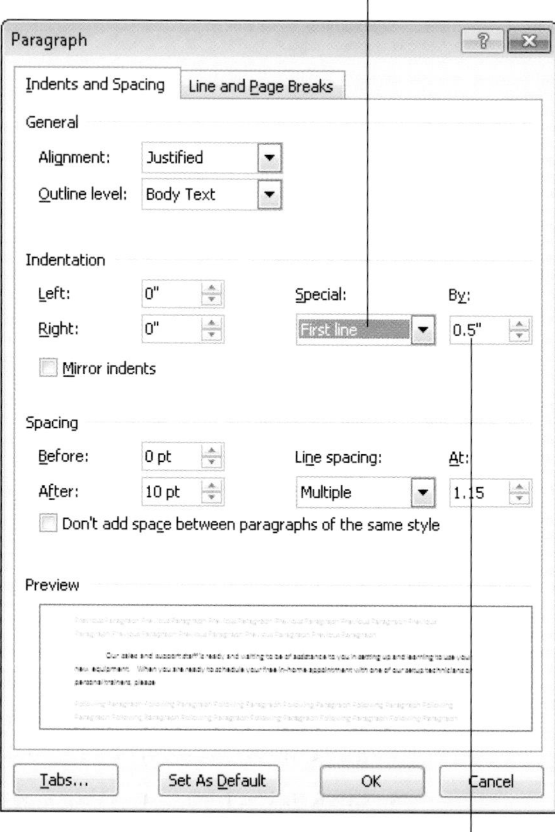

Figure 4-11

- **Down-pointing triangle at the left:** First-line indent. Drag this triangle to adjust the indent of only the first line.
- **Up-pointing triangle at the left:** Subsequent-lines indent. Drag this triangle to adjust the indent of all lines except the first one.
- **Rectangle at the left:** Left indent. Drag this rectangle to adjust the overall left indent for the paragraph. If the triangles at the left are not both at the same position, dragging the rectangle will adjust the left indent proportionally, keeping the current relationship between the two.
- **Up-pointing triangle at the right:** Right indent. Drag this triangle to adjust the right indent. You can't adjust the right indent for different lines in the same paragraph separately.

Figure 4-12 shows the indent markers on the Ruler for a paragraph that is indented 1 inch at both left and right and the first line is indented an additional 0.5 inch.

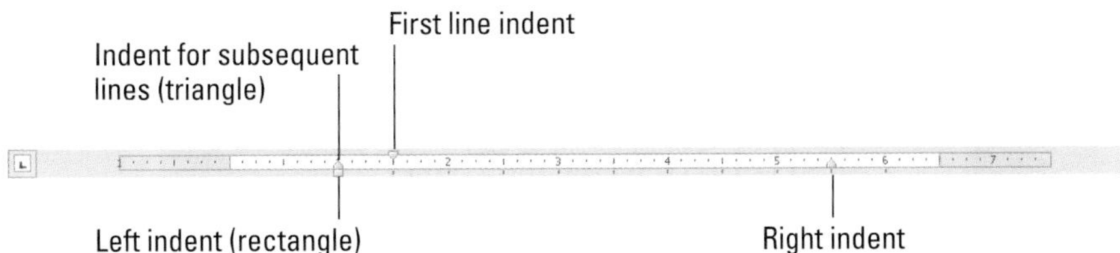

Figure 4-12

In the following exercise, you adjust indents using the Ruler.

Files needed: Lesson 4 Time Out Letter.docx

1. **In Lesson 4 Time Out Letter, click in the quotation paragraph.**

   The indent markers for that paragraph appear on the Ruler. If the Ruler doesn't appear, select the Ruler check box on the View tab.

2. **Drag the left indent marker (the rectangle at the left) to the 1" mark on the Ruler.**

   Be careful that you drag the rectangle, not one of the triangles.

3. **Drag the right indent marker (the triangle at the right) to the 5.5" mark on the Ruler (see Figure 4-13).**

4. **Click in the paragraph that begins *"Our sales and support . . ."***

   Note that the two triangles on the left end of the Ruler are not aligned with one another; the first-line indent is set at 0.5".

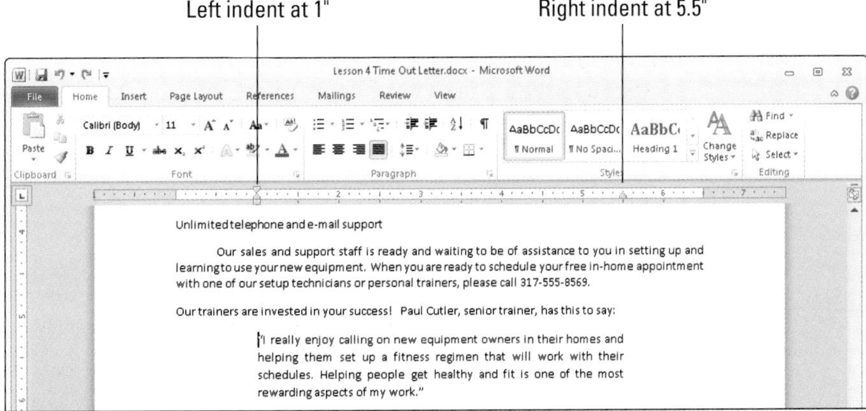

Figure 4-13

5. **Drag the first-line indent (the upper triangle) to the left margin (0" on the Ruler).**

   The first-line indent is removed from the paragraph.

6. **Save and close the document.**

Leave Word open for the next exercise.

Setting tab stops

Tab stops are position markers in a paragraph that specify where the insertion point will move when you press the Tab key. By default, a paragraph has tab stops every 0.5 inch, but you can change to some other interval or create custom tab stops.

> **LINGO**
>
> **Tab stops** are position markers in a paragraph that specify where the insertion point will move when you press the Tab key.

Tab stops can have different alignments:

- **Left:** The default alignment is left, which means that when you press the Tab key and then type some text, the text begins at the tab stop position.
- **Right:** In contrast, with a right-aligned tab stop, the text you type after pressing Tab moves over so that its end aligns with the tab stop.
- **Center:** A center tab stop centers the text from the tab stop position.
- **Decimal:** A decimal tab stop aligns numbers so that their decimal points are at the tab stop position.

If you have the Ruler turned on in Word, you can see tab stops on the Ruler. A left tab stop looks like an L, a right tab stop looks like a backward L, and a center tab stop looks like an upside-down T. A decimal tab stop looks like a center tab stop with a black dot in its lower-right corner. Figure 4-14 shows some text that uses tab stops, and the associated symbols on the Ruler.

A tab leader is a character that repeats to form a line that helps guide the reader's eye across the page. Any tab stop can have a leader applied to it. The leader fills in the space between that tab and the preceding one with the leader character. For example, in Figure 4-15, a leader has been applied to the tab stop at the 6" position on the Ruler.

> **LINGO**
>
> A **tab leader** repeats to form a line that guides the reader's eye across the page.

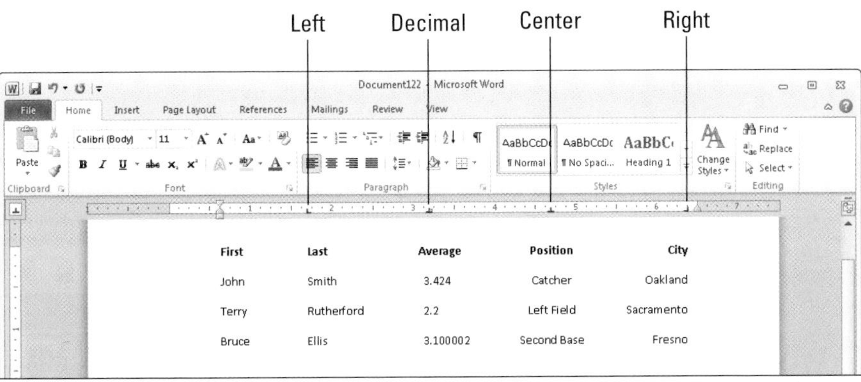

Figure 4-14

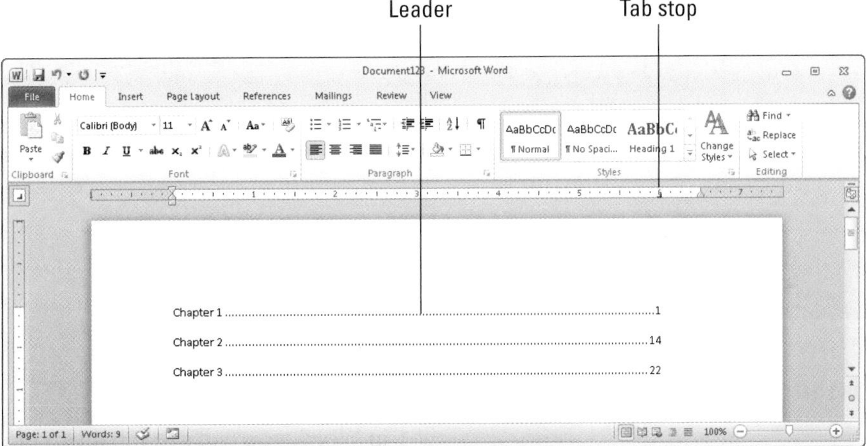

Figure 4-15

You can create tab stops with the Ruler or with the Tabs dialog box. The following exercise shows both methods.

In the following exercise, you create tab stops and then use them to create a multi-column list.

Files needed: None

1. **In Word, press Ctrl+N to start a new blank document and then press the Tab key several times.**

   Notice that the insertion point moves 0.5" to the right each time you press Tab. That's because the default tab stops are at 0.5" intervals.

2. **Press the Backspace key until the insertion point returns to the left margin, removing all the tabs you typed.**
3. **On the Home tab, click the dialog box launcher in the Paragraph group to open the Paragraph dialog box and then click the Tabs button.**

   The Tabs dialog box opens.
4. **In the Default Tab Stops box, click the up arrow until the setting is 1.0".**

   Default tab stops are now at 1" intervals.
5. **In the Tab Stop Position box, type** 5"**; in the Alignment area, click Right; in the Leader area, click 2 (the dotted line); and then click Set.**

   The new tab stop appears on the list below the Tab Stop Position box. See Figure 4-16.

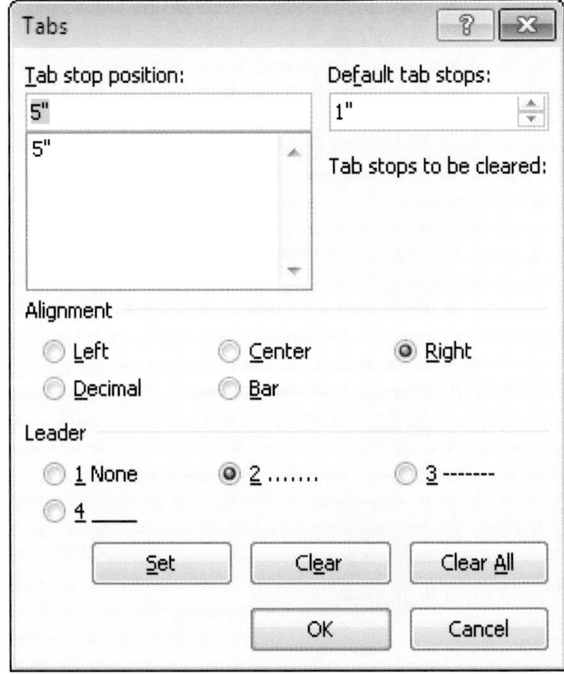

Figure 4-16

6. **Click OK to close the dialog box.**
7. **Type** Lesson 1 **and press the Tab key once.**

   The insertion point moves to the 5" tab stop.
8. **Type** 1 **and then press Enter.**

   The new paragraph has the same tab stops as the preceding one unless you change them.
9. **Choose Home➪Clear Formatting.**

   The right-aligned tab stop at 5" is removed from the new paragraph, leaving only the default tab stops.
10. **Press the Tab key twice.**

    Notice that the insertion point moves 1 inch each time you press Tab because you redefined the default tab stops in Step 4.

11. **Press the Backspace key twice to remove the two tabs you typed and then click the Tab Type button at the far left of the Ruler until the tab type is center (an upside-down T).**

12. **Click the Ruler at the 2.5" mark to set a center-aligned tab stop there and then press the Tab key once to move the insertion point to the new tab stop.**

13. **Type** Note: Page numbers are preliminary**.**

    The text you type center-aligns with the tab stop. See Figure 4-17.

14. **Save the document as Lesson 4 Tabs.**

Leave the document open for the next exercise.

EXTRA INFO

The Tab Type button toggles among several tab and other settings. If you accidentally click past the center tab stop type, keep clicking and it will come back around again.

EXTRA INFO

When you set a custom tab stop, all the default tab stops to the left of that position are eliminated, so the first stop is your custom one.

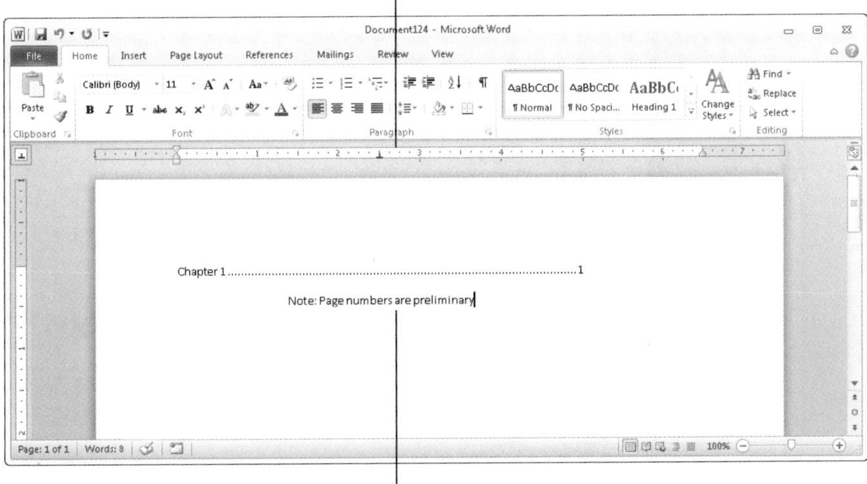

Figure 4-17

Changing and removing tab stops

The easiest way to change and remove tab stops is to work with them directly on the Ruler. You can drag a tab stop to the right or left to shift its position, or you can drag it off the Ruler entirely (up or down) to remove it.

To change a tab stop's type, double-click the tab stop on the Ruler to open the Tabs dialog box and make your changes there.

In the following exercise, you modify and remove tab stops.

Files needed: Lesson 4 Tabs.docx, open from the preceding exercise

1. **In the Lesson 4 Tabs document, click in the paragraph that begins with *"Note. . ."***

   The Ruler shows one custom tab stop for that paragraph: a center-aligned tab at the 2.5" mark.

2. **Drag the tab stop down off the Ruler to delete it.**

   The text reverts to left-aligned with the default tab stop at the 1-inch mark.

When no custom tab stops are set for a paragraph, the paragraph reverts to the default tab stops. This paragraph has default tab stops every 1 inch because in an earlier exercise, you changed the default from its original 0.5" setting.

3. **Click in the Lesson 1 paragraph.**

   The Ruler shows a custom tab stop at the 5" mark.

4. **Drag the custom tab stop from the 5" mark to the 6" mark on the Ruler.**

   The number 1 moves to the 6" mark on the Ruler, and the leader extends to fill the extra space. See Figure 4-18.

5. **Save the document and close it.**

Leave Word open for the next exercise.

Drag right tab stop to 6" mark

Figure 4-18

Creating Bulleted and Numbered Lists

Word makes it easy to create bulleted and numbered lists in your documents:

- **Use a bulleted list for lists where the order of items isn't significant.** The same "bullet" character (such as •) is used in front of each item. You might use a bulleted list for a packing list for a trip, for example, or a go-forward list.
- **Use a numbered list for lists where the order of items *is* significant and a where sequential step number is used to indicate order.** For example, a numbered list might contain the steps for a recipe or a meeting agenda.

LINGO

A **bulleted list** is a list in which each paragraph is preceded by a symbol. A **numbered list** is a list in which each paragraph is preceded by a number.

You can create a list from existing paragraphs, or you can turn on the list feature and type the list as you go. Either way, you're working with the Bullets button or the Numbering button on the Home tab.

Creating a basic numbered or bulleted list

In the following exercise, you convert some paragraphs into a numbered list and then change it to a bulleted list.

Files needed: Lesson 4 Time Out Letter.docx

1. **Open the Lesson 4 Time Out Letter file, created throughout much of this lesson.**
2. **Select the list of four benefits, starting with *"Free in-home setup . . ."* and then choose Home➪Numbering.**

   The list becomes numbered.
3. **Click the Bullets button.**

   The list switches to a bulleted list. See Figure 4-19.

Leave the document open for the next exercise.

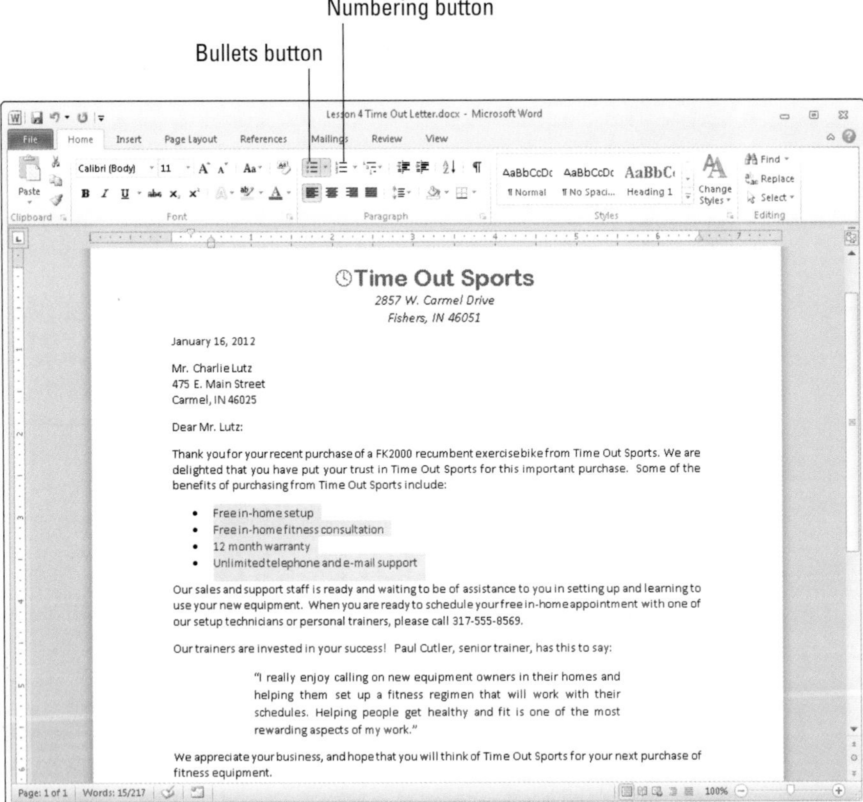

Figure 4-19

Changing the bullet character

You can use any character you like for the bullets in a bulleted list; you're not limited to the standard black circle. Word offers a choice of several common characters on the Bullets button's palette, and you can also select any picture or character from any font to use.

In the following exercise, you change the bullet character to several that are text-based or graphical.

Files needed: Lesson 4 Time Out Letter.docx, open from the preceding exercise

1. **In the Lesson 4 Time Out Letter document, select the four bulleted paragraphs.**
2. **From the Home tab, click the down arrow on the Bullets button, opening its palette (see Figure 4-20), and then choose the check mark bullet.**

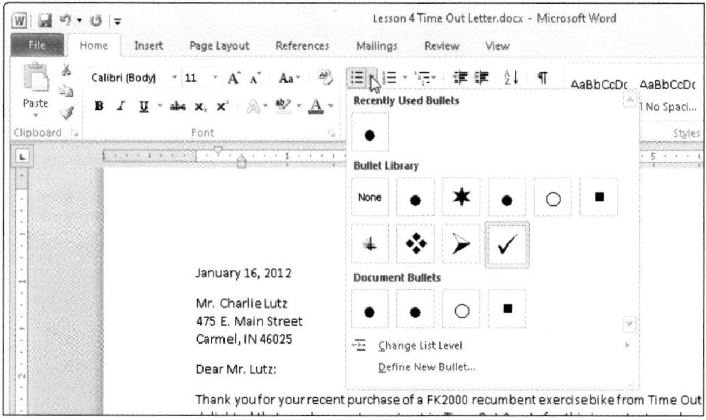

Figure 4-20

The list uses that character.

3. **Click the down arrow on the Bullets button again, reopening its palette and choose Define New Bullet.**

   The Define New Bullet dialog box opens.

4. **Click the Symbol button to open the Symbol dialog box opens and then from the Font drop-down list, choose Wingdings (see Figure 4-21).**

5. **Click the six-pointed black star, click OK to close the Symbol dialog box, and then click OK to close the Define New Bullet dialog box.**

   The bulleted list appears with the new star bullets.

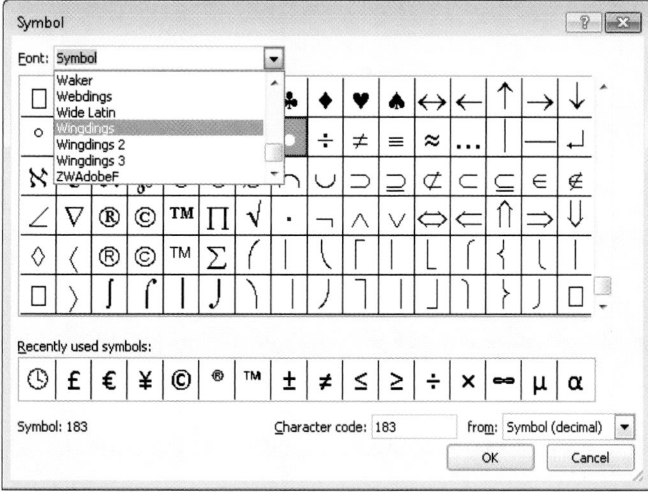

Figure 4-21

6. **Click the down arrow on the Bullets button again, reopening its palette and then choose Define New Bullet.**

   The Define New Bullet dialog box opens.

7. **Click the Picture button.**

   The Picture Bullet dialog box opens. See Figure 4-22.

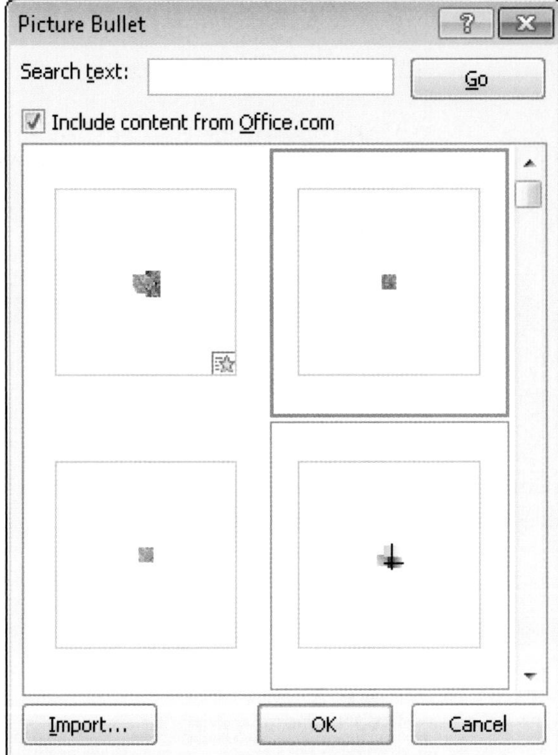

Figure 4-22

8. **Click any of the picture bullets that appeal to you, click OK to close the Picture Bullet dialog box, and then click OK to close the Define New Bullet dialog box.**

   The picture bullets appear on the list.

9. **Save the changes to the document.**

Leave the document open for the next exercise.

Changing the numbering style

Changing the numbering style is much like changing the bullet character, except you have a few extra options, such as choosing a starting number. You can select from various styles of numbering that include uppercase or lowercase letters, Roman numerals, or Arabic (regular) numerals.

In the following exercise, you change the numbering format for a numbered list.

Files needed: Lesson 4 Time Out Letter.docx, open from the preceding exercise

1. **In the Lesson 4 Time Out Letter document, select the four bulleted paragraphs if they aren't already selected.**
2. **From the Home tab, click the down arrow on the Numbering button to open its palette.**
3. **In the Numbering Library section, choose the numbering style that uses uppercase letters followed by periods (see Figure 4-23).**

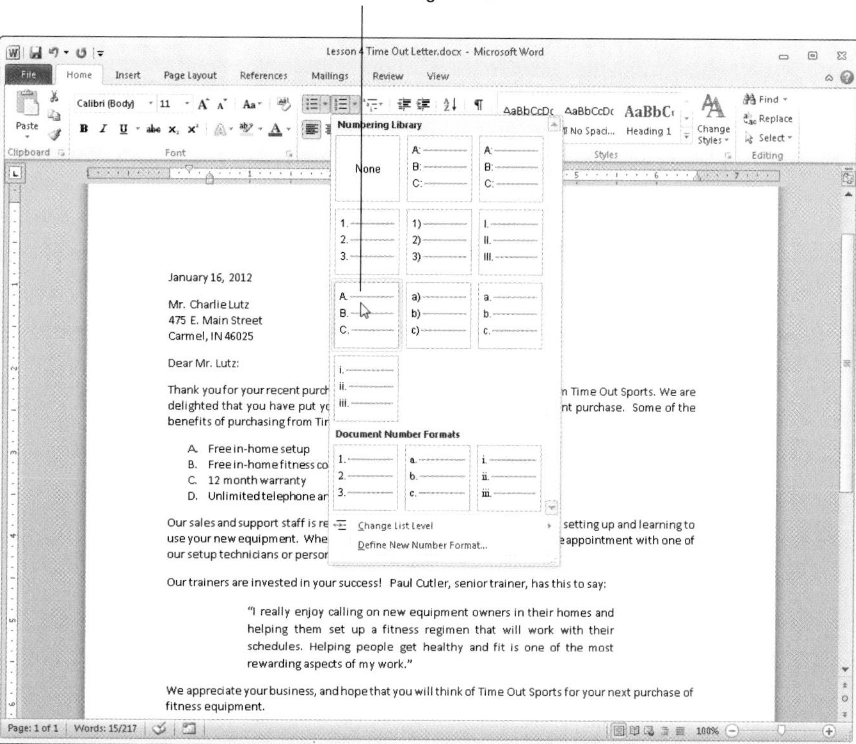

Figure 4-23

4. **Click the down arrow on the Numbering button and then choose Define New Number Format.**

   The Define New Number Format dialog box appears.

5. **In the Number Format text box, delete the period following the shaded A and type a colon (:), as shown in Figure 4-24.**

Change the period to a colon here

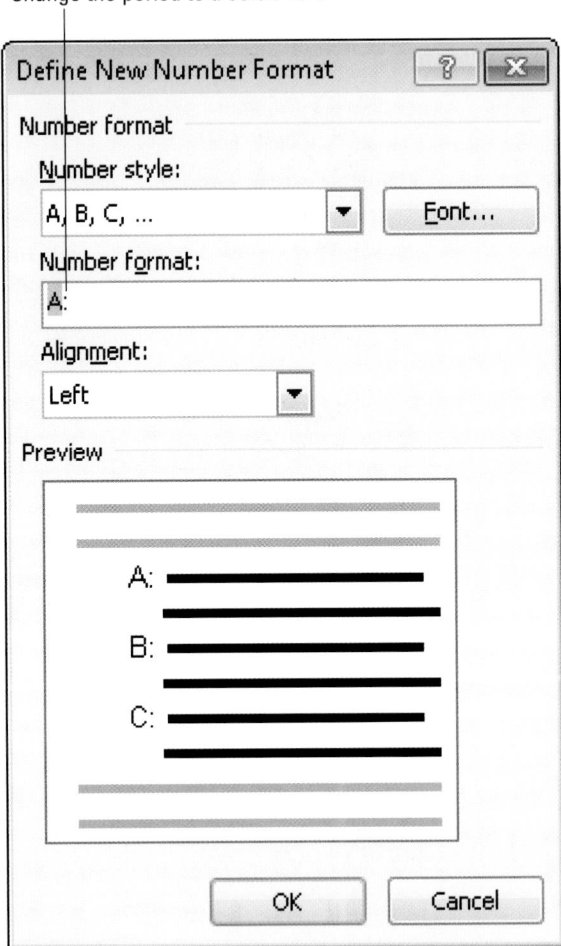

Figure 4-24

6. **Click the Font button to open the Font dialog box, set the font size to 14 points (see Figure 4-25), click OK to return to the Define New Number Format dialog box, and then click OK to accept the new format.**

   The list appears with extra-large letters, followed by colons. See Figure 4-26.

7. **Save the changes to the document.**

Leave the document open for the next exercise.

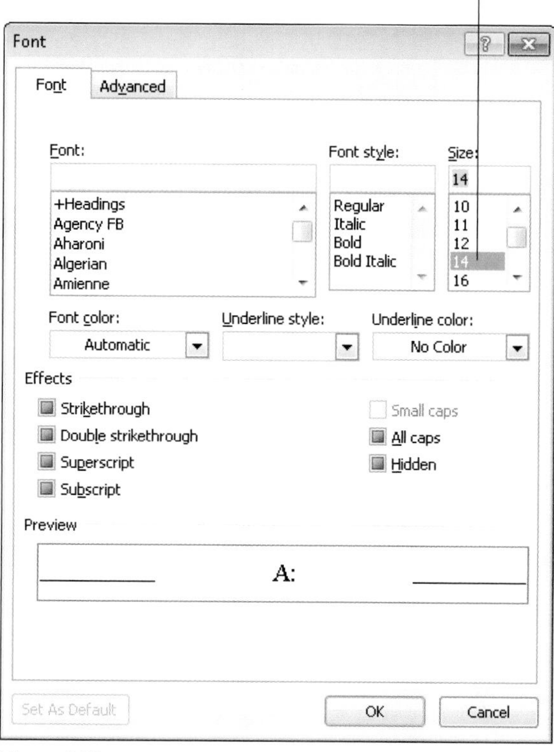

Figure 4-25

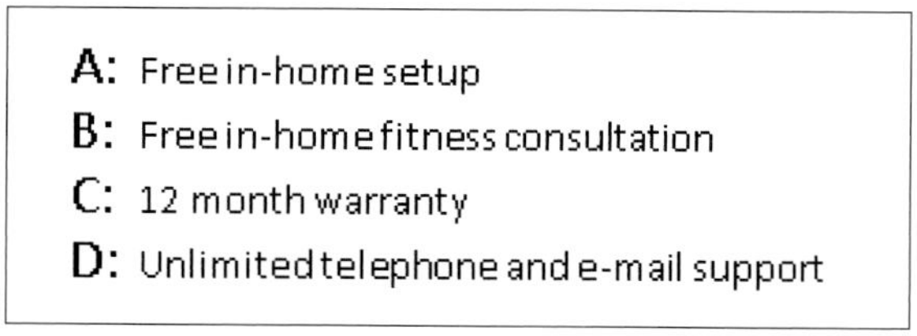

A: Free in-home setup
B: Free in-home fitness consultation
C: 12 month warranty
D: Unlimited telephone and e-mail support

Figure 4-26

Adding Borders and Shading

By default, a paragraph has no border or shading. You can add either or both to a single paragraph or any group of paragraphs to make them stand out from the rest of the document. You can use any border thickness, style, and color you like, and any color of shading.

Placing a border around a paragraph

A paragraph border appears around the outside of a single paragraph. If the paragraph is indented, the border will also be indented (left and right only; the indent doesn't change for hanging or first-line indents).

If you place the same border around two or more consecutive paragraphs, the border surrounds them as a group. That way you can create groups of paragraphs that appear "boxed" together for special emphasis.

In the following exercise, you add a border around a paragraph.

Files needed: Lesson 4 Time Out Letter.docx, open from the preceding exercise

1. **In the Lesson 4 Time Out Letter document, click anywhere within the quotation paragraph.**
2. **On the Home tab, in the Paragraph group, open the Border button's drop-down list and choose Outside Borders.**

   A plain black border appears around the quotation paragraph. See Figure 4-27. You could stop here if you wanted a plain border, but the next steps show you how to format the border in different ways.

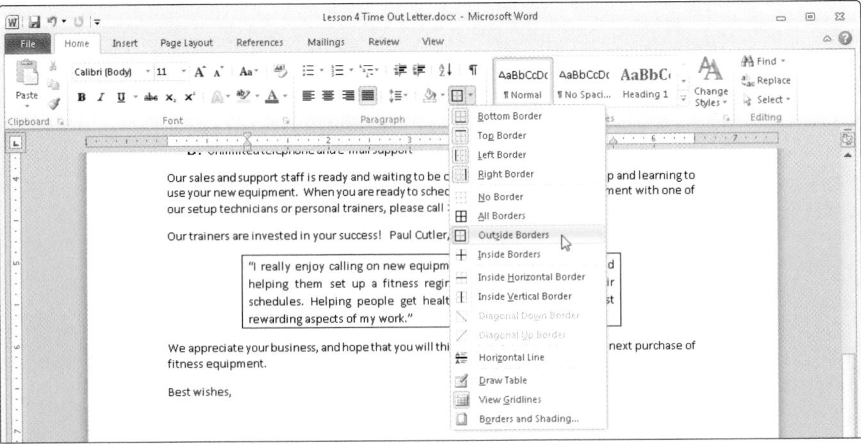

Figure 4-27

3. **From the Border button's drop-down list, choose Borders and Shading.**

   The Borders and Shading dialog box opens.
4. **Click the Shadow button.**

   The border becomes thicker at the bottom and right sides, simulating a shadow.

Check the results in the preview in the dialog box.

5. **Click the Box button.**

   The border once again has the same thickness on all sides. Check the results in the preview.

6. **From the Color drop-down list, choose the Blue, Accent 1 theme color; from the Width drop-down list, choose ½pt; in the Style area, click one of the dashed lines; and in the Preview area, click the buttons that represent the right and left sides, turning off those sides (see Figure 4-28).**

7. **Click OK to apply the border to the paragraph and then save the document.**

Leave the document open for the next exercise.

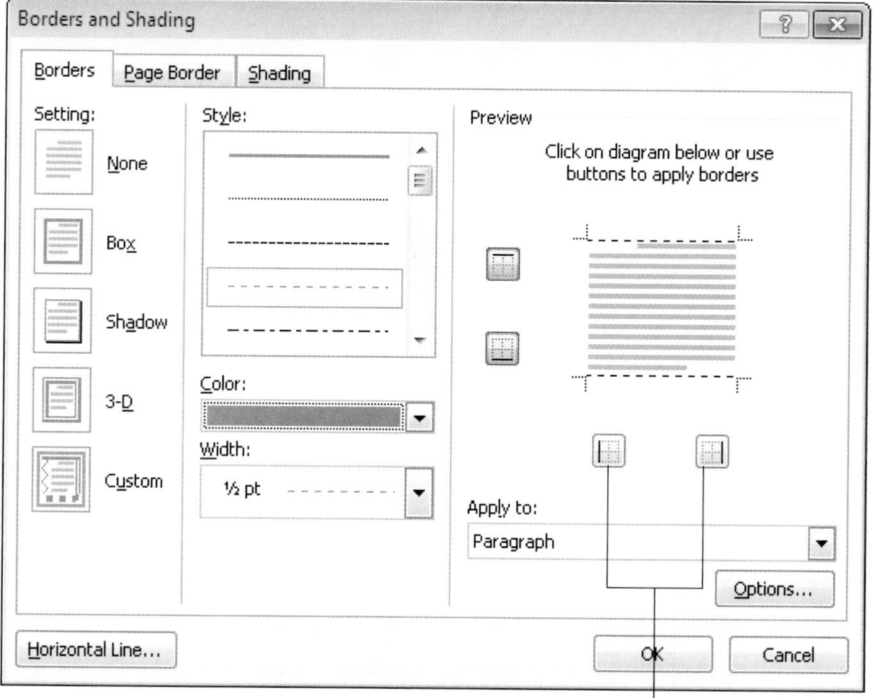

Figure 4-28

Shading a paragraph's background

Shading a paragraph helps it stand out from the rest of the document and adds visual interest to the document. You can use shading with or without a border.

As with a border, shading follows along with any indent settings you may have specified for the paragraph. If the paragraph is indented, the shading is also.

Word applies only solid-color shading to paragraphs. If you want a gradient shading behind a paragraph, or some other special shading effect such as a pattern, texture, or graphic, place a text box (choose Insert⇨Text Box) and then apply the desired shading to the text box as a Fill, like you would with a graphic. See Lesson 8 for more information.

In the following exercise, you add shading to a paragraph.

Files needed: Lesson 4 Time Out Letter.docx, open from the preceding exercise

1. **In the Lesson 4 Time Out Letter document, click anywhere within the quotation paragraph.**
2. **On the Home tab, in the Paragraph group, open the Shading drop-down list and choose Blue, Accent 1, Lighter 80%, as shown in Figure 4-29.**

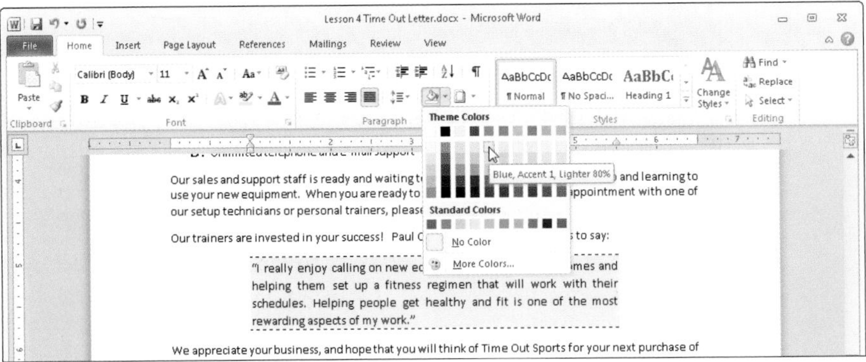

Figure 4-29

3. **Reopen the Shading drop-down list and choose More Colors.**

   The Colors dialog box opens.

4. **Click the Standard tab, click a light yellow square (see Figure 4-30), and then click OK to accept the new color choice.**
5. **Save and close the document.**

Exit Word.

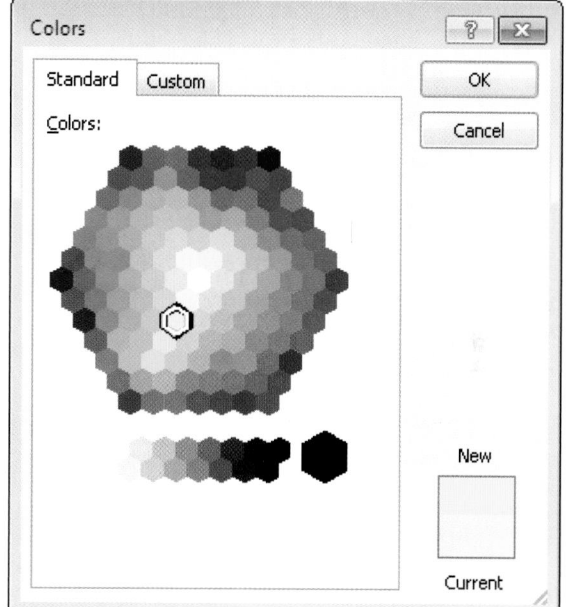

Figure 4-30

Summing Up

Word provides several ways to format paragraphs and tables and to help automate formatting. Here are the key points from this lesson:

- To apply horizontal alignment, use the buttons in the Paragraph group on the Home tab. Your choices are Align Text Left, Align Text Right, Center, and Justify.
- You can set vertical spacing from the Paragraph dialog box.
- A paragraph can be indented at the left or right (all lines) and can have a first-line or hanging indent applied.
- To indent the entire paragraph at the left, you can use the Increase Indent button in the Paragraph group on the Home tab.
- To set other indentation, open the Paragraph dialog box by clicking the dialog box launcher in the Paragraph group.
- To set tab stops, click the Ruler. To remove tab stops, drag them off the Ruler. You can also work with tab stops in the Tabs dialog box, accessed from the Paragraph dialog box.
- To create a default numbered or bulleted list, use their respective buttons on the Home tab. Each button has a drop-down list from which you can choose other bullet or numbering styles.

- To add a border to a paragraph, use the Border button's drop-down list on the Home tab.
- To add shading to a paragraph, use the Shading button's drop-down list on the Home tab.

Try-it-yourself lab

For more practice with the features covered in this lesson, try the following exercise on your own:

1. **In a new document, type** Shopping List **and then center the paragraph.**
2. **Place a border and shading around the Shopping List text.**
3. **Below that paragraph, create a bulleted list consisting of at least eight items you'd buy at a grocery store.**
4. **Indent the paragraphs of the bulleted list by 0.5" more than its default.**
5. **Save your document with a name of your choice and close Word.**

Know this tech talk

border: An outline around an object.

bulleted list: A list in which each paragraph is preceded by the same symbol.

first-line indent: A positive indent that affects only the first line of the paragraph. When negative, it's a *hanging indent.*

hanging indent: A negative indent that affects only the first line of the paragraph. When positive, it's a *first-line indent.*

horizontal alignment: The positioning of a paragraph between the right and left margins.

indentation: The amount that a paragraph is offset from the left or right margin.

justified: A horizontal alignment that stretches out the text so that it touches both the right and left margins.

leading: Vertical spacing between the lines of text.

numbered list: A list in which each paragraph is preceded by a consecutive number.

paragraph formatting: Formatting that affects whole paragraphs and cannot be applied to individual characters.

shading: The background fill in a paragraph or object.

tab stop: A position marker for a paragraph that indicates where the insertion point should move when the Tab key is pressed.

Lesson 5

Working with Styles and Templates

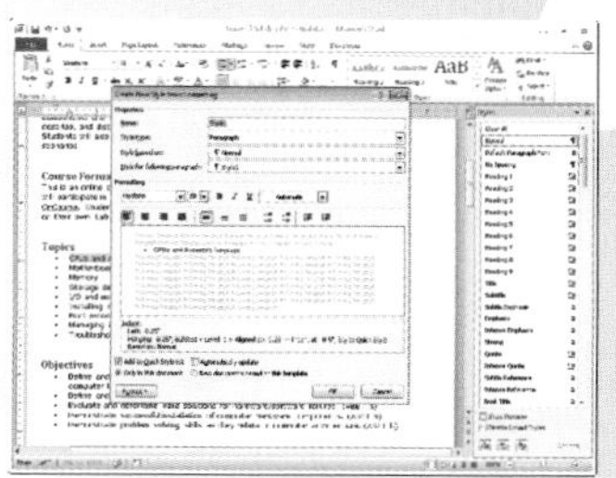

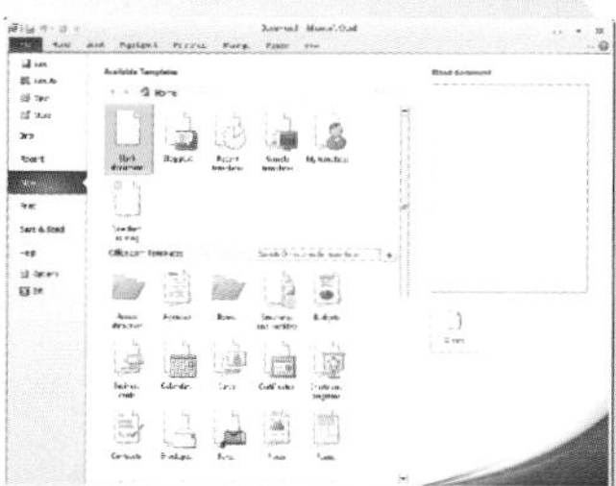

- Styles make consistent formatting quick and easy to apply.
- You can create your own styles to consistently apply your own custom formatting.
- The Style Inspector enables you to see exactly what formatting has been applied to selected text.
- You can modify templates to create your own custom versions of the templates that come with Word.

1. How do you apply a style to a paragraph?

   You'll be stylin' on page 137

2. How do you modify a style?

   Make that change on page 140

3. How do you create your own styles?

   Show off your creativity on page 143

4. How can you copy styles between documents?

   Make the copy on page 147

5. What does the Style Inspector do?

   Inspect page 151

6. What's the file extension on a Word template?

   That knowledge extends to page 154

7. How can you create a customized version of one of the Office.com templates?

   Express your custom flair on page 154

Styles and templates are two ways of standardizing documents. A *template* is a sample that you can base new documents on; it can contain sample content, styles, margin settings, and other formatting that jump-starts the document creation. A *style* is a formatting specification for an individual paragraph, list item, or character of text. You can store styles in templates so that when you start a document with a certain template, that set of styles is automatically available to you.

In this lesson, you learn how to apply styles as well as how to modify existing style definitions and create new ones. You also learn how to modify a template and how to create your own templates.

Apply Styles

Using a style makes it easy to apply consistent formatting throughout a document. For example, you might apply the Heading 1 style to all headings in the document and the Normal style to all the regular body text. Here are the advantages of this approach:

LINGO

A **style** is a named set of formatting specifications.

- **Ease:** Applying a style is easier than manually applying formatting. And changing the formatting is a snap. If you want the headings to look different, for example, you can modify the Heading 1 style to change them all at once.
- **Consistency:** You don't have to worry about all the headings being formatted consistently; because they're all using the same style, they're automatically all the same.

By default, each paragraph is assigned a Normal style. The template in use determines the styles available and how they're defined.

In Word 2010 in documents that use the default blank (Normal) template, the Normal style uses Calibri 11 point font and left-aligns the text, with no indentation.

You can redefine the styles in a document, and you can also create your own new styles.

Apply a style

In the Styles group on the Home tab is a Quick Style gallery. The first row appears in the Ribbon itself, and you can see the rest of it by clicking the More button to open the full gallery.

LINGO

The **Quick Style gallery** on the Home tab contains shortcuts for commonly used styles.

Not all styles appear in the Quick Style gallery — only the ones that are designated as quick styles. The rest of them appear in the Styles pane. To open the Styles pane, click the dialog box launcher on the Styles group.

To apply a style, select the paragraph(s) that you want to affect or move the insertion point into the paragraph. Then click the style you want to apply, either in the Quick Style gallery or in the Styles pane. Some styles also have keyboard shortcuts assigned to them, for quick applying.

In the following exercise, you apply styles to the paragraphs in a document.

Files needed: Lesson 5 Syllabus.docx

1. **In Word, open Lesson 5 Syllabus and save it as Lesson 5 Syllabus Formatted.**
2. **Click in the first paragraph *(CIT 233)*. Then on the Home tab, in the Styles group, click the More button (see Figure 5-1) to open the Quick Styles gallery.**

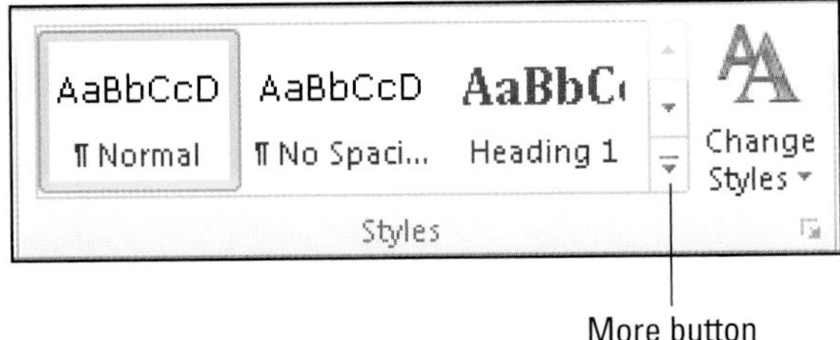

Figure 5-1

3. **Click the Title style (see Figure 5-2).**

   The style is applied to the first paragraph.

4. **Using the same procedure as Steps 2–3, apply the Subtitle style to the second paragraph.**
5. **Apply the Heading 1 style to each of the orange paragraphs by clicking Heading 1 in the Quick Style gallery.**

Figure 5-2

Here's a shortcut: Click to the left of the first orange paragraph to select it, and then hold down the Ctrl key and do the same for each of the remaining orange paragraphs. After they're all selected, apply the style to them all at once.

6. **Click the dialog box launcher to open the Styles pane.**

   The Styles pane is a floating pane to the right of the document.

7. **Scroll through the Styles pane and locate the Heading 2 style; then click in one of the green paragraphs near the end of the document and click the Heading 2 style in the Styles pane to apply it.**
8. **Apply the Heading 2 style to all the remaining green paragraphs.**

   The last page of the document resembles Figure 5-3.

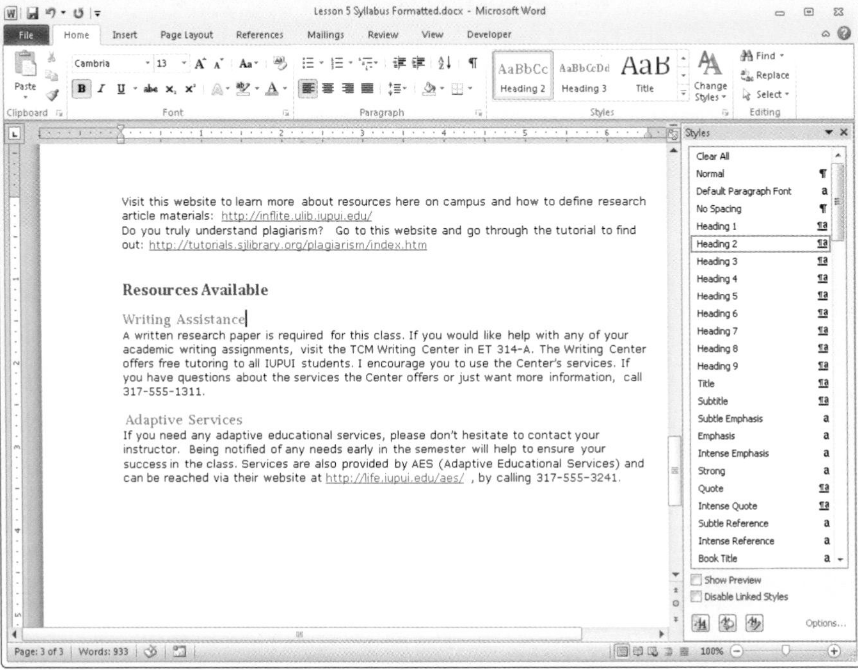

Figure 5-3

9. **Save the changes to the document.**

Leave the document open for the next exercise.

EXTRA INFO

Scroll through the Styles pane's list, and look at the symbols to the right of each style. Most of the styles in the Styles pane have a paragraph symbol (¶) to their right. This means that they are *paragraph styles* — they apply to entire paragraphs at once. They may include both paragraph and character formatting in their definitions, but if you click in a paragraph and then apply the style, the style will be applied to the whole paragraph. In contrast, some styles may have a lowercase *a* to their right on the list; these are *character styles,* or *text-level styles,* and they apply only to the text that you select before applying them. A character style can contain only character-based formatting.

Modify a style

You can modify a style in two ways: by example or by manually changing the style's definition. The by-example method is much easier, but somewhat less flexible. The following exercise shows both methods.

In the following exercise, you change the definitions of some styles.

Files needed: Lesson 5 Syllabus Formatted.docx, open from the preceding exercise

1. **Triple-click the document subtitle (the second paragraph) to select it and then change the font size to 18 point.**
2. **In the Styles pane, click the down arrow to the right of the Subtitle style, or right-click the Subtitle style.**
3. **In the menu that appears, choose Update Subtitle to Match Selection, as shown in Figure 5-4.**

   The style is updated with the new font size.

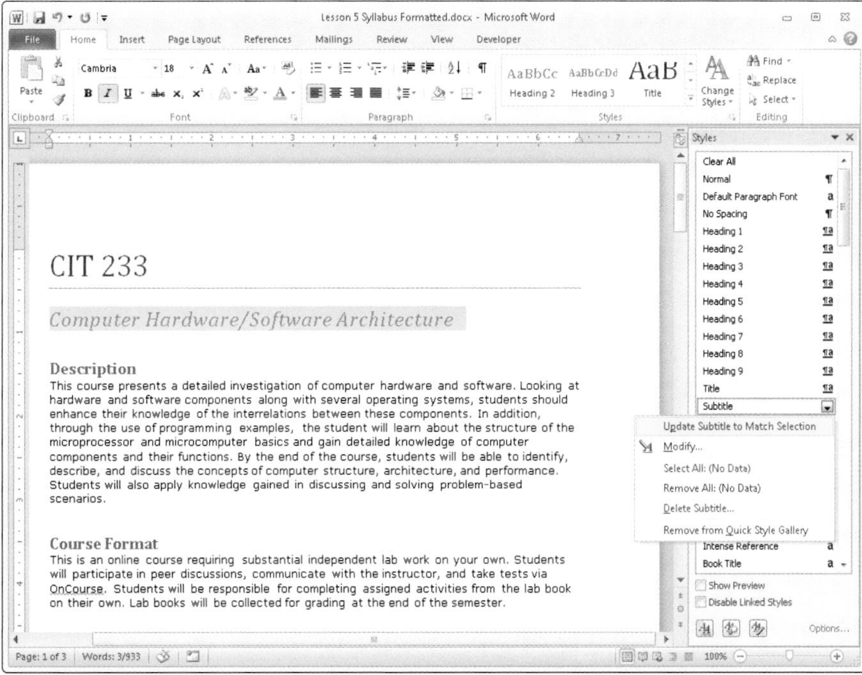

Figure 5-4

4. **Reopen the Subtitle style's menu and choose Modify.**

   The Modify Style dialog box opens.

For more practice, make other changes to the style's definition using the font controls in the Modify Style dialog box. The buttons and lists in the dialog box correspond to the tools in the Font and Paragraph groups on the Home tab.

5. **In the bottom-left corner of the dialog box, click the Format button and choose Font (see Figure 5-5) to open the Font dialog box.**

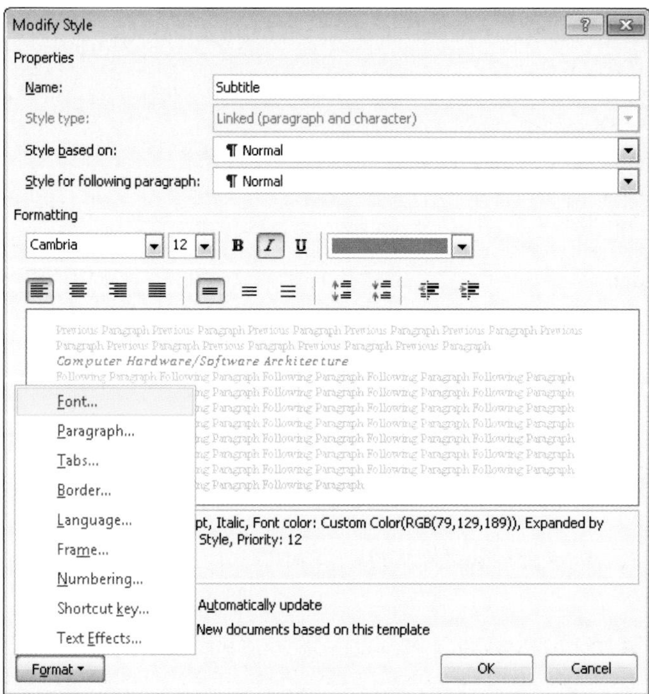

Figure 5-5

6. **Select the Small Caps check box, as shown in Figure 5-6, and then click OK to return to the Modify Style dialog box.**

Figure 5-6

Notice the Add to Quick Style List check box in the bottom-left corner of the Modify Style dialog box. This check box's status is what determines whether a particular style appears in the Quick Style gallery.

7. **Click OK to close the Modify Style dialog box.**

   The style definition is updated.

8. **Save the changes to the document.**

Leave the document open for the next exercise.

Because the Subtitle style is used only once in this document, you didn't get to see one of the biggest benefits of styles in this exercise: the fact that when you update a style, all text that has that style applied to it updates immediately. For more practice, change the definition of the Heading 1 or Heading 2 style, and watch all the instances change.

Create a new style

You can also create your own styles. This is especially useful if you want to build a template that you can give to other people to make sure that everyone formats documents the same way, such as in a group where each person assembles a different section of a report.

When you create your own styles, you can name them anything you like. Most people like to name styles based on their purposes, to make it easier to choose which style to apply. For example, *Figure Caption* would be a good name; *Style13* would not.

Just like when modifying a style, you can create a new style either by example or by manually specifying a style definition.

If you go with the definition method, you can specify some additional options that aren't available with the by-example method, such as defining which style follows this style. (In other words, if someone types a paragraph using this style and then presses Enter, what style will the next new paragraph be? The paragraph that follows a heading style is usually a body paragraph style. The paragraph that follows a body paragraph is usually another body paragraph.)

Each new style is based on an existing style (usually the Normal style) so that if there's a particular formatting aspect you don't specify, it trickles down from the parent style. For example, suppose you create a new style dubbed Important, and you base it on the Normal style. The Important style starts out with identical formatting to the Normal style, which is Calibri 11-point font. You might then modify it to have bold, red text. The definition of Important is Normal+bold+red. That's significant if you later change the definition of Normal to 12-point font. That font size change trickles down to Important automatically, and all text formatted with the Important style becomes 12 points in size.

In the following exercise, you create a new style.

Files needed: Lesson 5 Syllabus Formatted.docx, open from the preceding exercise

1. **Triple-click the first bulleted item *(CPUs and Assembly Language)* to select it.**

2. **At the bottom of the Styles pane, click the New Style button.**

   The Create New Style from Formatting dialog box opens (see Figure 5-7).

3. **In the Name box, type** Bulleted List**, and then click the Format button in the lower-left corner of the dialog box and choose Numbering.**

   The Numbering and Bullets dialog box appears.

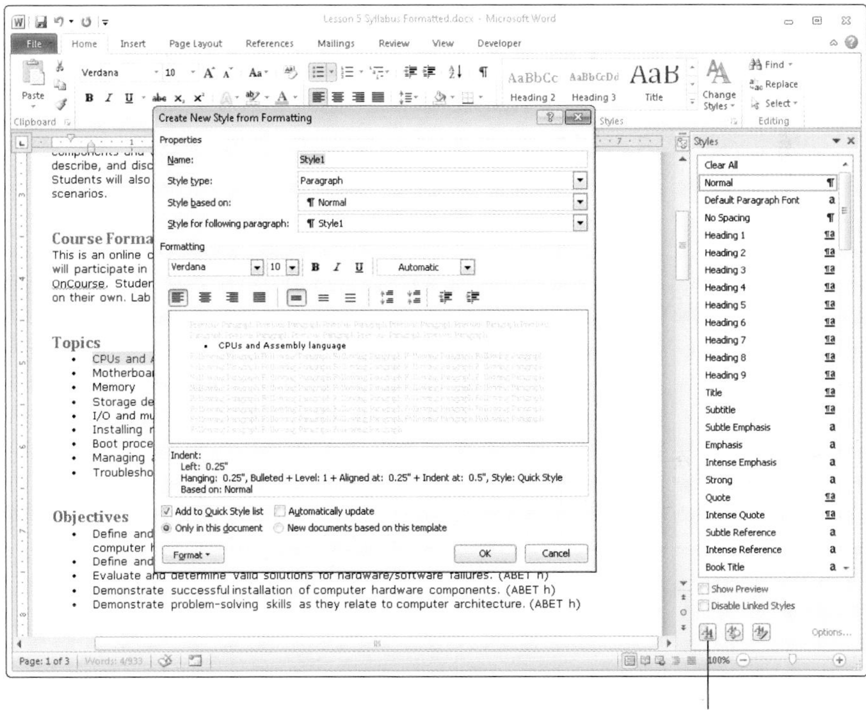

Figure 5-7

4. **Click the Bullets tab (see Figure 5-8), click the white circle bullet character, and then click OK.**
5. **Click the Format button again and choose Shortcut Key.**

   The Customize Keyboard dialog box opens.
6. **Press Ctrl+Q.**

   That key combination appears in the Press New Shortcut Key box.
7. **Open the Save Changes In drop-down list and choose Lesson 5 Syllabus Formatted.docx, as shown in Figure 5-9.**

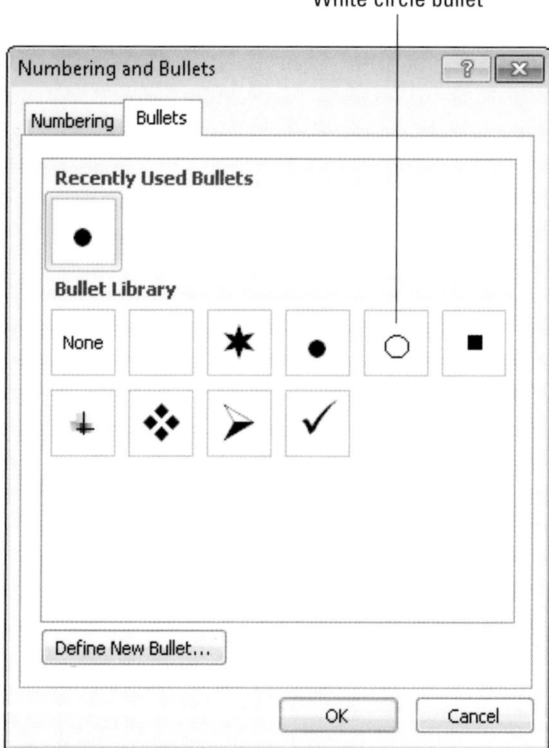

Figure 5-8

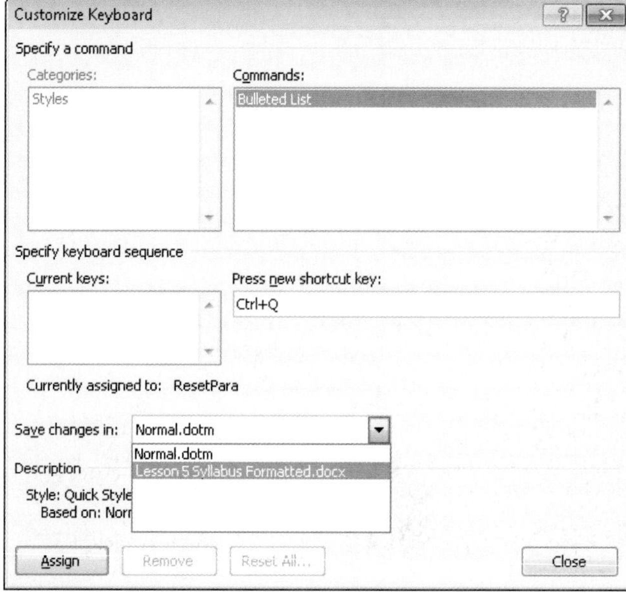

Figure 5-9

8. **Click the Assign button to assign the keyboard shortcut to the style, click Close to close the Customize Keyboard dialog box, and then click OK to accept the new style definition.**
9. **Using any method (for example, the Ctrl+Q shortcut), apply the new style, Bulleted List, to all the remaining bulleted paragraphs in the document.**
10. **Save the changes to the document and close it.**

Leave Word open for the next exercise.

Import styles from other documents

Each document stores its own styles. These styles originate from the template on which the document is based, but ultimately each document's styles are its own. So, for example, if you make a change to a style's definition in one document, or create new styles in that document, those changes, and those new styles, will not be available in any other documents.

You might, therefore, want to import styles from one document into another one to save yourself the time and effort of re-creating new styles that you want to use in both documents.

You can start in either document — the source of the styles or the destination of them — but the process is shorter by a few steps if you start in the document that already contains the styles you want to copy elsewhere.

In the following exercise, you copy styles from one document to another.

Files needed: Lesson 5 Styles.docx and Lesson 5 Syllabus Formatted.docx from previous exercises

1. **Open Lesson 5 Styles.**

   This document contains three new styles: Report Heading 1, Report Heading 2, and Report Heading 3.

You don't need to save Lesson 5 Styles with a different name because you don't modify it in this exercise.

2. **On the Home tab, click the dialog box launcher in the Styles group to open the Styles pane and then click the Manage Styles button at the bottom (see Figure 5-10).**

   The Manage Styles dialog box opens.

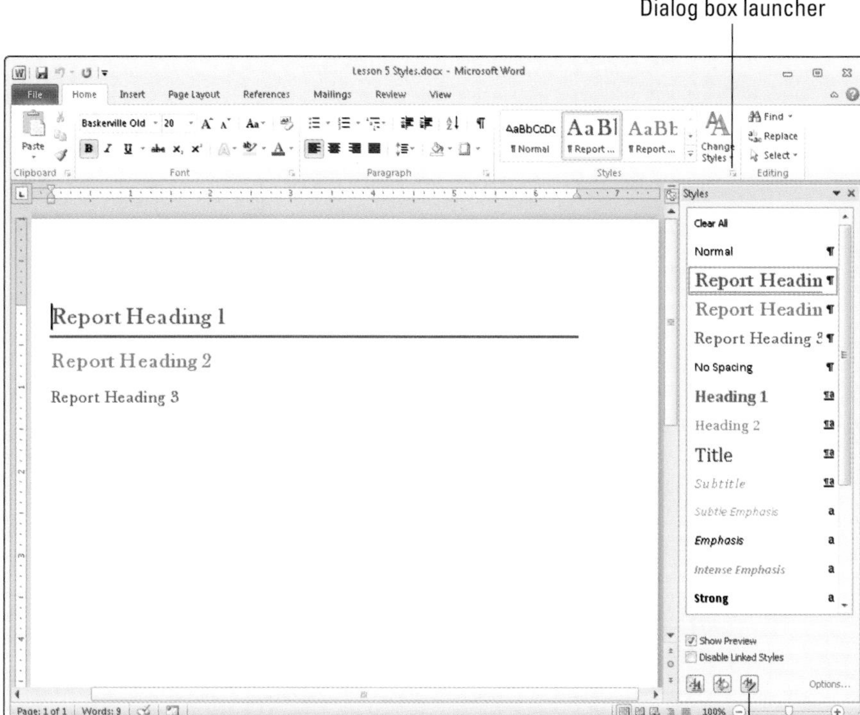

Figure 5-10

3. **At the bottom of the Manage Styles dialog box, click the Import/Export button.**

   The Organizer dialog box opens. See Figure 5-11.

4. **Click the Close File button on the right (under Normal.dotm) and then click the Open File button.**

   The Open dialog box appears.

5. **Click All Word Templates to open a list of file types and then choose All Word Documents (see Figure 5-12).**

6. **Navigate to the folder where you stored the file Lesson 5 Syllabus Formatted, select that file, and click Open.**

   A list of the styles in that document appears in the right pane. See Figure 5-13.

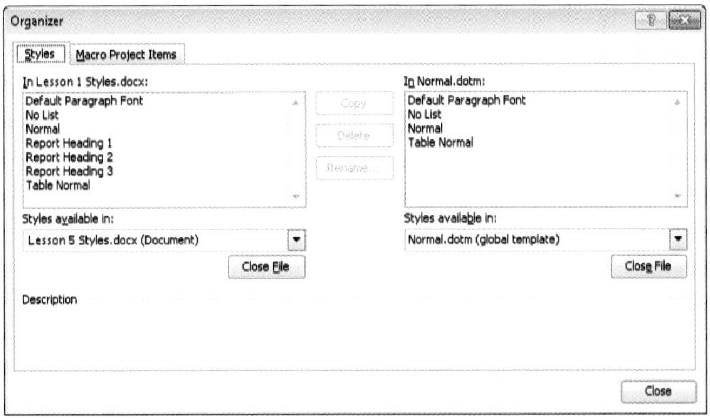

Figure 5-11

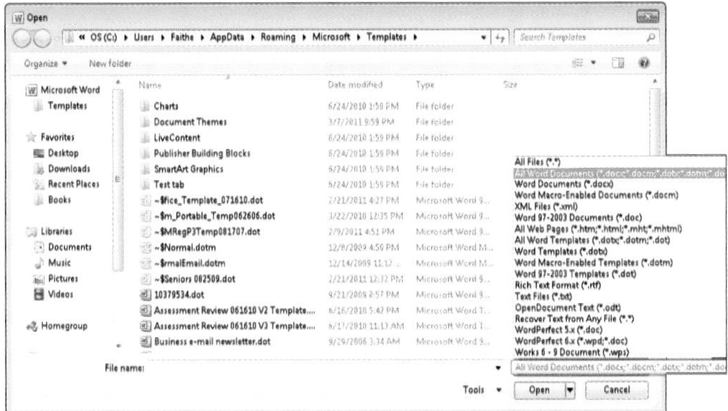

Figure 5-12

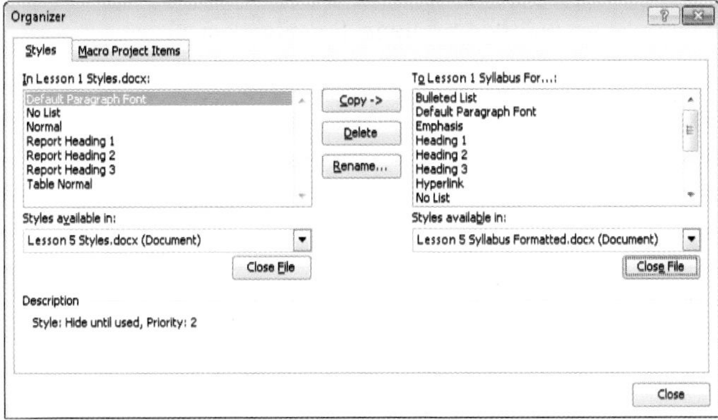

Figure 5-13

7. **Click Report Heading 1 in the left pane. Press the Shift key and click Report Heading 3.**

   All three of the custom styles are selected.

8. **Click the Copy button.**

   Those styles are copied to Lesson 5 Syllabus Formatted in the right pane.

9. **In the right pane, scroll down to confirm that the new styles appear on the list and then click Close.**

10. **If you see a prompt asking whether you want to save the changes to Lesson 5 Syllabus Formatted, click Save.**

    The styles are saved.

11. **Close Lesson 5 Styles without saving the changes.**

12. **Open Lesson 5 Syllabus Formatted, and on the Home tab, click the dialog box launcher in the Styles group, opening the Styles pane.**

13. **Scroll through the list of styles and locate the three newly copied styles (see Figure 5-14).**

Leave the document open for the next exercise.

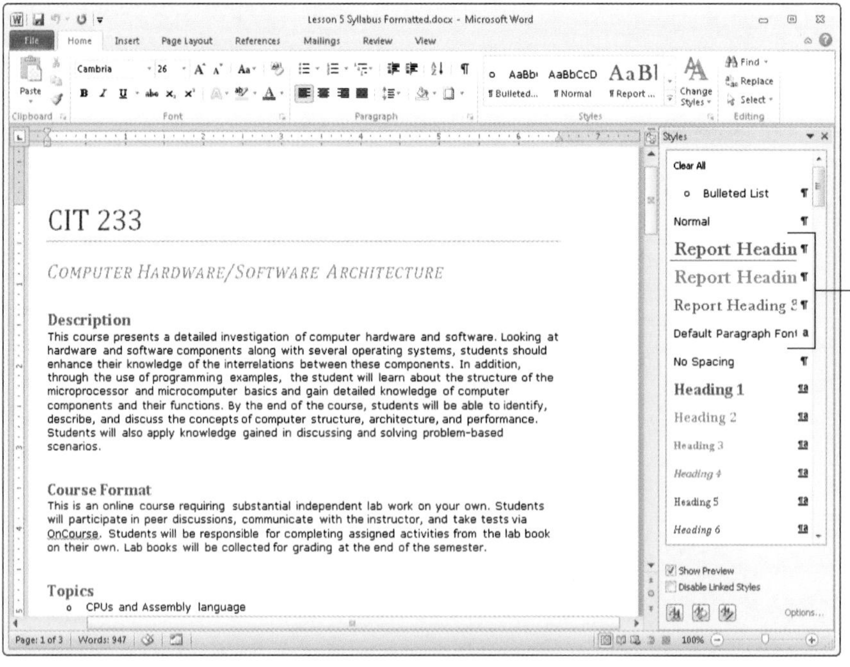

Figure 5-14

Use the Style Inspector

The Style Inspector is handy for examining the formatting that's applied to text. For example, you can see at a glance whether additional manual formatting has been applied to the text in addition to the formatting it receives from the style applied to it. You can also use the Style Inspector to quickly strip all the character or paragraph formatting for the text.

> **LINGO**
>
> The **Style Inspector** is a floating pane you can enable that shows what paragraph-level and text-level formatting is applied to the selected text.

In the following exercise, you use the Style Inspector to check the formatting on some text.

Files needed: Lesson 5 Syllabus Formatted.docx, open from the preceding exercise

1. **If the Styles pane is not already visible, on the Home tab, click the dialog box launcher in the Styles group to display it.**
2. **At the bottom of the Styles pane, click the Style Inspector button.**

   The Style Inspector pane opens. See Figure 5-15.

Dialog box launcher

Style Inspector button

Figure 5-15

3. **Click in the *CIT 233* paragraph if the insertion point is not already there.**

   The Style Inspector shows that the paragraph formatting is the Title style and the text-level formatting is the default paragraph font with no additional formatting, as shown in Figure 5-15.

4. **Press the down-arrow key once to move the insertion point to the next paragraph.**

   Its information appears in the Style Inspector window. See Figure 5-16.

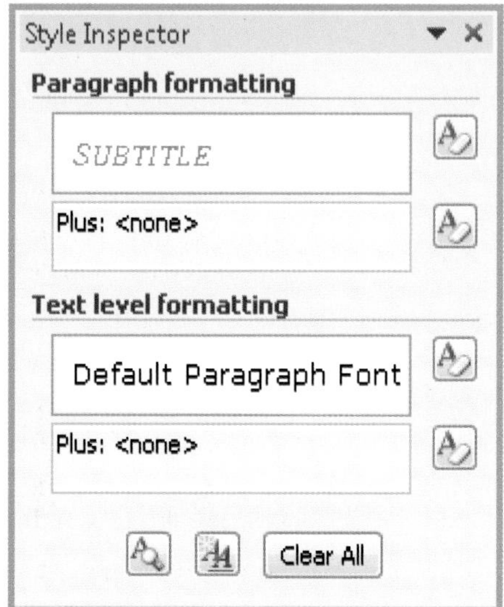

Figure 5-16

5. **Click the Reveal Formatting button at the bottom of the Style Inspector pane.**

   A Reveal Formatting pane appears, showing details about the formatting of the text where the insertion point currently rests. See Figure 5-17.

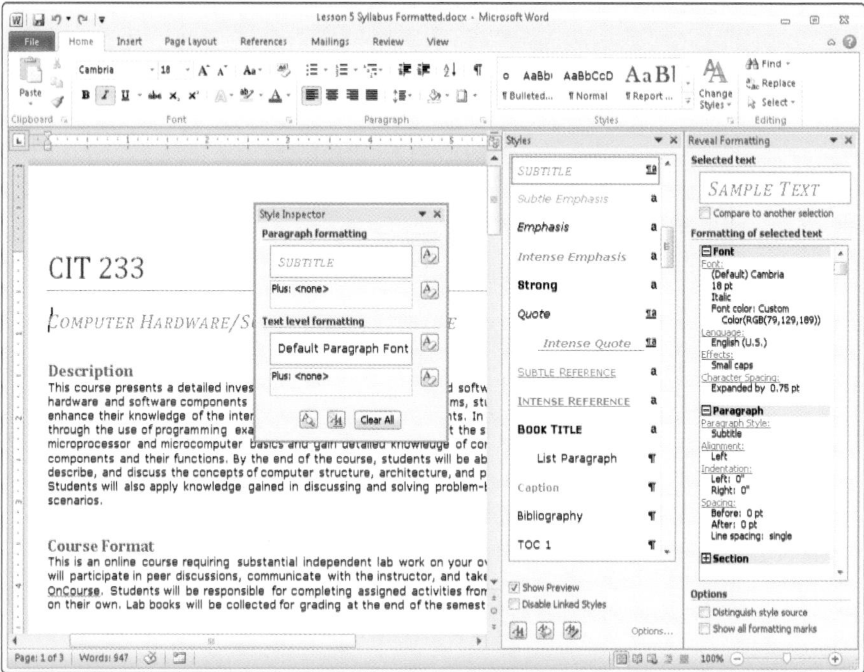

Figure 5-17

6. **Triple-click the paragraph to select all the text in it and then change the font size to 12.**
7. **Look in the Reveal Formatting task pane at the font size, which shows 12 points.**
8. **In the Style Inspector, click the Clear Character Formatting button.**

   The font size changes because the definition of the Subtitle style calls for 18-point font. See Figure 5-18.
9. **In the Style Inspector pane, click the Reset to Normal Paragraph Style button.**

   The Subtitle style is removed from the selected text, and the text appears using Normal style.
10. **Press Ctrl+Z or click the Undo button on the Quick Access toolbar to reverse the last action.**
11. **Save the document and close it.**

Leave Word open for the next exercise.

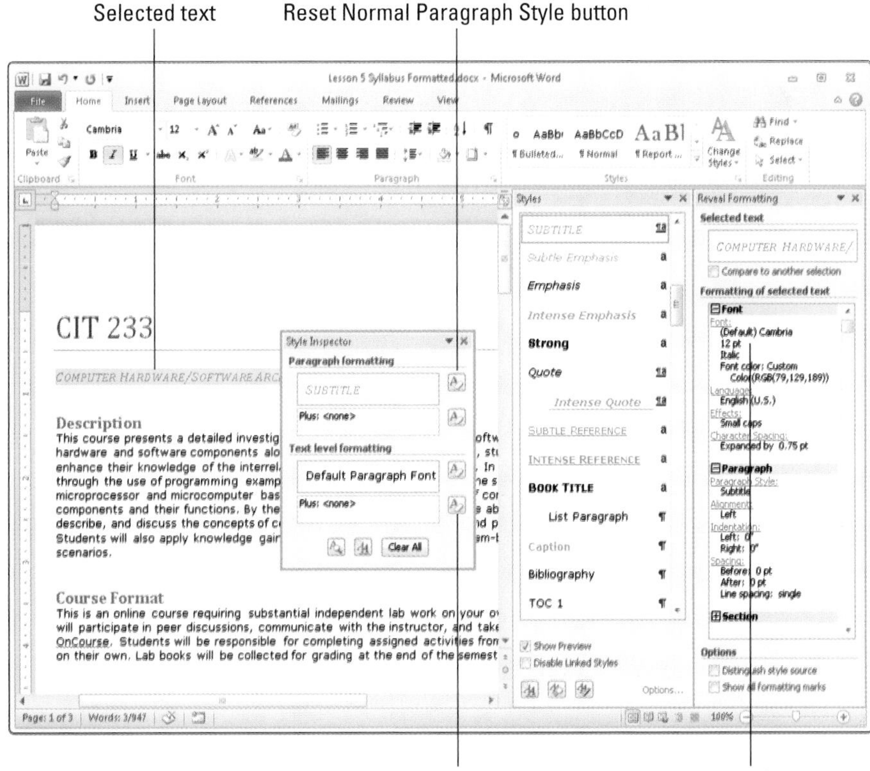

Figure 5-18

Modify and Create Templates

Every document has a template that it references. The template provides such basics as the margin settings and the definition of the Normal paragraph style. The template also may provide a list of styles. In addition, some templates also provide sample content, including text, graphics, text boxes, and hyperlinks.

> **LINGO**
>
> A **template** is a special type of document that stores formatting settings and boilerplate text on which you can base new documents.

Many templates are available via Office.com; you can select one by choosing File⇨New and then browsing the list of them. You can also customize templates to meet your own needs and even create your own templates.

Template files use a `.dotx` extension, rather than the regular `.docx` for documents. Word 2010 can also use templates from Word 2003 and earlier, which have `.dot` extensions, and macro-enabled templates, which have `.dotm` extensions.

Modify an existing template

Templates provide great shortcuts to document formatting, but if a template isn't exactly what you want it to be, you waste time each time you use it, making the same modifications over and over. For example, perhaps you find yourself changing the colors each time or filling in the same placeholders with your company's data. It is often easier to make changes to the template itself once.

In this exercise, you open a template and make changes to it, and then save the changes and start a new document based upon it.

Files needed: Lesson 5 Certificate.dotx

1. **Open the template Lesson 5 Certificate.**

   Don't just start a new document based upon it, but open the template itself. To do so:

   a. *Choose File⇨Open and then navigate to the folder containing the data files for this lesson.*

   b. *In the Open dialog box, click All Word Documents and then choose Word Templates to limit the list of files to those with a template extension (`.dotx`). See Figure 5-19.*

   c. *Click Lesson 5 Certificate.dotx and then click Open.*

   The template opens for editing.

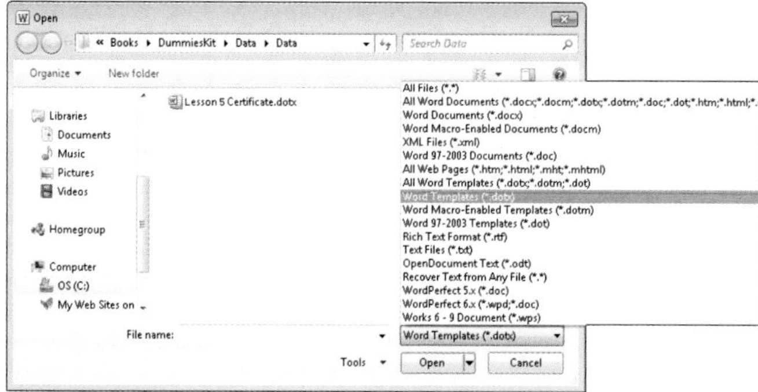

Figure 5-19

2. **Save the template file as Lesson 5 Certificate Template, in the following location, (*Username* is your Windows username):**

   `C:\Users\`*`Username`*`\AppData\Roaming\Microsoft\Templates`

3. **Triple-click the *[Your Jr. High School]* placeholder to select it and then type** Dayton Junior High School.

4. **Save the template and close it.**

5. **Choose File➪New and then click My Templates (see Figure 5-20).**

   The New dialog box opens.

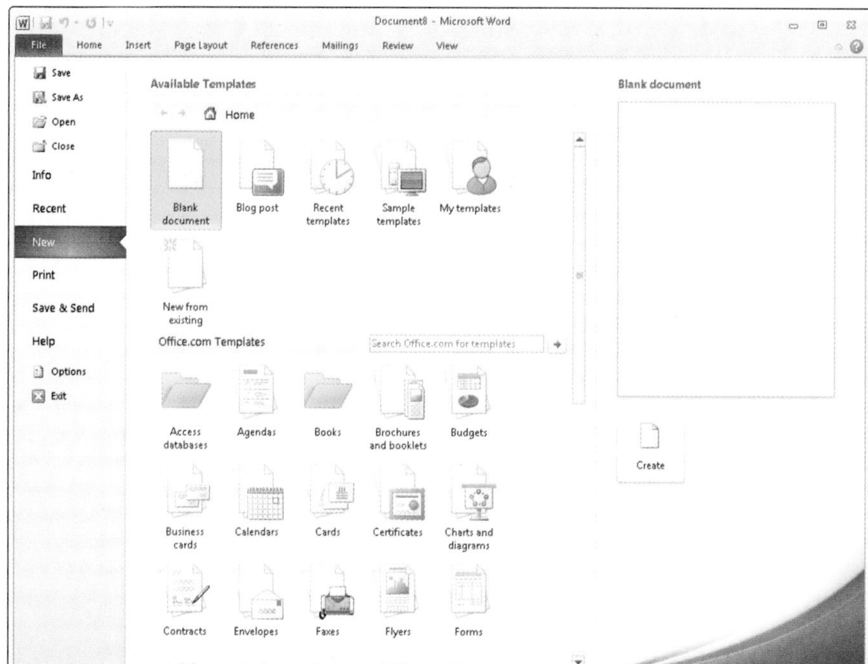

Figure 5-20

6. **Click the Lesson 5 Certificate.dotx template if it's not selected already (see Figure 5-21) and then click OK.**

   A new document opens that uses the customized version of the template.

7. **Close the new document without saving the changes to it.**

Leave Word open for the next exercise.

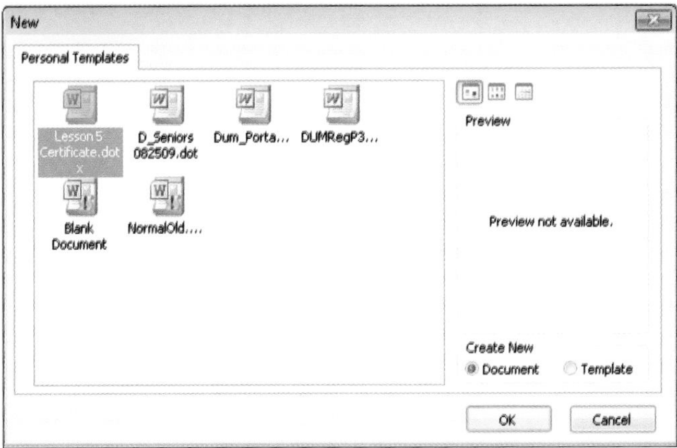

Figure 5-21

Create a new template

You can create your own templates whenever you like. These might contain sample content you've created, plus special margin settings, extra styles, or anything else that you want to reuse.

In this exercise, you create a new template with custom margin settings and a custom header.

Files needed: None

1. **Press Ctrl+N to start a new document based on the Normal template (a blank document with default settings).**
2. **Choose Page Layout⇨Margins⇨Moderate to change the document margins (see Figure 5-22).**
3. **Choose Page Layout⇨Page Color and select a pale blue (see Figure 5-23).**

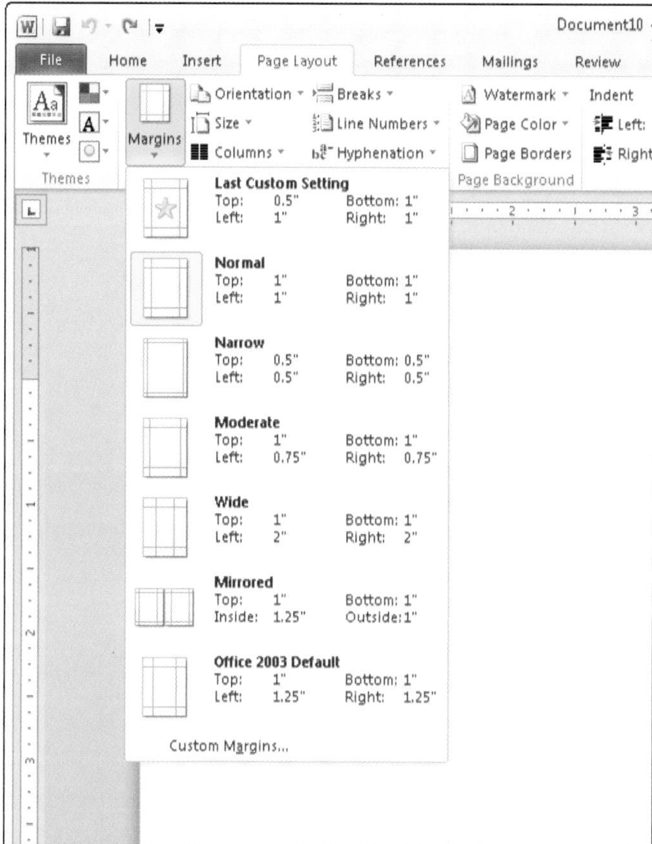

Figure 5-22

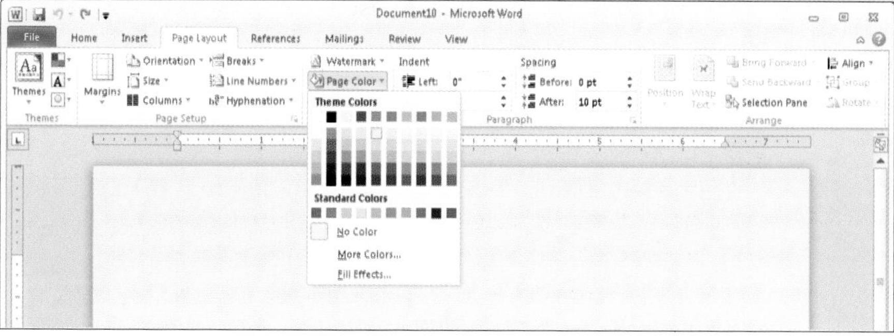

Figure 5-23

4. **Choose Insert➪Header➪Motion (Even Page) (see Figure 5-24).**

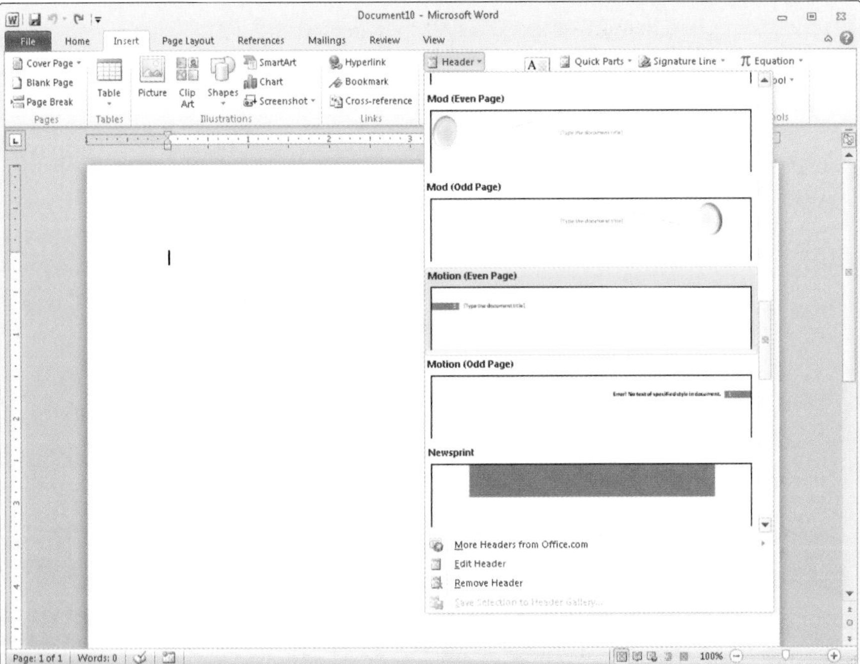

Figure 5-24

5. **Choose File➪Save & Send➪Change File Type➪Template.**
6. **Click the Save As button.**

   The Save As dialog box opens, with the appropriate file type and location already selected.

   The appropriate location is `C:\Users\`*`Username`*`\AppData\Roaming\Microsoft\Templates`. *Username* is your Windows username. If that's not the location that appears in the Save As dialog box, navigate to that location.

7. **In the File Name box, type** Lesson 5 Blue **and then click Save.**

   The new template is saved.

8. **Choose File➪Close to close the template.**
9. **Choose File➪New and then click My Templates.**

   The New dialog box opens. Your new template appears there.

10. **Click the Lesson 5 Blue template and then click OK to create a new document based upon it.**

11. **Close the new document without saving.**

Exit Word.

Summing Up

Styles and templates are two time-saving features in Word that help you easily and quickly apply consistent formatting and other settings. Here are the key points from this lesson:

- You can apply styles from the Quick Styles list on the Home tab or from the Styles pane.
- To modify a style, select it in the Styles pane, and then open its shortcut menu (right-click or use the arrow) and choose Modify.
- To create a new style, use the New Style button at the bottom of the Styles pane.
- You can define a new style by example or by manually specifying a style definition.
- To import styles from other documents, click the Manage Styles button at the bottom of the Styles pane and then click Import/Export.
- Use the Style Inspector to check a paragraph's formatting. Click the Style Inspector button at the bottom of the Styles pane to open it.
- To modify an existing template, open it in Word and make changes. Make sure you open it as a template rather than just starting a new document based upon it.
- To create a new template, format a document the way you want it and then click Save As to save it as a template.

Try-it-yourself lab

For more practice with the features covered in this lesson, try the following exercise on your own:

1. **Research a new technology or medical advance on the Internet that interests you.**
2. **Using Word, write a report that summarizes what you learned. Use Word's built-in styles to format the report (Title, Heading 1, Heading 2, and so on).**

3. **Create a new style, and name it *Body*. Format it using a different font than the Normal style uses and apply the Body style to all the body paragraphs in your document.**
4. **Center the document title at the top of the document.**
5. **Write your name above the title, format it with the Subtitle style, and right-align it. Then redefine the Subtitle style to include the right-alignment.**
6. **Save your document as Lesson 5 Lab Report.**
7. **Delete all the text from the document and save the empty document (containing the different style definitions) as a template dubbed Lab Reports.**
8. **Close Word, saving all changes if prompted.**

Know this tech talk

character style: A style that contains only text-level formatting.

paragraph style: A style that contains paragraph-level formatting; it may or may not also contain text-level formatting.

Quick Style gallery: A short list of commonly used styles appearing on the Home tab.

style: A named set of formatting specifications stored with a template or document.

Style Inspector: A floating pane you can enable that shows what paragraph-level and text-level formatting is applied to the selected text.

Lesson 6

Working with Pages and Sections

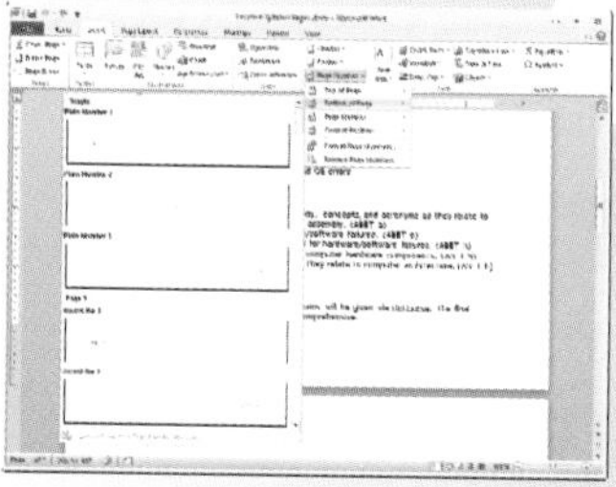

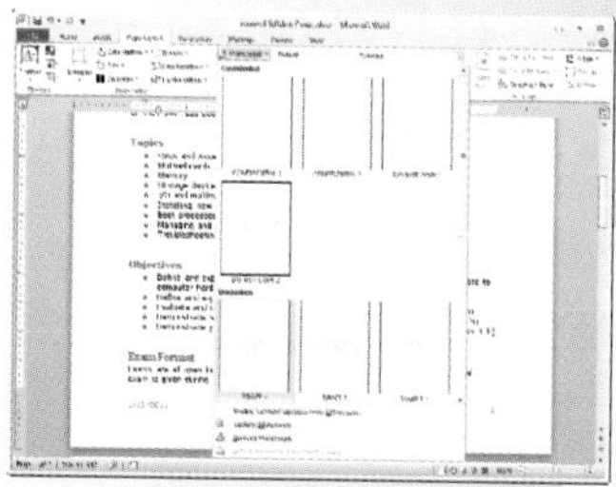

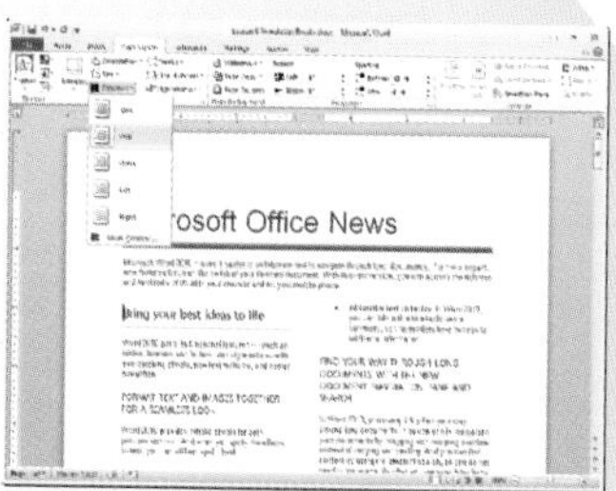

- Adding a page border or background makes a text-heavy page look more attractive and graphical.
- Headers and footers enable you to place repeated information at the top or bottom of each page, respectively.
- Inserting section breaks in a document enables you to use different page settings for different parts of the same document.
- Formatting text in multiple columns allows you to create interesting and complex newsletter-type layouts.

This lesson covers a variety of page-level formatting techniques. You learn how to apply a page border to a document, use page backgrounds, and set a page's vertical alignment. You also learn how to place running headers and footers on every page of a document, how to number pages, and many more useful page-layout skills.

Format Pages

Each document has some basic properties that describe its pages, such as paper size, page orientation, and margins. You learn about these in Lesson 1. In this lesson, you look at a few of the less common page formatting settings, including borders, backgrounds, and vertical alignment.

Page settings are usually document-wide, but you can use sections (which I cover later in this lesson) to enable you to have different page border, page background, and/or vertical alignment settings within the same document.

Add a page border

Page borders are primarily for decoration; you can use any style, color, and line thickness you want. You can also apply graphical borders (or border art) that repeat a small image as a pattern.

The border art supplied with Word includes a variety of small graphics that look good when repeated around the edges of the page. One nice thing about using these, as opposed to manually placing images around the border, is that you can resize the entire border at once by changing the value in the Width box.

LINGO

A **page border** is a border that appears outside the margins on each page. **Border art** is a repeated small image that forms a border around the outside of the document margins.

In the following exercise, you create several types of page borders.

Files needed: None

1. **Start Word, if necessary. If a blank document is not already onscreen, press Ctrl+N to create one. Save the document as Lesson 6 Pages.**
2. **Choose Page Layout➪Page Borders.**

   The Borders and Shading dialog box opens with the Page Border tab selected.
3. **In the Style section, scroll down and select the double wavy line; from the Color drop-down list, choose Purple, Accent 4.**
4. **If a preview of a purple wavy line doesn't appear in the Preview area, click the Box icon to apply the current settings to all sides of the page (see Figure 6-1).**

EXTRA INFO

Some line styles have a variety of widths you can choose from; the double wavy line you selected in Step 3 has only one width available.

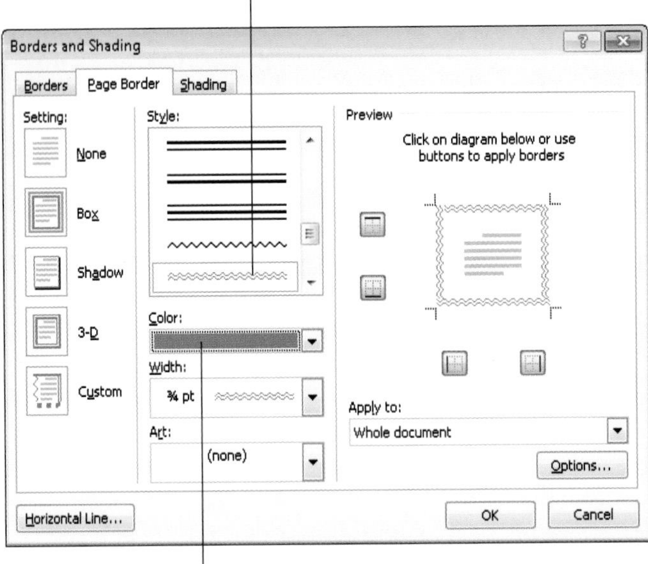

Figure 6-1

For extra practice, try clicking the None icon and then clicking one or more individual sides in the Preview area. This is how you apply a page border to only certain sides of the page. When you're done experimenting with that, click the Box icon again to apply the border to all sides again.

5. **Click OK.**

   The border is applied to the blank page. See Figure 6-2.

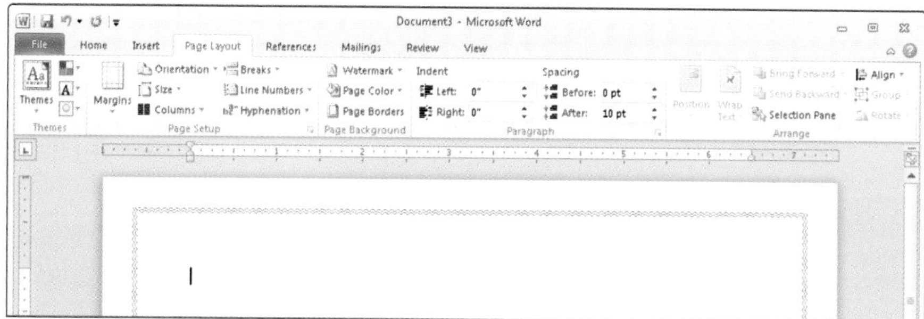

Figure 6-2

Page borders, like many page-level formatting elements, appear only in certain views. You don't see them in Draft, Web Layout, or Outline view.

6. **Choose Page Layout➪Page Borders to reopen the Borders and Shading dialog box.**
7. **From the Art drop-down list, choose the palm trees; click the down increment arrow on the Width box to set the width to 28 points; and then click OK.**

   The palm tree border is applied to the page, as shown in Figure 6-3.

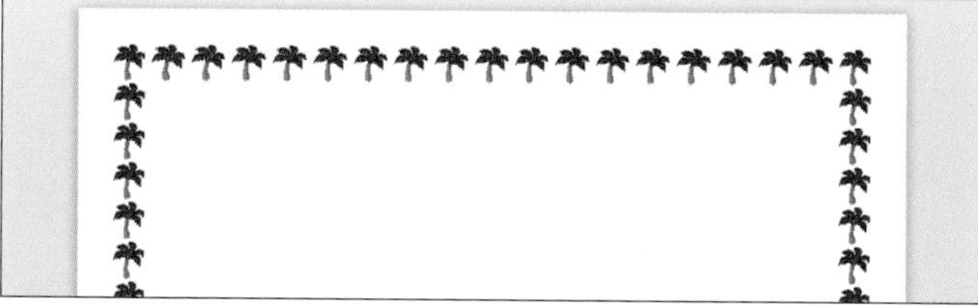

Figure 6-3

Leave the document open for the next exercise.

Apply a page background

Page backgrounds enable you to apply a color fill to the background of each page. This color fill can be a solid color, a gradient, a pattern, a texture, or even a picture. By default, this background doesn't print, but you can change Word's settings to make the background print if you want. In Word 2010, the page background is referred to as the page color.

Printing the background may use a lot of ink in your printer. This can get expensive, especially if you use an inkjet printer.

LINGO

A **page background,** or **page color,** is a fill to the background of a page.

In the following exercise, you apply a page background and set up Word to print it.

Files needed: Lesson 6 Pages.docx, open from the preceding exercise

1. **In the Lesson 6 Pages document, choose Page Layout➪Page Color.**

   A palette of colors appears. See Figure 6-4.

2. **Click any color you like.**

   The page background changes to that color.

3. **Choose Page Layout➪Page Color➪More Colors.**

   The Colors dialog box opens.

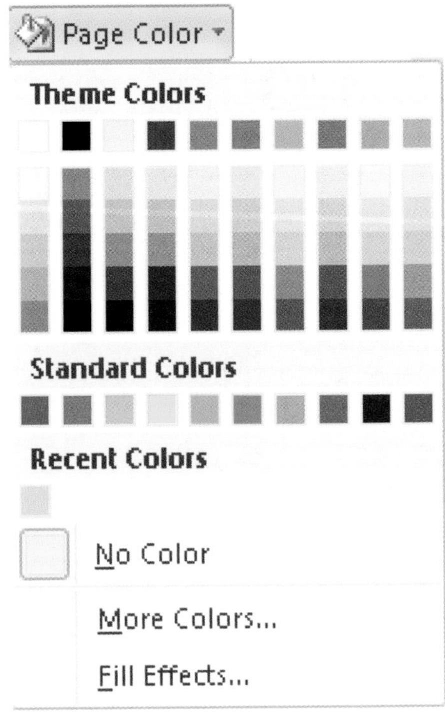

Figure 6-4

4. **Click the Custom tab; enter the following values: Red 230, Green 230, Blue 100 (see Figure 6-5); and then click OK.**

   The background changes to a shade of yellow.

5. **Choose Page Layout➪Page Color➪Fill Effects.**

   The Fill Effects dialog box opens.

6. **Click the Texture tab, click the Newsprint texture (see Figure 6-6), and then click OK.**

   The background changes to the Newsprint texture.

If you have your own texture files, you can use them. Click the Other Texture button to browse for the files on your hard drive.

7. **Choose Page Layout➪Page Color➪Fill Effects.**

   The Fill Effects dialog box opens.

8. **Click the Gradient tab and then select the Preset option.**

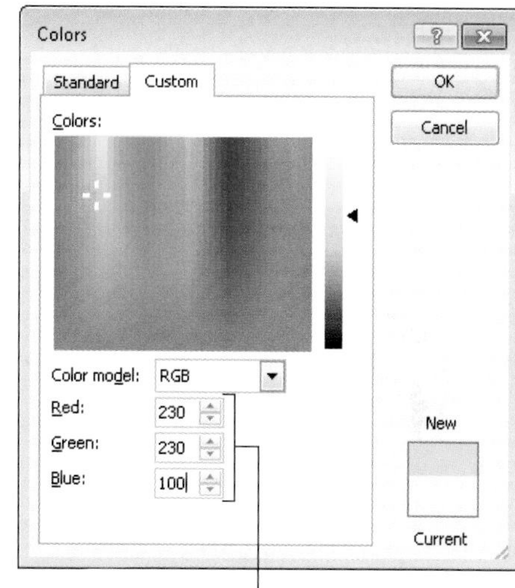

Figure 6-5

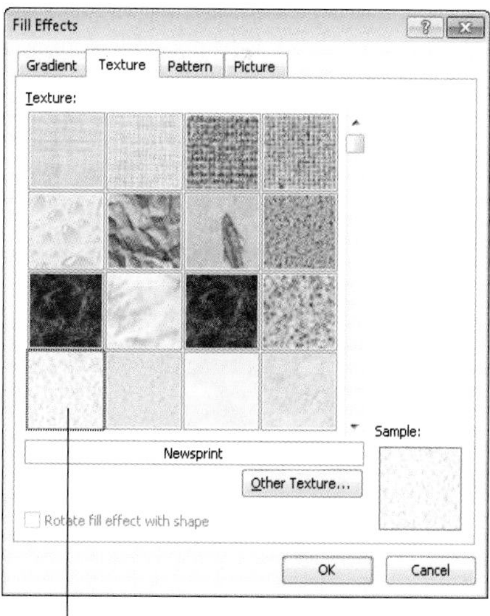

Figure 6-6

9. **From the Preset Colors drop-down list, choose Calm Water; in the Shading Styles area, select Diagonal Up (see Figure 6-7); and then click OK to apply the gradient background to the document.**

You can also define your own gradients by selecting One Color or Two Colors and then picking the colors to use. For more practice, try creating a gradient out of two of your favorite colors.

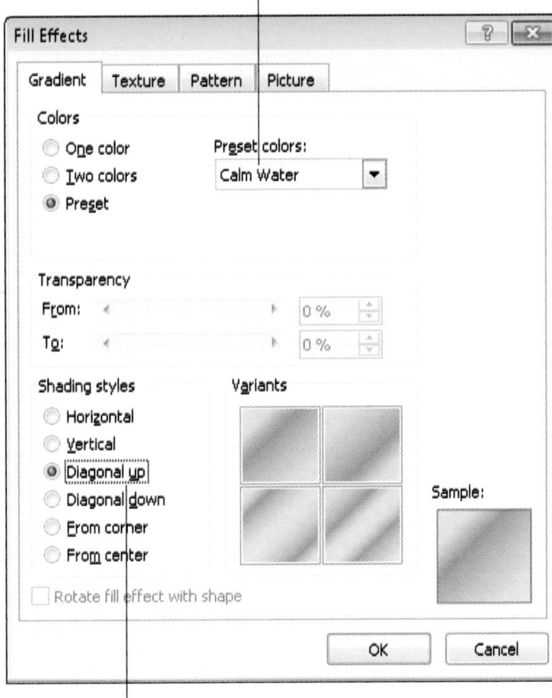

Figure 6-7

10. **Choose File⇨Print.**

    Notice that the print preview doesn't include the background.

11. **Click the Home tab to leave Backstage view.**
12. **Choose File⇨Options and click the Display tab.**
13. **Select the Print Background Colors and Images check box (see Figure 6-8) and then click OK.**
14. **Choose File⇨Print again.**

    Notice that this time print preview does include the background.

15. **Click the Home tab to leave Backstage view without printing, repeat Steps 12–13, and deselect the Print Background Colors and Images check box.**
16. **Save the document and close it.**

Leave Word open for the next exercise.

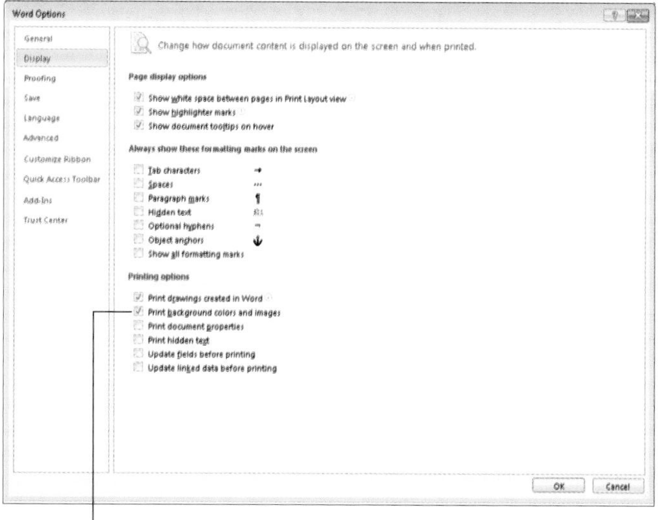

Mark this check box

Figure 6-8

Set vertical alignment for the page

As you learn in Lesson 4, each paragraph has a horizontal alignment setting such as left-aligned, right-aligned, centered, or justified. This setting controls where the paragraph aligns in relation to the left and right margins.

Similarly, a document page has a vertical alignment that determines how the page's content aligns in relation to the top and bottom margins. The default setting is Top, which means the text begins at the top margin, but you can change that. For example, when typing a business letter or making a poster or sign, you might want the text centered vertically.

Vertical alignment is the way the page's content aligns with the top and bottom margins.

In the following exercise, you set the vertical alignment in a document.

Files needed: Lesson 6 Sign.docx

1. **Open the Lesson 6 Sign document and save it as Lesson 6 Door Sign.**
2. **Choose View⇨One Page so you can see the entire page at once.**

   Notice the text is top-aligned on the page.

3. **On the Page Layout tab, click the dialog box launcher in the Page Setup group.**

   The Page Setup dialog box opens.

4. **Click the Layout tab, choose Center from the Vertical Alignment drop-down list (see Figure 6-9), and then click OK.**

   The text is centered vertically on the page.

5. **Save the document and close it.**

Leave Word open for the next exercise.

Set vertical alignment to Center

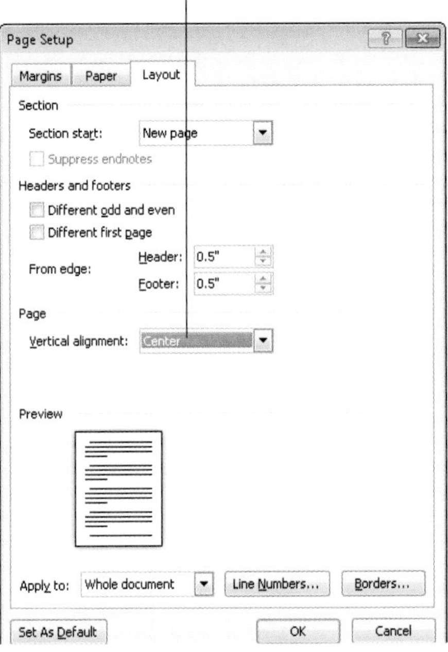

Figure 6-9

Use Headers and Footers

The header is the area at the top of a page, and the footer is the area at the bottom, outside of the top and bottom margins. Every document has a header and footer area, which are both empty by default. The header and footer appear in Print Layout view, Full Screen Reading view, and Web Layout view, and also on the printed page. (If you're in Draft view, you might want to switch to Print Layout view to follow along in this section more easily.)

> **LINGO**
>
> **Headers** and **footers** contain content that repeats at the top and bottom of each page, respectively, outside of the top and bottom margins.

You can place text in the header and footer that repeats on every page, and you can insert a variety of codes in them that display information like page numbers, dates, and times.

Number the pages

Have you ever dropped a stack of papers that needed to stay in a certain order? If the pages were numbered, putting them back together was fairly simple. If not, what a frustrating, time-consuming task.

Fortunately, Word makes it very easy to number your document pages. And you can choose from a variety of numbering styles and formats. When you number pages in Word, you don't have to manually type the numbers onto each page. Instead, you place a code in the document that numbers the pages automatically. Sweet!

When you use the Page Numbering feature in Word, it automatically inserts the proper code in either the header or the footer so that each page is numbered consecutively.

Page numbers are visible only in Print Layout view, Full Screen Reading view, Print Preview, and on the printouts themselves. You don't see the page numbers if you're working in Draft view or Web Layout view, even though they're there.

In the following exercise, you place a page numbering code in a document's footer.

Files needed: Lesson 6 Syllabus.docx

1. **Open the Lesson 6 Syllabus document and save it as Lesson 6 Syllabus Pages.**
2. **Choose Insert⇨Page Number⇨Bottom of Page⇨Plain Number 3 (see Figure 6-10).**

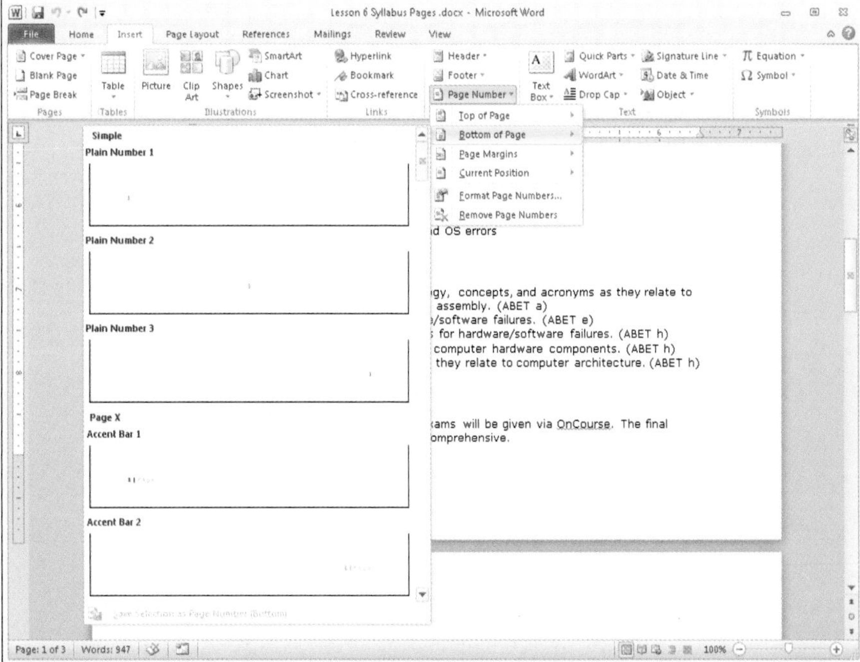

Figure 6-10

A page number code is placed at the right side of the footer, and the footer becomes active. See Figure 6-11.

You can't edit the body of the document while you're in this mode. To resume working within the main part of the document, double-click the main document (anywhere below the header or above the footer).

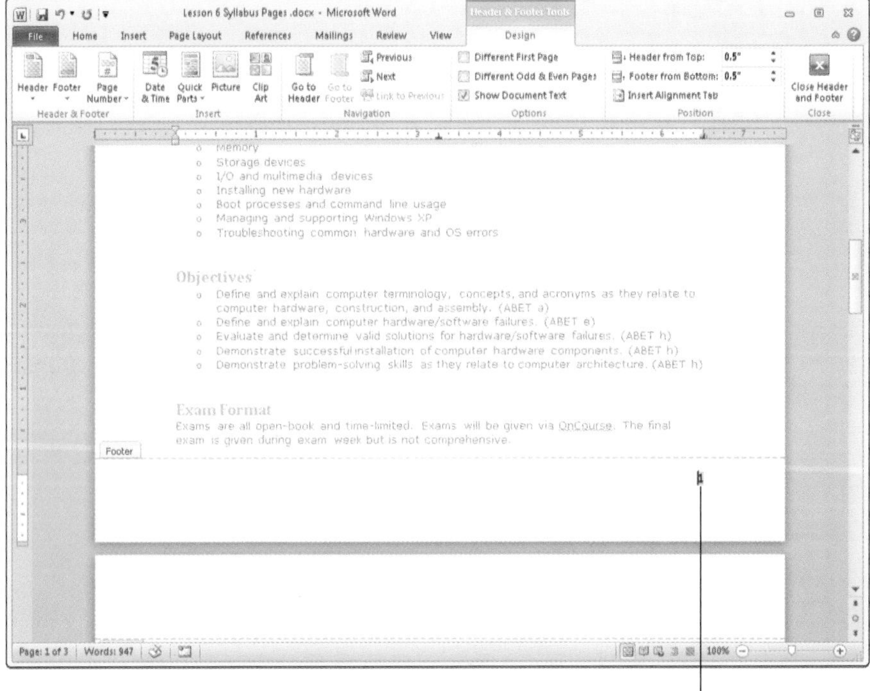

Figure 6-11

The page number code is gray when you select it; that's your clue that it's a code and not regular text.

3. **Double-click anywhere in the main part of the document to leave the footer.**

   The body of the document becomes editable again, and the actual page numbers appear at the bottoms of the pages.

For more practice, choose Insert⇨Page Number⇨Remove Page Numbers to undo the page number insertion and then choose a different preset from the Bottom of Page submenu. Not all the presets are plain; some of them add formatting.

Leave the document open for the next exercise.

Notice in Figure 6-10 the other page number position options instead of Bottom of Page:

- **Top of Page:** Places the page number code in the *header* (at the top of the page). The page numbers appear on every page.
- **Page Margins:** Places the page number code on the side of the page. The page numbers appear on every page.
- **Current Position:** Places the page number code at the insertion point in the document (as a one-time thing). Because the code is not in the header or footer, it doesn't repeat on each page. You might use this to create a cross-reference to content that's on another page, for example.
- **Format Page Numbers:** Opens a dialog box where you can fine-tune the formatting of the page numbering code, such as using Roman numerals or letters instead of digits.
- **Remove Page Numbers:** Removes existing page numbering code(s).

Use a header or footer preset

In addition to a page number, you can put other content in the header and footer areas of your document. For example, if you're typing the minutes of a club meeting, you might want to put the club's name in the header so that it appears across the top of each page.

Here are two ways of putting content into them: You can use presets to insert codes and formatting, or you can type text and insert codes manually into the headers and footers.

In the following exercise, you use a header preset.

Files needed: Lesson 6 Syllabus.docx, open from the preceding exercise

1. **In the Lesson 6 Syllabus document, choose Insert⇨Header⇨Alphabet.**

   Placeholder text and a colored bar appear in the Header section, and the Header section becomes active. See Figure 6-12.

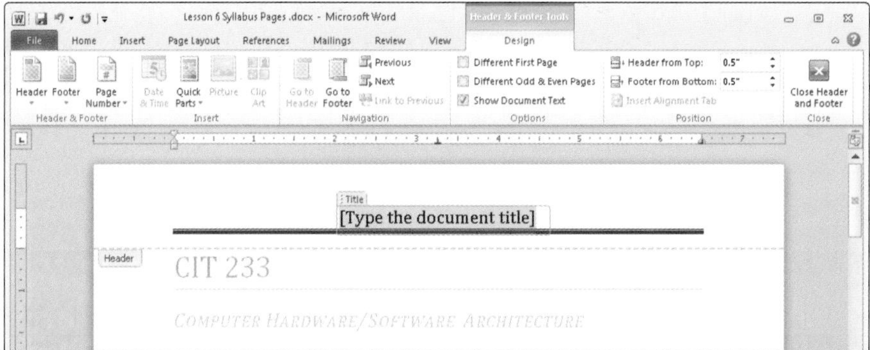

Figure 6-12

Some of the presets for headers and footers also insert a page-numbering code. This saves you the step of inserting the page-numbering code separately.

2. **Click in the *Type the document title* placeholder and then type** CIT 233 Syllabus**.**
3. **Choose Header & Footer Tools Design➪Close Header and Footer.**

   This is an alternate way of returning to normal editing mode.

Leave the document open for the next exercise.

Create a custom header or footer

The header and footer presets are great if they happen to match what you want to place there, but you can also create your own custom headers and footers that contain the exact combination of text and codes that you need. To do so, open the header or footer, click in it, and then type the text you want. Use the buttons on the Header & Footer Tools Design tab to insert codes.

In the following exercise, you create a custom footer that uses a combination of date/time codes, page numbers, and typed text.

Files needed: Lesson 6 Syllabus.docx, open from the preceding exercise

1. **In the Lesson 6 Syllabus document, double-click at the bottom of the first page to open the footer and move the insertion point into it.**
2. **Select the page number that's already there and press the Delete key.**
3. **Press the Backspace key twice to move the insertion point to the left side of the footer.**

4. **Choose Header & Footer Tools Design⇨Date & Time.**

   The Date and Time dialog box opens (see Figure 6-13).

5. **Make sure that the Update Automatically check box is selected, click the first date format on the list, and then click OK.**

   A code for the date appears in the footer.

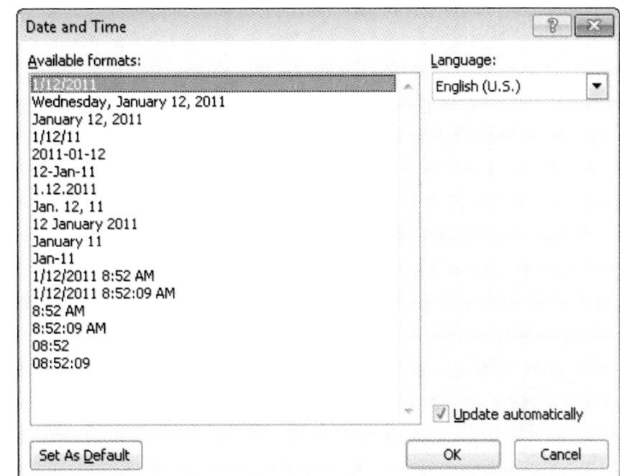

Figure 6-13

You can tell it's a code, rather than plain text, because when you point to it, it appears with a gray background.

6. **Right-click the date code and choose Toggle Field Codes.**

   This lets you see the code that creates the date. See Figure 6-14.

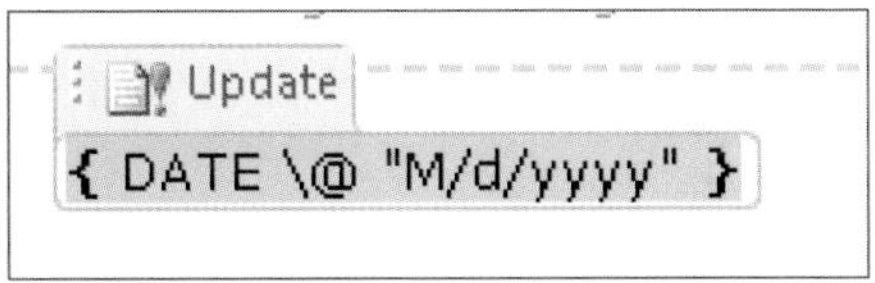

Figure 6-14

7. **Click in the date code and click the Update text that appears above it.**

   The date code is updated and returns to showing the date itself rather than the code.

8. **Click to the right of the date code to move the insertion point there and then press the Tab key to move to the center of the footer.**

9. **Type** Lawrence College **and press Tab to move to the right of the footer.**

The headers and footers have preset tab stops — a center-aligned one in the center, and a right-aligned one at the right. When you press Tab in Steps 8 and 9, you're moving to those existing tab stops.

10. **Choose Header & Footer Tools Design⇨Page Number⇨Current Position⇨Plain Number.**

    A page number code is inserted.

If you're curious about the code behind the page number, right-click it and choose Toggle Field Codes, as you did with the date in Step 6.

11. **Choose Header & Footer Tools Design➪Close Header and Footer and then choose File➪Print and check the preview at the right.**

    Notice that the codes in the footer produce today's date and the current page number on each page.

12. **Click the Home tab to leave Backstage view without printing.**

Leave the document open for the next exercise.

In a complex document, you can get very fancy with headers and footers. For example, you can choose to have a different header and footer on the first page, and you can have different headers and footers on odd and even pages. That's handy when you're printing a double-sided booklet, for example, so the page numbers can always be on the outside edges. To set either of those options, select their check boxes on the Header & Footer Tools Design tab. See Figure 6-15.

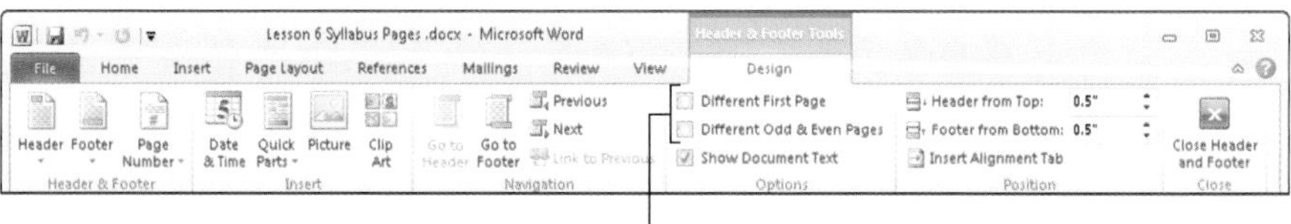

You can use these options to apply different headers and footers.

Figure 6-15

You can also create section breaks, and have a different header and footer in each section. (I cover sections later in this lesson.) When you use multiple headers and footers in a document, you can move between them by clicking the Previous and Next buttons on the Header & Footer Tools Design tab.

To adjust the header and footer size and positioning, use the settings in the Position group on the Header & Footer Tools Design tab. See Figure 6-15. You can specify a Header from Top and Footer from Bottom position there. For example, if you want a taller header section, increase the Header from Top setting.

Insert a watermark

Watermarks, which display a faint picture or text phrase behind the regular text, are used for a variety of purposes in documents. Some high-end paper has an embossed logo on it, and a watermark created via computer can approximate that look. Watermarks are also used to mark documents with designations, such as DRAFT or CONFIDENTIAL.

> **LINGO**
>
> A **watermark** is a faint image that appears behind the regular text on the page.

Watermarks are stored in a document's header/footer, so you can edit a watermark, including adjusting its position, when in Header and Footer editing mode.

In the following exercise, you place a watermark on a document.

Files needed: Lesson 6 Syllabus.docx, open from the preceding exercise

1. **In the Lesson 6 Syllabus document, choose Page Layout⇨Watermark⇨Draft 1.**

   See Figure 6-16. DRAFT appears in gray behind the text on each page.

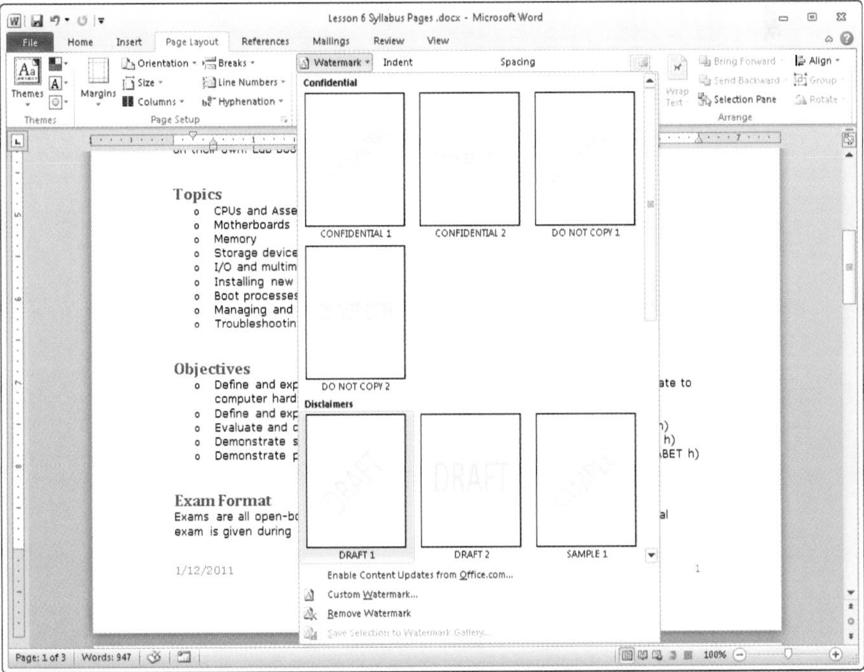

Figure 6-16

2. **Choose Page Layout⇨Watermark⇨Remove Watermark.**
3. **Choose Page Layout⇨Watermark⇨Custom Watermark.**

   The Printed Watermark dialog box opens.
4. **Select the Text Watermark option; in the Text box, delete the existing text and type** Lawrence College **(see Figure 6-17); and then click OK.**

   The watermark is inserted.

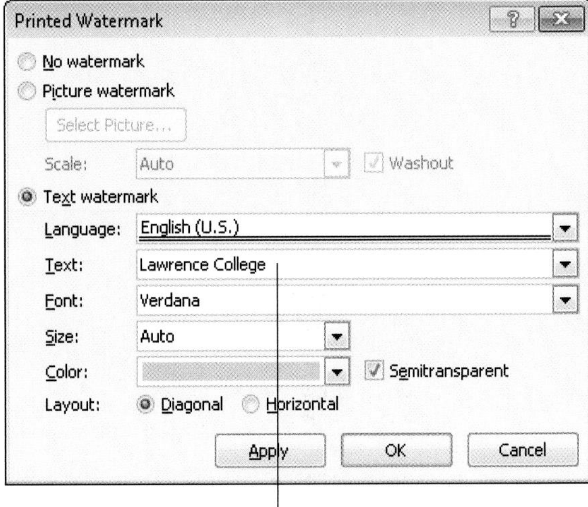

Figure 6-17

5. **Double-click the document's header area to enter Header and Footer editing mode and then click the watermark.**

   Notice that selection handles appear around the watermark.

A watermark is really just a piece of WordArt; you can edit its text, including rotating it, changing its color, and so on, as you would any WordArt. Notice that the WordArt Tools Format tab becomes available when you select the watermark.

6. **Choose WordArt Tools Format⇨Shape Fill and then click the Red, Accent 2, Lighter 80% color (see Figure 6-18).**

For more practice, try some of the other WordArt formatting options on the watermark, such as WordArt Styles or Change Shape.

7. **Choose Header & Footer Tools Design⇨Close Header and Footer to return to normal editing.**
8. **Save the document and close it.**

Leave Word open for the next exercise.

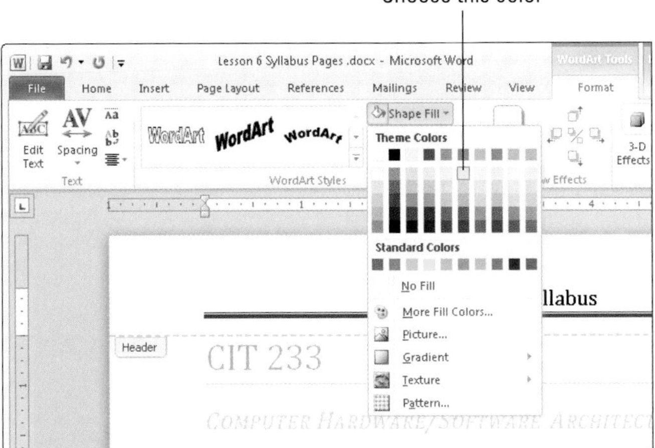

Figure 6-18

Work with Multi-Section Documents

You can set many page layout properties, such as margins, number of columns, headers and footers, paper size, and page orientation, for the entire document. However, in some situations, you might like to have different page layout settings within the same document, such as with a letter and envelope stored together in one file.

> **LINGO**
>
> A **section break** is a non-printing marker in a document that indicates where new settings, such as different margins, page orientation, or column numbers, should take effect.

When you need to have different page layout settings in the same document, you can create a section break. A section break enables you to define different settings for different areas of a document.

View section breaks and other hidden characters

Word automatically creates section breaks when you use certain features, so you may have created section breaks in the past and not realized it. For example, when you add an envelope to the document, which I cover in Lesson 9, a section break is automatically inserted to separate the envelope from the letter. When you select some paragraphs and choose a different number of columns for them, as you learn later in this lesson, section breaks are created before and after the selected paragraphs, and the new number-of-columns setting is applied to only the midsection between the two section breaks. There are lots of examples within Word of features that create section breaks automatically for you.

In the following exercise, you view a section break and turn on the display of other hidden characters.

Files needed: Lesson 6 Envelope.docx

1. **Open the Lesson 6 Envelope document and then choose View⇨Draft to switch to Draft view.**

   A section break line becomes visible between the envelope text and the letter text.

2. **On the Home tab, click the Show/Hide button.**

   Hidden characters, such as paragraph breaks and line breaks, appear. See Figure 6-19.

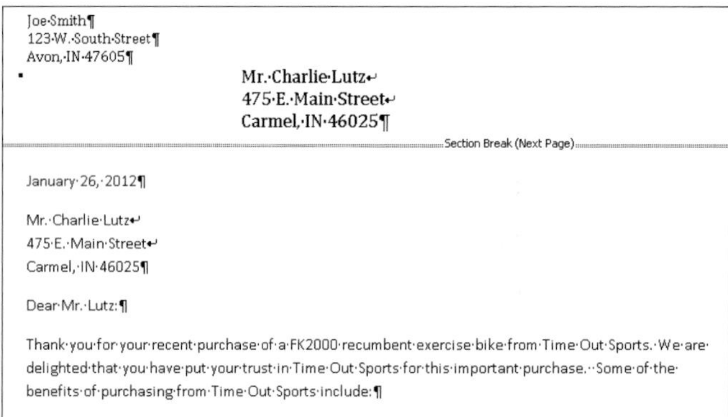

Joe·Smith¶
123·W.·South·Street¶
Avon,·IN·47605¶

Mr.·Charlie·Lutz↵
475·E.·Main·Street↵
Carmel,·IN·46025¶

Section Break (Next Page)

January·26,·2012¶

Mr.·Charlie·Lutz↵
475·E.·Main·Street↵
Carmel,·IN·46025¶

Dear·Mr.·Lutz:¶

Thank·you·for·your·recent·purchase·of·a·FK2000·recumbent·exercise·bike·from·Time·Out·Sports.·We·are·delighted·that·you·have·put·your·trust·in·Time·Out·Sports·for·this·important·purchase.··Some·of·the·benefits·of·purchasing·from·Time·Out·Sports·include:¶

Figure 6-19

3. **Click the Show/Hide button again to toggle off the hidden characters and then choose View⇨Print Layout to switch back to Print Layout view.**

4. **Close the document. Do not save changes if prompted.**

Leave Word open for the next exercise.

Insert a section break

Word enables you to create several types of section breaks:

- **Next page:** A combination of a section break and a page break. This starts the new section on a new page. This type was used to separate the envelope from the letter in the preceding exercise.
- **Continuous:** A section break that does not start a new page. You could use this type of break to separate a one-column masthead on a newsletter from a three-column news story beneath it, for example.
- **Even page:** Like a Next page break, except it starts the new section on an even-numbered page. If the current page is odd-numbered, it's the same as a regular Next page break. If the current page is even-numbered, it results in two page breaks.
- **Odd page:** The opposite of an Even page break. Odd starts the new section on an odd-numbered page.

In this exercise, you create a Next page section break.

Files needed: Lesson 6 Newsletter.docx

1. **Open the Lesson 6 Newsletter document and save it as Lesson 6 Newsletter Breaks.**
2. **Scroll down to the Ink heading on page 4, and the insertion point immediately before it, and choose Page Layout⇨Breaks⇨Next Page.**

   A section break and page break combo is inserted.
3. **Choose View⇨Draft to switch to Draft view so you can see the break (see Figure 6-20).**

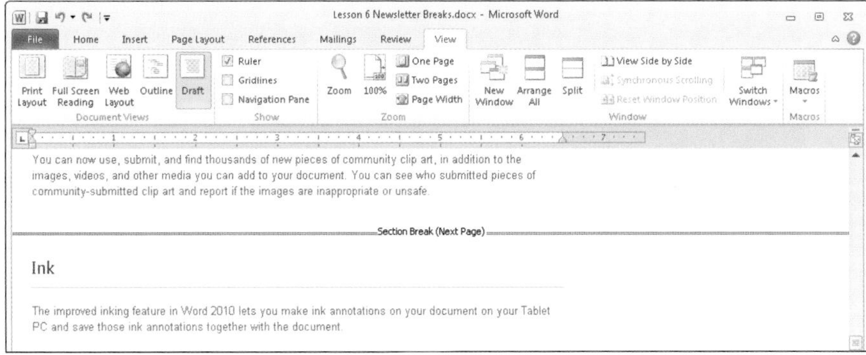

Figure 6-20

4. **Click the break to select it and then press the Delete key.**

   The break is removed.

5. **Choose View➪Print Layout to return to Print Layout view.**

Leave the document open for the next exercise.

Format Text in Multiple Columns

One of the benefits of a section break is that it lets you set certain areas of a document in different columns than the rest. You can create the section break first and then change the number of columns in that section; or you can select the text that should be differently columned and then change the column setting, and Word will create the section breaks as needed.

In this exercise, you change the Columns setting for part of a document.

Files needed: Lesson 6 Newsletter Breaks.docx, open from the preceding exercise

1. **In the Lesson 6 Newsletter Breaks document, choose View➪Draft to switch to Draft view, if you're not already in Draft view.**
2. **Scroll to the top of the first page and place the insertion point at the beginning of the *Bring your best ideas to life* heading line.**
3. **Choose Page Layout➪Breaks➪Continuous.**

   A continuous section break is inserted. Because you're in Draft view, you can see it; you couldn't see it in Print Layout view.

To check, switch to Print Layout view and then switch back to Draft view.

4. **Choose Page Layout➪Columns➪Two.**

   The text in the section that follows the section break changes to a two-column layout, and the view switches automatically to Print Layout.

For more practice, try each of the other settings on the Columns menu. Return to the Two setting when finished experimenting.

5. **Select the THE MICROSOFT OFFICE BACKSTAGE VIEW heading, and everything below it to the next heading.**
6. **Choose Page Layout⇨Columns One.**

   The selected text changes to a single-column layout; the rest of the document stays the same.
7. **Choose View⇨Draft and notice the section breaks that Word automatically inserted.**

   Continuous section breaks appear at the beginning and end of the selected text.
8. **Choose View⇨Print Layout to return to Print Layout view.**
9. **Save the document and close it.**

Exit Word.

Summing Up

Word's Page Layout features enable you to set up each page with the exact borders, margins, columns, headers, and footers you want. Here's a summary of what you learn in this lesson:

- To create a page border, choose Page Layout⇨Page Borders. You can either use a regular line as a border (with any color, thickness, and style you want), or choose one of the border art images Word provides.
- To apply a page background, choose Page Layout⇨Page Color. You can use a plain color, a pattern, a gradient, a texture, or a picture.
- To set the vertical alignment for the page layout, click the dialog box launcher in the Page Setup group on the Page Layout tab, and then on the Layout tab, set the Vertical Alignment setting.
- Choose Insert⇨Header or Insert⇨Footer to use preset headers and footers, respectively.
- Choose Insert⇨Page Number to place page numbering codes in the header or footer.
- To edit a header or footer manually, in Print Layout view, double-click the header or footer area to open it for editing.
- A watermark is a faint image that appears behind the regular text. Choose Page Layout⇨Watermark to insert one.
- Watermarks are stored in the header/footer of the document, so while the header and footer are active, you can also edit the watermark.

- You can insert section breaks by choosing Page Layout⇨Breaks. You can then apply different page layout formatting to each section.
- Section breaks are also automatically created when you select text and then change the number of columns for that text (choose Page Layout⇨Columns).

Try-it-yourself lab

For more practice with the features covered in this lesson, try the following exercise on your own:

1. **Start Word and type the title of a newsletter that you want to create.**

   The newsletter can be on any subject of interest to you. Make the title big and bold, so it stretches all the way across the page.

2. **Below the title, type a newsletter article.**
3. **Using section breaks and the Columns feature, format the article so that it appears in three columns under the newsletter title, while the title itself remains in one column.**
4. **Save your document as Lesson 6 Lab and close it.**
5. **Close all documents and exit Word.**

Know this tech talk

footer: The area below the bottom margin of a page, where repeated information can optionally be placed.

header: The area above the top margin of a page, where repeated information can optionally be placed.

page border: A border that appears outside the margins on each page of the document.

section break: A marker in a document that divides the document into multiple sections. Each section can have its own page layout settings.

vertical alignment: The alignment of the page's content in relation to its top and bottom margins.

Lesson 7

Creating and Formatting Tables

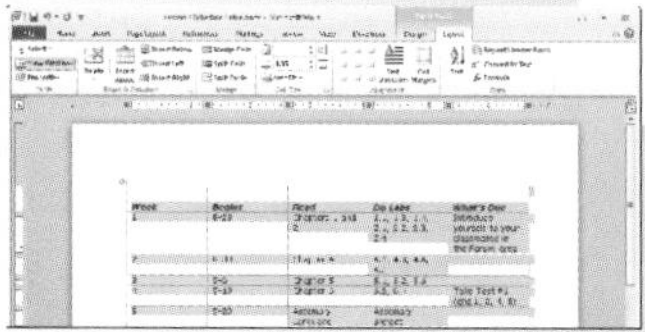

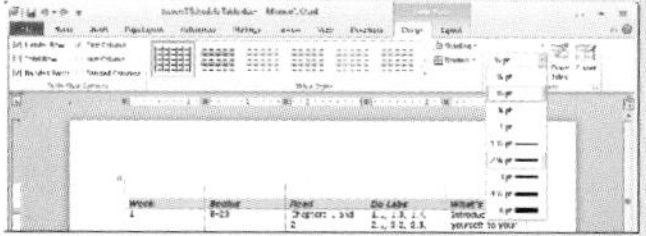

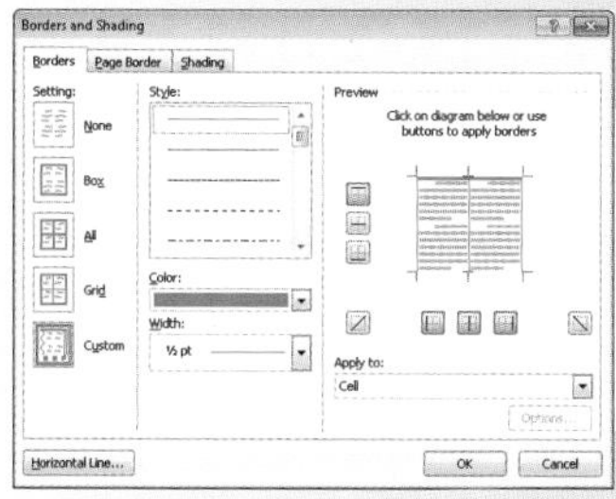

- Using tables allows you to organize complex sets of data in an orderly fashion.
- Inserting a table is an easy way to create a standard table of any size.
- Drawing a table enables you to customize the row and column dividers.
- You can resize rows and columns to make a table's structure meet your needs.
- Formatting table borders allows you to emphasize or hide certain lines of the table.

1. How do you draw a table by dragging with the mouse?

Drag yourself over to page 187

2. What is a delimited file?

Look for de answer on page 189

3. How do you convert existing text to a table?

Make the conversion on page 189

4. How can you select an entire table with one click?

Select that info from page.. 191

5. How do you resize a row or column in a table?

Check out page.. 192

6. What's the difference between borders and gridlines?

Learn the difference on page... 196

Tables are useful for displaying information in multicolumn layouts, such as address lists and schedules. You may be surprised at all the uses you can find for tables in your documents!

In this lesson, you learn how to insert tables in several ways. You also learn how to modify a table, and how to apply formatting to it that makes it easier to read and understand.

LINGO

A **table** is a grid of rows and columns, somewhat like a spreadsheet.

Create a Table

To create a table, you can either insert one as a whole or draw one line-by-line. In most cases, if you want a *standard-looking table* (that is, one with equally sized rows and columns), your best bet is to insert it. If you want an *unusual-looking table,* such as with different numbers of columns in some rows, you may be better off drawing the table.

When inserting a new table, you can specify a number of rows and columns to create a blank grid, and then fill in the grid by typing. Press the Tab key to move to the next cell. When you reach the end of the last row, you can press Tab to add a row to the table.

In the following exercise, you create a new table in two ways.

Files needed: None

1. **Start a new blank document in Word and save it as Lesson 7 Table.**
2. **Choose Insert⇨Table, and in the menu that appears with a grid, drag across the grid to select three rows and three columns, as shown in Figure 7-1, and then release the mouse button to create the table.**

Drag across the grid

Figure 7-1

For extra practice, delete the table you just inserted (press Ctrl+Z to undo the last action) and then insert the table by choosing Insert⇨Table⇨Insert Table. A dialog box where you can enter the number of rows and columns as digits opens.

3. **In the first cell of the first row, type** Name **and then press the Tab key to move to the next column.**
4. **Type** Position, **press Tab, type** Active?, **and press Tab.**

   The insertion point moves to the first cell in the next row.
5. **Type the rest of the entries shown in Figure 7-2 into the table. When you reach the bottom-left cell, press Tab again.**

   A new row appears at the bottom of the table.
6. **Click below the table to move the insertion point and then choose Insert⇨Table⇨Draw Table.**

   The mouse pointer turns into a pencil symbol.

Name	Position	Active?
Sheldon Peterson	Catcher	Yes
Brendon Lowe	Pitcher	Yes
Peter Fitzgerald	First Base	Yes
John Wilson	Second Base	No

Figure 7-2

7. **Drag to draw a box that is approximately the same height and width as the table you created earlier.**

   A box appears, and the mouse pointer remains a pencil.

8. **Drag within the box to draw three vertical lines and two horizontal lines, as shown in Figure 7-3.**

   Notice that the rightmost vertical line spans only the bottom two rows.

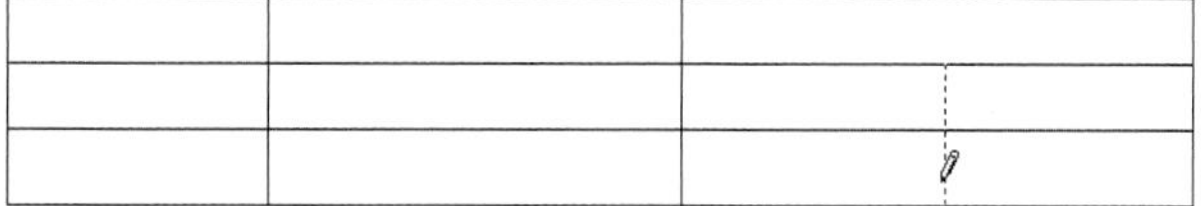

Figure 7-3

9. **Type the text shown in Figure 7-4 into the new table.**

Shift	Location	Worker	
Day	Clermont	Tom	Jones
Day	Clermont	Alice	Little

Figure 7-4

10. **Save the changes to the document and close it.**

Leave Word open for the next exercise.

Convert text to a table

If you already have some text that's separated into rows and columns with tabs, commas, or some other consistent character, you can convert it to a table with a few simple clicks.

LINGO

Delimited means separated via a consistent scheme.

For conversion to work, the existing text must be delimited with a consistent character to separate the columns. For example, the text in Figure 7-5 shows the data from the preceding exercise as a delimited text file, three columns with tab stops marking where each column should break.

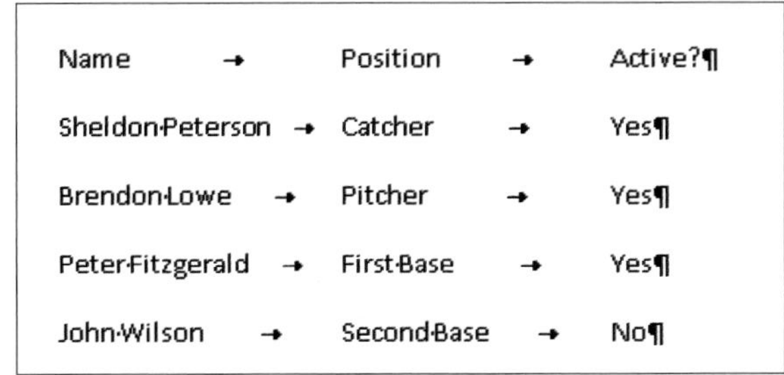

Name →	Position →	Active?¶
Sheldon Peterson →	Catcher →	Yes¶
Brendon Lowe →	Pitcher →	Yes¶
Peter Fitzgerald →	First Base →	Yes¶
John Wilson →	Second Base →	No¶

Figure 7-5

In the following exercise, you convert some existing delimited text into a table.

Files needed: Lesson 7 Schedule.docx.

1. **Open Lesson 7 Schedule and save it as Lesson 7 Schedule Table.**
2. **Select all the text in the document and then choose Insert➪Table➪Convert Text to Table.**

   The Convert Text to Table dialog box opens. See Figure 7-6.

Convert Text to Table

Table size

Number of columns: 5

Number of rows: 18

AutoFit behavior

Fixed column width: Auto

AutoFit to contents

AutoFit to window

Separate text at

Paragraphs Commas

Tabs Other: -

OK Cancel

Figure 7-6

3. **Click OK.**

   The text converts to a five-column table.
4. **Save the changes to the document.**

Leave the document open for the next exercise.

If you don't get the results you expect when converting text to a table, the problem is probably that not all rows have the same number of delimiters in them. You may be missing a tab, or have two tabs in a row, for example. Press Ctrl+Z to undo the table creation, check your column markers, and try again. You can turn on the display of hidden characters from the Home tab's Show/Hide button to make it easier to see where the tabs are.

Select rows and columns

Working with a table often involves selecting one or more cells, rows, or columns. Here are the many ways to do this:

- Drag across the cells you want to select.
- Click in the upper-left cell you want to select and then press the Shift key and press arrow keys to extend the selection.
- Click outside of the table on the left side to select an entire row.
- Click outside of the table above the table to select an entire column.
- Click the table selector icon (the four-headed arrow in a box; see Figure 7-7) in the upper-left corner of the table to select the entire table.

Week	Begins	Read	Do Labs	What's Due
1	8-23	Chapters 1 and 2	1.1, 1.3, 1.4, 2.1, 2.2, 2.3, 2.4	Introduce yourself to your classmates in the Forum area
2	8-30	Chapter 4	4.1, 4.3, 4.4, 4.5	

Figure 7-7

In the following exercise, you practice selecting various parts of a table.

Files needed: Lesson 7 Schedule Table.docx, open from the preceding exercise

1. **In Lesson 7 Schedule Table, click inside any cell of the table and then click the table selector icon (refer to Figure 7-7).**

   The entire table is selected.

2. **Click away from the table to deselect it.**

3. **Position the mouse pointer to the left of the table, next to the second row, and click.**

   That row becomes selected. See Figure 7-8.

Week	Begins	Read	Do Labs	What's Due
1	8-23	Chapters 1 and 2	1.1, 1.3, 1.4, 2.1, 2.2, 2.3, 2.4	Introduce yourself to your classmates in the Forum area
2	8-30	Chapter 4	4.1, 4.3, 4.4, 4.5	
3	9-6	Chapter 5	5.1, 5.2, 5.6	
4	9-13	Chapter 6	6.2, 6.4	Take Test #1 (chs 1, 2, 4, 5)
5	9-20	Assembly Language	Assembly project	

Figure 7-8

4. **Drag the mouse downward to row 4.**

   Rows 3 and 4 also become selected.

5. **Position the mouse pointer above the first column so the pointer becomes a black down-pointing arrow, and click.**

   The first column becomes selected.

6. **Click in the first cell and press the Shift key. Press the left-arrow key twice to extend the selection and then press the down-arrow key once to extend the selection.**

7. **Click in the first cell again and drag down to the third cell in the third row to extend the selection.**

Leave the document open for the next exercise.

Resize rows and columns

Word handles row height automatically for you, so you usually don't have to think about it. The row height changes as needed to accommodate the font size of the text in the cells of that row. Text in a cell wraps automatically to the next line when it runs out of room horizontally, so you can expect your table rows to expand in height as you type more text into them.

If you manually resize a row's height, the ability to auto-resize to fit content is turned off for that row. Therefore, if you add more text to that row later, Word doesn't automatically expand that row's height to accommodate it, and some text may be truncated.

In contrast, column width remains fixed until you change it, regardless of the cell's content. If you want the width of a column to change, you must change it yourself.

In the following exercise, you resize the rows and columns of a table.

Files needed: Lesson 7 Schedule Table.docx, open from the preceding exercise

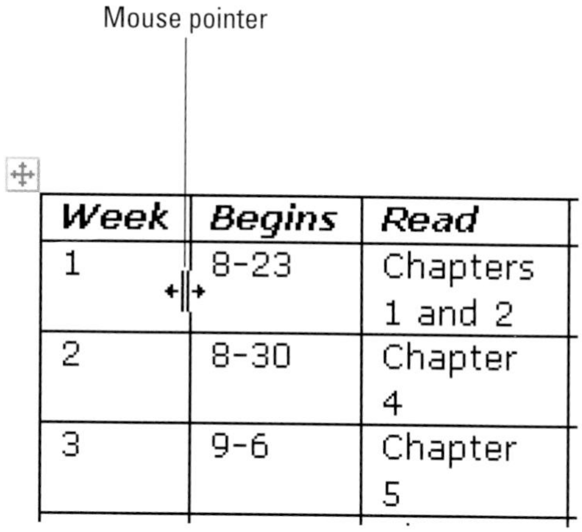

Mouse pointer

Week	Begins	Read
1	8-23	Chapters 1 and 2
2	8-30	Chapter 4
3	9-6	Chapter 5

Figure 7-9

1. **In Lesson 7 Schedule Table, position the mouse pointer over the column divider between the first and second columns.**

   The mouse pointer becomes a double-headed arrow, as shown in Figure 7-9.

2. **Drag to the right slightly to increase the width of the first column by about ¼ inch.**

   Notice that the second column's text now wraps unattractively, as shown in Figure 7-10.

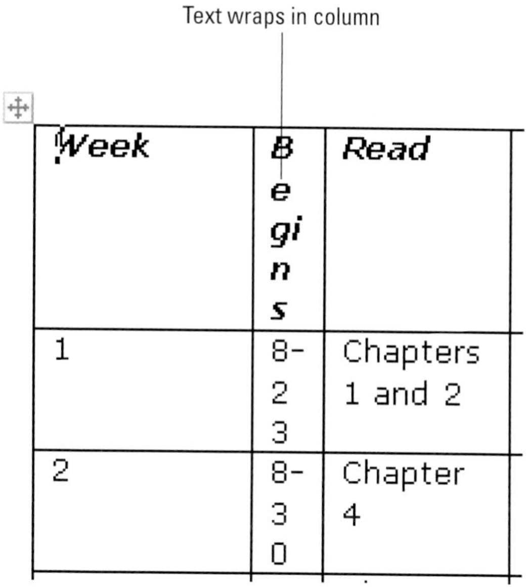

Text wraps in column

Week	B e gi n s	Read
1	8- 2 3	Chapters 1 and 2
2	8- 3 0	Chapter 4

Figure 7-10

3. **Press Ctrl+Z to undo the column width change; while pressing the Shift key, repeat Steps 1–2.**

   The other columns shift to the right to make room for the new width.

4. **Select the cells containing 1 and 2 in the first column.**

5. **Drag the column divider between the first and second columns to the left about ¼ inch, dragging that column back to its original position.**

   Only the two rows where cells were selected are affected, as shown in Figure 7-11.

Column width changed for only the selected rows

Week	*Begins*	*Read*
1	8-23	Chapters 1 and 2
2	8-30	Chapter 4
3	9-6	Chapter 5

Figure 7-11

6. **Press Ctrl+Z to undo the column change; click to move the insertion point inside any cell in the first column.**

7. **Choose Table Tools⇨Layout⇨AutoFit⇨AutoFit Contents.**

   All the column widths are adjusted in the table to fit the content more compactly. See Figure 7-12.

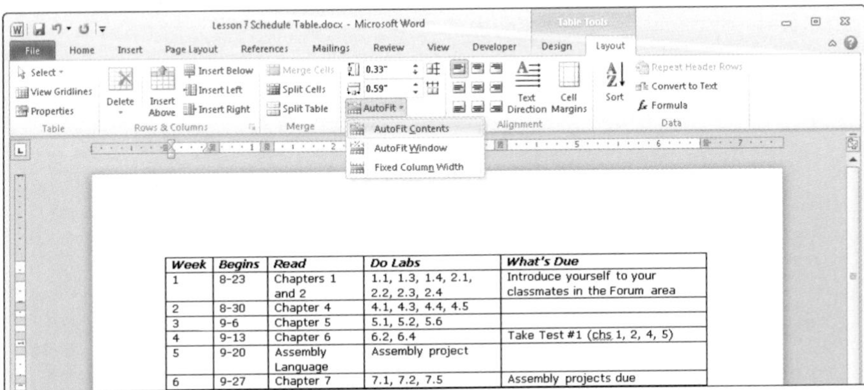

Week	*Begins*	*Read*	*Do Labs*	*What's Due*
1	8-23	Chapters 1 and 2	1.1, 1.3, 1.4, 2.1, 2.2, 2.3, 2.4	Introduce yourself to your classmates in the Forum area
2	8-30	Chapter 4	4.1, 4.3, 4.4, 4.5	
3	9-6	Chapter 5	5.1, 5.2, 5.6	
4	9-13	Chapter 6	6.2, 6.4	Take Test #1 (chs 1, 2, 4, 5)
5	9-20	Assembly Language	Assembly project	
6	9-27	Chapter 7	7.1, 7.2, 7.5	Assembly projects due

Figure 7-12

8. **Press Ctrl+Z to undo the resizing; double-click the column divider between the first and second columns.**

   This time only column 1 resizes to fit its contents more compactly.

9. **Position the mouse pointer over the horizontal divider between the heading row at the top and the first data row.**

   The mouse pointer becomes a two-headed arrow (see Figure 7-13).

Mouse pointer

Week	Begins	Read	Do Labs
1	8-23	Chapters 1 and 2	1.1, 1.3, 1.4, 2.1, 2.2, 2.3, 2.4
2	8-30	Chapter 4	4.1, 4.3, 4.4, 4.5
3	9-6	Chapter 5	5.1, 5.2, 5.6

Figure 7-13

10. **Drag downward to increase the height of the heading row by about ¼ inch.**

11. **Select the heading row, and choose Table Tools Layout➪Align Bottom Left.**

    The headings are bottom-aligned in their cells (see Figure 7-14). Vertical alignment was not an issue previously because the height of the row was auto-fitted to the content.

Align Bottom Left button

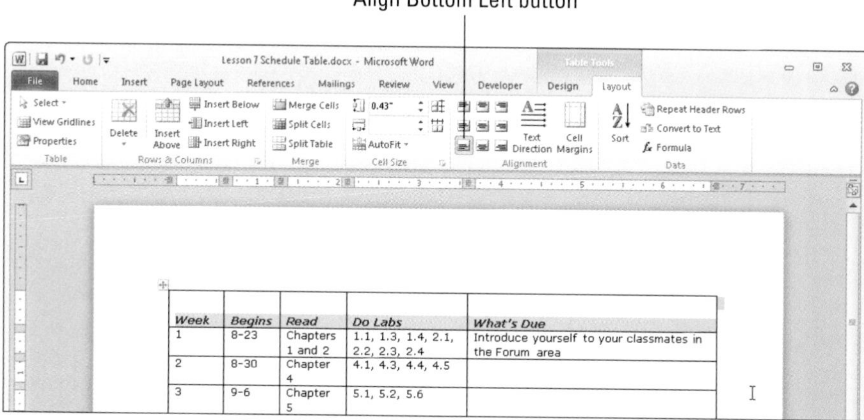

Figure 7-14

12. **Click the table selector icon in the upper-left corner of the table to select the entire table.**

13. **Choose Table Tools⇨Layout⇨Distribute Columns to evenly distribute the space among all the columns (see Figure 7-15).**
14. **Press Ctrl+Z to undo the resizing.**
15. **Save the changes to the document.**

Leave the document open for the next exercise.

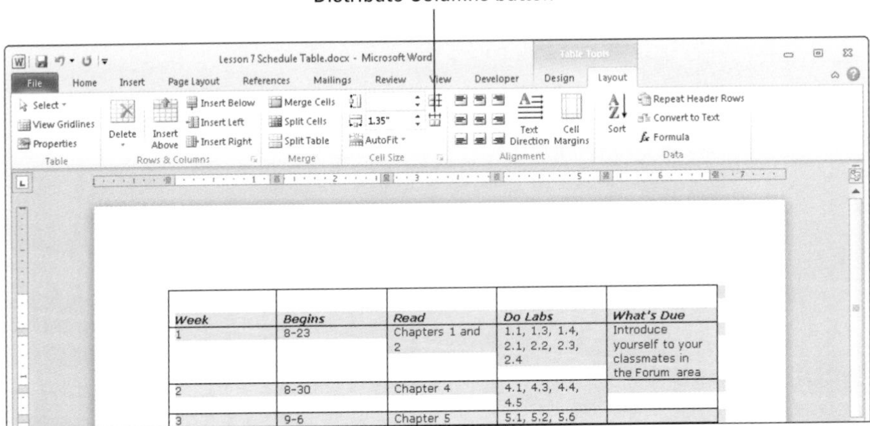

Figure 7-15

Format table borders

Gridlines can be displayed or hidden onscreen (via Table Tools Layout⇨View Gridlines). Gridlines do not print, and when displayed onscreen, they appear as thin blue or gray dashed lines. You probably won't see the gridlines in most tables because they're covered by borders. By default, table gridlines have plain black borders. You can change the borders to different colors, styles (such as dotted or dashed), and thicknesses or remove the borders altogether.

> **LINGO**
>
> **Gridlines** are the dividers that separate a table's rows and columns. A **border** is formatting applied to a gridline that makes it appear when printed.

In the following exercise, you apply formatting to table borders.

Files needed: Lesson 7 Schedule Table.docx, open from the preceding exercise

1. **In Lesson 7 Schedule Table, select the entire table and then choose Table Tools Design➪Borders➪No Border (see Figure 7-16).**
2. **If the gridlines aren't already visible, choose Table Tools Layout➪View Gridlines.**

   Dashed lines appear for the table's row and column dividers. See Figure 7-17.

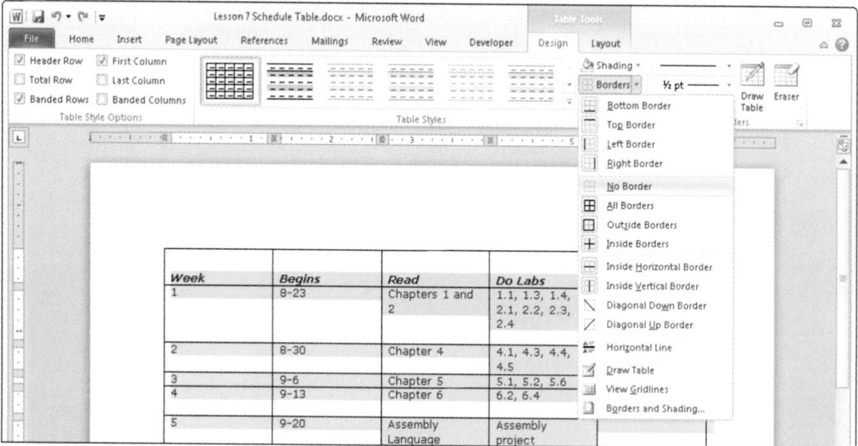

Figure 7-16

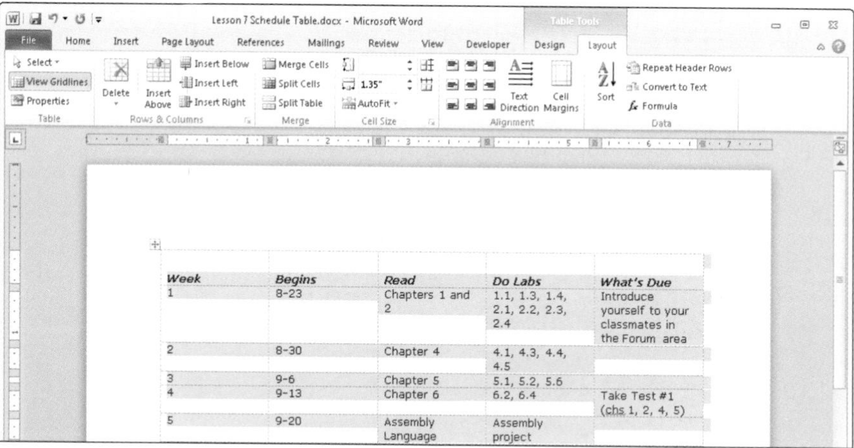

Figure 7-17

3. **Select the header row of the table and then choose Table Tools Design➪Line Weight➪2¼ Pt (see Figure 7-18).**

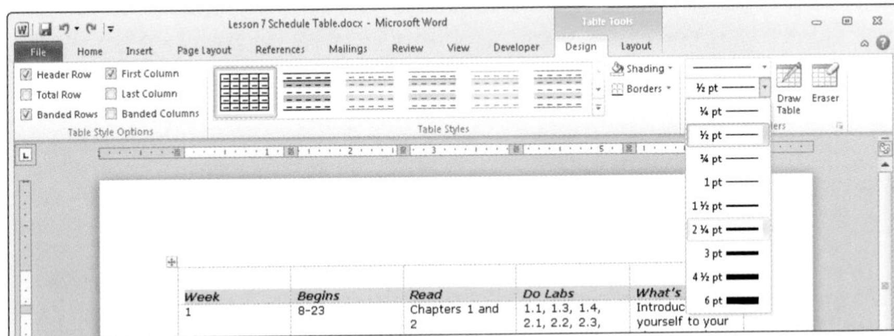

Figure 7-18

4. **Choose Table Tools DesignPen Color and click a red square.**
5. **Choose Table Tools DesignBordersBottom Border.**

   A red bottom border with 2¼-inch thickness appears on that row only.

6. **Select all the rows in the table *except* the header row, and then click the dialog box launcher for the Draw Borders group on the Table Tools Design tab.**

   The Borders and Shading dialog box opens, with the Borders tab displayed. A red border shows in the sample for the top of the selection; when you applied the red border, the first row was selected and the border was at its bottom. The new selection has that same border as its top.

7. **From the Width drop-down list, choose ½ Pt.**
8. **In the Preview area, click the areas where vertical borders might appear (see Figure 7-19) and then click OK.**
9. **Turn off the gridlines again by choosing Table Tools Layout➪View Gridlines, and then click away from the table to deselect it.**

   The table now has a thick, top border separating the header from the rest of the table, and red vertical lines separating the columns. See Figure 7-20.

10. **Save the changes to the document.**

Exit Word.

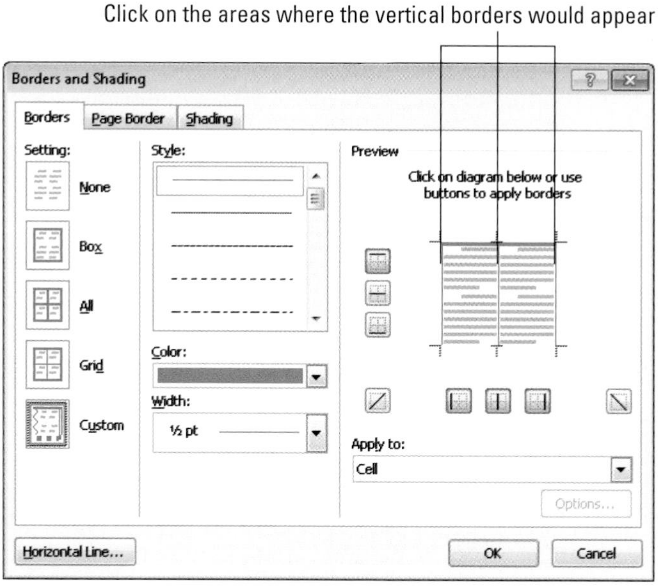

Click on the areas where the vertical borders would appear

Figure 7-19

Week	Begins	Read	Do Labs	What's Due
1	8-23	Chapters 1 and 2	1.1, 1.3, 1.4, 2.1, 2.2, 2.3, 2.4	Introduce yourself to your classmates in the Forum area
2	8-30	Chapter 4	4.1, 4.3, 4.4, 4.5	
3	9-6	Chapter 5	5.1, 5.2, 5.6	
4	9-13	Chapter 6	6.2, 6.4	Take Test #1 (chs 1, 2, 4, 5)
5	9-20	Assembly Language	Assembly project	
6	9-27	Chapter 7	7.1, 7.2, 7.5	Assembly projects due
7	10-4	Chapter 8	8.1, 8.2, 8.4, 8.6	
8	10-11	Chapter 9	9.1, 9.2, 9.3,	
9	10-18	Chapter 10	10.3, 10.6	
10	10-25	Chapter 11	11.1, 11.2, 11.3, 11.5, 11.8	Take Test #2 (Chs 6, 7, 8, 9, 10)
11	11-1	Chapter 12 and 13	13.1, 13.2, 13.4, 13.6, 13.7	
12	11-8	Chapter 14	14.1, 14.2, 14.3, 14.4, 14.5, 14.6	
13	11-15	Chapter 15	15.1, 15.2, 15.3	Take test #3

Figure 7-20

Summing Up

Tables can be a great way to organize data into multiple rows and columns. Here are the key points from this lesson:

- You can create a new table from the Insert tab, either by specifying a number of rows and columns, or by drawing the table.
- You can also convert existing delimited text into a table with the Convert Text to Table command.
- Drag the borders of a table to resize rows and columns.
- Tables have *gridlines* (or non-printing lines that show where the rows and columns are) and, optionally, *borders* (formatting applied to the gridlines).
- Format a table's borders from the Table Tools Design tab.

Try-it-yourself lab

For more practice with the features covered in this lesson, try the following exercise on your own:

1. **In a new document, create a table with two columns and ten rows.**
2. **In the left column, type a list of items you want to purchase for your home.**
3. **In the right column, type the approximate price for each item.**
4. **Add a new row at the top of the table, and in the new row, type the columns' headings.**
5. **Format the table attractively.**
6. **Save your document with a name of your choice and then close Word.**

Know this tech talk

border: Formatting applied to the outer edge or gridline of a table cell or other object.

delimited: Multi-column data where the columns are separated using a consistent character, such as a tab.

gridlines: The non-printing lines that (optionally) show onscreen where the edges of a table's rows and columns are.

Lesson 8

Inserting and Formatting Graphics

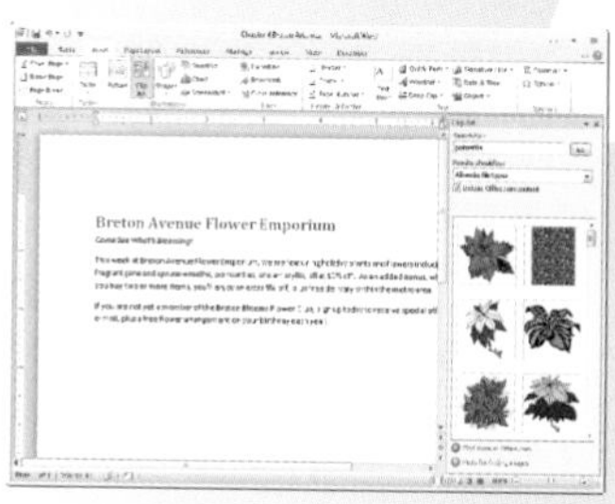

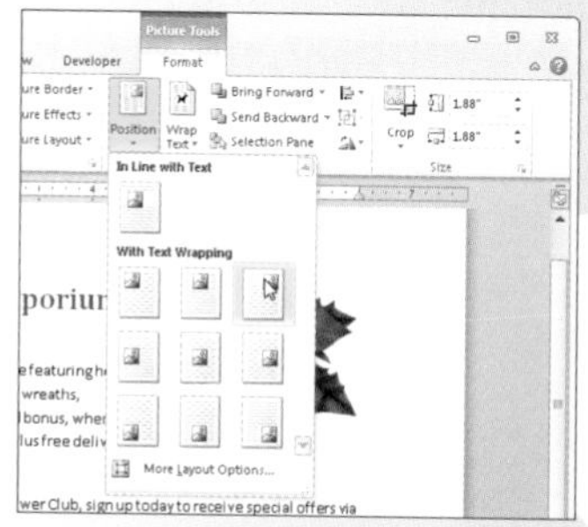

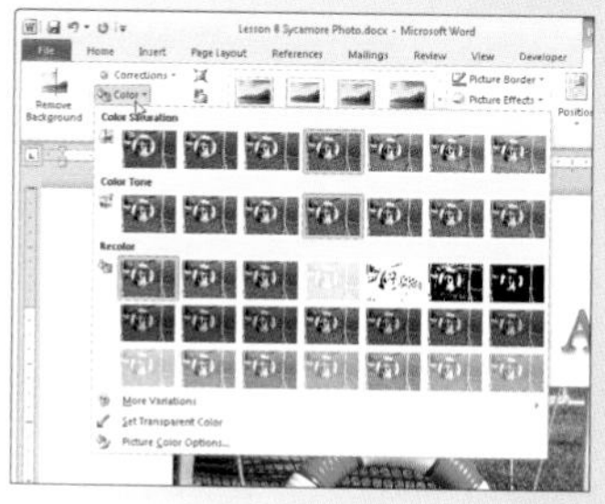

- Find and insert clip art from Microsoft's online collection to use professionally designed artwork without paying royalties or usage fees.
- Insert your own photos and other artwork in a Word document to personalize your work and make it more interesting to view.
- Change the text wrap settings for graphics to fine-tune the way that the text in the document wraps around and interacts with the graphics.
- Drawing lines and shapes with Word's Shapes tool creates custom artwork that you may not otherwise be able to find, such as unique logos.
- Apply fill colors and effects to drawn shapes to make the drawings stand out.

You can dress up Word documents with a variety of types of graphics, by either importing pictures from other sources or creating them yourself inside Word. Graphics can make a document more interesting and can explain visual concepts more easily than text alone. (You know the old saying . . . a picture is worth a thousand words.)

In this lesson, you learn how to insert clip art and photos from your own files and how to position and format pictures in a document. You also learn about the drawing tools, which are available not only in Word, but also in Excel and PowerPoint.

Insert Clip Art

When you buy any of the Office applications, you get free access to a large online library of clip art maintained by Microsoft. Each of the main Office applications has a Clip Art command that opens a task pane in which you can search the library and insert clips from it into your documents.

The Clip Art library that Microsoft provides contains plenty of clip art, but that's not all; it also contains stock photos, sounds, and video clips you can use for free. The four types of content offered are

- **Illustrations:** Resizable line drawings (in other words, traditional clip art)
- **Photographs:** Pictures taken with a digital camera
- **Video:** Digital movie clips
- **Audio:** Digital sound clips

LINGO

Clip art is generic, predrawn artwork.

EXTRA INFO

In the days before most businesses had computers, companies that needed stock artwork would buy large books of line drawings, and when they needed an image, they'd clip it out of the book with scissors and then glue it to a paste-up layout. That's where the name comes from.

People don't use audio and video in Word because most Word documents are printed for distribution, and audio and video can't be printed. PowerPoint, on the other hand, makes great use of audio and video because its output is designed to be shown on a computer screen.

When you install Office 2010, a few clip art images are installed on your hard drive, but the majority of the collection is stored online. When you use the Clip Art feature in an Office application, it automatically connects to Microsoft's online collection.

Computers can display two classes of graphics: vector and raster. They're very different from one another, and each is best suited for a different purpose.

Clip art is a type of vector graphic. A vector graphic is created behind the scenes by using math formulas; if you've taken a geometry class where you plotted a function on graph paper, you get the idea. Computerized clip art builds images by layering and combining individual lines and shapes, each one constructed via a math formula. As a result, the clips can be resized without losing any quality because resizing simply changes the math formula. Clip art files are also very small compared with raster graphics. The main drawback of clip art is that the images don't look real; they look like drawings.

> **LINGO**
>
> A **vector graphic** is a graphic that's drawn using math formulas to create its lines and shapes. A **raster graphic** is a graphic comprised of a grid of **pixels,** or colored dots.

Photos from digital cameras are examples of raster graphics. A raster graphic is a densely packed collection of colored dots that together form an image. If you zoom in on a photo on a computer, you can see these dots individually. In a raster graphic, each dot is a pixel, and its color is represented by a numeric code (usually 24 or 32 binary digits in length per pixel). Raster graphics can be photorealistic, but because so much data is required to define each pixel, the file sizes tend to be large.

Microsoft Office uses the terms *image* and *graphic* interchangeably in its documentation and help system, and so does this book. Both refer generically to any picture, regardless of its type or source.

Find and insert clips

In the following exercise, you practice searching for various types of clips with the Clip Art task pane and inserting them in a document.

Files needed: Lesson 8 Breton.docx

1. **Start Word, if necessary, and then open Lesson 8 Breton and save it as Lesson 8 Breton Art.**
2. **Choose Insert⇨Clip Art.**

   The Clip Art task pane opens at the right.
3. **Select All Media Types from the Results Should Be drop-down list; in the Search For text box, type** poinsettia; **and then click Go.**

Word remembers your settings from previous searches, so when you open the Clip Art task pane, a keyword may be entered already; if so, delete it before typing **poinsettia**.

A selection of clips that have *poinsettia* as a keyword appear in the task pane. See Figure 8-1.

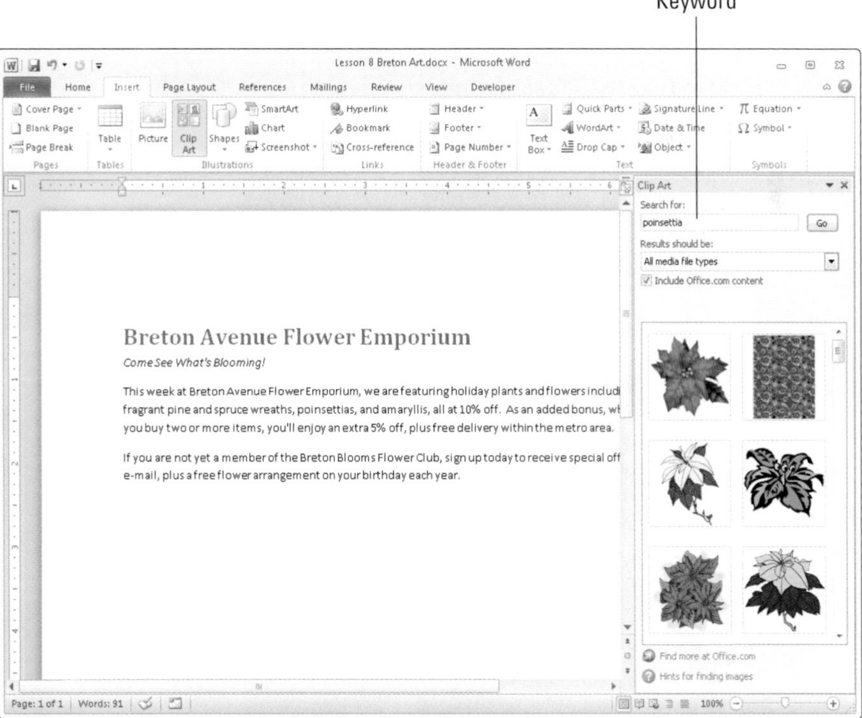

Figure 8-1

4. **Scroll through the resulting clips.**

   Notice that the results are a mixture of line drawings and photographs.

If you don't have an Internet connection or aren't connected to the Internet when you use the Clip Art feature, you're limited to the clips stored on your hard drive.

5. **From the Results Should Be drop-down list, deselect the All Media Types check box; then select only the Illustrations check box (see Figure 8-2).**

Figure 8-2

EXTRA INFO

Click the Find More at Office.com link at the bottom of the task pane if you want to browse the complete clip art collection via a web interface.

6. **Click Go again to rerun the search.**

   This time the results include only clip art.

7. **Position the insertion point at the beginning of the first body paragraph ("This week . . .").**

The picture is placed wherever the insertion point is. If the insertion point is in the middle of a paragraph, the picture will split the paragraph in two, possibly creating an awkward look that you didn't intend. For best results in most cases, position the insertion point on its own line, between two paragraphs, or at least at the beginning or end of a paragraph.

8. **Click one of the clips to insert it.**

   The clip appears in the document, as shown in Figure 8-3.

Breton Avenue Flower Emporium
Come See What's Blooming!

This week at Breton Avenue Flower Emporium, we are featuring hol
plants and flowers including fragrant pine and spruce wreaths, poinsettias, and amaryllis, all at 10
As an added bonus, when you buy two or more items, you'll enjoy an extra 5% off, plus free deliv
within the metro area.
If you are not yet a member of the Breton Blooms Flower Club, sign up today to receive special of
e-mail, plus a free flower arrangement on your birthday each year.

Figure 8-3

9. **Press the Delete key to remove the inserted clip, press Enter to create a new paragraph, and then press the up-arrow key once to move the insertion point into that new paragraph.**
10. **In the Clip Art task pane, click a different clip to insert it in the new paragraph.**

    This time the clip appears on its own line.
11. **Press Delete to remove the inserted clip and then press Delete again to remove the empty paragraph.**
12. **Save the document.**

For more practice, perform some additional searches. For example, you can specify different file types, such as only audio or only video files, and you can search for multiple keywords at once.

Leave the document open for the next exercise.

LINGO

An **inline image** is an image that is treated as a text character in a paragraph.

EXTRA INFO

In this example, the clip is placed in the document as an inline image. An inline image is treated like a really large character of text. The height of the image makes the first line of the paragraph extra tall, as you can see in Figure 8-3. Later in this lesson, you learn how to make text wrap more gracefully around a picture.

Make a clip available offline

The Clip Art feature relies heavily on the Internet to deliver clips from Microsoft's online collection of clips. You can't always be certain that the Internet will be available, however, so if you know you will need certain clips later, you should make those clips available offline. Doing so copies the clips to your hard drive. When a clip is stored on your hard drive, you can also change its keywords so that it appears when you search for different words.

In the following exercise, you make a clip available offline and add a keyword to it.

Files needed: Lesson 8 Breton Art.docx, open from the preceding exercise

1. **In the Lesson 8 Breton Art document, confirm that the Clip Art task pane is open and *poinsettia* appears in the Search For text box.**
2. **Deselect the Include Office.Com Content check box and then click Go to rerun the search.**

   This time no results are found.
3. **Select the Include Office.Com Content check box again and then click Go to rerun the search.**
4. **Right-click one of the clips and choose Make Available Offline from the contextual menu.**

   The Copy to Collection dialog box opens, as shown in Figure 8-4.
5. **Click Favorites and then click OK.**

   The clip is copied to your hard drive.

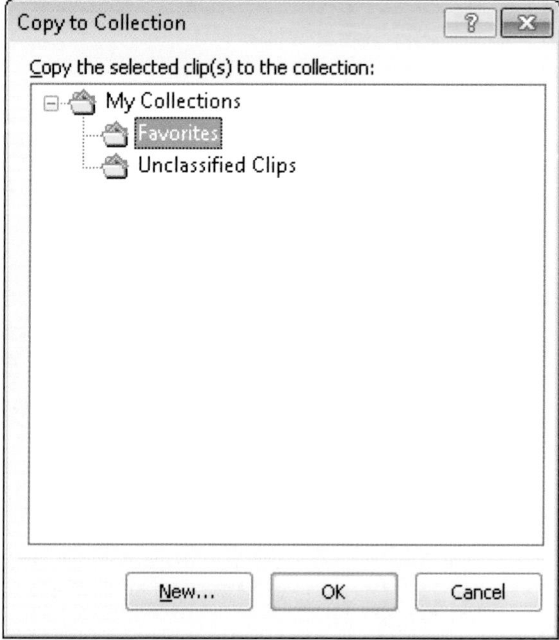

Figure 8-4

6. **Deselect the Include Office.Com Content check box and then click Go to rerun the search.**

   The clip you chose appears in the search results.

7. **Right-click the clip and choose Edit Keywords.**

   The Keywords dialog box appears.

8. **In the Keyword box, type** Christmas **(see Figure 8-5); click Add to add the keyword to the clip; click OK to close the dialog box.**

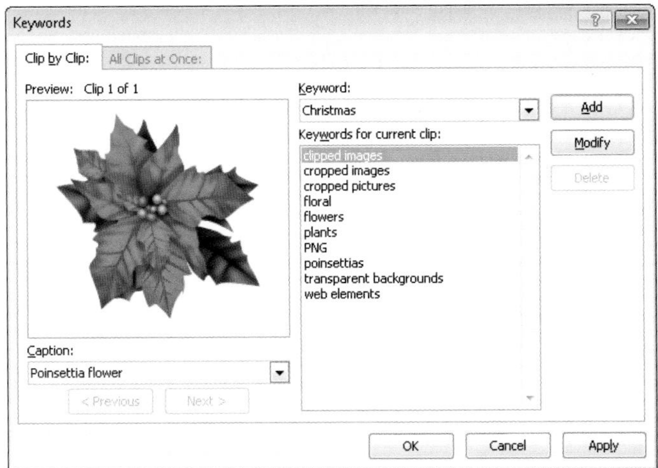

Figure 8-5

Try editing the keywords for a clip that's not available offline. You can't edit them because you don't have your own copy, and you can't change the properties of the communal copy stored at Microsoft.

9. **In the Search For text box, replace *poinsettia* by typing** Christmas **and then click Go to rerun the search.**

   The search results include the poinsettia clip you made available as well as a Santa Claus clip.

10. **Close the Clip Art task pane.**

To close the task pane, click the Close (X) button in the upper-right corner of the task pane or choose Insert⇨Clip Art again.

11. **Save the document.**

Leave the document open for the next exercise.

Insert Photos from Files

The clips available via the Clip Art task pane are pretty generic. Sometimes, you might want to insert a more personal picture, such as a digital photo you took or a picture that a friend or co-worker sent you via e-mail.

In the following exercise, you insert a photograph from a file stored on your hard drive.

Files needed: Lesson 8 Breton Art.docx, open from the preceding exercise

1. **In the Lesson 8 Breton Art document, click at the end of the document and then press Enter to start a new paragraph.**
2. **Choose Insert⇨Picture.**

   The Insert Picture dialog box opens.
3. **Navigate to the folder containing the data files for this lesson and select `08graphic01.jpg` (see Figure 8-6).**
4. **Click the Insert button.**

   The picture is inserted in the document.
5. **Save the document.**

Leave the document open for the next exercise.

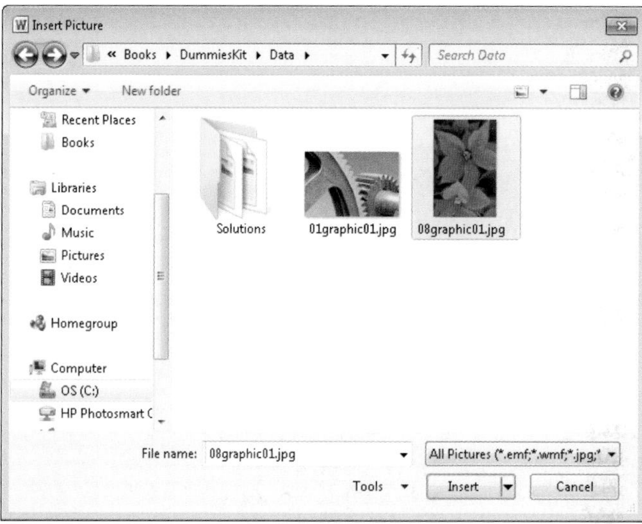

Figure 8-6

Manage Picture Size and Placement

After you insert a graphic in a document, you may decide you want to move it or change how the text around it interacts with it. For example, you might want the text to wrap around the graphic or even run on top of it.

You can size and position a graphic in several ways. You can manually size or move by dragging; you can specify exact values for height, width, and/or position on the page; or you can use Word's placement commands to place the image in relation to other content.

Change a picture's text wrap setting

By default, as I mention earlier, a picture is inserted as an inline image, which means it's treated like a text character. That's not usually the best way for an image to interact with the text, though. More often you want the text to flow around the image so that, if the text moves (because of editing), the graphic stays where you put it. You can change a picture's text wrap setting to control this.

LINGO

Text wrap is the way in which the surrounding text interacts with the graphic.

In the following exercise, you change the text wrap setting for a picture.

Files needed: Lesson 8 Breton Art.docx, open from the preceding exercise

1. **In the Lesson 8 Breton Art document, select the picture that you inserted in the preceding exercise.**

   The Picture Tools tabs become available.

2. **Choose Picture Tools Format⇨Wrap Text⇨Square (see Figure 8-7).**

   The text in the last line wraps around the picture.

3. **Drag the picture upward and drop it at the left margin so that its top aligns with the top of the first body paragraph (see Figure 8-8).**

For extra practice, try each of the other text wrap settings and then compare their results. You don't have to select each of the settings; just pointing at a setting shows a preview of it in the document.

The photo currently in the document is rectangular, so you don't see any difference between some of the settings. To understand the differences between them, you must use a piece of clip art with a transparent background for your experiments.

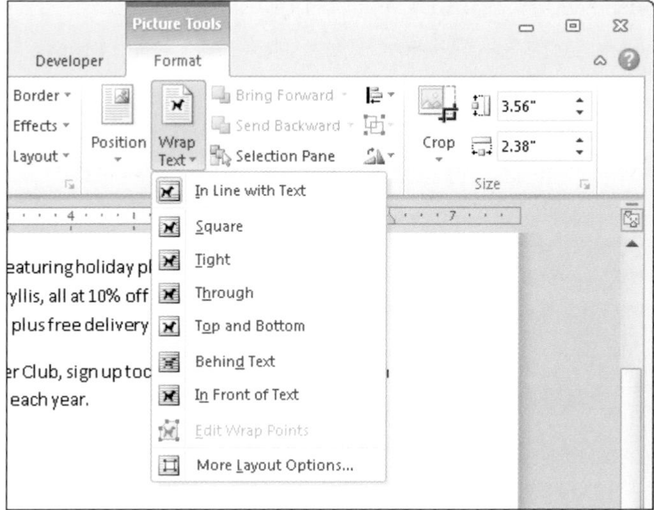
Picture Tools
Developer
Format
Border
Effects
Layout
Position
Wrap Text
Bring Forward
Send Backward
Selection Pane
Crop
3.56"
2.38"
Size
In Line with Text
Square
Tight
Through
Top and Bottom
Behind Text
In Front of Text
Edit Wrap Points
More Layout Options...

Figure 8-7

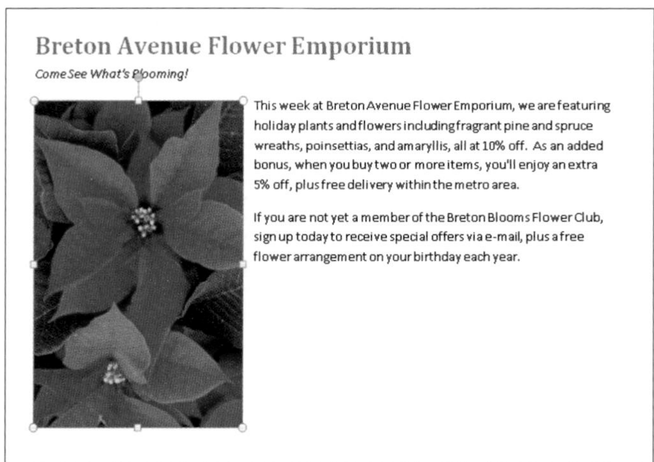
Breton Avenue Flower Emporium
Come See What's Blooming!
This week at Breton Avenue Flower Emporium, we are featuring holiday plants and flowers including fragrant pine and spruce wreaths, poinsettias, and amaryllis, all at 10% off. As an added bonus, when you buy two or more items, you'll enjoy an extra 5% off, plus free delivery within the metro area.
If you are not yet a member of the Breton Blooms Flower Club, sign up today to receive special offers via e-mail, plus a free flower arrangement on your birthday each year.

Figure 8-8

4. **Press the Delete key to delete the picture, reopen the Clip Art task pane, and search for illustrations with the keyword *poinsettia.***

5. **Locate and insert a clip art image that has a white (transparent) background and then close the Clip Art task pane.**

6. **Choose Picture Tools Format➪Wrap Text➪Square.**

   The text wraps around the clip art with a rectangular border, as shown in Figure 8-9.

7. **Click the Wrap Text button again and choose Tight.**

   The text wraps around the image itself, not its rectangular frame, as shown in Figure 8-10.

Breton Avenue Flower Emporium
Come See What's Blooming!
This week at Breton Avenue Flower Emporium, we are featuring holiday plants and flowers including fragrant pine and spruce wreaths, poinsettias, and amaryllis, all at 10% off. As an added bonus, when you buy two or more items, you'll enjoy an extra 5% off, plus free delivery within the metro area.
If you are not yet a member of the Breton Blooms Flower Club, sign up today to receive special offers via e-mail, plus a free flower arrangement on your birthday each year.

Figure 8-9

Stray text may wrap around image inappropriately

Breton Avenue Flower Emporium
Come See What's Blooming!
This week at Breton Avenue Flower Emporium, we are featuring holiday plants and flowers including fragrant pine and spruce wreaths, poinsettias, and amaryllis, all at 10% off. As an added bonus, when you buy two or more items, you'll enjoy an extra 5% off, plus free delivery within the metro area.
If
you are not yet a member of the Breton Blooms Flower Club, sign up today to receive special offers via e-mail, plus a free flower arrangement
on
your birthday each year.

Figure 8-10

8. **Click the Wrap Text button and choose Edit Wrap Points.**

   Black squares and a dotted red outline appear around the clip art image.

   These usually invisible points determine where the text is allowed to flow when text is set to Tight (that is, to wrap tightly around the image). See Figure 8-11.

EXTRA INFO

Depending on the image you chose, some stray bits of text may appear below and to the left of the image, as shown in Figure 8-10. You can fix the stray text by adjusting the image's wrap points.

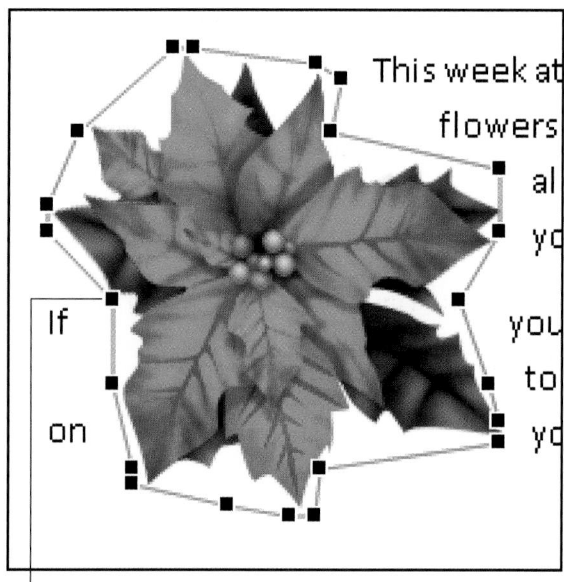

Drag a black square outward to prohibit the text from wrapping in that space

Figure 8-11

9. **Drag one or more of the black squares outward to block out the space where the stray text appears so that it can't flow there anymore.**

   See Figure 8-12 for an example.

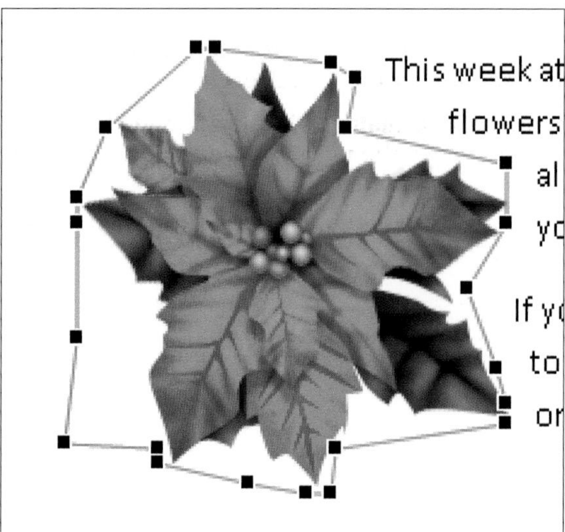

Figure 8-12

10. **Click away from the image to deselect it and finalize the change in its wrap points.**
11. **Save the changes to the document.**

Leave the document open for the next exercise.

Move a picture

You can move a picture by dragging it where you want it to go. The way a picture moves when you drag it varies, depending on the text wrap setting you've chosen for the picture. If the default setting of In Line with Text is in effect, you can drag a picture only to a spot where you can also drag text:

- Within existing paragraphs
- Before or after existing paragraphs

You can't place a picture outside the document margins or below the end-of-document marker. If any other text wrapping setting is in effect, you can drag a picture anywhere on the page.

You can also move a picture by specifying an exact position for it, from the Format Picture dialog box, or by using one of the presets in the Position drop-down list on the Picture Tools Format tab.

In the following exercise, you move a picture.

Files needed: Lesson 8 Breton Art.docx, open from the preceding exercise

1. **In the Lesson 8 Breton Art document, select the clip art that you worked with in the preceding exercise.**
2. **Choose Picture Tools Format⇨Position and then choose the position that shows the picture in the upper-right corner of the document (see Figure 8-13).**
3. **Drag the picture downward slightly so that its top aligns with the top of the first body paragraph.**
4. **Click the Position button again and choose More Layout Options.**

   The Layout dialog box opens with the Position tab displayed.

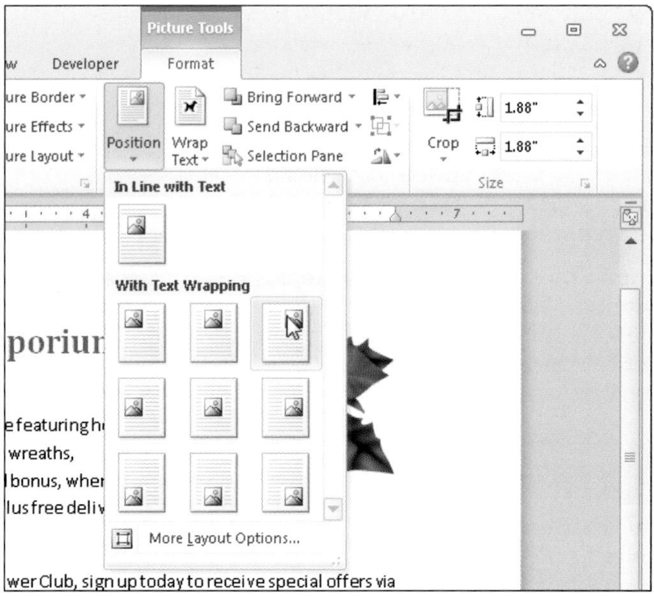

Figure 8-13

5. **In the Horizontal section, in the Absolute Position text box, type** 5 **and in the Vertical section, in the Absolute Position text box, type** 1 **(see Figure 8-14); click OK to close the dialog box.**

Inches are the default units of measurement for picture settings unless otherwise specified.

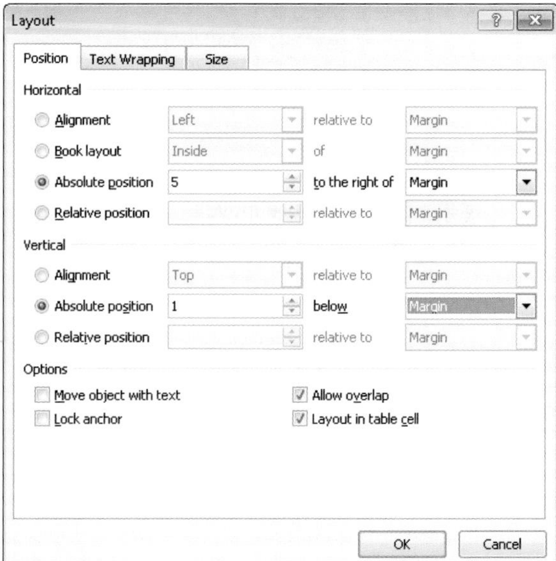

Figure 8-14

But what if you want the picture to move with the text, if you add or delete more text in the document so the text that's next to the picture now might not later be? The following steps show how to set that up.

6. **Click the Position button and choose More Layout Options to reopen the Layout dialog box.**
7. **In the Vertical section, for the Absolute Position setting, change the value in the Absolute Position text box to 0.2" and choose Paragraph in the Below drop-down list.**

EXTRA INFO

Are you wondering why you're offsetting the picture by 0.2 inch rather than setting it to zero to top-align? It's because you're attaching the picture to the document subheading, not the first body paragraph, and 0.2 inch below the subheading happens to correspond to the top of the first body paragraph's vertical position.

8. **Select the Move Object with Text check box (see Figure 8-15) and then click OK.**
9. **Click at the beginning of the paragraph that contains the document subheading ("Come see . . .") and press Enter twice.**

Notice that the picture moves with that paragraph.

10. **Press the Backspace key twice to delete the extra paragraphs just created.**

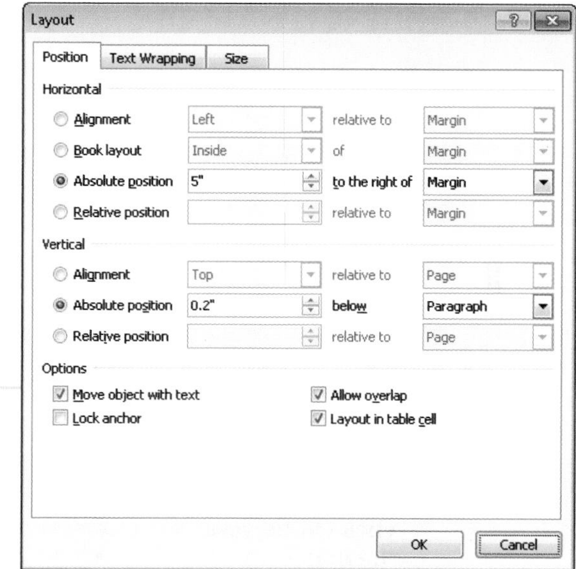

Figure 8-15

11. **Save the changes to the document.**

Leave the document open for the next exercise.

Resize a picture

You can resize a picture by dragging its selection handles or by specifying an exact height and width for the picture from the Layout dialog box.

> **LINGO**
>
> The **aspect ratio** is the proportion of width to height.

When you resize a picture, its aspect ratio can change. A photo may not look right if you don't maintain the aspect ratio; clip art is less likely to suffer from small differences in the ratio. When you drag a corner selection handle, the aspect ratio is maintained; when you drag a side selection handle, it is not.

Most image types maintain the aspect ratio automatically if you drag a corner selection handle. If the aspect ratio doesn't stay constant when you drag a corner selection handle, hold down the Shift key as you drag to force it to do so.

Raster images look fuzzy if you enlarge them past their original size. That's one advantage of vector images: They remain crisp and sharp at any size.

In the following exercise, you resize a picture.

Files needed: Lesson 8 Breton Art.docx, open from the preceding exercise

1. **In the Lesson 8 Breton Art document, select the clip art image that you worked with in the preceding exercise if it isn't already selected.**

Notice its selection handles: circles in the corners and squares on the sides.

2. **Hover the mouse over the lower-left selection handle.**

   The mouse pointer becomes a double-headed diagonal arrow.

3. **Drag out and downward, enlarging the image by about ½ inch.**

   See Figure 8-16. Use the onscreen ruler to gauge the distance.

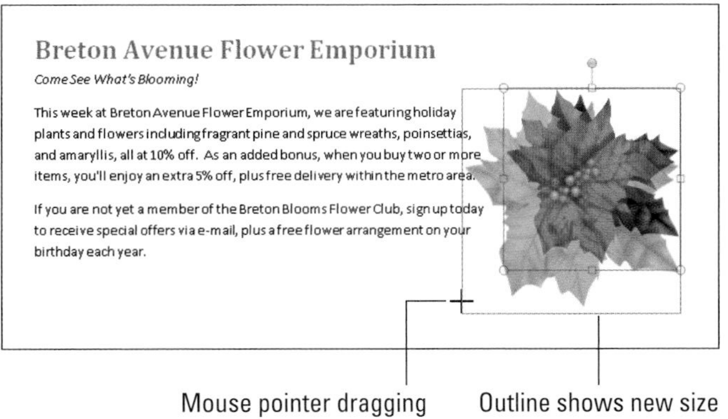
Breton Avenue Flower Emporium
Come See What's Blooming!
This week at Breton Avenue Flower Emporium, we are featuring holiday plants and flowers including fragrant pine and spruce wreaths, poinsettias, and amaryllis, all at 10% off. As an added bonus, when you buy two or more items, you'll enjoy an extra 5% off, plus free delivery within the metro area.
If you are not yet a member of the Breton Blooms Flower Club, sign up today to receive special offers via e-mail, plus a free flower arrangement on your birthday each year.
Mouse pointer dragging
Outline shows new size

Figure 8-16

4. **Right-click the picture and choose Size and Position.**

   The Layout dialog box opens with the Size tab displayed.

5. **In the Height section, set the Absolute setting to 2". Do the same in the Width section (see Figure 8-17). Click OK.**

6. **Save the changes to the document and close it.**

Exit Word.

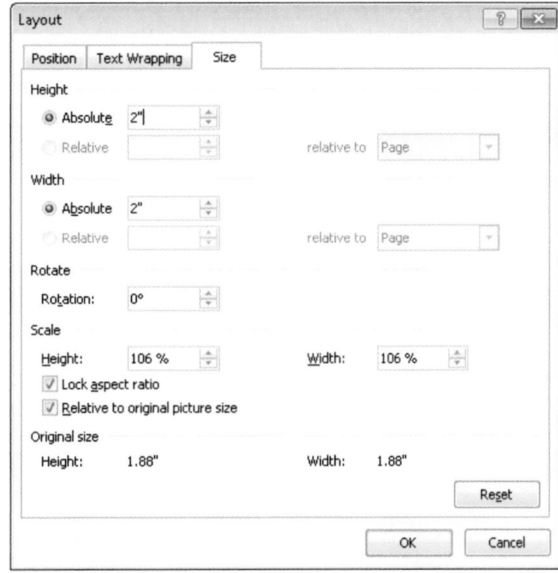
Layout
Position
Text Wrapping
Size
Height
Absolute 2"
Relative
relative to Page
Width
Absolute 2"
Relative
relative to Page
Rotate
Rotation: 0°
Scale
Height: 106 %
Width: 106 %
Lock aspect ratio
Relative to original picture size
Original size
Height: 1.88"
Width: 1.88"
Reset
OK
Cancel

Figure 8-17

Modify a Picture

The original picture you insert in a Word document is just a starting point; you can modify that picture in a variety of ways to create special effects and to improve the picture's appearance. For example, you can adjust the picture's brightness and contrast, apply a color wash to it, and/or apply artistic effects to the picture that give it interesting new looks, such as making a photo look like a pencil sketch or a watercolor painting.

Adjust brightness and contrast

If a photo suffers from being too light or too dark, you can make adjustments in Word that may help it. If a picture looks washed-out and faded, increasing its contrast may enhance it. You can also choose to sharpen or soften an image.

In the following exercise, you adjust the brightness, contrast, and sharpness of a picture.

> **LINGO**
>
> **Brightness** refers to the overall lightness or darkness of the image, whereas **contrast** refers to the difference between the light and dark areas of a picture.

Files needed: Lesson 8 Sycamore.docx

1. **In Word, open Lesson 8 Sycamore and save it as Lesson 8 Sycamore Photo.**
2. **Select the photo and then choose Picture Tools Format⇨Corrections to open a menu of samples (see Figure 8-18).**

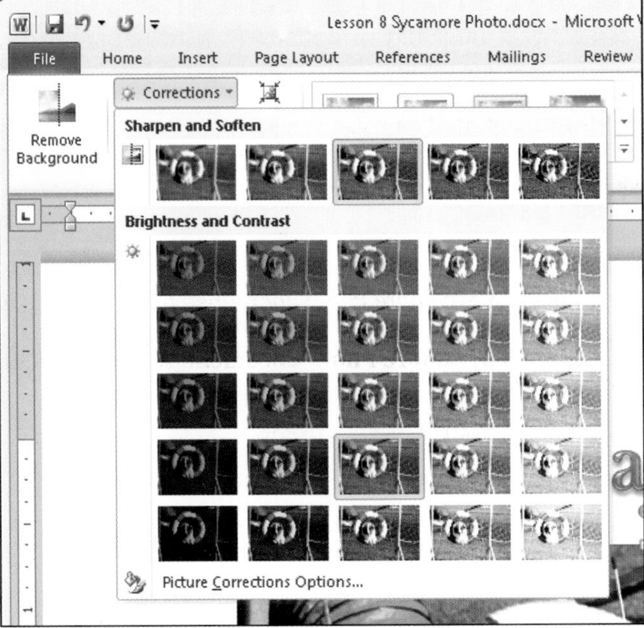

Figure 8-18

3. **Point the mouse at several of the samples and observe the preview on the picture; then in the Brightness and Contrast section, choose the Brightness 0, Contrast +20% sample (third sample in the fourth row).**
4. **Click the Corrections button again to reopen the menu and in the Sharpen and Soften section, click the Sharpen 25% sample (fourth sample in the first row).**
5. **Save the changes to the document.**

Leave the document open for the next exercise.

Adjust colors

You can make adjustments — subtle or dramatic — to a picture's colors from within Word. You can adjust the color saturation and the color tone. The color tone is described by "temperature" in Office applications, with lower numbers being more blue (think: frozen) and higher numbers being more orange (think: heated like a flame). For example, a strongly blue tone would be 4700K, and a strongly orange tone would be 11200K. You can also make an image grayscale or black-and-white, or apply a color wash, which makes the image monochrome (like grayscale) but with some other color than gray.

LINGO

Color saturation is the vividness of the color. **Color tone** is the subtle change in the tint of the image (red, green, or blue). **Color wash** is an effect that changes an image to a monochrome version with the chosen color as the single color that comprises it.

In the following exercise, you modify a photo's colors.

Files needed: Lesson 8 Sycamore Photo.docx, open from the preceding exercise

1. **In the Lesson 8 Sycamore Photo document, select the picture if it's not already selected.**
2. **Choose Picture Tools Format⇨Color.**

   A palette of color change options appears. See Figure 8-19.
3. **Point to several of the options, and observe their effect on the image behind the open menu; then in the Color Tone section on the Color button's menu, choose Temperature: 5900 K.**
4. **Choose Picture Tools Format⇨Color again, and in the Recolor section, choose Olive Green, Accent Color 3 Dark.**

   The picture appears as a monochrome image in olive green.

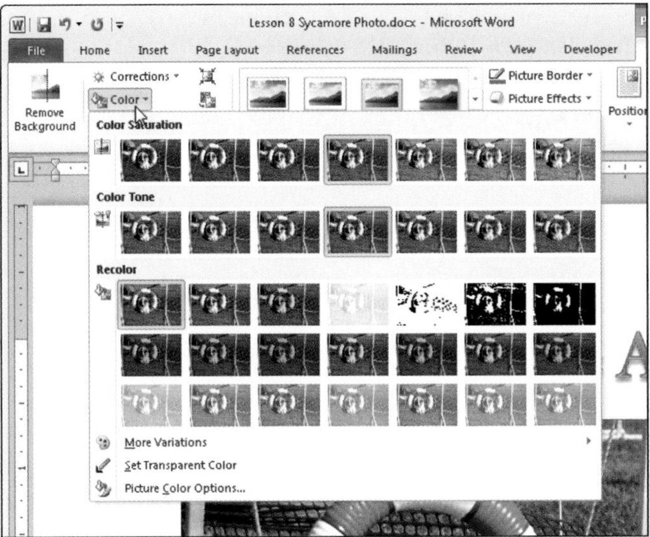

Figure 8-19

5. **In the Recolor section, click the full-color sample (No Recolor) to return the image to multi-color.**
6. **Save the changes to the document.**

Leave the document open for the next exercise.

Apply artistic effects

Many effects are designed to make a photograph appear as if it were drawn or painted by an artist.

In the following exercise, you apply artistic effects to a photo.

Files needed: Lesson 8 Sycamore Photo.docx, open from the preceding exercise

1. **In the Lesson 8 Sycamore Photo document, select the picture if it's not already selected.**
2. **Choose Picture Tools Format⇨Artistic Effects.**

   A palette of effect options appears. See Figure 8-20.

LINGO

An **artistic effect** is a transformation that gives the image an altered appearance in some way. For example, some of the artistic effects include Pencil Grayscale, Line Drawing, and Watercolor Sponge.

3. **Point at several effects to see them applied to the image and then choose Pencil Sketch.**

   The image's appearance takes on the qualities of a pencil sketch, as shown in Figure 8-21.

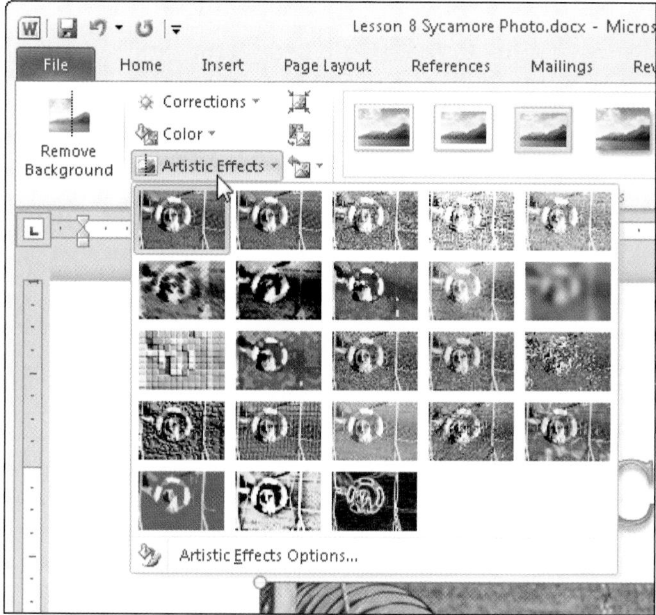

Figure 8-20

Figure 8-21

4. Save the file and close it.

Leave Word open for the next exercise.

Draw Lines and Shapes

In addition to importing other people's images, you can also draw your own via the Shapes tool in Word. By combining and formatting shapes, you can create simple illustrations and annotate other artwork with lines and shapes that call attention to certain areas.

Word doesn't differentiate between lines and shapes in its drawing tools: They're all generically called *shapes.* Therefore when this book refers to shapes, it also includes lines.

The lines and shapes that you draw in Word are vector graphics, which means they can be drawn at any size, and moved, sized, and formatted freely after their initial placement. Drawn shapes are similar to clip art images in most ways; most of the formatting you can apply to a clip art image, you can also apply to drawn lines and shapes.

The drawing tools in Office applications are quite rudimentary, and you may find it difficult to create complex artwork using them. You can use other applications to create your artwork and then import the finished images into Office applications.

Draw shapes

To draw a shape, use the Shapes command to open a palette of shapes and then click the one you want to draw. Then either click or drag in the Word document to create the chosen line or shape.

So which is, it — click or drag? Either one will work, but they produce different results. If you click in the document, a shape of default dimensions appears. You can then resize and format it as you like. If you drag in the document, you can control the shape's dimensions by the amount you drag vertically and horizontally.

Certain shapes, such as circles and squares, are the same height and width by default, but if you drag to create them, you can distort their original aspect ratios to make ovals and rectangles. If you want to *constrain* a shape to its default aspect ratio as you draw it, hold down the Shift key while you drag.

In the following exercise, you draw some lines and shapes to create a simple picture.

Files needed: None

1. **Press Ctrl+N to start a new blank document in Word and save it as Lesson 8 Drawings.**
2. **Choose Insert⇨Shapes, and on the menu that appears, examine the available categories of shapes and the individual shapes within each one (see Figure 8-22).**

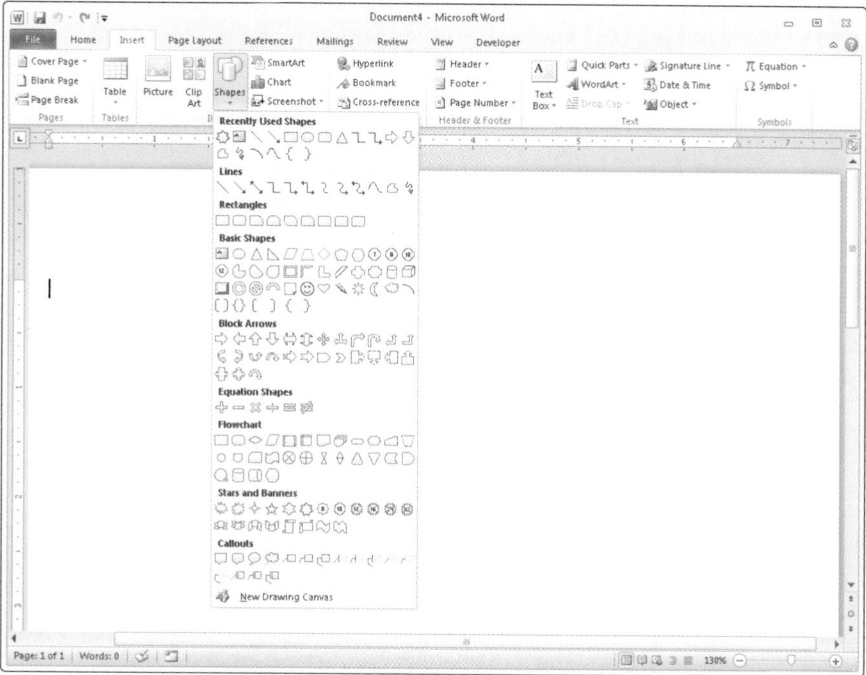

Figure 8-22

3. **In the Rectangles section, choose Rounded Rectangle.**
4. **Click anywhere on the document to place a 1-inch rounded square and then drag a side selection handle outward to increase the shape's width to 2 inches.**
5. **Choose Insert⇨Shapes again and then choose the isosceles triangle.**
6. **Hold down the Shift key and drag on the document to create a triangle that is 1.5-inches wide at its base.**

   Holding down Shift maintains the original aspect ratio of the shape. Place the triangle and the rectangle side-by-side with the triangle on the right.

7. **Choose Insert⇨Shapes again, and in the Lines section, choose Curve.**
8. **Move the mouse pointer to the document and then follow these steps to place the curve:**
   a. *Click below the rectangle to place the beginning of the line.*
   b. *Move the mouse pointer about 1 inch down and 1.5 inches to the right of the original point, and then click again to place the center of the curve.*
   c. *Move the mouse pointer 1 inch up and 1.5 inches to the right of the previous point, and then double-click to end the drawing of the curve.*

   Figure 8-23 shows the drawings at this point. Your curve may look different from the one shown.

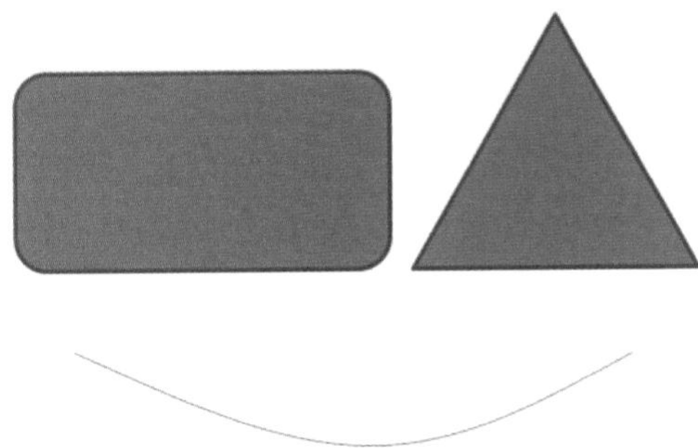

Figure 8-23

9. **Select the curve and press the Delete key to remove it.**
10. **Choose Insert⇨Shapes again, and in the Stars and Banners section, choose Up Ribbon.**
11. **Drag to draw a ribbon below the remaining shapes, approximately 5.5 inches wide and .5 inch high.**
12. **Save the document.**

Leave the document open for the next exercise.

Choose a shape outline and shape fill

For a shape to be seen, it needs to have an outline, a fill, or both. By default, shapes you draw have both. The default fill color comes from the color scheme that's in use; it's the Accent 1 color (the fifth color from the left in the color palette).

> **LINGO**
>
> A **fill** is an inside color or pattern for a shape, whereas an **outline** is a colored border around the outside of a shape.

The shape outline, if present, has a color, a weight (thickness), and a style (such as solid, dotted, or dashed). You can control all those options from the Drawing Tools Format tab.

Any shape (except a line) can also have a fill. This fill can be any of the following:

- A solid color
- A texture
- A pattern, such as a checkerboard or pinstripe
- A gradient
- A picture

LINGO

A **texture** is a repeating graphic that makes the fill look like a certain type of surface, such as marble, wood, or newsprint. A **gradient** is a gradual blending from one color to another.

Lines don't have a fill. Their appearance is controlled by their Shape Outline setting.

In addition to the standard outline and fill choices, you can also apply Shape Effects, such as beveled edges, glow, shadows, reflection, and 3-D rotation, to drawn shapes. By combining different shapes, fills, and borders, you can create some very interesting effects.

As a shortcut to object formatting, you can apply one of the Shape Styles, available from the Drawing Tools Format tab.

In the following exercise, you format some shapes.

Files needed: Lesson 8 Drawings.docx, open from the preceding exercise

1. **In the Lesson 8 Drawings document, select the rounded rectangle.**
2. **On the Drawing Tools Format tab, click the More button in the Shape Styles group, opening the palette of shape styles and then click the Intense Effect — Red, Accent 2 style.**

   The style is applied to the rounded rectangle.
3. **Select the triangle; then choose Drawing Tools Format⇨Shape Fill and click the Yellow standard color.**

4. **Choose Drawing Tools Format⇨Shape Outline and click the Orange standard color.**

5. **Choose Drawing Tools Format⇨Shape Outline⇨Weight and click the ¼ point weight.**

6. **Choose Drawing Tools Format⇨Shape Effects⇨Glow⇨More Glow Colors and then click the Orange standard color.**

   The triangle and rectangle resemble Figure 8-24 at this point.

Figure 8-24

7. **Select the banner shape; then choose Drawing Tools Format⇨Shape Fill⇨Texture⇨ White Marble.**

8. **Choose Drawing Tools Format⇨Shape Outline⇨No Outline.**

9. **Choose Drawing Tools Format⇨Shape Fill⇨Gradient⇨More Gradients.**

   The Format Picture dialog box opens.

TIP

You can drag the dialog box aside and see the changes you make applied immediately to the banner shape.

10. **Select the Gradient Fill option if it's not already selected.**

11. **From the Preset Colors drop-down list, choose Gold; from the Type drop-down list, choose Radial; and from the Direction drop-down list, choose From Top Left Corner.**

12. **Click Close.**

    The banner looks like Figure 8-25.

Figure 8-25

13. **Save the changes to the document.**

Leave the document open for the next exercise.

Rotate and modify a shape, and add text

Each shape, when selected, has a small green selection handle at its top. This is a *rotation handle;* you can drag it to rotate the shape. You can also rotate a shape by exactly 90 degrees with the Rotate button (on the Drawing Tools Format tab), or rotate it by a precise amount in the Format Shape dialog box.

Some shapes also have one or more yellow diamonds on them when selected. These diamonds are for modifying the shape's dimensions; you can drag one of the diamonds to change a certain part of the shape. For example, on a block arrow are separate diamonds for changing the size of the arrow head and the arrow shaft.

To add text to a shape, just select the shape and begin typing. The text is placed in the center of the shape. The shape is a type of text box, and can be formatted in much the same way as any other text box.

In the following exercise, you rotate and modify some shapes.

Files needed: Lesson 8 Drawings.docx, open from the preceding exercise

1. **In the Lesson 8 Drawings document, select the triangle and then choose Drawing Tools Format⇨Rotate⇨Rotate Right 90° (see Figure 8-26).**

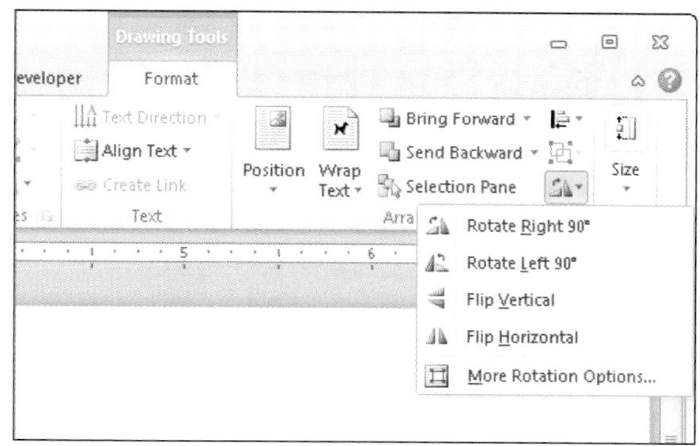

Figure 8-26

2. **Choose Drawing Tools Format⇨Rotate⇨Rotate Right 90° again to rotate the triangle another 90 degrees.**
3. **Choose Drawing Tools Format⇨Rotate⇨Flip Vertical.**

   The triangle returns to its original appearance.

Flipping is not the same as rotating for some shapes. It happens to have the same effect for this triangle, but if you try it on an irregular shape, such as Explosion 2, you will see the difference.

4. **Drag the green rotation handle on the triangle to rotate it so that the tip of the triangle (the point closest to the rotation handle) points to the right.**
5. **Right-click the triangle and choose Format Shape.**
6. **Click the 3-D Rotation category at the left and in the Z text box, type** 270 **(see Figure 8-27) so that the shape is rotated for the tip to point downward. Click Close to close the dialog box.**

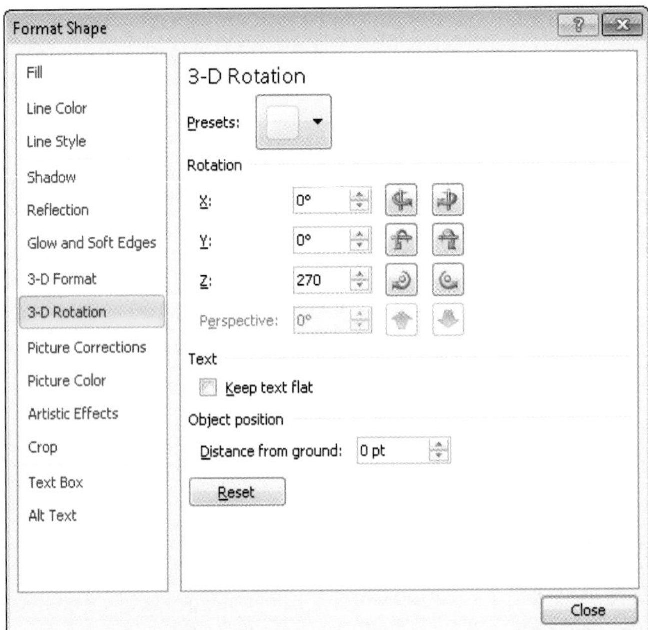

Figure 8-27

7. **Click the banner shape and then drag the leftmost diamond to the left as far as possible, increasing the middle section of the banner.**
8. **Drag the middle diamond up as far as possible, shrinking the height of the middle section of the banner; double-click in the banner and type** ACME Corporation. **Drag the diamond down slightly to make the bottoms of the letters appear if needed.**

9. **Select the text you just typed; choose Home⇨Font Color and choose black for the text color.**

   The banner looks like Figure 8-28.

Figure 8-28

10. **Save the changes to the document.**

Leave the document open for the next exercise.

Stack and group shapes

Single shapes may sometimes be useful in a document, but the real power of the Shapes feature can be found by combining shapes to create more complex drawings and logos. You can stack the shapes on top of each other, and control the order in which they appear in the stack. After you have a group of shapes arranged just the way you want them, you can then use the Group command to meld them together into one object that you can move and resize as a whole.

In the following exercise, you combine several shapes into a logo and then group them into a single object.

Files needed: Lesson 8 Drawings.docx, open from the preceding exercise

1. **In the Lesson 8 Drawings document, change the triangle's height and width to 1.75 inches each.**

   You can do this by dragging its side selection handles and using the ruler to gauge the measurement, or by choosing Drawing Tools Format⇨Size and entering precise measurements.

2. **Drag the triangle on top of the rounded rectangle, and then center the triangle vertically and horizontally over the rectangle (see Figure 8-29).**

Figure 8-29

3. **With the triangle selected, choose Drawing Tools Format⇨Send Backward to move the triangle behind the rectangle.**

4. **Choose Drawing Tools Format⇨Bring Forward⇨Bring to Front.**

   The triangle moves forward again, in front of the rectangle.

5. **Drag the banner on top of the other shapes, and then center it vertically and horizontally.**

   The triangle obscures the banner because the triangle is set to be the front object.

6. **With the banner selected, click Bring Forward until the banner is fully visible.**

   The logo looks like Figure 8-30.

Figure 8-30

7. **Hold down the Shift key and click each of the three shapes, selecting them all; then choose Drawing Tools Format⇨Group⇨Group.**

   The shapes are grouped into one object.

8. **Save the changes to the document and close it.**

Exit Word.

Summing Up

Word accepts a variety of graphics, including clip art, photographs, and drawn lines and shapes. Here are the important skills and concepts in this lesson:

- The Clip Art task pane, which you access by choosing Insert⇨Clip Art, searches for clips in Microsoft's extensive online collection.

- The Clip Art collection that Microsoft provides includes illustrations, photographs, video, and audio clips, but clip art is traditionally vector-based line drawings (what Word dubs *illustrations*).
- When you search for clip art, you can specify one or more keywords and optionally narrow down the search to a particular type of clip.
- You can make a clip available offline by right-clicking it in the Clip Art task pane and choosing Make Available Offline.
- A picture's text wrap setting determines whether it will be an inline image or will interact with surrounding text (and in what manner).
- To move a picture, drag it with the mouse. You can also specify an exact position for it in the Layout dialog box.
- To resize a picture, drag one of its selection handles. Drag a corner to resize it proportionally (that is, maintaining its aspect ratio).
- The Picture Tools Format tab contains buttons for modifying a picture in several ways, including adjusting its brightness, contrast, and sharpness, and changing its color.
- You can apply artistic effects to a picture from the Picture Tools Format tab. These effects make a photo seem like it has been drawn or painted by hand.
- Draw your own lines and shapes by choosing Insert⇨Shapes. You can then format these graphics via the Drawing Tools Format tab.
- The green circle on a graphic is its rotation handle; drag it to rotate the graphic.
- On a drawn line or shape, the yellow diamond(s), if present, are shape-changing handles; drag one of them to modify the shape.
- To group shapes, select them and then choose Drawing Tools Format⇨Group⇨Group.

Try-it-yourself lab

For more practice with the features covered in this lesson, try the following exercise on your own:

1. **Start Word and begin creating a flyer that advertises a yard sale. Type the appropriate text, including a location, the date and time, and a list of items to be sold.**
2. **Find and insert two pieces of clip art that would be appropriate for this flyer.**
3. **Set the text wrapping on the clip art so that the text wraps around the clips and then position and size the clips attractively.**

4. **Enhance the flyer further by drawing at least two shapes on the flyer and formatting them to match the look of the rest of the flyer.**

For example, you might use starbursts or arrows to call attention to important text.

5. **Save your document as Lesson 8 Flyer.**
6. **Close the document and exit Word.**

Know this tech talk

aspect ratio: The proportion of height to width of an image.

brightness: The overall lightness or darkness of an image.

clip art: Generic, predrawn artwork, available from third-party sources or from Microsoft's Office.com collection.

color saturation: The vividness of the color in an image.

color tone: The tint of an image.

color wash: An effect applied to an image that makes it monochrome but with some other color than gray.

contrast: The difference between the light and dark areas of an image.

fill: The color of the inside of a shape.

inline image: A picture that's placed within the document's paragraph structure and is treated as a character of text.

outline: The color and other properties of the outside border of a shape, or of a line.

pixel: An individual dot or data point in a raster graphic.

raster graphic: A type of graphic that defines the color of each pixel (or dot) that makes up the image individually.

text wrap: The setting that determines how the surrounding text interacts with an image, if it isn't an inline image.

vector graphic: A type of graphic that defines each line or fill with a math formula.

Lesson 9
Managing Correspondence

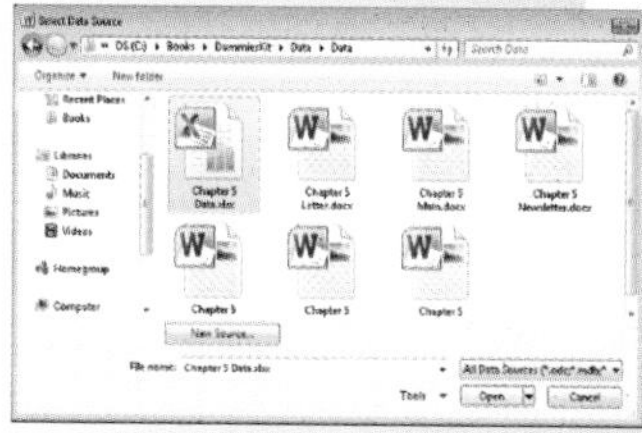

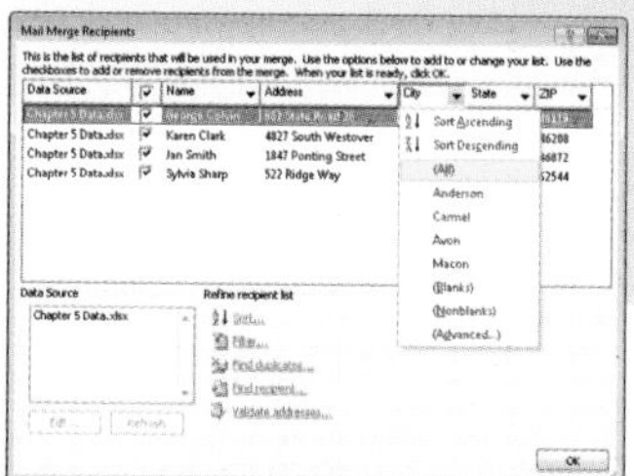

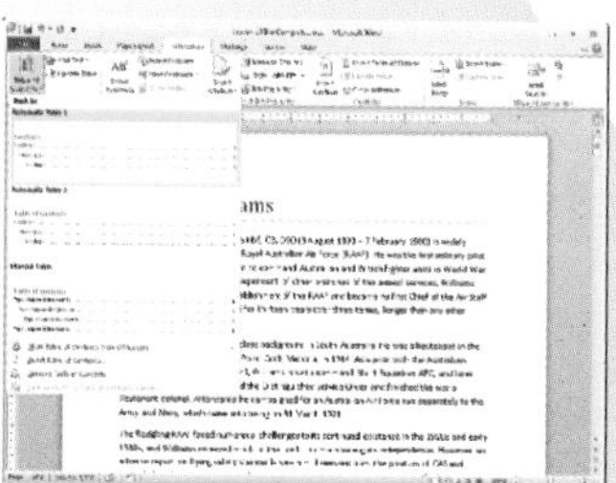

- Word can print envelopes that match your business correspondence in font and style.
- Saving a return address enables you to create other envelopes later without retyping the return address.
- Mail merge enables you to combine a list of addresses with a form for labels, envelopes, or letters.
- Sorting the records in a mail merge allows them to print in the order you specify.
- Filtering the records in a mail merge enables you to exclude certain records from displaying or printing.

This lesson covers creating special-purpose documents, such as envelopes, and creating mail merges that enable you to customize multiple copies of an envelope, label, or document from a separately stored data list. You learn how to set up basic merges, and how to sort and filter a mail merge data source.

Create Envelopes

Envelopes are the natural companions of business and personal letters. Most of the time, when you print a letter, you also want an envelope for it. You can address the envelope by hand, of course, but printing an envelope is quick and easy in Word.

One nice thing about the Envelopes feature in Word is that it can automatically extract the mailing address from the letter, so you don't have to retype it. Envelopes also stores your return address and recalls it for you each time you print an envelope.

An envelope has a different paper size and orientation than a business letter, so how does Word manage to store them both in the same file? Word creates a section break between the letter and the envelope. Each section, such as headers/footers, watermarks, page numbers, and more, can have its own settings that would normally apply to the entire document. You learn more about sections later in this lesson; for now, just appreciate the capability they add to the process of creating an envelope.

Add an envelope to a document

In the following exercise, you add an envelope to a document.

Files needed: Lesson 9 Letter.docx

1. **Open the Lesson 9 Letter document and save it as Lesson 9 Letter Envelope.**
2. **Choose Mailings⇨Envelopes.**

   The Envelopes and Labels dialog box opens. Word attempts to fill in the correct address in the Delivery Address box, but in this case, it fails; it fills in the bulleted list instead of the mailing address.
3. **Click Cancel to close the dialog box.**
4. **Select the recipient name and address in the letter *(Mr. Charlie Lutz, 475 E Main St., Carmel, IN 46025)* and then choose Mailings⇨Envelopes again.**

   This time Word fills in the address correctly.
5. **Type your own return address, or make one up, in the Return Address box** (see **Figure 9-1**), **click Add to Document (or Change Document), and if prompted to save the return address as the default, click Yes.**

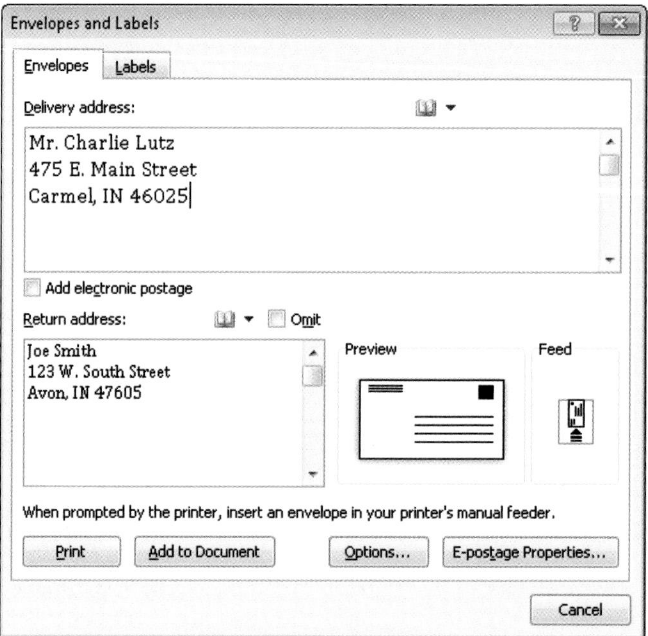

Figure 9-1

A new section is created at the beginning of the document, and the envelope is placed there. Notice in Figure 9-2 that the new section has a different paper size, orientation, and margins than the letter.

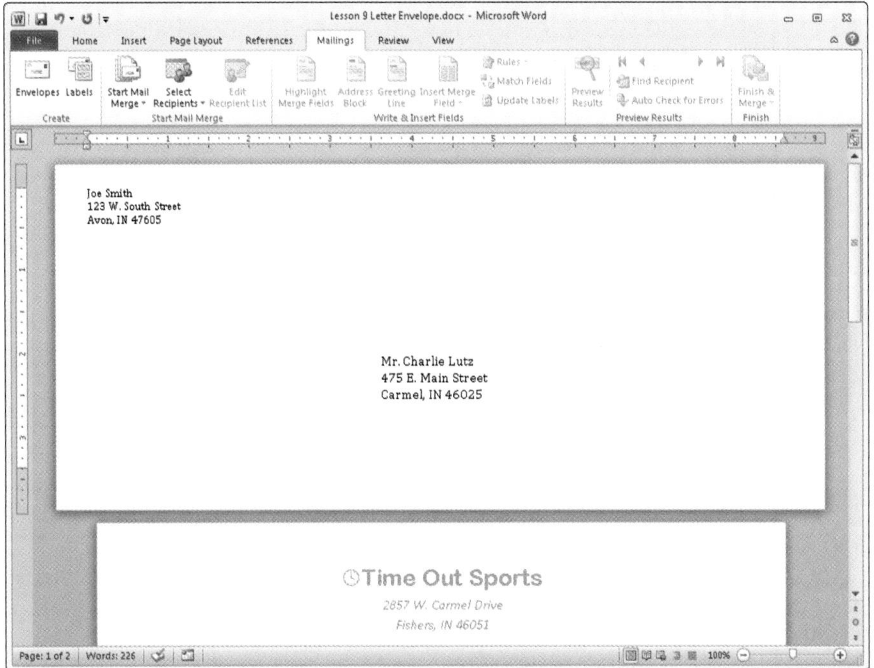

Figure 9-2

To understand how the document can have two different page sizes, switch to Draft view. Notice the section break between the two pages. Switch back to Print Layout view when finished.

Leave the document open for the next exercise.

EXTRA INFO

In the future, this same return address will be filled in for you automatically. If you don't want to use the return address for the current envelope but may want to use it in the future, you can select the Omit check box. If you don't want to use the address anymore permanently, delete it from the Return Address box.

Change the envelope size

There are many different shapes and sizes of envelopes, and Word can print on any of them. However, you must tell Word the dimensions of the envelope you're using so it can size the document appropriately.

In the following exercise, you change the size of an envelope definition stored in a Word document.

Files needed: Lesson 9 Letter Envelope.docx, open from the preceding exercise

1. **In the Lesson 9 Letter Envelope document, choose Mailings➪Envelopes to reopen the Envelopes and Labels dialog box and then click the Options button.**

   The Envelope Options dialog box opens. See Figure 9-3.

2. **From the Envelope Size drop-down list, choose Monarch, and then click OK to return to the Envelopes and Labels dialog box.**

3. **Click the Change Document button.**

   The envelope size changes in the document.

4. **Change the envelope size to Size 10.**

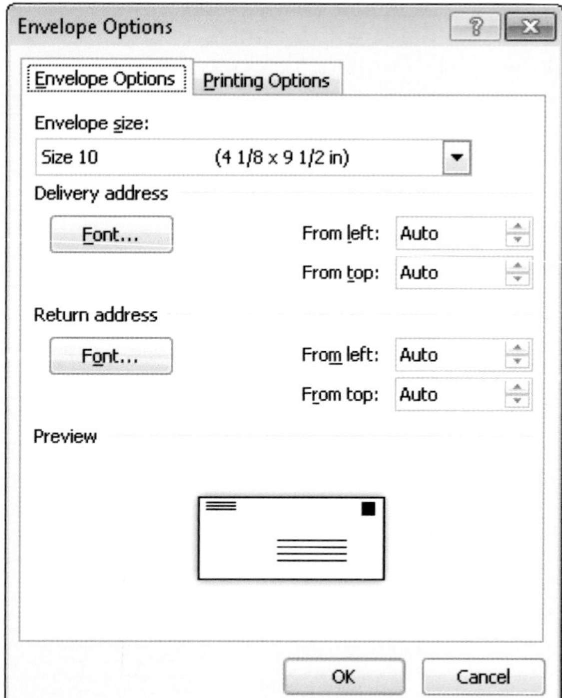

Figure 9-3

Leave the document open for the next exercise.

Print an envelope

To print an envelope, feed an envelope into your printer and then print the section of the document that contains the envelope. You can either do this manually (by choosing File⇨Print and then selecting only page 1 to print) or you can reopen the Envelopes and Labels dialog box and print from there, in which case only the envelope (not the letter) prints.

In the following exercise, you print an envelope.

Files needed: Lesson 9 Letter Envelope.docx, open from the preceding exercise

1. **Choose Mailings⇨Envelopes to reopen the Envelopes and Labels dialog box (see Figure 9-4).**
2. **Feed an envelope into your printer and then click the Print button.**

   The envelope prints.
3. **Save and close the document.**

Leave Word open for the next exercise.

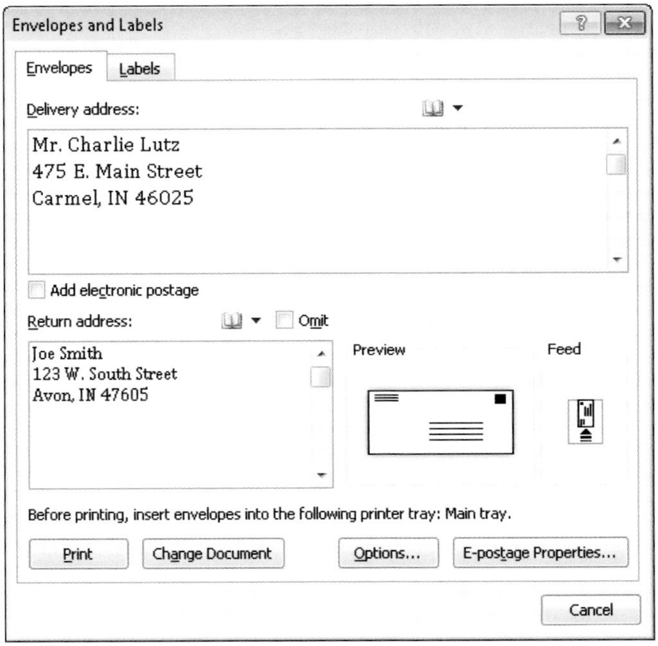

Figure 9-4

If the envelope printing doesn't go as you expected — say, it prints on the wrong side, or it's not lined up correctly — you might need to try again and change the orientation at which you feed it into the printer. For example, you might need to feed the envelope sideways, rotated 180 degrees, or upside-down.

To avoid wasting an envelope, do a test print with plain paper. Draw an arrow on a piece of paper, and put it into your printer's paper tray, face up, arrow facing in. Then print what will appear on your envelope on that paper. The relationship between the printout and the arrow can tell you how to orient the envelopes you feed in. For example, if the arrow is on the reverse side from the printing, you know that envelopes need to be fed into the printer flap up.

Perform a Mail Merge

Big companies use mail merge to mail customized advertisements, but it's not just for businesses. Home users can take advantage of mail merge for Christmas card mailing labels, party invitations, club newsletters, and more.

The three steps to a mail merge are

1. Create (or identify) the data source.
2. Create the main document and then insert the merge codes in it.
3. Perform the merge operation between the data source and the main document.

The data source must be a delimited file. In other words, there has to be some consistent way that it distinguishes between one column or row of data and the next. Here are some possible data source types:

LINGO

A **mail merge** combines a data list, usually of names and addresses (that is, mailing information), with a form letter, a label, or an envelope template to produce customized copies of the letter for each person.

LINGO

The **data source** is the file that contains the names to be merged, whereas the **main document** is the file that contains the text that will be the same for each copy, plus the codes to link to the data source.

- **Excel or Word table:** If the data source is an Excel spreadsheet, each type of information is in a separate column, as shown in Figure 9-5. The same goes if the data source is a Word table.

- **Plain text:** If the data source is a plain text file, each column is delimited (separated) by a specific character, such as tab or a comma. When a delimited text file uses commas, it's a Comma Separated Values, or CSV, file. The example in Figure 9-6 uses a comma.
- **Outlook:** If the data source is an Outlook Contacts list, each type of information is in a separate field.
- **Word list:** If you don't have a data source already, choose Mailings⇨Select Recipients⇨Type New List to create one with the Type New List feature in Word.

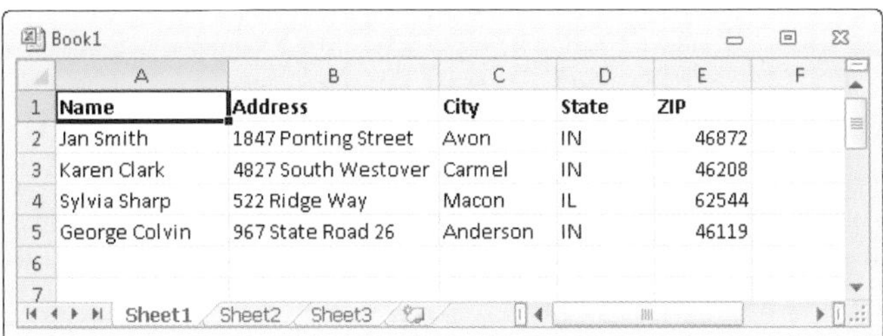

Figure 9-5

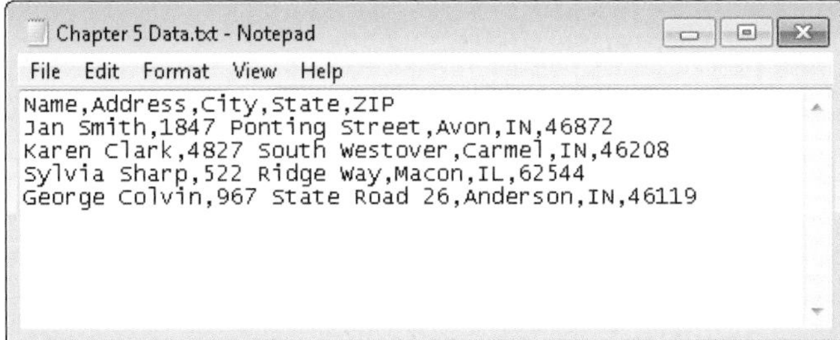

Figure 9-6

A data file shouldn't contain anything except the data (and perhaps a single row of field labels, as in Figure 9-6 with Name, Address, City, State, and ZIP). Don't use any blank rows or titles at the top of the page because that confuses the Mail Merge utility. Check your data file to remove extraneous rows before using the file as your mail merge source.

After preparing the data file, you set up the main document. You can either create the main document from scratch, or you can start with an existing document and convert it to be a mail merge main document. The main document consists of regular text plus codes that show where the merge fields should be inserted. Figure 9-7 shows an example.

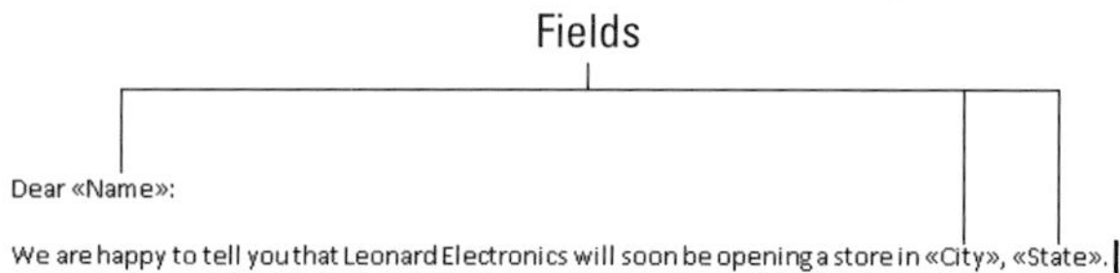

Figure 9-7

Then, as the final step in the merge process, you bring together the two pieces. You can do so either by sending the results directly to the printer or by creating a new document that contains the merge, which you can then edit as needed and then print.

Create mail-merged letters

Letters are one of the most commonly mail-merged document types. Typically the merge fields are used to generate the mailing address. In some letters, fields are also used to customize the letter itself (refer to Figure 9-7).

Word 2010 provides some time-saving code blocks that you can use if you like. For example, you can insert an `<<AddressBlock>>` code, which sets up a standard mailing address for you, or you can insert individual codes to create the mailing address block yourself. For example, the following are equivalent:

```
<<AddressBlock>>        <<Name>>
                        <<Address>>
                        <<City>>, <<State>> <<ZIP>>
```

Word also provides a `<<greeting line>>` code block that inserts a greeting, such as *Dear <<title>> <<lastname>>*. You can customize the greeting line code to use any combination of titles, first names, and last names.

The following exercise doesn't use the greeting line code because the data file doesn't have separate fields for first and last names, and the `<<greeting line>>` code works best when those names are separate.

In this exercise, you create mail-merged letters.

Files needed: Lesson 9 Main.docx and Lesson 9 Data.xlsx

1. **Open Lesson 9 Main and save it as Lesson 9 Main Merge.**
2. **Choose Mailings⇨Start Mail Merge⇨Letters.**
3. **Choose Mailings⇨Select Recipients⇨Use Existing List.**

   The Select Data Source dialog box opens. See Figure 9-8.

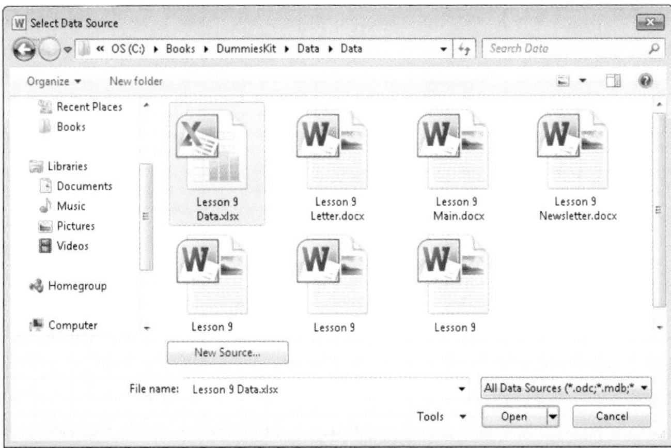

Figure 9-8

4. **Navigate to the folder containing the data files for this class. Select Lesson 9 Data.xlsx and click Open.**

   The Select Table dialog box opens, prompting you to choose which worksheet you want to use.

5. **In the Select Table dialog box, make sure Sheet1 is selected and click OK.**

6. **Move the insertion point to the line immediately after the date and then choose Mailings⇨Address Block.**

   The Insert Address Block dialog box opens. See Figure 9-9.

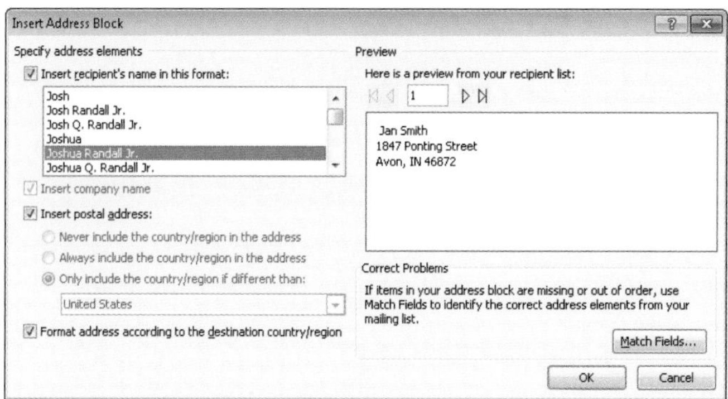

Figure 9-9

7. **Confirm that the address in the Preview area looks correctly formed and then click OK to accept the default settings.**

   An `<<AddressBlock>>` code appears in the document.

8. **Press Enter to start a new line after the `<<AddressBlock>>` code, type** Dear, **and press the spacebar once.**

> **EXTRA INFO**
>
> If the sample in the Preview area is not right, click the Match Fields button and specify which fields should be associated with which parts of the address block.

9. **Choose Mailings⇨Insert Merge Field⇨Name.**

   A `<<Name>>` code is inserted.

10. **Type a comma after the code and then click to move the insertion point immediately before the word *store* in the first paragraph.**

11. **Choose Mailings⇨Insert Merge Field⇨City.**

    A `<<City>>` code is inserted at the insertion point.

12. **Press the spacebar once to add a space after the code.**

    The letter looks like Figure 9-10.

13. **Choose Mailings⇨Preview Results.**

    The first letter appears as it will be printed. Notice that extra space is between the lines of the address block.

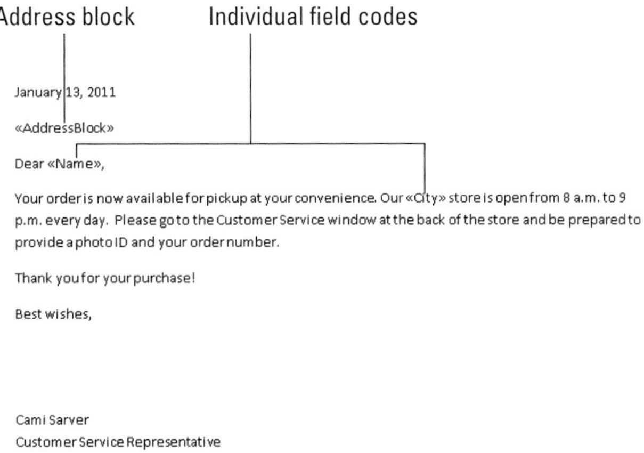

Figure 9-10

14. **Select all the lines of the address block on the previewed letter and then choose Home⇨Line and Paragraph Spacing⇨Remove Space after Paragraph (see Figure 9-11).**

    This takes care of the spacing problem for all letters in the merge file.

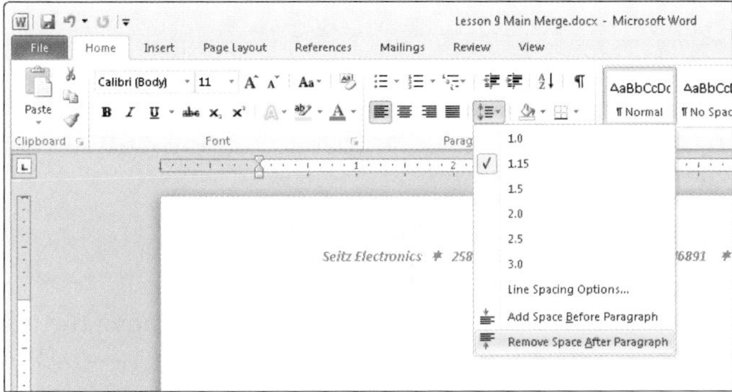

Figure 9-11

15. **Click at the end of the last line of the address block and press Enter once, creating an extra line of space between the address and the greeting.**
16. **Choose Mailings⇨Next Record to see a preview of the next letter (see Figure 9-12).**

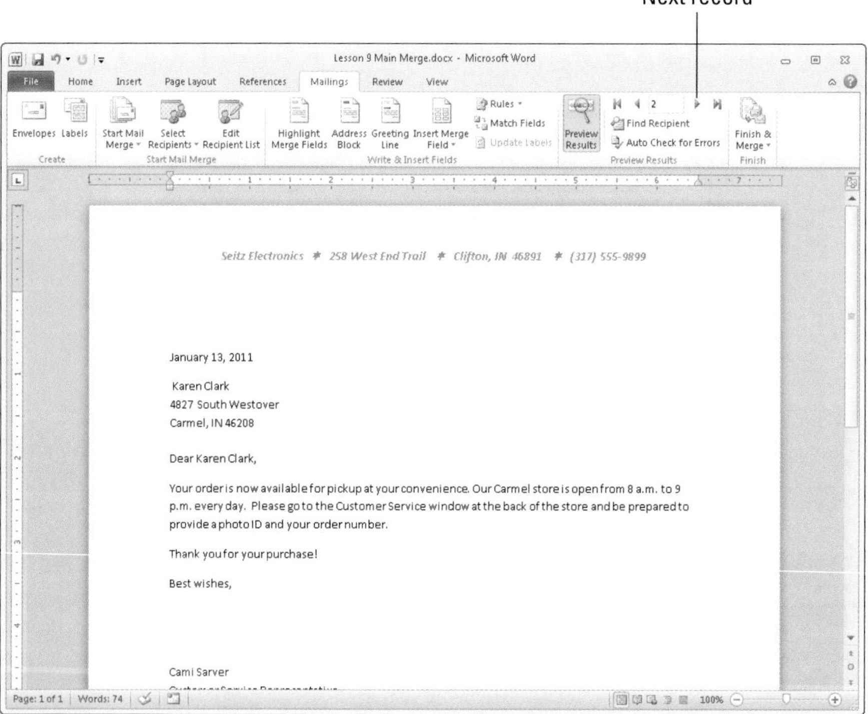

Figure 9-12

To make the letters look better, you could center them vertically on the page, as you learn to do in Lesson 4.

17. **Keep clicking Next Record until you have seen all records and then choose Mailings➪Finish & Merge➪Edit Individual Documents.**

    The Merge to New Document dialog box opens.

18. **Click OK to merge all the copies into one document.**

    A new document — Letters1 — opens.

19. **Scroll through the new document to check the letters; then close it without saving changes to it.**

20. **Save your changes to the Lesson 9 Main Merge file and then close it.**

Leave Word open for the next exercise.

Create mail-merged labels

Another type of mail merge involves printing on sticky-backed labels, which you can then pull apart and use for package mailing, name tags, or any other purpose you might use labels for.

The mail merge process is much the same for labels, except that you specify a label type and size and then Word creates a table that mimics the labels. The merge fields are placed into the upper-left corner cell of the table and copied into the other cells.

In this exercise, you create mail-merged labels.

Files needed: Lesson 9 Data.xlsx

1. **In Word, press Ctrl+N to start a new blank document, save it as Lesson 9 Labels.docx, and then choose Mailings⇨Start Mail Merge⇨Labels.**

   The Label Options dialog box appears.

2. **From the Label Vendors drop-down list, choose Avery US Letter; in the Product Number list, choose 5160 Easy Peel Address Labels (see Figure 9-13); click OK.**

Figure 9-13

3. **If you don't see the gridlines of the table onscreen, choose Table Tools Layout⇨View Gridlines.**

4. **Choose Mailings⇨Select Recipients⇨Use Existing List.**

   The Select Data Source dialog box opens (refer to Figure 9-8).

5. **Navigate to the folder containing the data files for this class. Select Lesson 9 Data.xlsx and click Open.**

   The Select Table dialog box opens, prompting you to choose which worksheet you will use for the data source.

6. **In the Select Table dialog box, make sure Sheet1 is selected and then click OK.**

   The data source is attached. In the table, `<<Next Record>>` codes appear in every cell except the upper-left one. See Figure 9-14.

7. **Choose Mailings⇨Address Block, and in the Insert Address Block dialog box that appears, click OK to accept the default address block settings.**

   The `<<AddressBlock>>` code appears only in the upper-left cell.

For more practice, you could delete the `<<AddressBlock>>` code and construct your own address block manually by inserting the `<<Name>>` field, pressing Shift+Enter, inserting the `<<Address>>` field, pressing Shift+Enter, inserting the `<<City>>` field, typing a comma and a space, inserting the `<<State>>` field, typing two spaces, and inserting the `<<ZIP>>` field.

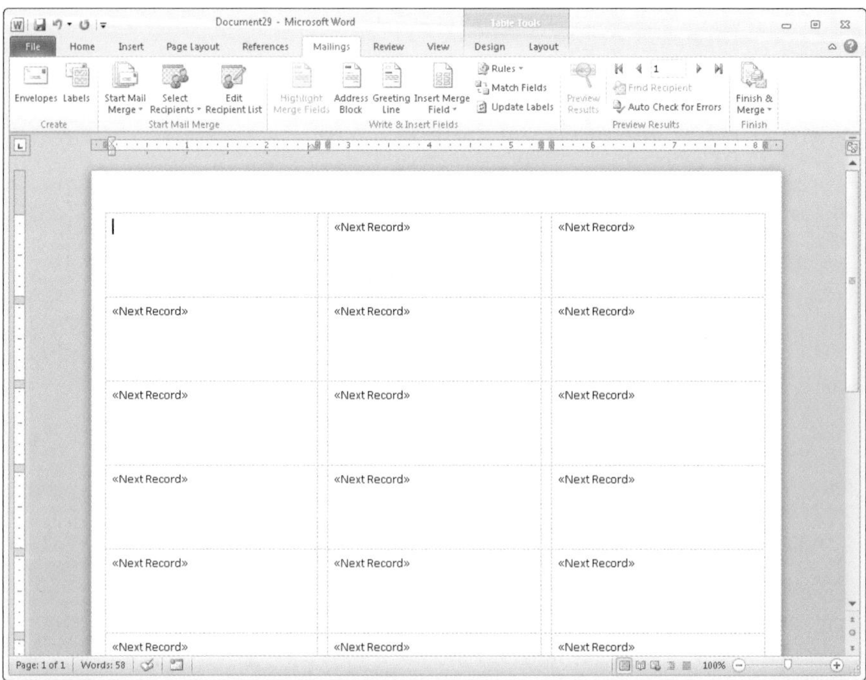

Figure 9-14

8. **Choose Mailings⇨Update Labels.**

   The code from the upper-left cell is copied to each of the other cells.

9. **Choose Mailings⇨Preview Results.**

   The four label results appear, as shown in Figure 9-15.

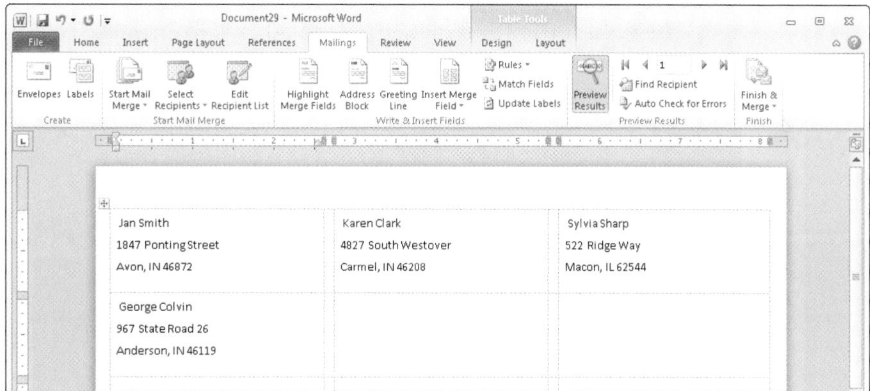

Figure 9-15

10. **Save the document.**

Leave the document open for the next exercise.

Sort and Filter Mail Merge Records

If you pull data from a large database to create your mail merge or pull from a data source that includes more records than you need for your purposes, you may find it helpful to sort and/or filter the data to show only what you want, in the order you want it. In the following exercises, you sort and filter your data.

Sort a merge data source

Sorting the records in the data source places them in alphabetical order (or numeric order) based on one or more fields. For example, you might want to print mailing labels in zip code order, or by last name.

In this exercise, you sort the records in a mail merge by zip code.

Files needed: Lesson 9 Labels.xlsx, open from the preceding exercise

1. **In the Lesson 9 Labels document, choose Mailings⇨Edit Recipient List.**

   The Mail Merge Recipients dialog box opens.

2. **Click the down-pointing arrow on the ZIP field's column header, choose Sort Ascending (see Figure 9-16), and click OK.**

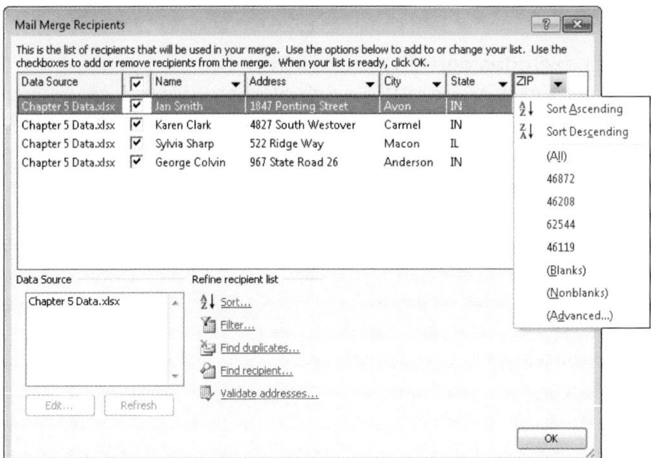

Figure 9-16

The records appear in zip code order, as shown in Figure 9-17.

If field codes appear instead of records, choose Mailings⇨Preview Results.

3. **Save the document.**

Leave the document open for the next exercise.

If you need a multi-level sort to break ties, such as sorting by last name if two records have the same zip code, click the Sort link in the Refine Recipient List section (see Figure 9-16), to set up your sort in a dialog box that allows multiple sort levels.

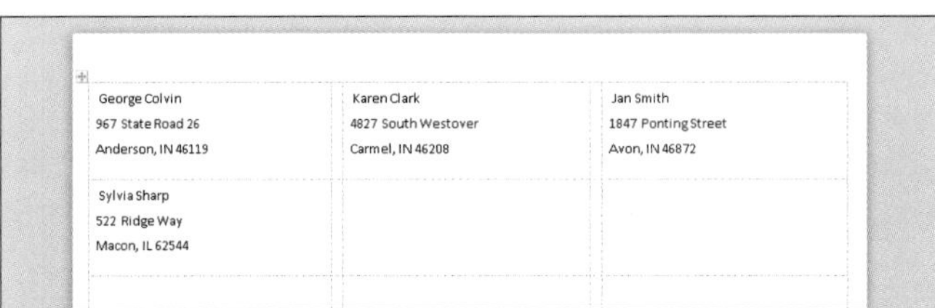

Figure 9-17

Filter a merge data source

Filtering a data source excludes certain records (or, to look at it another way, it includes only certain records) on the basis of one or more criteria you specify. For example, you might want only addresses from a certain city or state to be included, or only those that match a list of certain cities or states.

Filtering data excludes certain records from the merge results, but does not delete the rejected data from the original copy of the data source, so you can choose later to re-include it, or include it when using that same data set for other projects.

In this exercise, you filter the records in a mail merge to show only those with certain cities.

Files needed: Lesson 9 Labels.xlsx, open from the preceding exercise

1. **Choose Mailings⇨Edit Recipient List.**

   The Mail Merge Recipients dialog box opens.

2. **Click the down-pointing arrow on the City field's column header, choose Avon (see Figure 9-18), and click OK.**

   The label preview changes to show only one label.

3. **Choose Mailings⇨Edit Recipient List.**

   The Mail Merge Recipients dialog box opens.

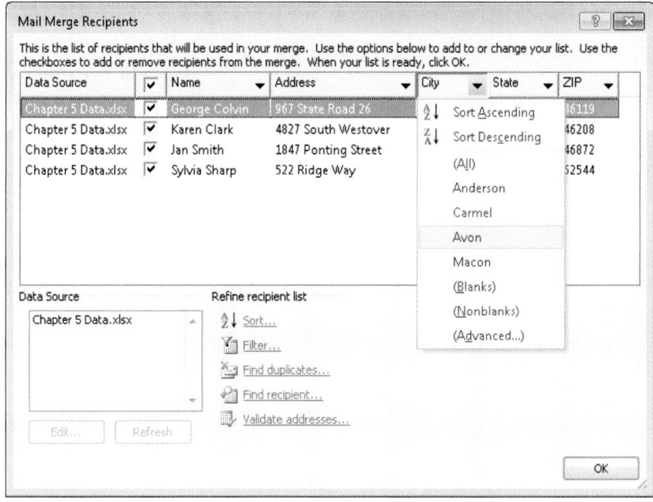

Figure 9-18

4. **Click the down-pointing arrow on the City field's column header and choose (All).**

   The complete list of all four records reappears. See Figure 9-19.

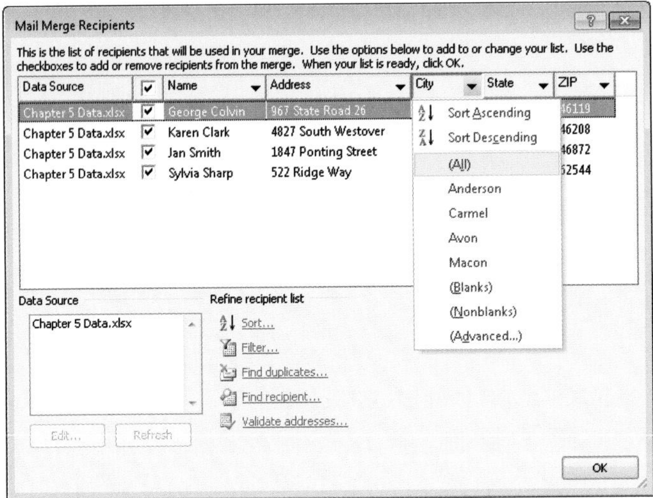

Figure 9-19

5. **Click the down-pointing arrow on the City field's column header and choose Advanced.**

   The Filter and Sort dialog box opens with the Filter Records tab displayed.

6. **Choose City from the first drop-down list in the Field column; in the Compare To column, in the first text box, type** Avon **(see Figure 9-20).**

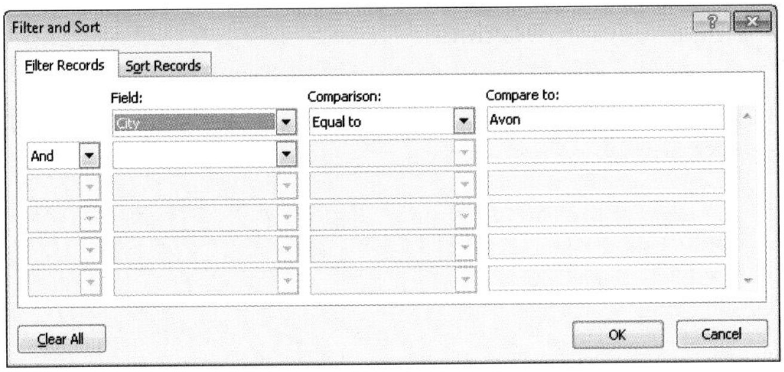

Filter and Sort
Filter Records | Sort Records
Field: City | Comparison: Equal to | Compare to: Avon
And
Clear All | OK | Cancel

Figure 9-20

7. **In the second row, choose Or from the And drop-down list; choose City from the Field drop-down list in the second row; and in the second row in the Compare To column, type** Carmel **(see Figure 9-21).**

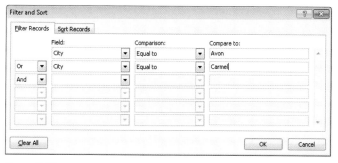

Figure 9-21

8. **Click OK to accept the new filtering criteria and then click OK to close the Mail Merge Recipients dialog box.**

   Two labels appear in the results: one for Avon and one for Carmel.

9. **Save the document and close it.**

Exit Word.

Summing Up

Here are the key points from this lesson:

- You can include an envelope in the same document as a letter. The envelope is in a different section, which enables it to have a different page size.
- To add an envelope to a document, change its size, or print it, choose Mailings⇨Envelopes.
- Mail merges combine a main document with a database listing to create customized copies of the main document. Use the commands on the Mailings tab to set up mail merges.
- To choose which type of document to mail merge, choose Mailings⇨Start Mail Merge and then choose either Letters or Labels.
- To select a data source for the mail merge, choose Mailings⇨Select Recipients⇨Use Existing List.

- To insert fields into the main document, choose Mailings⇨Address Block for a full address block, or choose Mailings⇨Insert Merge Field to select a specific field.
- To sort the recipients, choose Mailings⇨Edit Recipient List and then click the down arrow on one of the column headings to sort by that field.
- To filter the recipients, choose Mailings⇨Edit Recipient List and then open the menu for the field's column header and choose what values to include or exclude.

Try-it-yourself lab

For more practice with the features covered in this lesson, try the following exercise on your own:

1. **Start a new blank document and start a Labels mail merge. Use any size label you like. Save the document as Lesson 9 Label Main.**
2. **Using your Outlook Contacts list, or any delimited data file that contains names and addresses, create mailing labels that you could use to distribute your newsletter by postal mail.**

   If you don't have an appropriate data file, create one by choosing Mailings⇨Select Recipients⇨Type New List.
3. **Perform the mail merge to create the labels in a new document and save the new document as Lesson 9 Label Merge.**
4. **Close all documents and exit Word.**

Know this tech talk

address block: An `<<AddressBlock>>` code that creates a fully formed name and address for mailing in a mail merge document.

data source: The file containing the data to be used for a mail merge.

delimited: A file that uses a consistent character to separate data into multiple columns. A comma or a tab stop is commonly used as a delimiter character.

mail merge: Combining a data list with a form letter, label, or envelope template to produce customized copies.

main document: The document in a mail merge that contains the standardized text and the codes for linking to the data source.

Lesson 10

Preparing Professional Reports

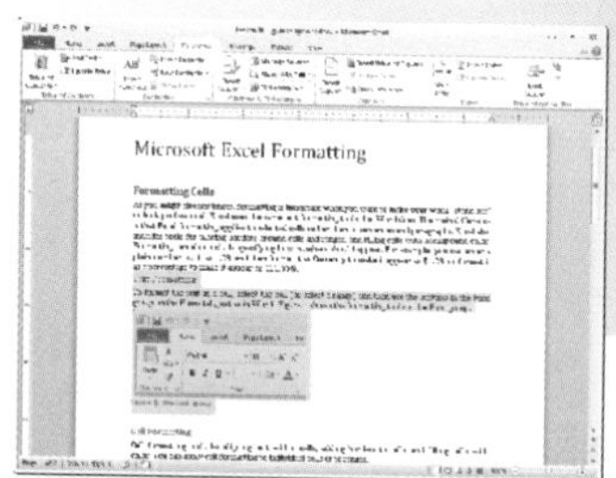

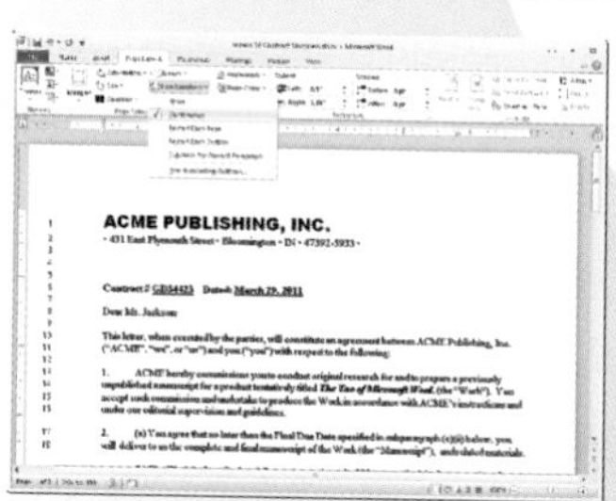

- A Table of Contents lets readers know the starting page numbers for each heading.
- An index provides an alphabetical listing of important terms and their page numbers.
- Figure captions make it easier to refer to a specific figure in the text.
- A Table of Authorities provides a list of legal citations in a document.
- Footnotes and endnotes provide background information separate from the main text.

When preparing long documents, you might want to take advantage of some of the many features that Word has for keeping things organized across multiple pages. For example, you can create footnotes, a Table of Contents, an index, and other helpers for your audience, as well as captioning and auto-numbering figures, to help yourself keep things numbered properly as you edit and move text.

Create a Table of Contents

Most technical and educational books include a Table of Contents, or TOC, to assist readers in quickly locating specific sections. A TOC lists each heading of the document, and either lists its page number (suitable for printed copies) or provides a live hyperlink to it (suitable for online copies).

LINGO

A **Table of Contents,** or **TOC,** is a chronological list of the main headings in the document, with page numbers or hyperlinks that provide quick access to the referenced sections.

Define heading levels

TOCs are created based on the styles in your document. Each of the built-in heading styles in Word has a specific TOC level pre-assigned to it, but you can change these.

You can also assign TOC levels to other styles as well, including styles that you wouldn't normally associate with headings. For example, you could assign a TOC level to a style you use for figure captions to include each figure caption in your TOC.

In this exercise, you modify the TOC levels for the styles used for headings in a document.

Files needed: Lesson 10 Bio.docx

1. **Open Lesson 10 Bio and save it as Lesson 10 Bio Complete.**
2. **On the Home tab, click the dialog box launcher in the Styles group.**

   The Styles pane opens.
3. **Scroll down in the document to the first heading: *Early Career.* Click to move the insertion point into it.**

   In the Styles pane, the Major style is highlighted.
4. **Point to the Major style in the Styles pane, and when a down arrow appears to its right, click the arrow to open its menu and choose Modify (see Figure 10-1).**

   The Modify Style dialog box opens.
5. **In the bottom-left corner of the dialog box, click the Format button and choose Paragraph (see Figure 10-2).**

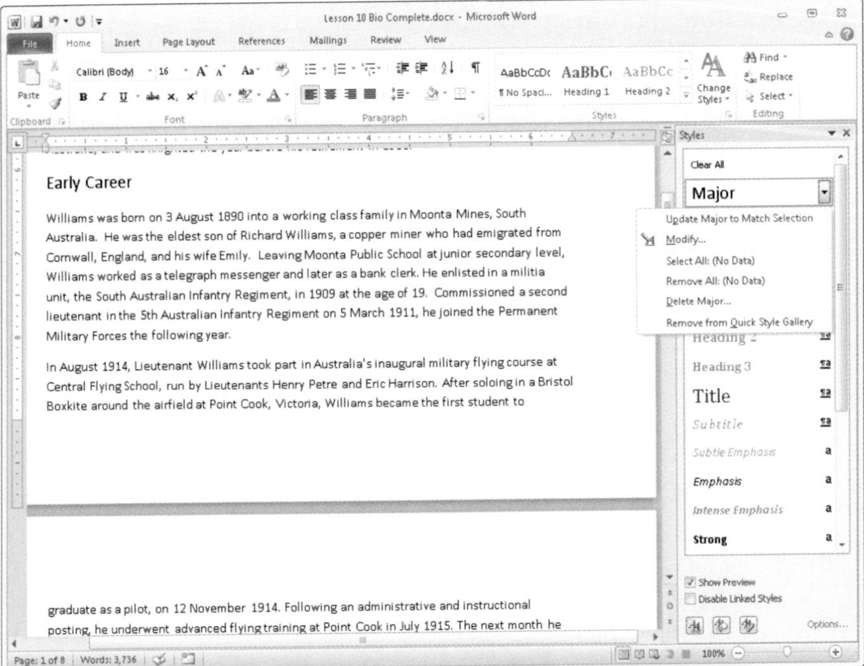
Lesson 10 Bio Complete.docx - Microsoft Word
File
Home
Insert
Page Layout
References
Mailings
Review
View
Paste
Clipboard
Calibri (Body)
16
Font
Paragraph
AaBbCcDc
AaBbC
AaBbCc
¶ No Spaci...
Heading 1
Heading 2
Change Styles
Styles
Find
Replace
Select
Editing
Early Career
Williams was born on 3 August 1890 into a working class family in Moonta Mines, South Australia. He was the eldest son of Richard Williams, a copper miner who had emigrated from Cornwall, England, and his wife Emily. Leaving Moonta Public School at junior secondary level, Williams worked as a telegraph messenger and later as a bank clerk. He enlisted in a militia unit, the South Australian Infantry Regiment, in 1909 at the age of 19. Commissioned a second lieutenant in the 5th Australian Infantry Regiment on 5 March 1911, he joined the Permanent Military Forces the following year.
In August 1914, Lieutenant Williams took part in Australia's inaugural military flying course at Central Flying School, run by Lieutenants Henry Petre and Eric Harrison. After soloing in a Bristol Boxkite around the airfield at Point Cook, Victoria, Williams became the first student to
graduate as a pilot, on 12 November 1914. Following an administrative and instructional posting, he underwent advanced flying training at Point Cook in July 1915. The next month he
Styles
Clear All
Major
Update Major to Match Selection
Modify...
Select All: (No Data)
Remove All: (No Data)
Delete Major...
Remove from Quick Style Gallery
Heading 2
Heading 3
Title
Subtitle
Subtle Emphasis
Emphasis
Intense Emphasis
Strong
Show Preview
Disable Linked Styles
Options...
Page: 1 of 8
Words: 3,736
100%

Figure 10-1

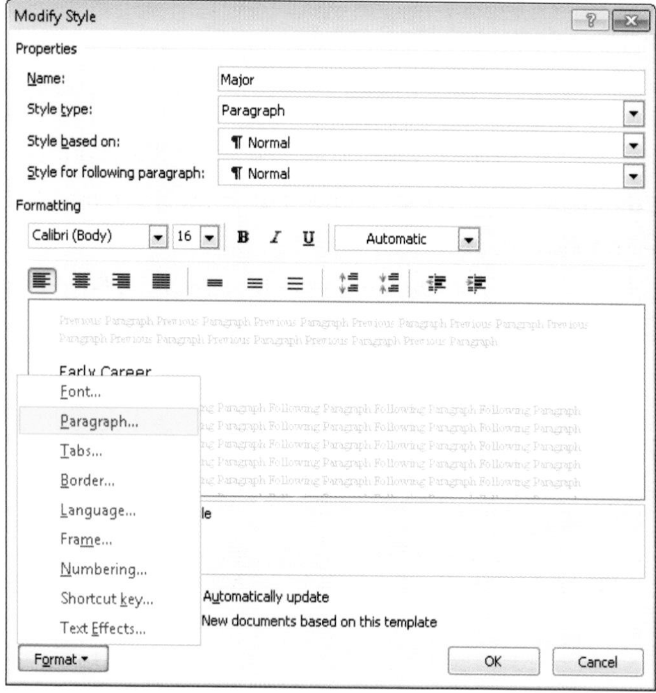

Figure 10-2

6. **In the Paragraph dialog box that appears, from the Outline Level drop-down list, choose Level 1 (see Figure 10-3), click OK to close the Paragraph dialog box, and then click OK to close the Modify Style dialog box.**
7. **Repeat Steps 4–6 to assign Level 2 to the Minor style and then click the Close (x) button on the Styles pane to close it.**
8. **Save the document.**

Leave the document open for the next exercise.

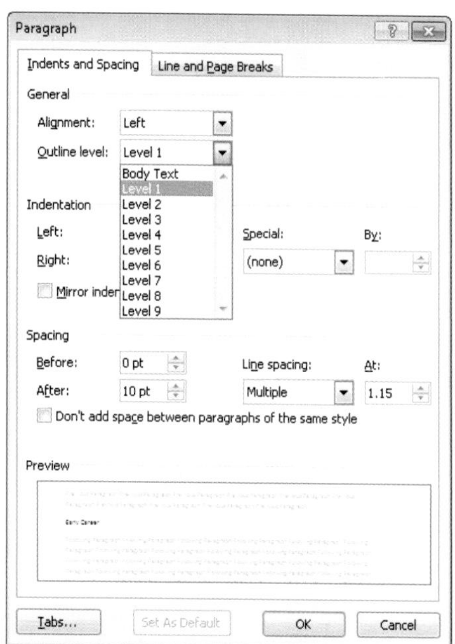

Figure 10-3

Generate a TOC

You can place a TOC anywhere in a document, but it's traditionally placed at the beginning, or at least near the beginning (for example, following a cover page). You have many options for generating the TOC, such as number alignment, hyperlinking, and the levels to include.

In this exercise, you generate a Table of Contents.

Files needed: Lesson 10 Bio Complete.docx, open from the preceding exercise

1. **Press Ctrl+Home to move the insertion point to the beginning of the Lesson 10 Bio Complete document.**
2. **Choose References⇨Table of Contents⇨Automatic Table 1 (see Figure 10-4).**

   A default-formatted TOC appears in the document, as shown in Figure 10-5.

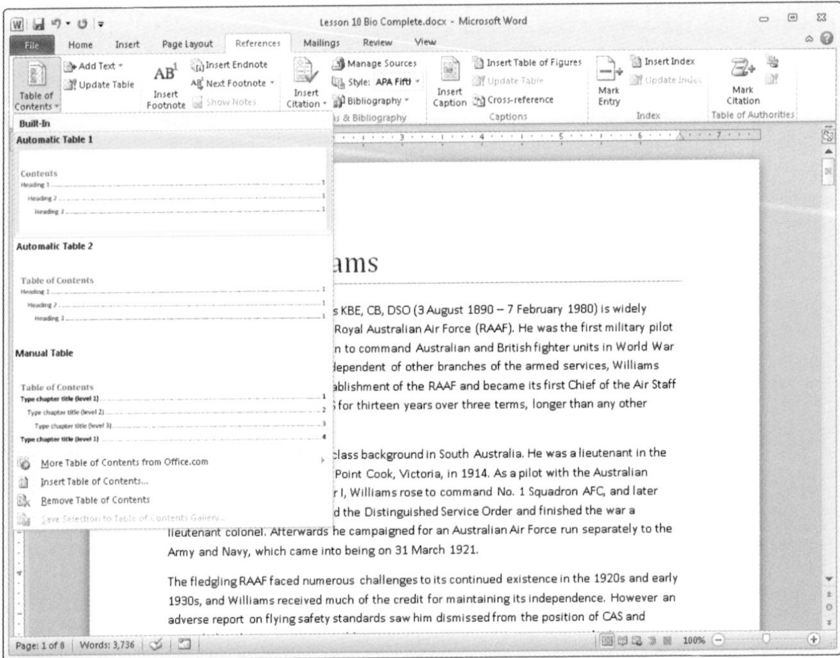

Figure 10-4

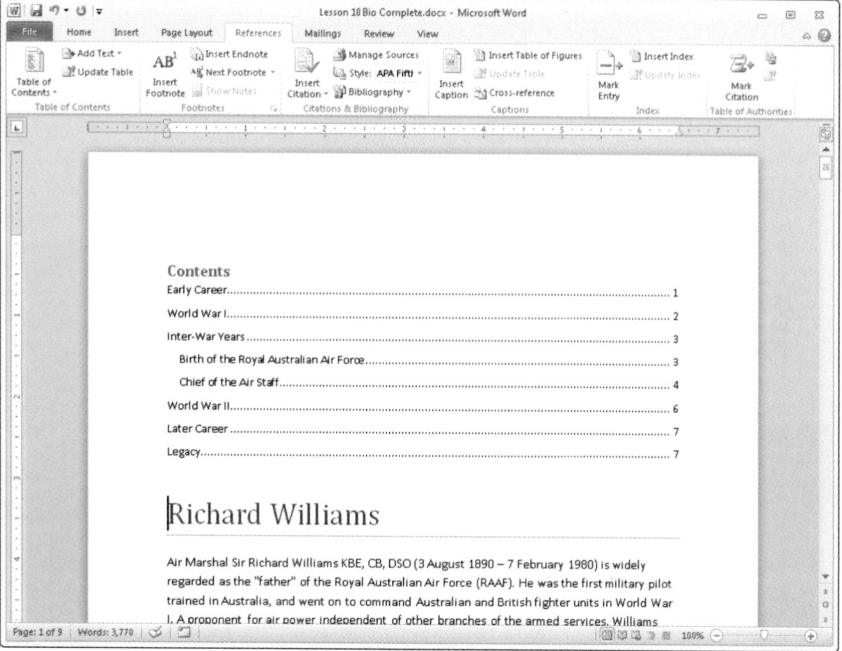

Figure 10-5

3. **Press Ctrl+Z or click the Undo button on the Quick Access toolbar to remove the TOC.**

   You re-create it via different settings next.

4. **Choose References⇨Table of Contents⇨Insert Table of Contents.**

   The Table of Contents dialog box opens.

5. **From the Formats drop-down list, choose Formal (see Figure 10-6) and then click OK.**

   A differently formatted TOC appears.

6. **Save the document.**

Leave the document open for the next exercise.

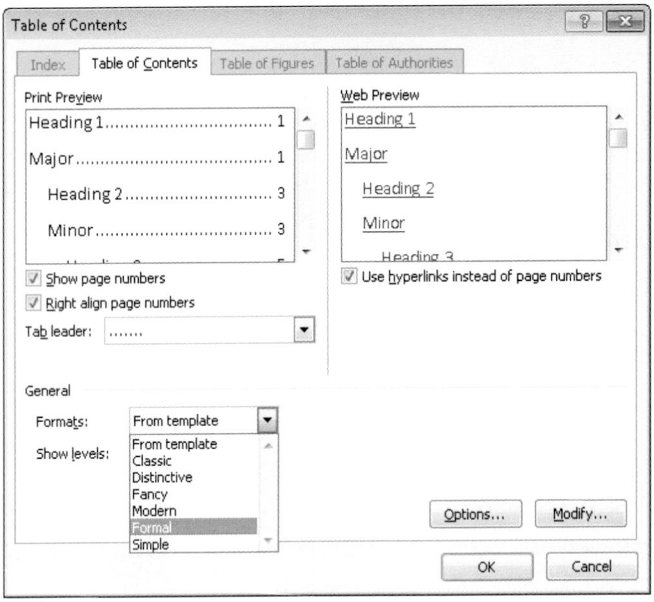

Figure 10-6

Update a TOC

When you make changes to the document, the TOC doesn't update automatically. You can refresh it at any time, however.

In this exercise, you update a Table of Contents.

Files needed: Lesson 10 Bio Complete.docx, open from the preceding exercise

1. **Scroll down to the first heading in the Lesson 10 Bio Complete document *(Early Career)* and edit it to** Early Life.
2. **Scroll back up to the top of the document and then choose References➪Update Table.**

   The Update Table of Contents dialog box opens. See Figure 10-7.

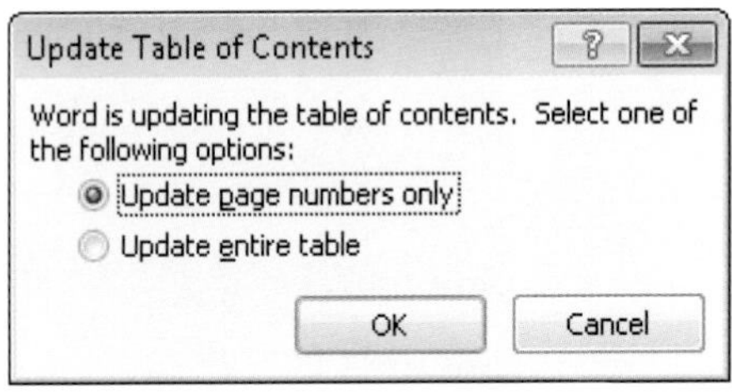

Figure 10-7

3. **Select Update Entire Table and then click OK.**

   The TOC updates to show the new wording.
4. **Save the document.**

Leave the document open for the next exercise.

Work with TOC styles

The text within the TOC is formatted according to special built-in TOC styles in Word. You can select a different format when creating the TOC (via the Formats drop-down list), as you did earlier in the "Generate a TOC" section. You can also fine-tune the TOC's styles by modifying the styles individually.

In this exercise, you modify a TOC style.

Files needed: Lesson 10 Bio Complete.docx, open from the preceding exercise

1. **In the TOC at the beginning of the Lesson 10 Bio Complete document, click in the first line *(Early Life).***
2. **On the Home tab, click the dialog box launcher in the Styles group, opening the Styles pane.**
3. **In the Styles pane, scroll down to the TOC styles (see Figure 10-8).**
4. **Right-click the TOC 1 style in the Styles pane and choose Modify Style.**

   The Modify dialog box opens.

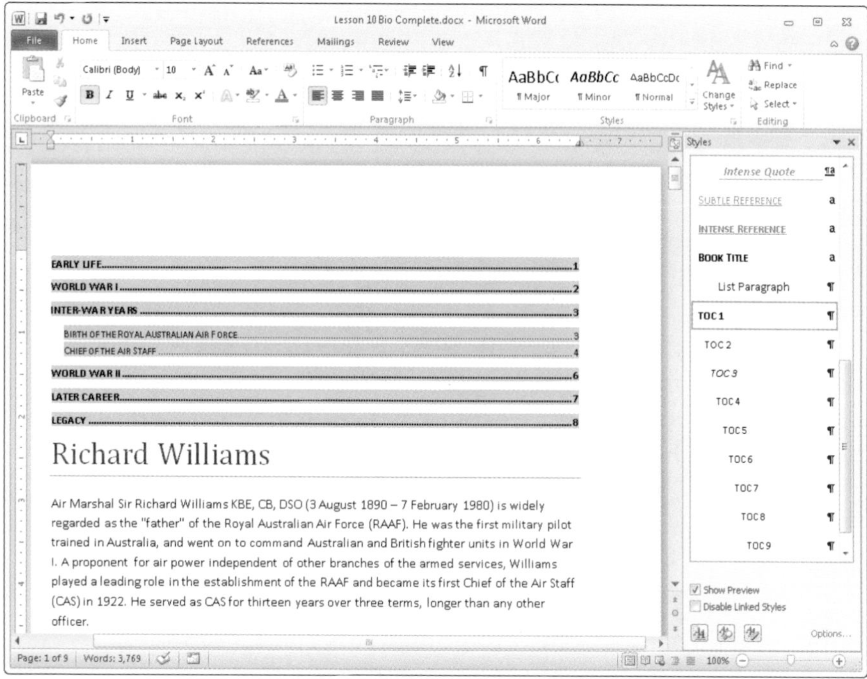

Figure 10-8

5. **Click the Bold button to turn off the Bold attribute (see Figure 10-9) and then click OK.**

   All text using that style is updated (that is, all the Level 1 text in the TOC).

6. **Click away from the TOC to deselect it (see Figure 10-10) and then click the Close (x) button on the Styles pane to close it.**

7. **Save the document.**

Leave the document open for the next exercise.

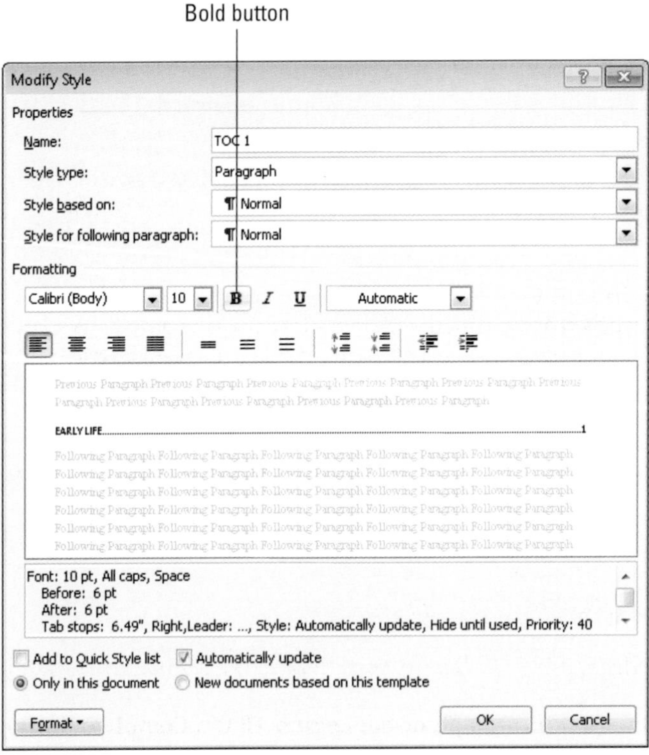

Figure 10-9

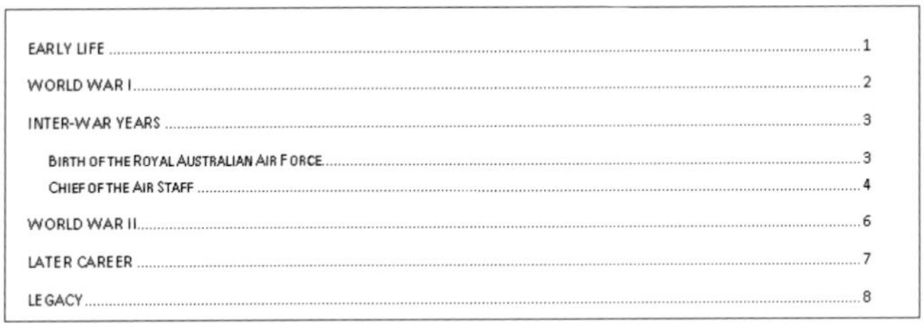

EARLY LIFE 1
WORLD WAR I 2
INTER-WAR YEARS 3
BIRTH OF THE ROYAL AUSTRALIAN AIR FORCE 3
CHIEF OF THE AIR STAFF 4
WORLD WAR II 6
LATER CAREER 7
LEGACY 8

Figure 10-10

Create an Index

Whereas a TOC helps readers find headings in the document, an index helps you find specific words and phrases. An index contains an alphabetical listing of important words in the document, along with the page numbers on which those words appear.

Creating an index is a two-step process. First you mark the index entries in the document and then you compile the index.

> **LINGO**
>
> An **index** is an alphabetical list of important words in the document, along with page numbers in which those words are featured.

Mark index entries

The first step in creating an index is to mark the words you plan to include. You do so by marking each entry, which places a hidden code in the document immediately following the word or phrase.

Marking the index entries can be a time-consuming task. You can mark all instances of a word at once with the Mark All option, but this isn't as good as marking each entry individually because the Mark All option tends to overmark, marking incidental uses of a word rather than only the important uses.

Professional-quality indexes are marked by professional indexers, and a large document, such as a book, can take many days to mark.

In this exercise, you mark index entries.

Files needed: Lesson 10 Bio Complete.docx, open from the preceding exercise

1. **In the first paragraph of the Lesson 10 Bio Complete document, select the text *World War I* and then choose References⇨Mark Entry.**

   The Mark Index Entry dialog box opens. See Figure 10-11.

2. **Click the Mark button.**

   An index entry code is inserted in the document. See Figure 10-12. Word displays hidden characters if they aren't already displayed so that the index code is visible. The dialog box remains open.

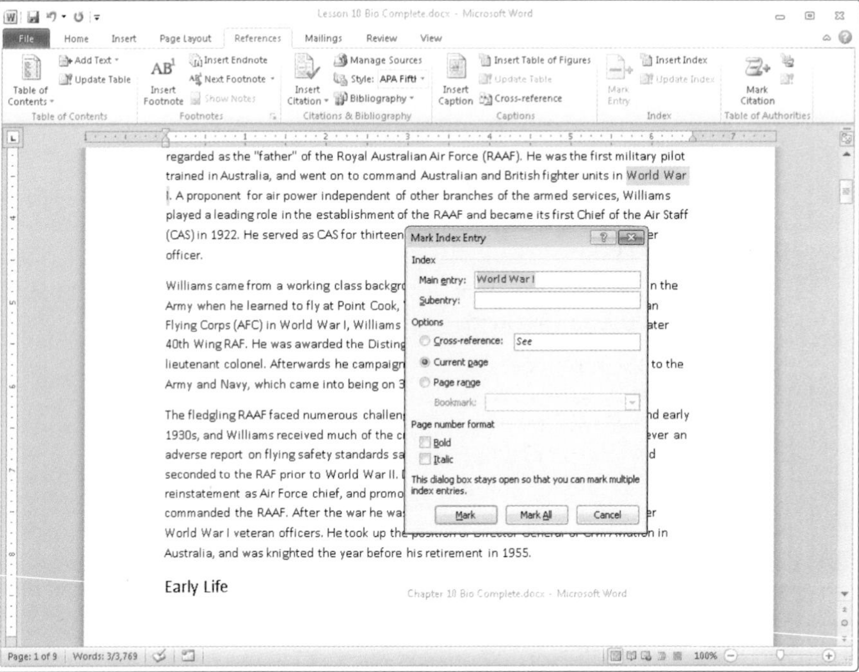

Figure 10-11

Air·Marshal·Sir·Richard·Williams·KBE,·CB,·DSO·(3·August·1890·—·7·February·1980)·is·widely· regarded·as·the·"father"·of·the·Royal·Australian·Air·Force·(RAAF).·He·was·the·first·military·pilot· trained·in·Australia,·and·went·on·to·command·Australian·and·British·fighter·units·in·World·War· I{·XE·"World·War·I"·}.·A·proponent·for·air·power·independent·of·other·branches·of·the·armed· services,·Williams·played·a·leading·role·in·the·establishment·of·the·RAAF·and·became·its·first· Chief·of·the·Air·Staff·(CAS)·in·1922.·He·served·as·CAS·for·thirteen·years·over·three·terms,·longer· than·any·other·officer.¶

Figure 10-12

3. **Click the Mark All button.**

   All other instances of *World War I* are also marked with the same code.

You can mark instances individually, or mark them all at once, depending on whether you want every instance to be indexed. Between entries, you can close the dialog box or leave it open. If you close it and then select some text, the selected text appears in the Main Entry text box automatically.

4. **Click the Close button to close the dialog box and then use the same process as in Steps 1–4 to mark all instances of *Royal Australian Air Force.***

   Leave the dialog box open when finished.

5. **In the first paragraph, select the text *RAAF,* and then in the Mark Index Entry dialog box, change the text in the Main Entry box to** RAAF**.**

6. **Select the Cross-Reference option and then click after *See* and type** Royal Australian Air Force **(see Figure 10-13).**

Figure 10-13

7. **Click the Mark button.**

8. **Save the document and close it.**

Leave Word open for the next exercise.

Generate an index

After the document has been fully marked up for indexing, you can generate the index. Compared to marking, generating the index is fast and easy, requiring just a few steps.

In this exercise, you generate an index.

Files needed: Lesson 10 Bio Indexed.docx

1. **Open Lesson 10 Bio Indexed and save it as Lesson 10 Bio Final.**

2. **Move the insertion point to the end of the document, press Ctrl+Enter to start a new page, and choose References⇨Insert Index.**

   The Index dialog box opens.

3. **From the Formats drop-down list, choose Classic (see Figure 10-14) and then click OK.**

   The index appears in the document. See Figure 10-15.

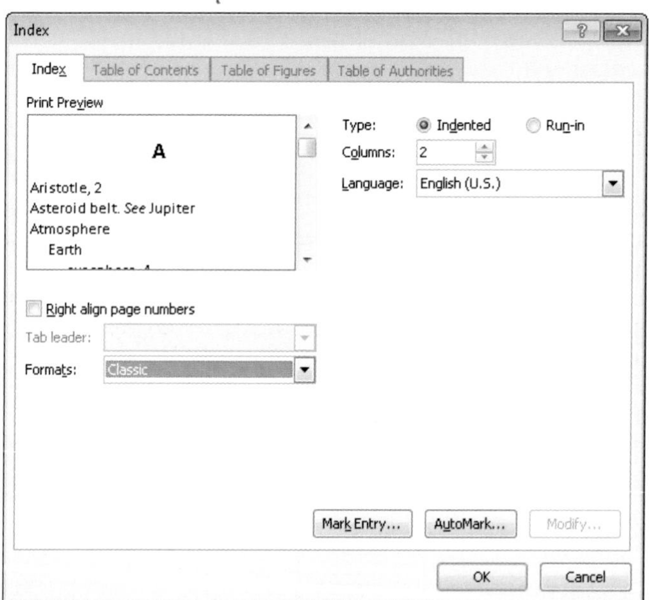

Figure 10-14

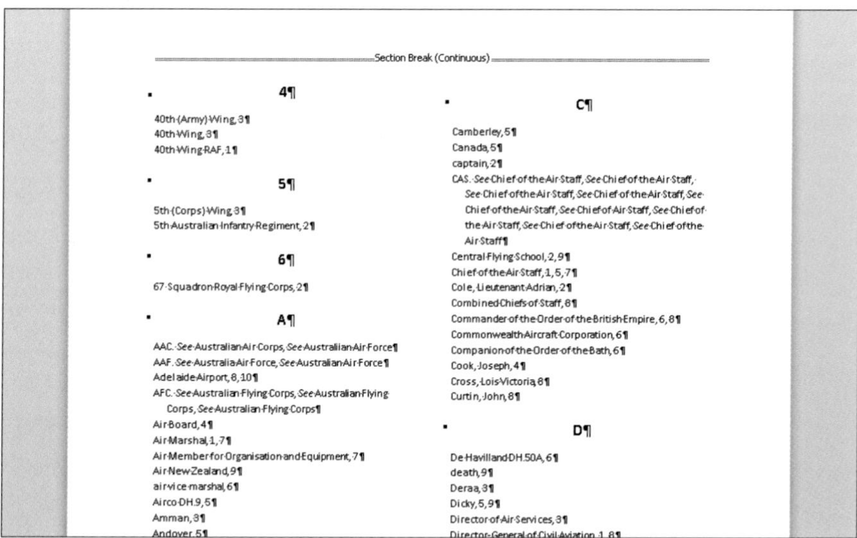

Figure 10-15

4. **Choose Home⇨Show/Hide to hide all the index codes and other nonprinting characters.**
5. **Save and close the document.**

Leave Word open for the next exercise.

Caption and Organize Figures

In a document that contains graphics that contribute to the content (that is, graphics that are more than just decoration), you may want to number and caption each one so you can keep track of them more easily. With automatically numbered figure captions, if you move a figure in the document so that the numbering wouldn't be consecutive anymore, the figure is renumbered automatically. Using figure captions can also enable you to easily create a Table of Figures, which is like a Table of Contents except it lists only the figures and their captions. You can also use figure captions to cross-reference figures in the document by number.

Attach a caption to a figure

When you attach a caption to a figure, you turn over to Word the task of keeping its numbering straight. You can optionally add descriptive text to the caption if you like, or modify the format of its numbering.

In this exercise, you attach captions to figures.

Files needed: Lesson 10 Figures.docx

LINGO

A **caption** is a text label that describes a picture's content. Captions are usually numbered, such as Figure 1, to help describe which picture you're referring to.

1. **Open Lesson 10 Figures and save it as Lesson 10 Figures Captions.**
2. **Click the first graphic to select it and then choose References⇨Insert Caption.**

   The Caption dialog box opens. In the Caption box, the caption Figure 1 already appears.

3. **Edit the caption to read Figure 1**: The Font group **(see Figure 10-16) and then click OK.**

   The caption is added below the figure, as shown in Figure 10-17.

4. **Scroll down to the next page, click the second figure, and choose References⇨Insert Caption.**

   In the Caption box, Figure 2 already appears.

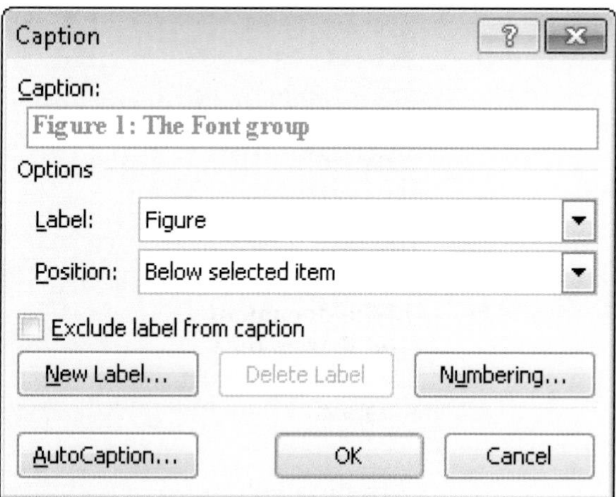

Figure 10-16

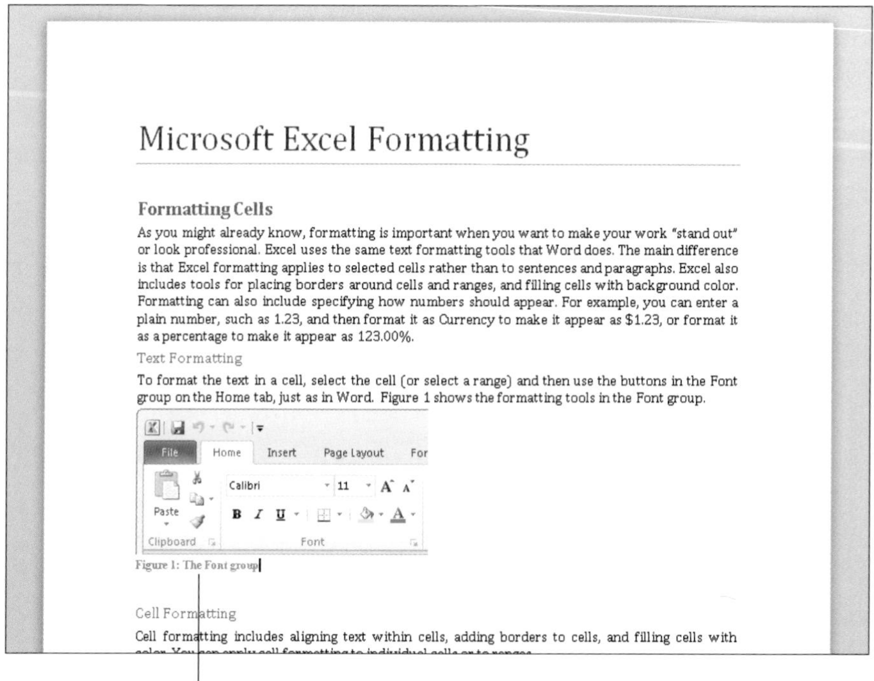

Figure 10-17

5. **Edit the caption to read Figure 2**: The Borders menu. **(See Figure 10-18.) Click OK.**

   The caption is added below the figure.

6. **Click the third figure in the document and then choose References➪Insert Caption.**

7. **Change the Figure 3 caption to Figure 3**: The Alignment group **and then click OK.**

   The caption is added below the figure.

Caption

Caption:

Figure 2: The Borders menu

Options

Label: Figure

Position: Below selected item

Exclude label from caption

New Label... | Delete Label | Numbering...

AutoCaption... | OK | Cancel

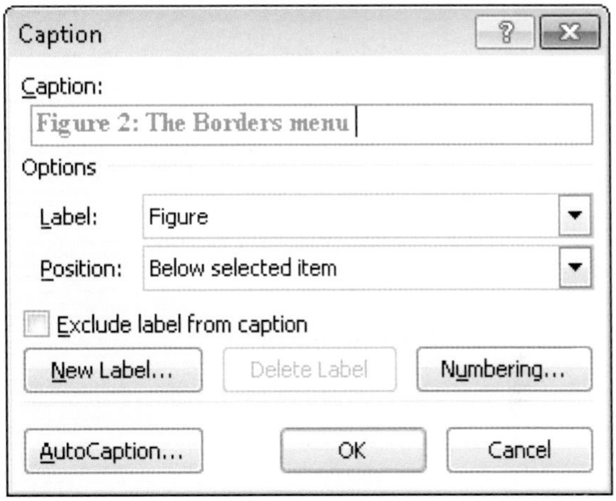

Figure 10-18

8. **Select the entire Text Formatting section of the document, from the Text Formatting heading through the figure caption below Figure 1 (see Figure 10-19).**

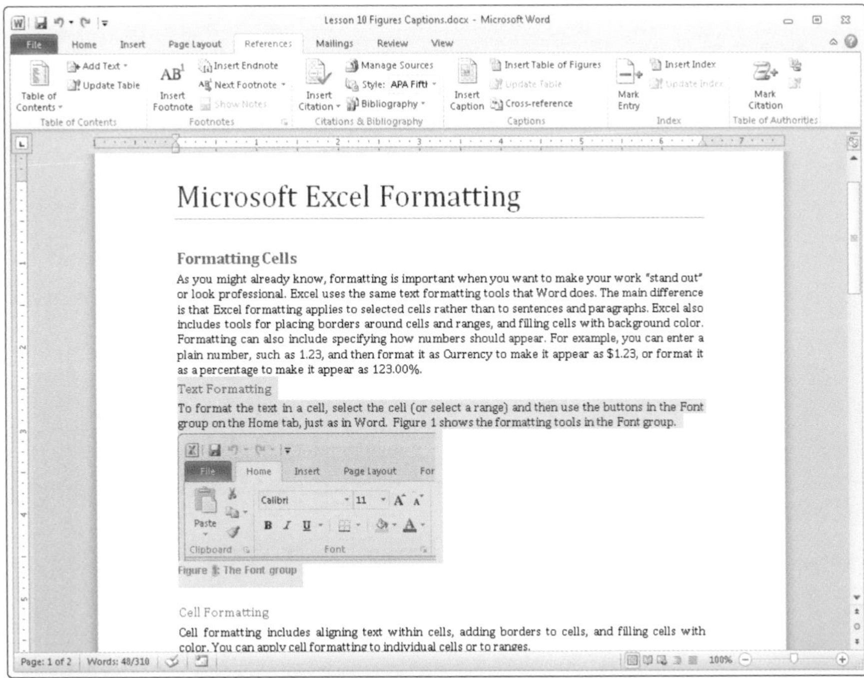

Figure 10-19

9. **Press Ctrl+X to cut the selected text to the Clipboard; then click at the end of the document and press Ctrl+V to paste the Clipboard content.**

   The figure captions have not yet renumbered themselves.

10. **Press Ctrl+A to select the entire document and then press the F9 key to update the fields.**

    The figure captions renumber according to their positions in the document.

You can also right-click the field code (the figure number, in this case) and choose Update Field on the shortcut menu.

11. **Save the document.**

Leave the document open for the next exercise.

If you want to make sure that the figure captions are always up-to-date when you print the document, choose File⇨Options, and on the Display tab, select the Update Fields before Printing check box.

Create a cross-reference

In the preceding exercise, when you moved a section of the document and then updated the figure numbering, the references in-text to the figures did not update, so those references are now out-of-sync. For example, the paragraph before Figure 1 says, "as shown in Figure 2." You can solve this problem by using cross-references in the text instead of manually typing the numbers of the figures to which you refer.

LINGO

A **cross-reference** is an active reference to content elsewhere in the document.

In this exercise, you set up cross-references to figures.

Files needed: Lesson 10 Figures Captions.docx, open from the preceding exercise

1. **In the third paragraph of the Lesson 10 Figures Caption document, select the text *Figure 2* and then choose References⇨Cross-Reference.**

   The Cross-Reference dialog box opens.

2. **From the Reference Type list, choose Figure; from the Insert Reference To list, choose Only Label and Number; from the For Which Caption list, choose Figure 1 (see Figure 10-20); and then click Insert.**
3. **Click Close to close the dialog box.**
4. **Scroll down to the next in-text figure reference (a reference to Figure 3 in the paragraph following the first figure), select the text *Figure 3*, and then choose References➪Cross-Reference.**
5. **In the For Which Caption List, choose Figure 2: The Alignment group and then click Insert.**
6. **Leave the Cross-Reference dialog box open and drag it to the side so the document behind it is visible.**
7. **Scroll down to the Text Formatting section of the document and select the text Figure 1; then in the Cross-Reference dialog box, select Figure 3: The Font group and click Insert.**
8. **Click Close to close the dialog box.**
9. **Save the document.**

Leave the document open for the next exercise.

Figure 10-20

Create a Table of Figures

A Table of Figures is not necessary in a short document, but in very long reports with dozens or hundreds of figures, it can help readers greatly by providing quick access to the numbered figures.

In this exercise, you create a Table of Figures.

Files needed: Lesson 10 Figures Captions.docx, open from the preceding exercise

LINGO

A **Table of Figures** is like a Table of Contents except it lists the document's figures and their captions.

1. **Click at the bottom of the Lesson 10 Figures Captions document to move the insertion point below the caption of the final figure and then press Ctrl+Enter to create a page break.**
2. **Type** Table of Figures, **and apply the Heading 1 style to the paragraph (from the Home tab, in the Styles group; see Figure 10-21).**

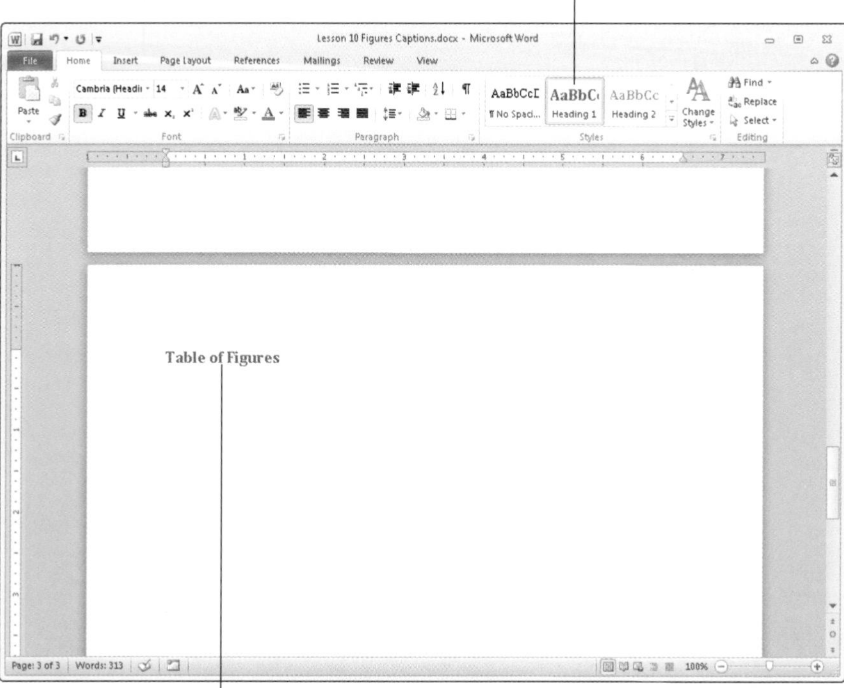

Figure 10-21

3. **Press Enter to start a new paragraph below the text you just typed and then choose References➪Insert Table of Figures.**

   The Table of Figures dialog box opens.

4. **Deselect the Use Hyperlinks Instead of Page Numbers check box (see Figure 10-22) and then click OK to insert the Table of Figures.**

   The Table of Figures appears in the document, as shown in Figure 10-23.

5. **Save the document and close it.**

Leave Word open for the next exercise.

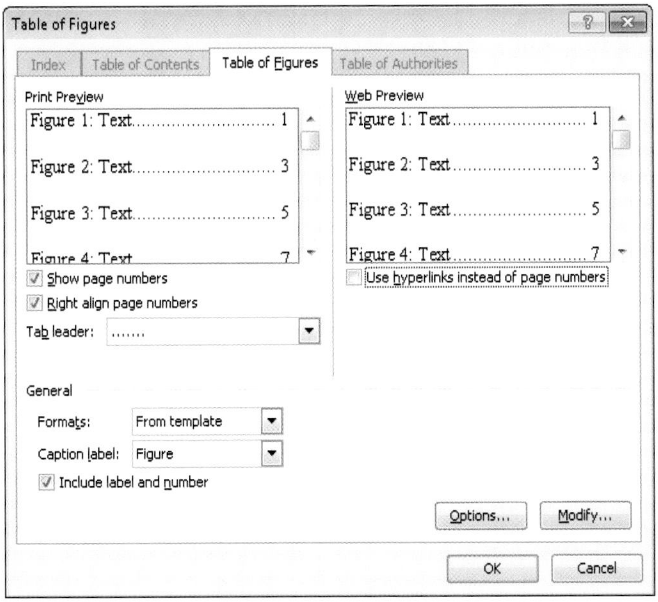

Figure 10-22

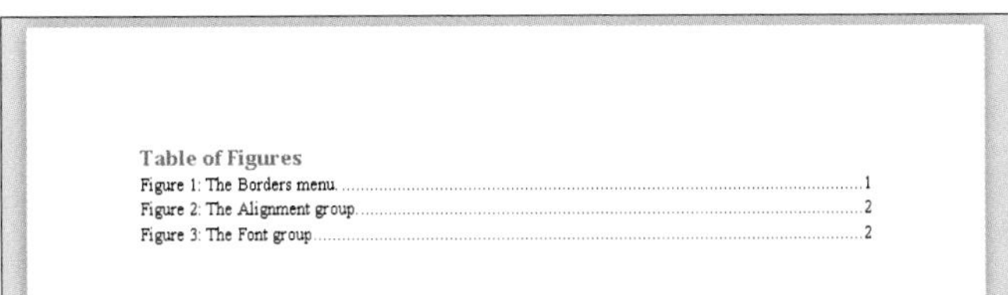

Table of Figures

Figure 10-23

Organize Legal Documents

Legal documents have some special requirements. For example, many legal documents use line numbering so that the parties reading them can easily refer to a specific line, and most legal documents include citations of court cases and other legal precedents. In the following sections, you learn how to use features in Word to accommodate those needs.

Turn on line numbering

Line numbering, if enabled, appears to the left of each line that contains text in your document. All lines are numbered except those in tables, footnotes, endnotes, text boxes, headers, and footers. You can choose to number every line individually or choose to display line numbers at intervals, such as every tenth line.

In this exercise, you create line numbering.

Files needed: Lesson 10 Contract.docx

1. **Open Lesson 10 Contract and save it as Lesson 10 Contract Numbers.**
2. **Choose Page Layout⇨Line Numbers⇨Continuous (see Figure 10-24).**

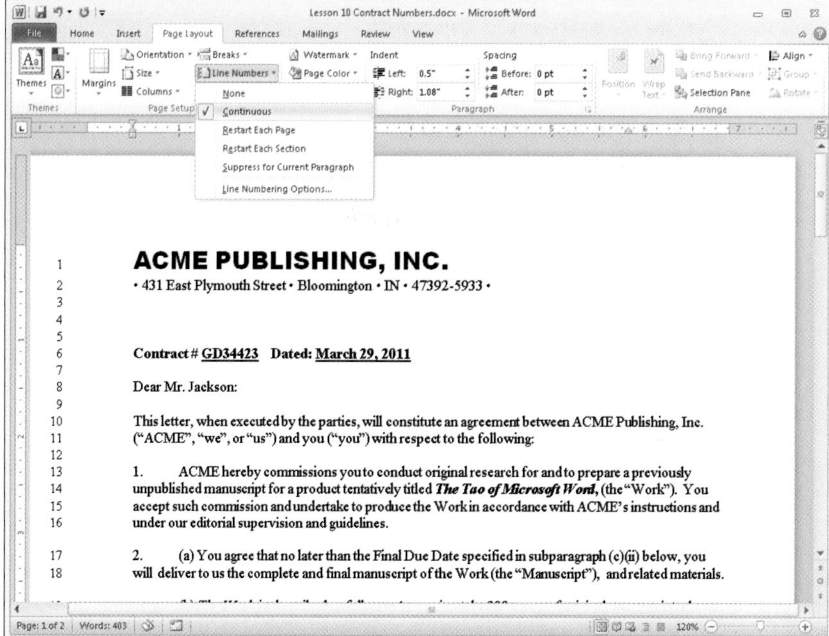

Figure 10-24

Blank lines created by pressing Enter are numbered along with other lines. However, blank lines created by applying extra spacing above or below a paragraph, or blank lines in-between the lines of a double-spaced paragraph, are not numbered. Notice in Figure 10-24, for example, that lines 3–5 are blank numbered lines, and the extra line of spacing between lines 16 and 17 is not numbered.

3. **Choose Page Layout⇨Line Numbers⇨Line Numbering Options.**

   The Page Setup dialog box opens with the Layout tab displayed.

4. **Click the Line Numbers button.**

   The Line Numbers dialog box opens.

5. **Change the Count By value to 10, as shown in Figure 10-25, click OK to close the Line Numbers dialog box, and then click OK to close the Page Setup dialog box.**

   The lines are now numbered every ten lines, instead of every line.

6. **Save the document and close it.**

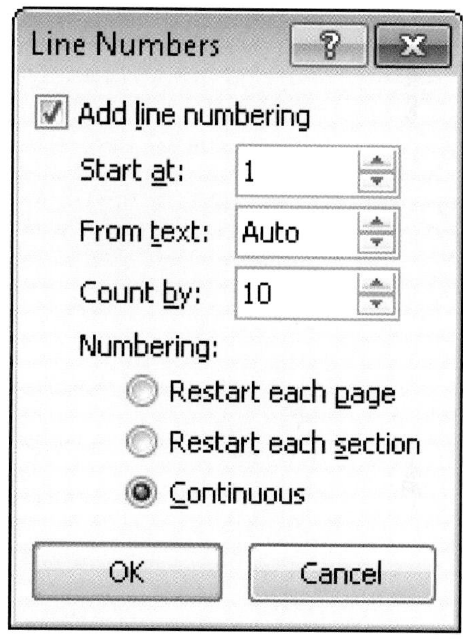

Figure 10-25

Leave Word open for the next exercise.

Create a Table of Authorities

A Table of Authorities is common in a very long legal document to summarize the sources cited by creating a Table of Authorities, as an aid to other legal professionals who may work with the document and need to verify the sources cited.

> **LINGO**
>
> A **Table of Authorities** is like a Table of Contents except it refers only to citations of legal precedents (also known as **authorities**).

To create a Table of Authorities, you first enter each citation within the body of the document. Then you mark each one as a citation via Word's Mark Citation feature. Finally, you assemble the Table of Authorities, compiling all the marked citations.

In this exercise, you mark some legal citations and create a Table of Authorities.

Files needed: Lesson 10 Legal.docx

1. **Open Lesson 10 Legal and save it as Lesson 10 Legal Authorities.**
2. **Select the first citation in the document and then choose References➪Mark Citation.**

   The Mark Citation dialog box opens. See Figure 10-26.

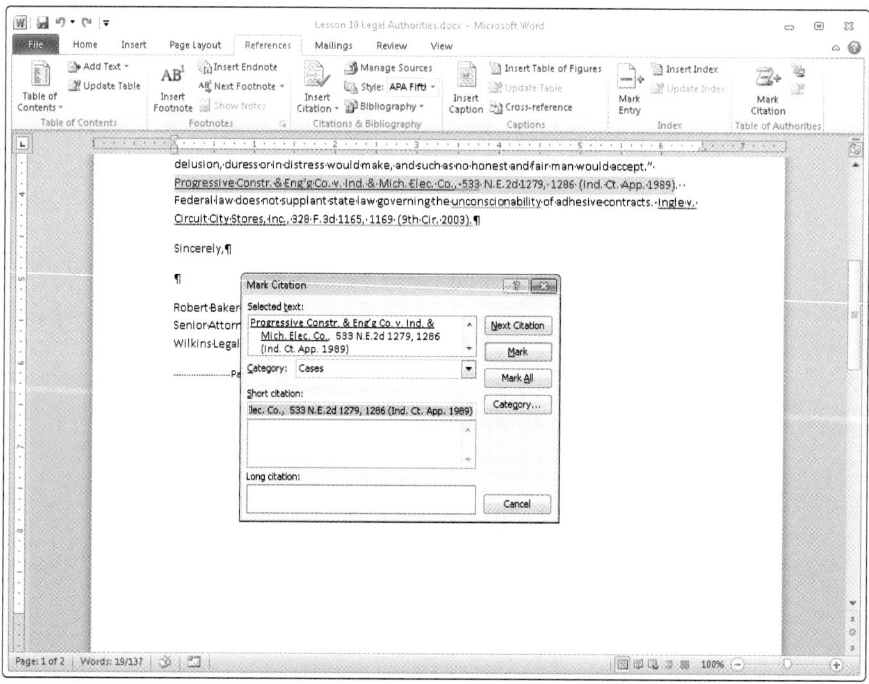

Figure 10-26

3. **Click the Mark button.**

   A field code is inserted into the document.
4. **Click Close and examine the code that was inserted.**

   The code is visible because Word switches to a view that includes hidden text and non-printing characters when you open the Mark Citation dialog box. Figure 10-27 shows the inserted code for the first citation.
5. **Select the second citation in the document (the last line of the paragraph) and choose References➪Mark Citation.**

   The Mark Citation dialog box opens, with the selected citation filled in. See Figure 10-28.

We received your letter of March 15, along with the proposed changes to the Anderson and DeWitt contract. These changes would be unconscionable and are therefore Mr. Anderson and Mr. DeWitt decline to include them. To be unconscionable, a contract "must be such as no sensible man not under delusion, duress or in distress would make, and such as no honest and fair man would accept." Progressive Constr. & Eng'g Co. v. Ind. & Mich. Elec. Co., 533 N.E.2d 1279, 1286 (Ind. Ct. App. 1989){ TA \l "Progressive Constr. & Eng'g Co. v. Ind. & Mich. Elec. Co., 533 N.E.2d 1279, 1286 (Ind. Ct. App. 1989)" \s "Progressive Constr. & Eng'g Co. v. Ind. & Mich. Elec. Co., 533 N.E.2d 1279, 1286 (Ind. Ct. App. 1989)" \c 1 }. Federal law does not supplant state law governing the unconscionability of adhesive contracts. Ingle v. Circuit City Stores, Inc., 328 F.3d 1165, 1169 (9th Cir. 2003).¶

Figure 10-27

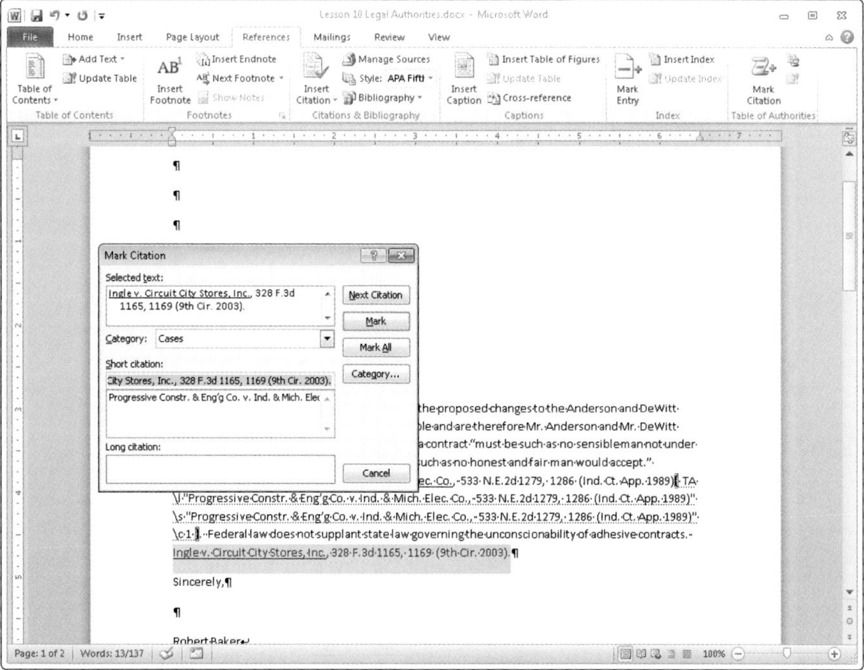

Figure 10-28

6. **Click the Mark button to mark the citation and then click Close to close the dialog box.**
7. **Choose Home tab⇨Show/Hide (see Figure 10-29) to toggle off the non-printing characters (including the codes for the citations).**
8. **Click at the bottom of the document to move the insertion point there, press Ctrl+Enter to start a new page, type** Table of Authorities, **and apply the Heading 1 style to it (see Figure 10-30).**

Figure 10-29

Figure 10-30

9. **Press Enter to start a new line and then choose References➪Insert Table of Authorities.**

   The Table of Authorities dialog box opens. See Figure 10-31.

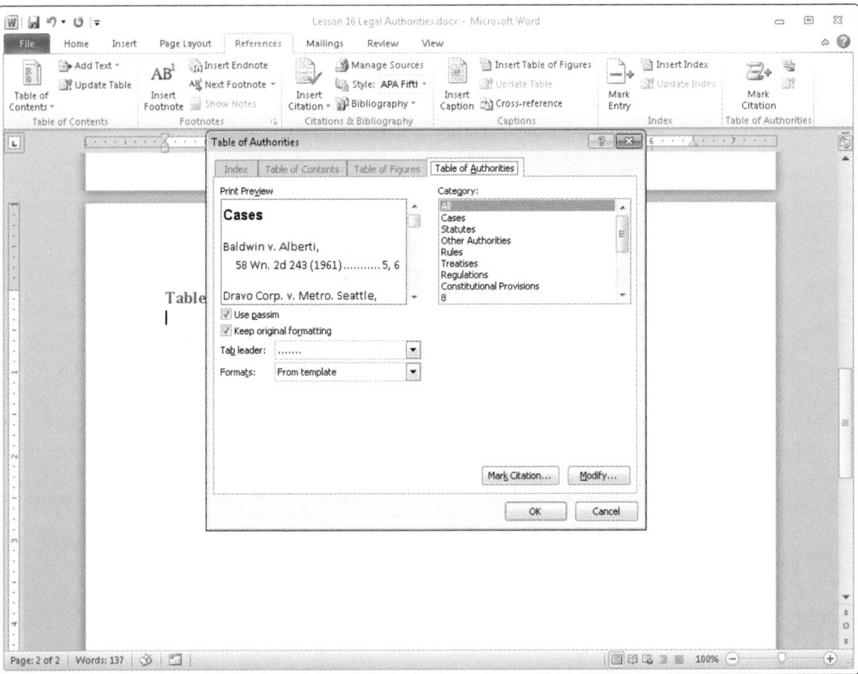

Figure 10-31

10. Click OK to insert the Table of Authorities with the default settings.

The Table of Authorities appears in the document. See Figure 10-32.

11. Save the document and close it.

Leave Word open for the next exercise.

Table of Authorities

Cases

Ingle v. Circuit City Stores, Inc., 328 F.3d 1165, 1169 (9th Cir. 2003).. 1
Progressive Constr. & Eng'g Co. v. Ind. & Mich. Elec. Co., 533 N.E.2d 1279, 1286 (Ind. Ct. App. 1989)..... 1

Figure 10-32

Create Footnotes and Endnotes

In Word, you can create either footnotes or endnotes in a variety of styles. Footnotes and endnotes can be used for bibliography information, such as citing the source of information or for explanatory information that may not be appropriate for inclusion in the body text.

> **LINGO**
>
> A **footnote** is an explanatory note that appears at the bottom of a page. An **endnote** is the same as a footnote except it appears at the end of the document.

Insert a footnote

A footnote is an explanatory note that appears at the bottom of the same page as the part of the document the reference applies to. When you use footnotes, the main part of the text stops a few lines earlier than normal on the page so there will be enough room for the footnote to appear. Word automatically adjusts the spacing for you to make the footnote appear in the right place.

Footnotes provide additional information that is not part of the main text. For example, a footnote could provide anecdotal information about a source you are citing. You can also use footnotes for source citations. Footnotes appear at the bottom of the page on which they are referenced.

In this exercise, you create a footnote.

Files needed: Lesson 10 Williams.docx

1. **Open Lesson 10 Williams and save it as Lesson 10 Williams Bio.**
2. **Click at the end of the first sentence in the first paragraph under the Early Career heading to move the insertion point immediately after its period and then choose References⇨Insert Footnote.**

   A small number 1 appears at the spot where the insertion point was, and a corresponding footnote appears at the bottom of the page. The insertion point moves into the footnote, so you can type its text. See Figure 10-33.

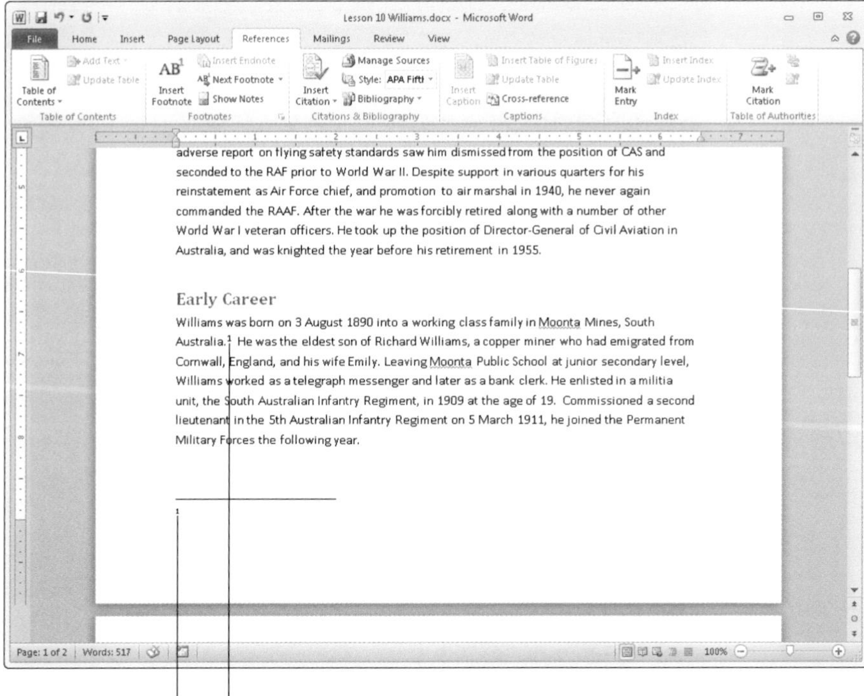

Figure 10-33

3. **Type** Garrison, Australian Dictionary of Biography, pp.502–505.
4. **Select the text *Australian Dictionary of Biography,* and then choose Home⇨Italic (or press Ctrl+I) to italicize it.**

   The footnote appears, as shown in Figure 10-34.

Early Career

Williams was born on 3 August 1890 into a working class family in Moonta Mines, South Australia.[1] He was the eldest son of Richard Williams, a copper miner who had emigrated from Cornwall, England, and his wife Emily. Leaving Moonta Public School at junior secondary level, Williams worked as a telegraph messenger and later as a bank clerk. He enlisted in a militia unit, the South Australian Infantry Regiment, in 1909 at the age of 19. Commissioned a second lieutenant in the 5th Australian Infantry Regiment on 5 March 1911, he joined the Permanent Military Forces the following year.

[1] Garrison, *Australian Dictionary of Biography*, pp.502–505

Figure 10-34

5. **Save the document.**

Leave the document open for the next exercise.

Insert an endnote

Endnotes are useful when you need to include footnotes but you don't want them to take up space at the bottom of each page. With endnotes, all the footnotes appear at the end of the document, in one list.

In this exercise, you create an endnote.

Files needed: Lesson 10 Williams Bio.docx, open from the preceding exercise

1. **In the Lesson 10 William Bio document, click at the end of the second sentence in the first paragraph under the heading Early Career to place the insertion point immediately after the period (see Figure 10-35).**

Place the insertion point here

Early Career

Williams was born on 3 August 1890 into a working class family in Moonta Mines, South Australia.[1] He was the eldest son of Richard Williams, a copper miner who had emigrated from Cornwall, England, and his wife Emily. Leaving Moonta Public School at junior secondary level, Williams worked as a telegraph messenger and later as a bank clerk. He enlisted in a militia unit, the South Australian Infantry Regiment, in 1909 at the age of 19. Commissioned a second lieutenant in the 5th Australian Infantry Regiment on 5 March 1911, he joined the Permanent Military Forces the following year.

Figure 10-35

2. **Choose References➪Insert Endnote.**

   A small i (actually a lowercase Roman numeral) appears where the insertion point was, and on the next page, below the last paragraph, an endnote section appears, and the insertion point moves into the note. See Figure 10-36.

Endnote number

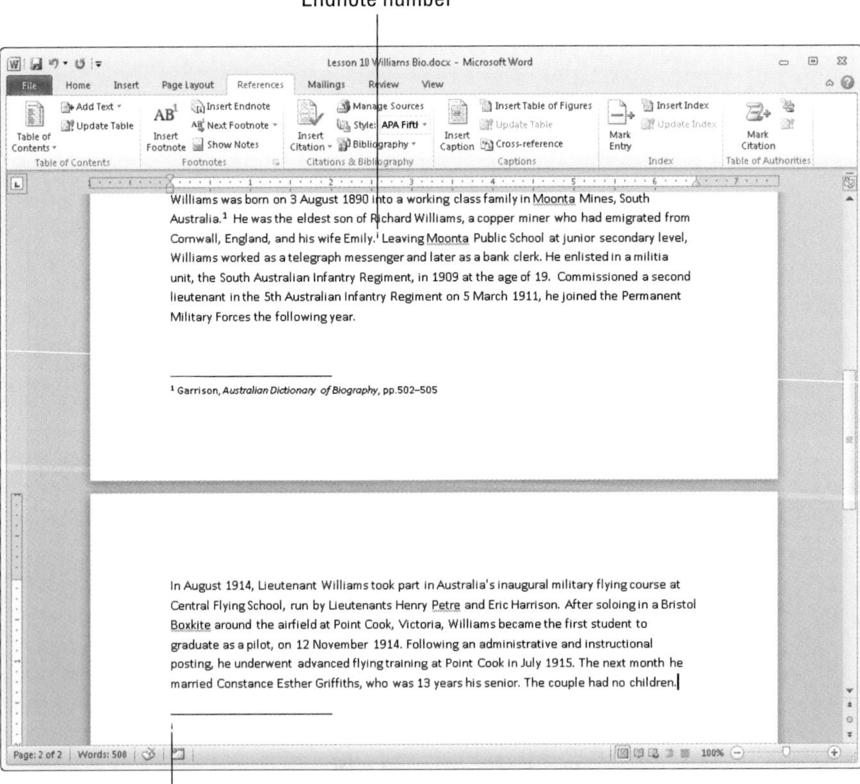

Endnote section of document

Figure 10-36

3. **Type** Odgers, The Royal Australian Air Force, p.49.

4. **Select *The Royal Australian Air Force*, and then choose Home➪Italic or press Ctrl+I to italicize it.**

   The endnote appears, as shown in Figure 10-37.

Word enables you to have both footnotes and endnotes in a document, but that can get confusing for your readers. Experts recommend that you stick with either footnotes or endnotes, one or the other, in a document.

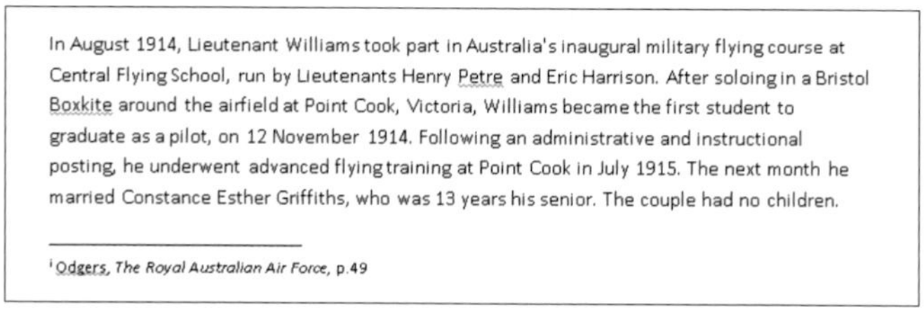

In August 1914, Lieutenant Williams took part in Australia's inaugural military flying course at Central Flying School, run by Lieutenants Henry Petre and Eric Harrison. After soloing in a Bristol Boxkite around the airfield at Point Cook, Victoria, Williams became the first student to graduate as a pilot, on 12 November 1914. Following an administrative and instructional posting, he underwent advanced flying training at Point Cook in July 1915. The next month he married Constance Esther Griffiths, who was 13 years his senior. The couple had no children.

[i] Odgers, *The Royal Australian Air Force*, p.49

Figure 10-37

5. **Save the document.**

Leave the document open for the next exercise.

Convert between footnotes and endnotes

Generally speaking, you should use one or the other in a document — footnotes or endnotes — but not both. Even though Word allows you to do use both, doing so can be confusing because the reader doesn't know where to look to find a note.

If you have used both footnotes and endnotes and now want to remedy that, or if you want to switch between using one or the other, Word makes it easy to do so.

In this exercise, you switch the endnotes in a document to footnotes.

Files needed: Lesson 10 Williams Bio.docx, open from the preceding exercise

1. **In the Lesson 10 Williams Bio document, on the References tab, click the dialog box launcher in the Footnotes group.**

   The Footnote and Endnote dialog box opens. See Figure 10-38.

Figure 10-38

2. **Click the Convert button.**

   The Convert Notes dialog box opens. See Figure 10-39.

3. **Select the Convert All Endnotes to Footnotes option and then click OK.**

   The endnote is converted to a footnote on page 1.

4. **Click Close to close the dialog box.**

5. **Save the document.**

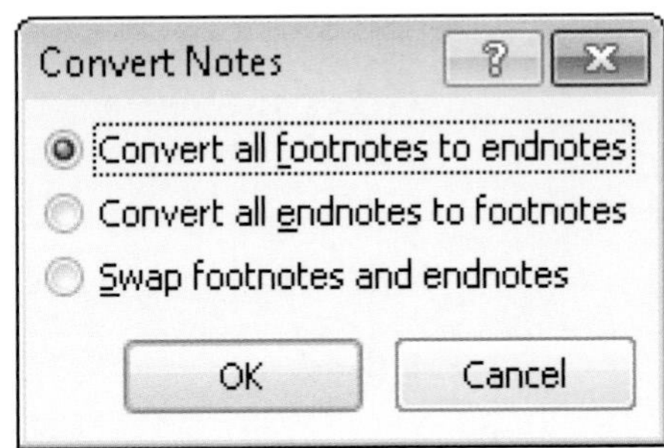

Figure 10-39

Leave the document open for the next exercise.

Format footnotes and endnotes

You can change many aspects of footnotes and endnotes in your document, including what numbering scheme will be used for them, what the starting number will be, whether the numbering restarts on each page, and so on.

In this exercise, you change the numbering of footnotes to Roman, and then change them again to use symbols instead of numbers.

Files needed: Lesson 10 Williams Bio.docx, open from the preceding exercise

1. **In the Lesson 10 Williams Bio document, on the References tab, click the dialog box launcher in the Footnotes group.**

   The Footnote and Endnote dialog box opens.

2. **From the Number Format drop-down list, choose the uppercase Roman numerals (I, II, III), as shown in Figure 10-40, and then click Apply.**

   The new numbering format is applied in the document.

3. **On the References tab, click the dialog box launcher in the Footnotes group.**

Footnote and Endnote
Location
Footnotes: Bottom of page
Endnotes: End of document
Convert...
Format
Number format: I, II, III, ...
Custom mark:
Symbol...
Start at: I
Numbering: Continuous
Apply changes
Apply changes to: Whole document
Insert
Cancel
Apply

Figure 10-40

The Footnote and Endnote dialog box opens.

4. **From the Number Format drop-down list, choose the set of symbols at the bottom of the menu and then click Apply.**

   The symbols are applied as footnote markers.

5. **Save the document and close it.**

Exit Word.

Summing Up

In this lesson, you learned some techniques for organizing and formatting long documents. Here are the key points from this lesson:

- A Table of Contents provides a quick reference at the beginning of a document, including the major headings and their page numbers. To generate a TOC, choose References⇨Table of Contents.
- A TOC is based on styles, so before generating your TOC, make sure your headings are formatted using heading styles.
- To update a TOC, choose References⇨Update Table.
- An index is an alphabetical listing of important terms and the page numbers on which they appear.
- To create an index, first mark the words to be made into entries by choosing References⇨Mark Entry. Then generate the index by choosing References⇨Insert Index.
- Captioning figures enables you to auto-number them sequentially in the document, and to create a Table of Figures. To add a figure caption, choose References⇨Insert Caption.
- To create a cross-reference, choose References⇨Cross-Reference.
- To create a Table of Figures, choose References⇨Insert Table of Figures.
- Legal documents often require line numbering. To number lines, choose Page Layout⇨Line Numbers⇨Continuous.
- A Table of Authorities is a summary of legal citations in a document. To create one, first mark the citations by choosing References⇨Mark Citation, and then choose References⇨Insert Table of Authorities to generate the table.
- To add a footnote, choose References⇨Insert Footnote. To add an endnote, choose References⇨Insert Endnote.

Try-it-yourself lab

For more practice with the features covered in this lesson, try the following exercise on your own:

1. **Open a multi-page document that you've created and save it as Lesson 10 Try It.**

   If you don't already have a multi-page document, copy some text from a web page into a new Word document to practice with.

2. **Add a Table of Contents, an index, and at least one footnote or endnote to the document.**
3. **Save all changes if prompted and exit Word.**

Know this tech talk

caption: A text label that describes a piece of artwork.

cross-reference: A reference to another location elsewhere in a document.

endnote: An explanatory note that appears at the end of a document.

footnote: An explanatory note that appears at the bottom of a page.

Table of Authorities: A Table of Contents that refers to citations of legal precedents.

Table of Contents: An ordered list of the headings or other major elements in a document.

Table of Figures: A listing of the figures in a document.

Lesson 11

Protecting and Sharing a Document

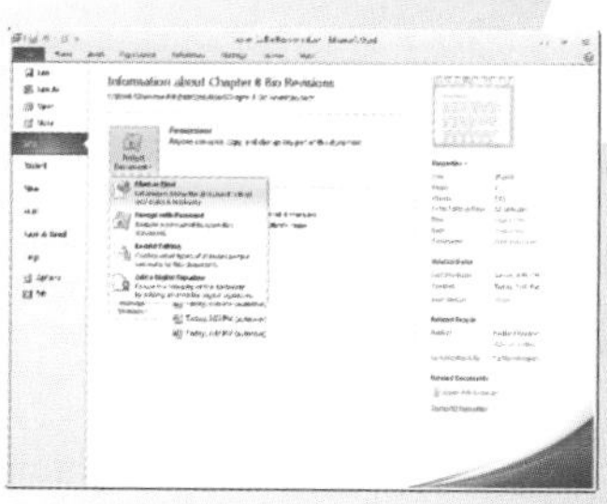

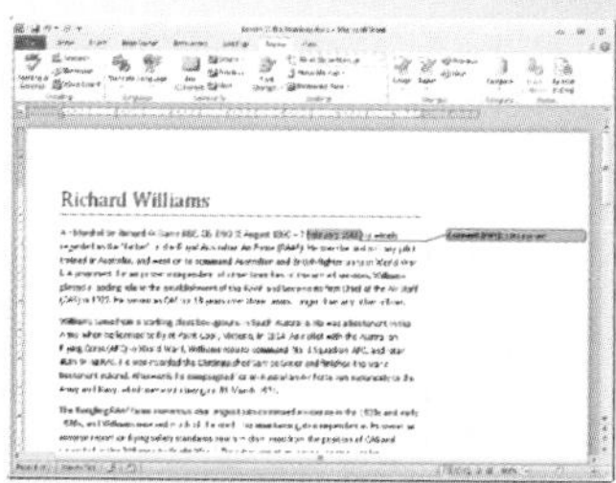

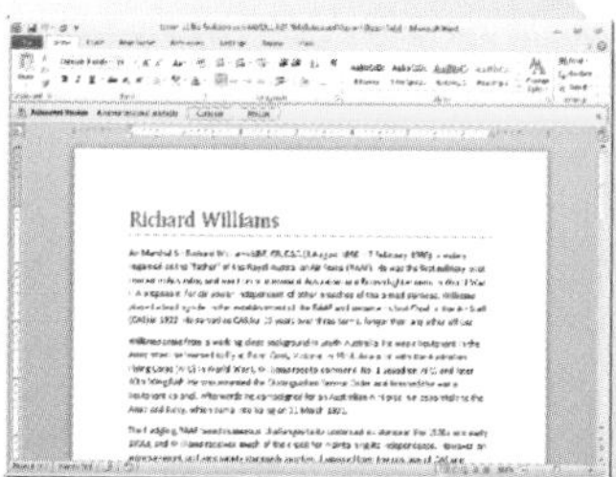

- Turning on change tracking enables you to see what other people have changed in your document.
- Accepting or rejecting revisions gives you control over the changes that others make.
- Comments allow multiple reviewers to communicate with each other.
- Reverting to an earlier version of a document restores content that may have been deleted erroneously.
- The Compatibility Checker helps determine whether people with earlier versions of Word can see your document the way you intended.

1. How do you turn change tracking on or off?

Track that down on page 293

2. How do you accept or reject revision marks?

Accept that info on page 298

3. How do you insert a comment?

That's commented on over on page 305

4. How can you revert to an earlier version of a document?

A version of that info is on page 309

5. How can you maximize document compatibility with earlier Word versions?

That info is compatible with page 311

This lesson covers many of Word's most popular features for managing the process of sharing your work with others. Word makes it easy to track the changes and comments made by multiple users, and then integrate them into a combined final version that takes everyone's changes into account. Word can also store and retrieve multiple versions of documents, and can remove certain features of a document to make it more compatible with earlier versions of Word — which can be very useful if some of the people on your editing team don't use the latest Office release.

Track Document Changes

Word can track many types of document changes, including insertions, deletions, moves, and formatting modifications. In the following sections, you learn how to enable and configure change tracking and revision mark display. You also learn how to accept or reject revisions.

Turn on change tracking

By default, change tracking is turned off. When you turn it on, Word begins notating each change you make, using a standard set of marks, such as double-underlining for insertions and strikethrough for deletions.

In this exercise, you enable change tracking in a document.

Files needed: Lesson 11 Bio.docx

1. **Open Lesson 11 Bio, save it as Lesson 11 Bio Revisions, and then choose Review⇨Track Changes.**

   The Track Changes button becomes highlighted. See Figure 11-1.

Figure 11-1

2. **Click the down arrow on the Track Changes button, opening a menu, and choose Change Tracking Options (see Figure 11-2).**

   The Track Changes Options dialog box opens.

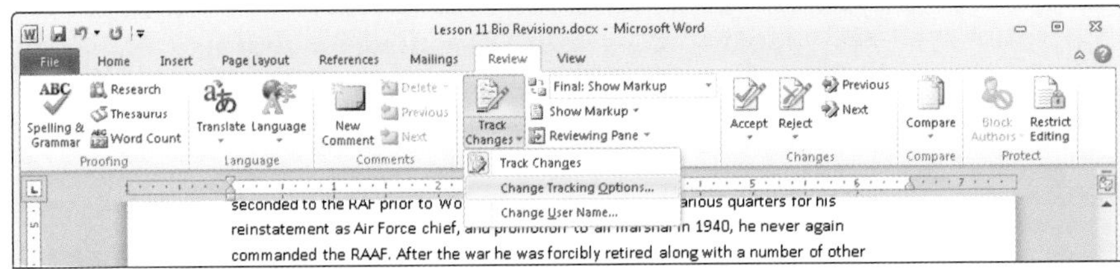

Figure 11-2

3. **Take note of the various colors and symbols that are set to mark the different types of changes.**

   For example, note that the color of insertions and deletions depends on the author (with a different color assigned to each author). See Figure 11-3.

4. **Click the Cancel button to close the dialog box without making any changes.**

5. **In the first paragraph, delete *British* and type** United Kingdom **in its place.**

   British turns red and appears in strikethrough, and *United Kingdom* appears underlined. See Figure 11-4.

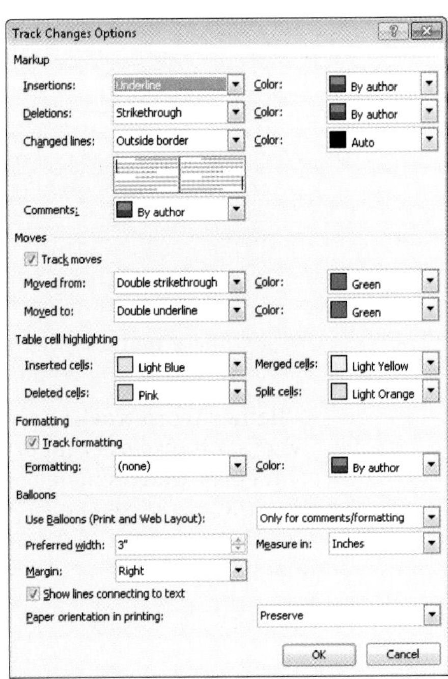

Figure 11-3

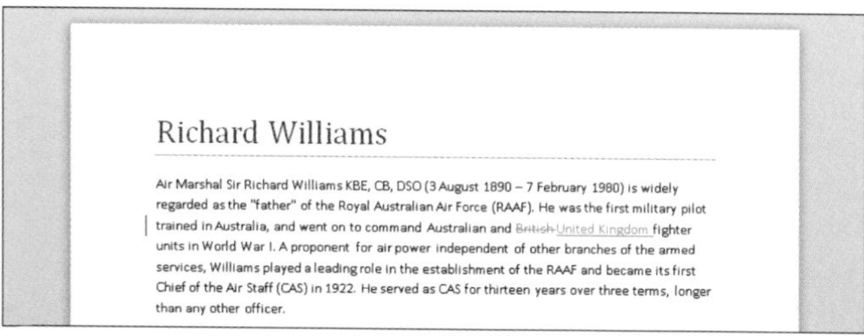

Figure 11-4

6. **On the first line of the first body paragraph, select *Sir Richard Williams* and press Ctrl+B to make it bold.**

   A balloon appears to the right of the paragraph showing the formatting change. See Figure 11-5.

7. **Save the document.**

Leave the document open for the next exercise.

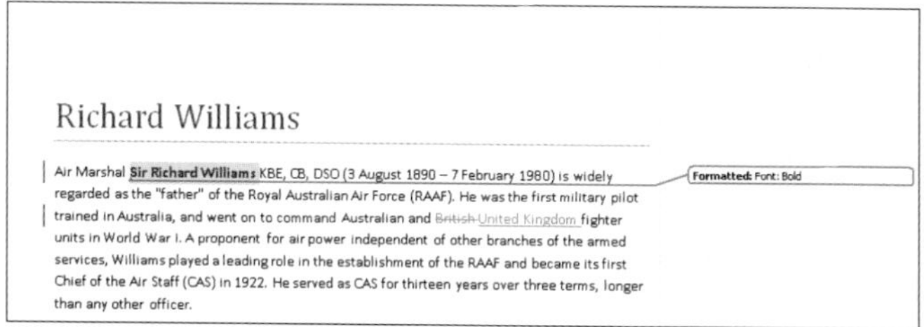

Figure 11-5

Display or hide different types of changes

Whether Word tracks a particular type of change or not is separate from whether it *displays* that type of change onscreen at any given time. You can hand-pick which change types appear onscreen, or set Word to show none of the change marks at all.

In this exercise, you set certain types of changes to display or hide.

Files needed: Lesson 11 Bio Revisions.docx, open from the preceding exercise

1. **Choose Review⇨Show Markup⇨Ink (see Figure 11-6) to deselect the Ink option.**

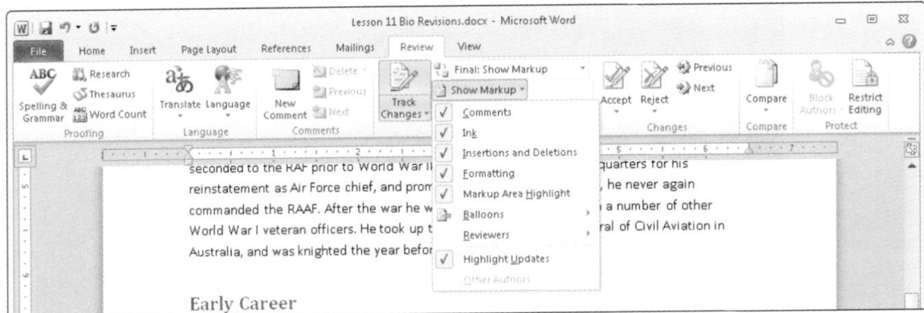

Figure 11-6

2. **Choose Review⇨Show Markup⇨Balloons⇨Show Revisions in Balloons.**

   See Figure 11-7. The deletion of *British* appears in a balloon. The addition of United Kingdom doesn't appear in a balloon because it's an insertion.

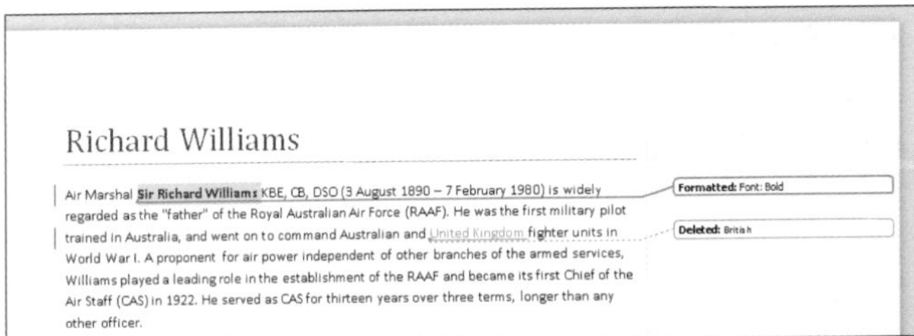

Figure 11-7

3. **Choose Review⇨Show Markup⇨Balloons⇨Show All Revisions Inline.**

   The markup area disappears from the right side of the document and all balloons disappear.

4. **From the Display for Review drop-down list, choose Final.**

   All revisions are shown, but all revision marks are hidden. See Figure 11-8.

5. **From the Display for Review drop-down list, choose Original.**

   All revisions are hidden, and all review marks are also hidden.

6. **From the Display for Review drop-down list, choose Final: Show Markup.**

   All revisions are displayed, and all review marks are also displayed.

Display for Review drop-down list

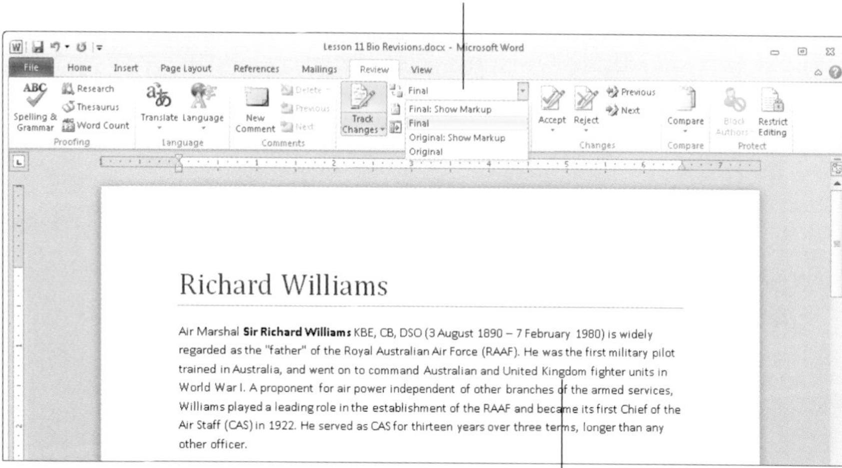

Changes are displayed, but not marked

Figure 11-8

7. **Choose Review➪Reviewing Pane➪Reviewing Pane Vertical.**

   A vertical task pane appears to the left of the document, showing each revision. See Figure 11-9.

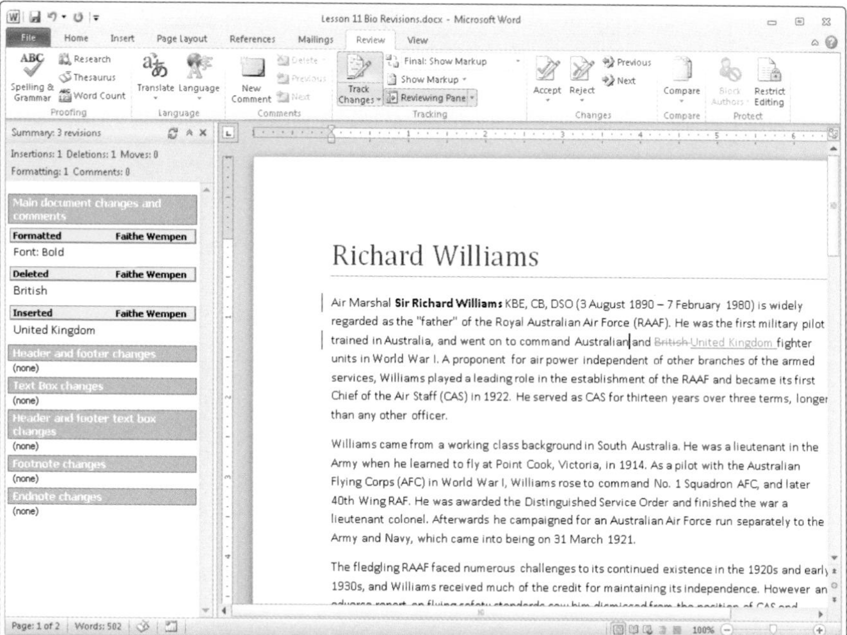

Figure 11-9

8. **Choose Review⇨Reviewing Pane⇨Reviewing Pane Horizontal.**

   The task pane moves to the bottom of the document.

9. **Choose Review⇨Reviewing Pane⇨Reviewing Pane Horizontal again.**

   The Reviewing pane disappears.

10. **Save the document.**

Leave the document open for the next exercise.

Accept or reject a revision

When you accept a revision, the change is incorporated into the document and the revision mark goes away. When you reject a revision, the change is discarded and the revision mark goes away. You can accept or reject each revision individually, or you can accept or reject all revisions in the entire document at once.

In this exercise, you make some revisions, and then accept or reject them.

Files needed: Lesson 11 Bio Revisions.docx, open from the preceding exercise

1. **In the Lesson 11 Bio Revisions document, in the first body paragraph, delete *thirteen* and type** 13 **to replace it.**

   The change appears with revision marks. See Figure 11-10.

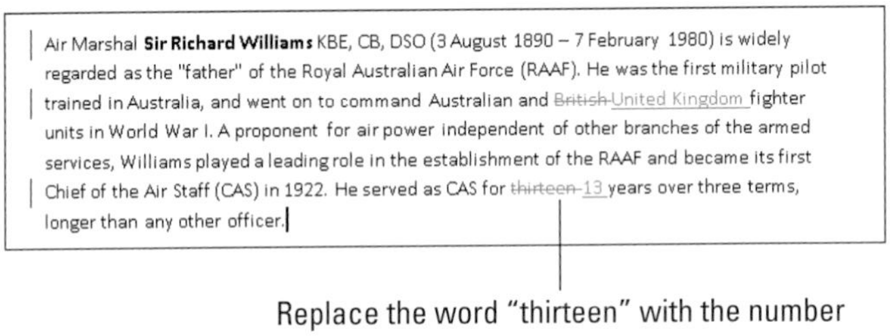

Air Marshal **Sir Richard Williams** KBE, CB, DSO (3 August 1890 – 7 February 1980) is widely regarded as the "father" of the Royal Australian Air Force (RAAF). He was the first military pilot trained in Australia, and went on to command Australian and ~~British~~ United Kingdom fighter units in World War I. A proponent for air power independent of other branches of the armed services, Williams played a leading role in the establishment of the RAAF and became its first Chief of the Air Staff (CAS) in 1922. He served as CAS for ~~thirteen~~ 13 years over three terms, longer than any other officer.

Replace the word "thirteen" with the number

Figure 11-10

2. **Click at the beginning of the first paragraph to move the insertion point there; then choose Review⇨Next, found in the Changes group, to move the insertion point to the first change (the bold text in the first line).**

3. **Choose Review⇨Reject to reject that change.**

   The next change is selected (the deletion of *British*).

4. **Click Reject.**

   The next change is highlighted (the insertion of *United Kingdom*).

5. **Click Reject.**

   The next change is highlighted (the deletion of *thirteen*).

6. **Click Accept.**

   The next change is highlighted (the insertion of *13*).

7. **Click Accept.**

   A dialog box appears telling you that there are no more changes. See Figure 11-11.

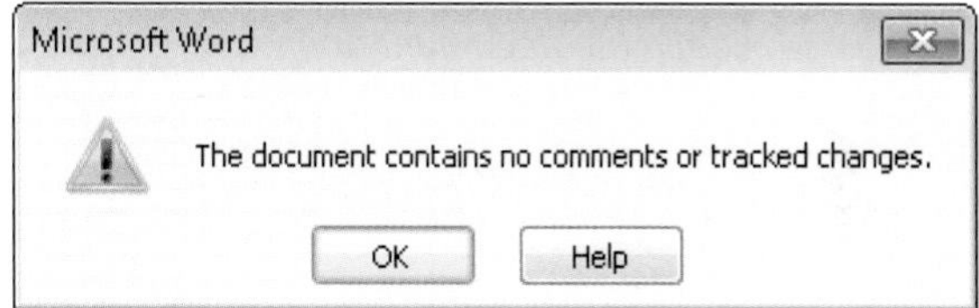

Figure 11-11

8. **Click OK.**

   The dialog box closes and the paragraph appears, as shown in Figure 11-12.

> Air Marshal Sir Richard Williams KBE, CB, DSO (3 August 1890 – 7 February 1980) is widely regarded as the "father" of the Royal Australian Air Force (RAAF). He was the first military pilot trained in Australia, and went on to command Australian and British fighter units in World War I. A proponent for air power independent of other branches of the armed services, Williams played a leading role in the establishment of the RAAF and became its first Chief of the Air Staff (CAS) in 1922. He served as CAS for 13 years over three terms, longer than any other officer.

Figure 11-12

9. **Save the document.**

Leave the document open for the next exercise.

Accept or reject all revisions

If you're confident about the revisions, you might want to accept them all at once. For example, if you made them all yourself, you might already know that they're all valid changes. Conversely, if you want to discard all the changes at once (for example, if someone heavily edited a document and you preferred it the original way), you can do that as well.

In this exercise, you make some revisions and then reject them all.

Files needed: Lesson 11 Bio Revisions.docx, open from the preceding exercise

1. **In the Lesson 11 Bio Revisions document, in the first body paragraph, in the first line, delete *1980* and type** 1982**; in the second body paragraph, delete *1914* and type** 1915**; and in the second body paragraph, capitalize Lieutenant Colonel (see Figure 11-13).**

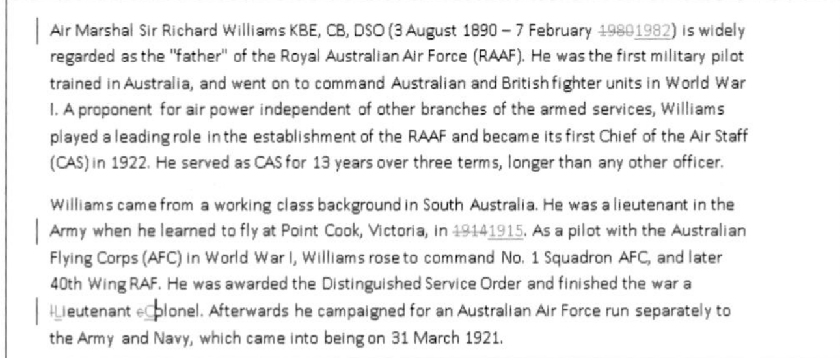

Air Marshal Sir Richard Williams KBE, CB, DSO (3 August 1890 – 7 February ~~1980~~1982) is widely regarded as the "father" of the Royal Australian Air Force (RAAF). He was the first military pilot trained in Australia, and went on to command Australian and British fighter units in World War I. A proponent for air power independent of other branches of the armed services, Williams played a leading role in the establishment of the RAAF and became its first Chief of the Air Staff (CAS) in 1922. He served as CAS for 13 years over three terms, longer than any other officer.

Williams came from a working class background in South Australia. He was a lieutenant in the Army when he learned to fly at Point Cook, Victoria, in ~~1914~~1915. As a pilot with the Australian Flying Corps (AFC) in World War I, Williams rose to command No. 1 Squadron AFC, and later 40th Wing RAF. He was awarded the Distinguished Service Order and finished the war a ~~l~~Lieutenant ~~c~~Colonel. Afterwards he campaigned for an Australian Air Force run separately to the Army and Navy, which came into being on 31 March 1921.

Figure 11-13

2. **Choose Review➪Reject➪Reject All Changes in Document (see Figure 11-14).**

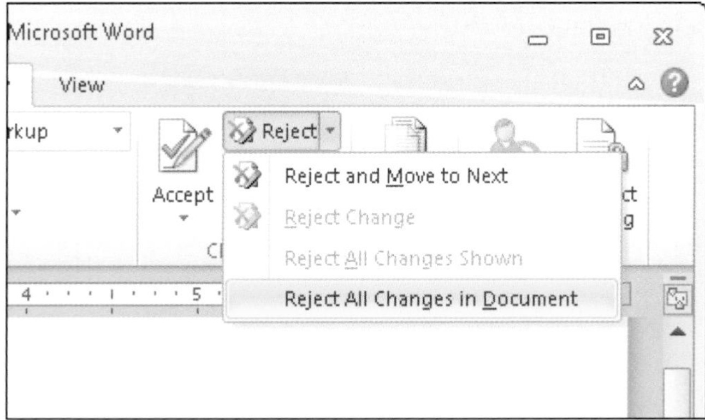

Figure 11-14

All the changes you made are reversed, and the revision marks disappear.

3. **Save the document.**

Leave the document open for the next exercise.

Mark a document as final

LINGO

Mark as Final disables editing for the document.

After accepting the edits in your document, you may want to discourage other people from making additional changes to it. One way to do this is to use the Mark as Final feature in Word to temporarily disable editing for that document.

Marking a document as final is not a security measure because anyone can easily override it; however, it does make the user stop and think before making an edit.

In this exercise, you mark a document as final, and then override that setting.

Files needed: Lesson 11 Bio Revisions.docx, open from the preceding exercise

1. **In the Lesson 11 Bio Revisions document, choose File⇨Info⇨Protect Document⇨Mark as Final (see Figure 11-15).**

   A message appears that the document will be marked as final and then saved (see Figure 11-16).

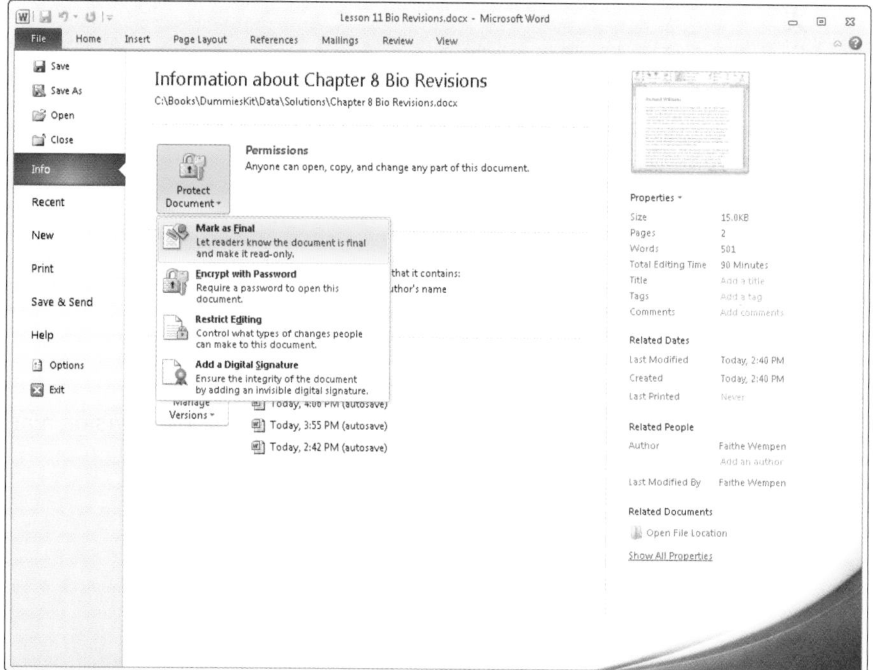

Figure 11-15

2. **Click OK.**

   A message appears that the document has been marked as final (see Figure 11-17).

3. **Click OK.**

4. **Click the Edit Anyway button.**

   The Ribbon returns, and the document is no longer marked as final. See Figure 11-18.

5. **Click the Home tab to exit Backstage view.**

   An information bar appears across the top of the document, and the Ribbon doesn't appear.

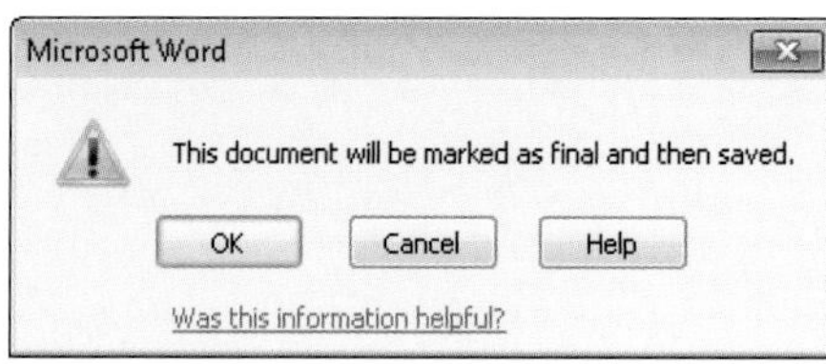

Figure 11-16

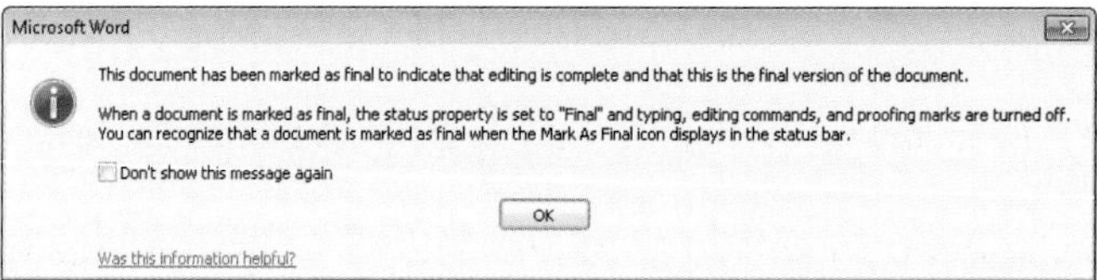

Microsoft Word
This document has been marked as final to indicate that editing is complete and that this is the final version of the document.
When a document is marked as final, the status property is set to "Final" and typing, editing commands, and proofing marks are turned off. You can recognize that a document is marked as final when the Mark As Final icon displays in the status bar.
Don't show this message again
OK
Was this information helpful?

Figure 11-17

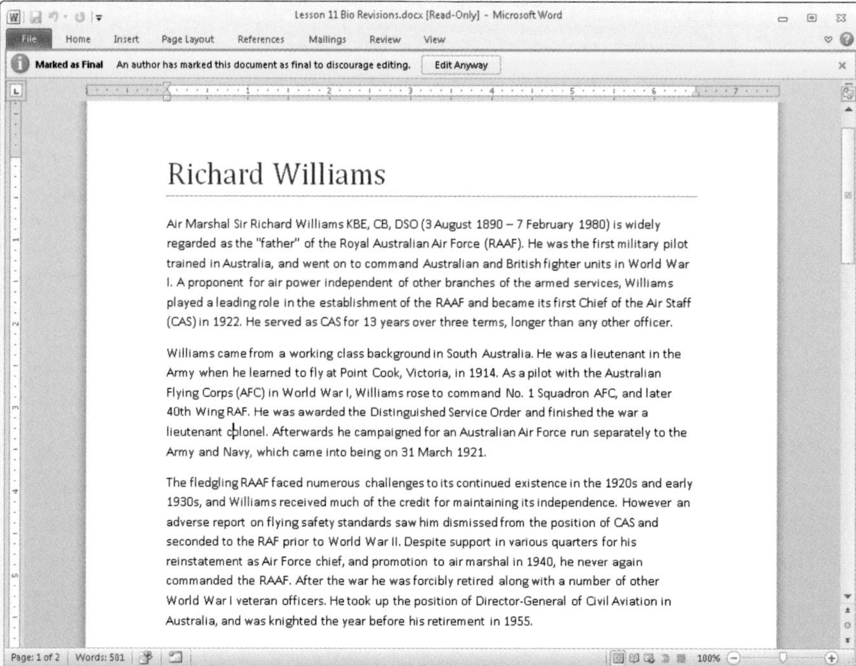

Lesson 11 Bio Revisions.docx [Read-Only] - Microsoft Word
File
Home
Insert
Page Layout
References
Mailings
Review
View
Marked as Final
An author has marked this document as final to discourage editing.
Edit Anyway
Richard Williams
Air Marshal Sir Richard Williams KBE, CB, DSO (3 August 1890 – 7 February 1980) is widely regarded as the "father" of the Royal Australian Air Force (RAAF). He was the first military pilot trained in Australia, and went on to command Australian and British fighter units in World War I. A proponent for air power independent of other branches of the armed services, Williams played a leading role in the establishment of the RAAF and became its first Chief of the Air Staff (CAS) in 1922. He served as CAS for 13 years over three terms, longer than any other officer.
Williams came from a working class background in South Australia. He was a lieutenant in the Army when he learned to fly at Point Cook, Victoria, in 1914. As a pilot with the Australian Flying Corps (AFC) in World War I, Williams rose to command No. 1 Squadron AFC, and later 40th Wing RAF. He was awarded the Distinguished Service Order and finished the war a lieutenant colonel. Afterwards he campaigned for an Australian Air Force run separately to the Army and Navy, which came into being on 31 March 1921.
The fledgling RAAF faced numerous challenges to its continued existence in the 1920s and early 1930s, and Williams received much of the credit for maintaining its independence. However an adverse report on flying safety standards saw him dismissed from the position of CAS and seconded to the RAF prior to World War II. Despite support in various quarters for his reinstatement as Air Force chief, and promotion to air marshal in 1940, he never again commanded the RAAF. After the war he was forcibly retired along with a number of other World War I veteran officers. He took up the position of Director-General of Civil Aviation in Australia, and was knighted the year before his retirement in 1955.
Page: 1 of 2
Words: 501
100%

Figure 11-18

6. Save the document.

Leave the document open for the next exercise.

Prevent untracked changes

If you're using the Track Changes feature in Word to ensure that nobody makes any unnoticed changes in a document, you may want to take a further security step and restrict changes to tracked ones only. You can also password-protect this restriction so that nobody can sneak changes into your document without them being tracked.

In this exercise, you prevent a document from being changed without change tracking.

Files needed: Lesson 11 Bio Revisions.docx, open from the preceding exercise

1. **In the Lesson 11 Bio Revisions, document, choose Review➪Restrict Editing.**

   The Restrict Formatting and Editing task pane opens to the right of the document. See Figure 11-19.

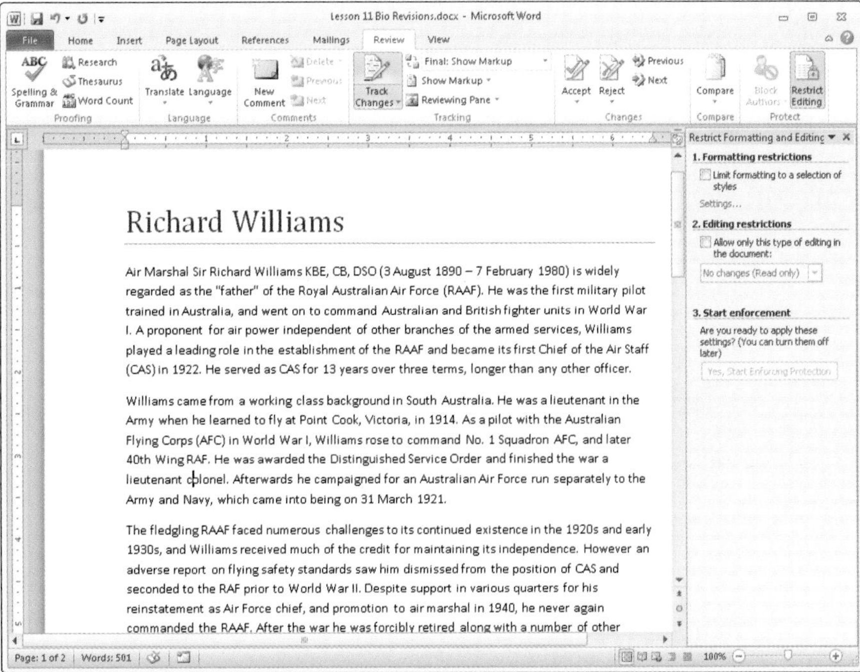

Figure 11-19

2. **In the Editing Restrictions section, select the Allow Only This Type of Editing in the Document check box, from the drop-down list, choose Tracked Changes, and then click the Yes, Start Enforcing Protection button.**

   The Start Enforcing Protection dialog box opens.

3. **In the Start Enforcing Protection box, click OK (see Figure 11-20).**

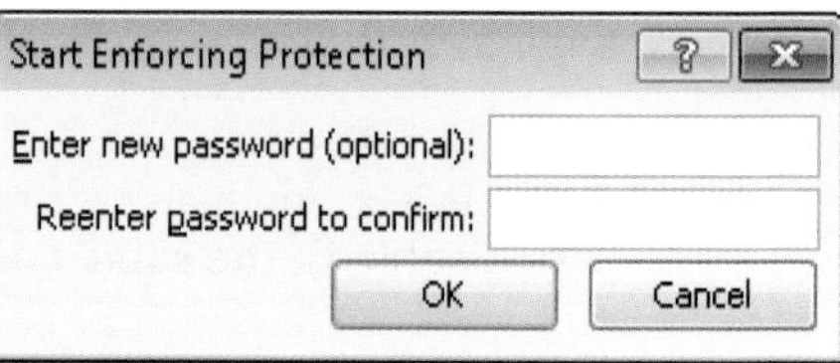

Figure 11-20

You can password-protect change tracking, but in this exercise, you don't.

4. **Try to choose Review⇨Track Changes.**

   The Track Changes button, however, is disabled.

5. **In the Restrict Formatting and Editing task pane, click the Stop Protection button.**

   The Track Changes button is once again clickable.

6. **Choose Review⇨Restrict Editing to close the task pane.**

7. **Save the document.**

Leave the document open for the next exercise.

Work with Document Comments

Comments enable users to write notes to each other within the document. You might create a comment to express an opinion about someone else's edit of a particular sentence, for example, or to explain the reasoning behind your edit. Then when you're ready to review the comments in the document, you can use the Review tab to easily move between comments.

> **LINGO**
>
> **Comments** are non-printing notes you can attach to certain parts of a document to exchange information with other contributors.

In the following exercises, you learn how to insert, review, and delete comments.

Insert a comment

Comments appear, by default, in balloons to the right of the document, like some revisions do. They also appear in the Reviewing pane, if enabled. When multiple users add comments to a document, each person's comments appear in a different color balloon (or bar in the Reviewing pane, if balloons are disabled), the same color as is used for that person's revisions.

In this exercise, you insert comments in a document.

Files needed: Lesson 11 Bio Revisions.docx, open from the preceding exercise

1. **In the Lesson 11 Bio Revisions document, in the first paragraph, select *February 1980* and then choose Review➪New Comment.**

   The Reviewing pane appears below the document (because that's the last location you specified for it). Balloons don't appear for comments because you turned off that feature in an earlier exercise. The insertion point moves to the comment.

2. **Type** Is this accurate?.

   The text you type appears in the Reviewing pane, under the Comment heading. See Figure 11-21.

Your initials appear as a comment marker, followed by a comment number

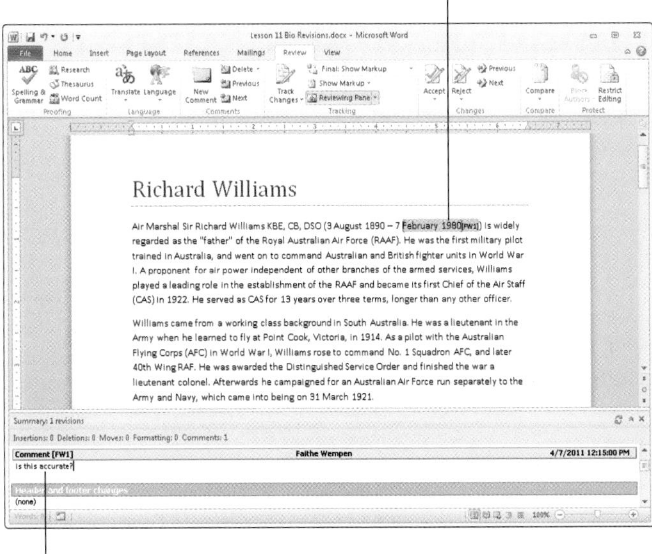

Comment appears in the Reviewing pane

Figure 11-21

3. **Choose Review⇨Track Changes⇨Change Tracking Options.**

   The Track Changes Options dialog box opens.

4. **From the Use Balloons (Print and Web Layout) drop-down list, choose Only for Comments/Formatting (see Figure 11-22) and then click OK.**

   The comment appears in a balloon to the right of the document.

5. **Choose Review⇨Reviewing Pane to turn off the Reviewing pane.**

   The Reviewing pane is no longer needed because the comments already appear. Figure 11-23 shows the comment in a balloon.

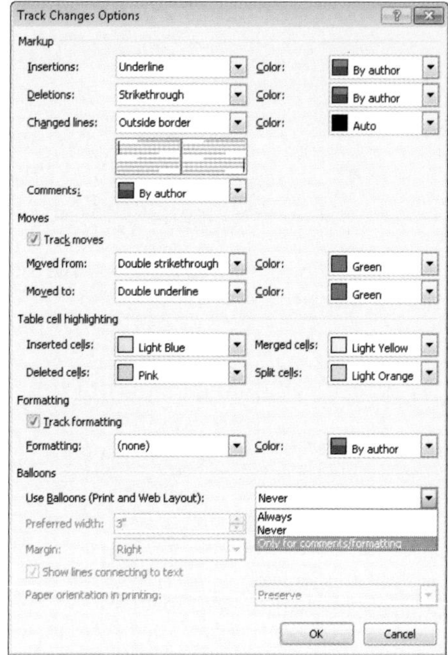

Figure 11-22

6. **Scroll to the bottom of the document, select *Constance Esther Griffiths,* and then choose Review⇨New Comment.**

   A new comment balloon appears.

7. **Type** Verify middle name **and then press Ctrl+Home to return to the top of the document.**

8. **Save the document.**

Leave the document open for the next exercise.

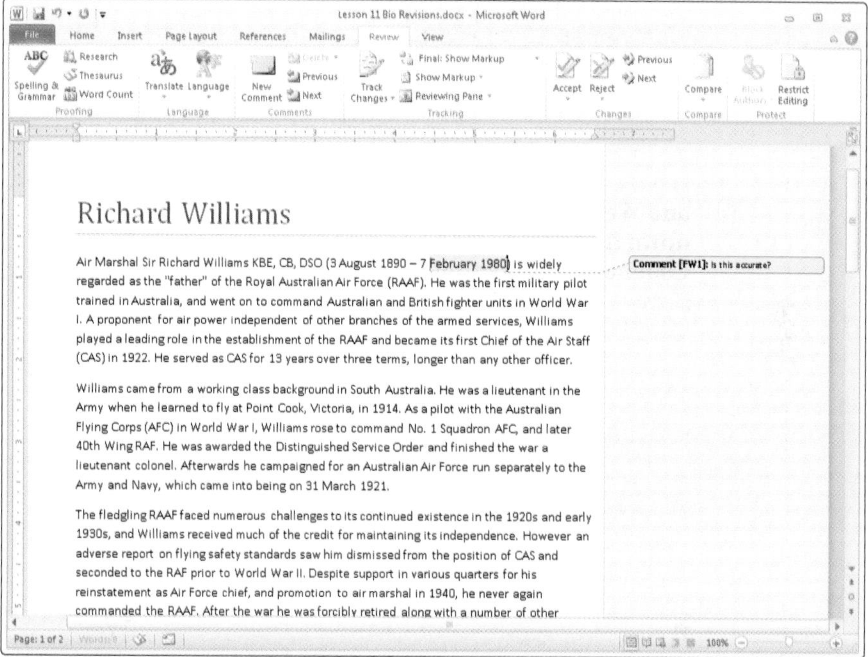

Figure 11-23

Review comments

In a short document, you can easily scroll through and examine the comments, especially if they're in balloons. In a very long document, however, you may find it easier to use the Next and Previous buttons on the Review tab's Comments group to move from one comment to another.

In this exercise, you review the comments in a document.

Files needed: Lesson 11 Bio Revisions.docx, open from the preceding exercise

1. **In the Lesson 11 Bio Revisions document, choose Review⇨Next, found in the Comments group.**

   Make sure you click the Next button in the Comments group, not in the Changes group. The first comment becomes selected. See Figure 11-24.

Comment selected

Figure 11-24

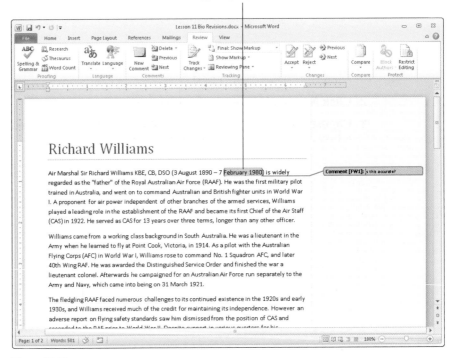

2. **Click Next again.**

   The next comment appears.

3. **Click Previous.**

   The previous comment appears.

4. **Press Ctrl+Home to return to the beginning of the document.**

Leave the document open for the next exercise.

Delete a comment

After you review a comment, you may want to delete it.

To choose whether to include comments when printing, choose File⇨Print and then click the Print All Pages button. At the bottom of the menu that appears is a Print Markup command. If this command is selected, comments will print; if it isn't, they won't. Click the command to toggle its setting.

In this exercise, you delete comments from a document.

Files needed: Lesson 11 Bio Revisions.docx, open from the preceding exercise

1. **In the Lesson 11 Bio Revisions document, choose Review⇨Next, found in the Comments section, to move to the first comment and then choose Review⇨Delete to delete the first comment.**
2. **Click Next again to go to the next comment.**
3. **Choose Review⇨Delete⇨Delete All Comments in Document to remove all remaining comments from the document (see Figure 11-25).**

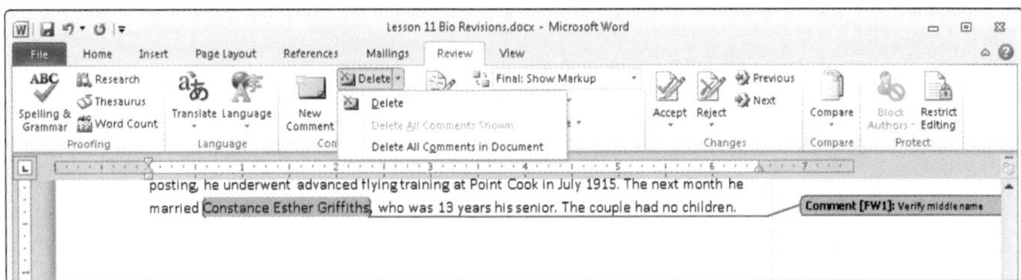

Figure 11-25

4. **Save the document.**

Leave the document open for the next exercise.

Manage Document Versions

Have you ever wished you could go back to an earlier version of your work, after you've made some edits to it? In Word 2010, you can.

When Word auto-saves your work, it retains those temporary files for a certain amount of time, so you can recover earlier versions of your work. If any of these files are available on your PC, they appear on the Info tab in Backstage view, under the Versions heading.

> **EXTRA INFO**
>
> Under the Versions heading, you see the last several auto-saves, but not necessarily all of them. To see them all, click the Manage Versions button, click Recover Unsaved Documents, and choose from a dialog box that shows all auto-saved copies.

In this exercise, you view and restore an earlier version of a document.

Files needed: Lesson 11 Bio Revisions.docx, open from the preceding exercise

1. **In the Lesson 11 Bio Revisions document, choose File➪Info and then look under the Versions heading.**

   Previous versions may appear there, as shown in Figure 11-26. (Yours may look different from Figure 11-26.)

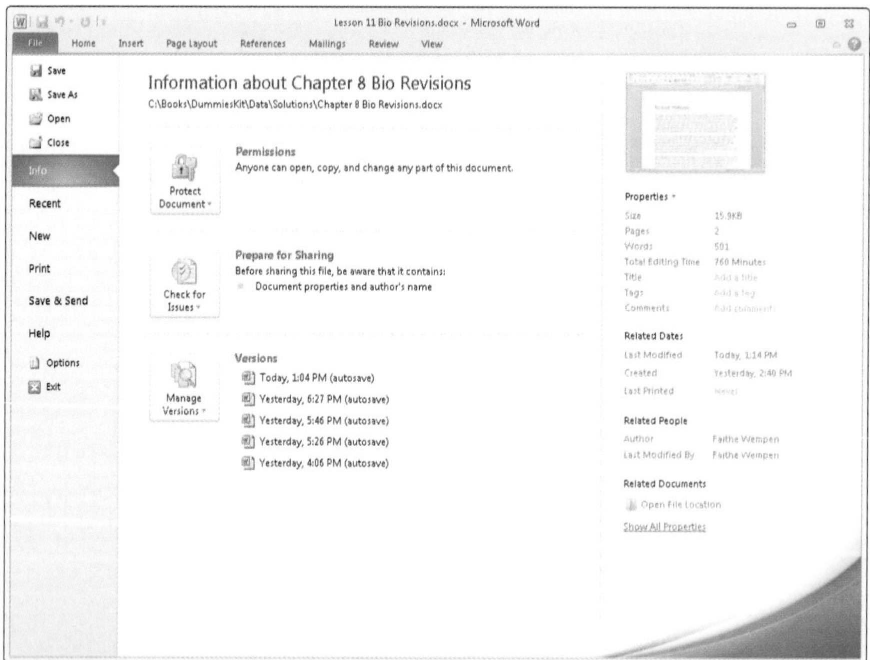

Figure 11-26

2. **Click one of the files listed there.**

   The file opens in Word in a separate window, as a read-only file. An information bar appears across the top, reminding you that it's not the latest version and offering two buttons: Compare and Restore. See Figure 11-27.

3. **Click the Restore button and in the confirmation box that appears, as shown in Figure 11-28, click OK.**

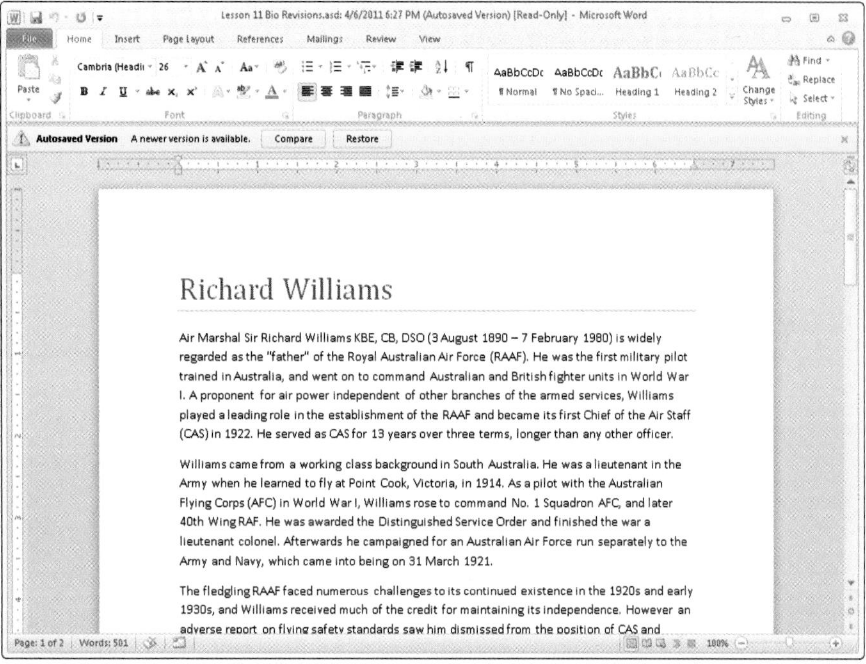

Figure 11-27

The newer version is overwritten by the older one.

4. **Close the document.**

Leave Word open for the next exercise.

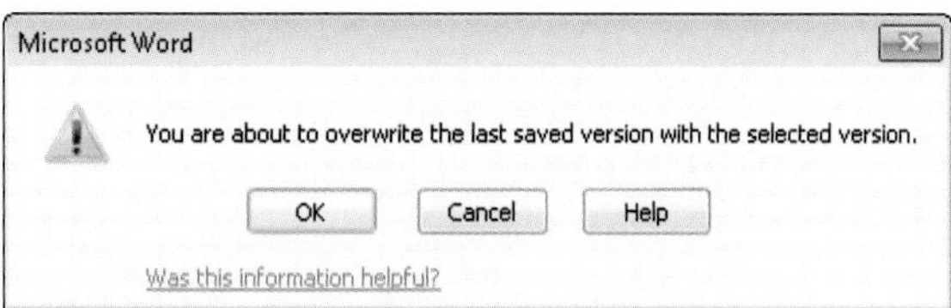

Figure 11-28

Use the Compatibility Checker

Word 2007 and 2010 use basically the same file format, but there are some new features in 2010 that Word 2007 doesn't support. In addition, if you want to share your work with someone who uses an even earlier version, you may have additional compatibility issues.

The Compatibility Checker in Word 2010 enables you to check whether a document will share without any problems. For each incompatibility, the Compatibility Checker explains what will be done to resolve the problem, but it doesn't make any changes to your document.

In this exercise, you run the Compatibility Checker for a document.

Files needed: Lesson 11 Compatibility.docx

1. **Open Lesson 11 Compatibility and save it as Lesson 11 Compatibility Checked.**
2. **Choose File➪Info➪Check for Issues➪Check Compatibility (see Figure 11-29).**

   The Microsoft Word Compatibility Checker dialog box opens, as shown in Figure 11-30.

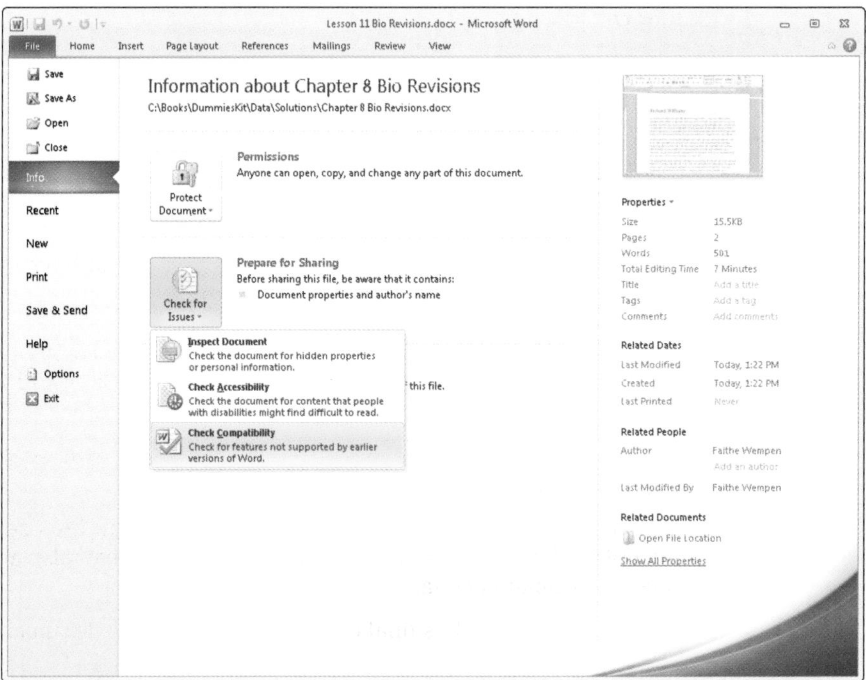

Figure 11-29

3. **Click the Help hyperlink.**

   The Word Help window opens, displaying an article that describes the compatibility issues that it looks for.

4. **Read the article and then close the Word Help window.**

5. **Click OK to close the dialog box.**

6. **Save the document and close it.**

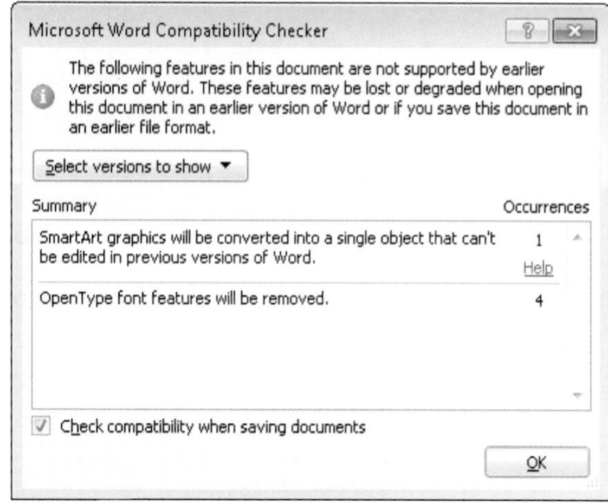

Figure 11-30

Exit Word.

Summing Up

This lesson covered methods of managing documents that have multiple contributors. Here are the key points from this lesson:

- To track changes in the document, choose Review➪Track Changes. You can use Change Tracking Options to fine-tune what is tracked and how it's tracked.
- To display or hide various types of change markup, choose Review➪Show Markup.
- You can accept or reject each change in a document. Choose Review➪Accept or Review➪Reject for individual edits. You can also accept or reject all remaining changes.
- Marking a document as final disables editing for the document; it isn't a security feature because it can be overridden easily. To mark a document as final, choose File➪Protect Document➪Mark as Final.
- You can prevent others from making untracked changes by choosing Review➪Restrict Editing.

- Comments enable contributors to leave messages for one another that aren't part of the main document. To insert a comment, choose Review⇨New Comment. To review comments in a document, choose Review⇨Next, in the Comments group.
- Older versions of a document are auto-saved. To access them, choose File⇨Info and look under the Versions heading.
- The Compatibility Checker checks a document to make sure people with earlier versions of Word can read it. Choose File⇨Info⇨Check for Issues⇨Check Compatibility.

Try-it-yourself lab

For more practice with the features covered in this lesson, try the following exercise on your own:

1. **Write a memo proposing a change to a policy at your workplace or school and save it as Lesson 11 Memo.**
2. **Add comments to the document and then turn on revision marks.**
3. **Send the document to a friend, and ask him to make at least one revision to it and send it back to you.**
4. **Review the changes, and then accept or reject them.**
5. **Review and delete the comments and then mark the document as final.**
6. **Close the document and exit Word.**

Know this tech talk

comment: A note inserted in a document, usually containing a question or explanation of a part of the document.

Mark as Final: To make a file uneditable, preventing accidental changes to it. The read-only aspect can be overridden easily.

About the CD

This README file contains information to help you get started using Dummies eLearning. This course requires no installation.

The practice files for the lessons in this book are at `www.dummies.com/go/word2010elearningkit`.

System Requirements

Dummies eLearning provides all required functionality on the following Microsoft operating systems: Windows 7, Windows Vista, Windows XP, Windows 2000, and Windows 2003 Server.

The following browsers are supported under Windows: Microsoft Internet Explorer 9.0 or higher and Mozilla Firefox 2.x or higher.

To run a QS3 CD-ROM, the system should have the following additional hardware/software minimums:

- Adobe Flash Player 8
- A Pentium III, 500 MHz processor
- 256MB of RAM
- A CD-ROM or DVD-ROM drive

A negligible amount of disk space must be available for tracking data. Less than 1MB will typically be used.

Launch Instructions

Setup instructions for Windows machines:

1. **Put the CD in the CD drive.**
2. **Double-click the My Computer icon to view the contents of the My Computer window.**
3. **Double-click the CD-ROM drive icon to view the contents of the Dummies eLearning CD.**
4. **Double-click the start.bat file to start the Dummies eLearning CBT.**

   Your computer may warn you about active content. Click Yes to continue starting the CD. The CD may create new tabs in your browser. Click the tab to see the content.

The browser offers the option of using the lessons from the CD or from the website:

- **To use the web version,** click that option and follow the instructions. The web version may require a registration code from the book.
- **To use the CD,** click that option and follow the instructions. Agree to the EULA and install Flash Player, if prompted. Allow disk space usage by clicking the Allow button, if prompted.

Operation

After you enter your username, the eLearning course displays a list of topics. Select any topic from the list by clicking its Launch button. When the topic opens, it plays an introductory animation. To watch more animations on the topic, click the Next button (the arrow pointing right) at the bottom of the screen to play the next one.

If you want to switch to another lesson or another topic, use the list on the left side of the topic window to open a lesson and select a topic.

Some topics have a hands-on activity section that lets you perform a task on your own. To see the activity from start to finish, click Show Me Full Demo. If you want to try the tasks for yourself, click Guide Me Through to see the animation in sections and repeat it yourself. If you're ready to solo, click Let

Me Try to work through all the steps yourself without coaching. (If you need a helping hand to finish, just click Hint at the bottom of the window, and then click Show Me Clue in the dialog box.) When you perform the activity, be sure to position the cursor directly over the subject you want to click; your computer may not respond the first time you click. To end the activity, click the X at the bottom of the Milestone box.

Some topics have an active tab for resources on the right side of the window. By default, Windows opens this content in a new window. If you have another compressed file manager installed, such as WinZip, your system may behave differently.

Troubleshooting

What do I do if the page does not load?

It's possible that you have a security setting enabled that isn't allowing the needed Flash file to run. Be sure that pop-up blockers are off, ActiveX content is enabled, and the correct versions of Shockwave and Flash are on the system you're using.

Please contact your system administrator or technical support group for assistance.

What do I do if the Add User window appears when the course loads and there are no names in the Learner Name list, but I have previously created a user account?

The course stores your information on the machine on which you create your account, so first make sure that you're using the eLearning For Dummies course on the same machine on which you created your Learner account. If you're using the course on a network and use a different machine than the one on which you created your account, the software will not be able to access your Learner record.

If you're on the machine on which you created your account, close the course browser window. Depending on the configuration of your machine, sometimes a course will load before accessing the user data.

If this still doesn't work, contact your network administrator for more assistance.

What do I do if I click a Launch button but nothing happens?

This may occur on machines that have AOL installed. If you're using the course from a CD-ROM and you're an AOL subscriber, follow these steps:

1. **Exit the course.**
2. **Log on to AOL.**
3. **Restart the course.**

What do I do if the Shockwave installer on the ROM says that I have a more recent version of the plug-in, but the software still says that I need to install version 8.5 or higher?

Download the latest version of the Shockwave plug-in directly from Adobe's website:

```
http://www.adobe.com/downloads/
```

If prompted to install Flash Player to view the CD's content, you can download the latest version from the same URL.

End-User License Agreement

READ THIS. You should carefully read these terms and conditions before opening the software packet(s) included with this book "Book". This is a license agreement "Agreement" between you and John Wiley & Sons, Inc. "WILEY". By opening the accompanying software packet(s), you acknowledge that you have read and accept the following terms and conditions. If you do not agree and do not want to be bound by such terms and conditions, promptly return the Book and the unopened software packet(s) to the place you obtained them for a full refund.

1. **License Grant.** WILEY grants to you (either an individual or entity) a nonexclusive license to use one copy of the enclosed software program(s) (collectively, the "Software") solely for your own personal or business purposes on a single computer (whether a standard computer or a workstation component of a multi-user network). The Software is in use on a computer when it is loaded into temporary memory (RAM) or installed into permanent memory (hard disk, CD-ROM, or other storage device). WILEY reserves all rights not expressly granted herein.

2. **Ownership.** WILEY is the owner of all right, title, and interest, including copyright, in and to the compilation of the Software recorded on the physical packet included with this Book "Software Media". Copyright to the individual programs recorded on the Software Media is owned by the author or other authorized copyright owner of each program. Ownership of the Software and all proprietary rights relating thereto remain with WILEY and its licensers.

3. **Restrictions on Use and Transfer.**

   (a) You may only (i) make one copy of the Software for backup or archival purposes, or (ii) transfer the Software to a single hard disk, provided that you keep the original for backup or archival purposes. You may not (i) rent or lease the Software, (ii) copy or reproduce the Software through a LAN or other network system or through any computer subscriber system or bulletin-board system, or (iii) modify, adapt, or create derivative works based on the Software.

   (b) You may not reverse engineer, decompile, or disassemble the Software. You may transfer the Software and user documentation on a permanent basis, provided that the transferee agrees to accept the terms and conditions of this Agreement and you retain no copies. If the Software is an update or has been updated, any transfer must include the most recent update and all prior versions.

4. **Restrictions on Use of Individual Programs.** You must follow the individual requirements and restrictions detailed for each individual program in the "About the CD" appendix of this Book or on the Software Media. These limitations are also contained in the individual license agreements recorded on the Software Media. These limitations may include a requirement that after using the program for a specified period of time, the user must pay a registration fee or discontinue use. By opening the Software packet(s), you agree to abide by the licenses and restrictions for these individual programs that are detailed in the "About the CD" appendix and/or on the Software Media. None of the material on this Software Media or listed in this Book may ever be redistributed, in original or modified form, for commercial purposes.

5. **Limited Warranty.**

   (a) WILEY warrants that the Software Media is free from defects in materials and workmanship under normal use for a period of sixty (60) days from the date of purchase of this Book. If WILEY receives notification within the warranty period of defects in materials or workmanship, WILEY will replace the defective Software Media.

(b) WILEY AND THE AUTHOR(S) OF THE BOOK DISCLAIM ALL OTHER WARRANTIES, EXPRESS OR IMPLIED, INCLUDING WITHOUT LIMITATION IMPLIED WARRANTIES OF MERCHANTABILITY AND FITNESS FOR A PARTICULAR PURPOSE, WITH RESPECT TO THE SOFTWARE, THE PROGRAMS, THE SOURCE CODE CONTAINED THEREIN, AND/OR THE TECHNIQUES DESCRIBED IN THIS BOOK. WILEY DOES NOT WARRANT THAT THE FUNCTIONS CONTAINED IN THE SOFTWARE WILL MEET YOUR REQUIREMENTS OR THAT THE OPERATION OF THE SOFTWARE WILL BE ERROR FREE.

(c) This limited warranty gives you specific legal rights, and you may have other rights that vary from jurisdiction to jurisdiction.

6. **Remedies.**

(a) WILEY's entire liability and your exclusive remedy for defects in materials and workmanship shall be limited to replacement of the Software Media, which may be returned to WILEY with a copy of your receipt at the following address: Software Media Fulfillment Department, Attn.: *Microsoft Word 2010 eLearning Kit For Dummies,* John Wiley & Sons, Inc., 10475 Crosspoint Blvd., Indianapolis, IN 46256, or call 1-800-762-2974. Please allow four to six weeks for delivery. This Limited Warranty is void if failure of the Software Media has resulted from accident, abuse, or misapplication. Any replacement Software Media will be warranted for the remainder of the original warranty period or thirty (30) days, whichever is longer.

(b) In no event shall WILEY or the author be liable for any damages whatsoever (including without limitation damages for loss of business profits, business interruption, loss of business information, or any other pecuniary loss) arising from the use of or inability to use the Book or the Software, even if WILEY has been advised of the possibility of such damages.

(c) Because some jurisdictions do not allow the exclusion or limitation of liability for consequential or incidental damages, the above limitation or exclusion may not apply to you.

7. **U.S. Government Restricted Rights.** Use, duplication, or disclosure of the Software for or on behalf of the United States of America, its agencies and/or instrumentalities "U.S. Government" is subject to restrictions as stated in paragraph (c)(1)(ii) of the Rights in Technical Data and Computer Software clause of DFARS 252.227-7013, or subparagraphs (c) (1) and (2) of the Commercial Computer Software - Restricted Rights clause at FAR 52.227-19, and in similar clauses in the NASA FAR supplement, as applicable.

8. **General.** This Agreement constitutes the entire understanding of the parties and revokes and supersedes all prior agreements, oral or written, between them and may not be modified or amended except in a writing signed by both parties hereto that specifically refers to this Agreement. This Agreement shall take precedence over any other documents that may be in conflict herewith. If any one or more provisions contained in this Agreement are held by any court or tribunal to be invalid, illegal, or otherwise unenforceable, each and every other provision shall remain in full force and effect.

Index

Numerics

A

B

C

D

E

F

G

J

K

L

M

N

O

P

Q

R

S

T

U

V

W

Z